Arabic Literary Salons in the Islamic Middle Ages

Poetics of Orality and Literacy

John Miles Foley, series editor

Arabic Literary Salons in the Islamic Middle Ages

Poetry, Public Performance, and the Presentation of the Past

Samer M. Ali

University of Notre Dame Press
Notre Dame, Indiana

University of Notre Dame Press
Notre Dame, Indiana 46556
www.undpress.nd.edu

Published in the United States of America

Reprinted in 2013

Library of Congress Cataloging-in-Publication Data

Ali, Samer M.
Arabic literary salons in the Islamic Middle Ages : poetry, public performance, and the presentation of the past / Samer M. Ali.
p. cm.—(Poetics of orality and literacy)
Originally presented as the author's thesis (doctoral)—Indiana University.
Includes bibliographical references and index.
ISBN-13: 978-0-268-02032-3 (pbk. : alk. paper)
ISBN-10: 0-268-02032-9 (pbk. : alk. paper)
1. Arabic poetry—750–1258—History and criticism.
2. Salons—Islamic Empire. 3. Oral tradition—Islamic Empire.
4. Islamic Empire—Intellectual life. I. Title.
PJ7553.A55 2010
892.7'13409—dc22

2010037737

∞ *The paper in this book meets the guidelines for permanence and durability of the Committee on Production Guidelines for Book Longevity of the Council on Library Resources.*

To my mother

and my father

My lute awake! perform the last
Labour that thou and I shall waste,
And end that I have now begun;
For when this song is sung and past,
My lute be still, for I have done.

—Sir Thomas Wyatt (1503–42),
"The Lover Complaineth the Unkindness of His Love"

Contents

Acknowledgments

The publication of this book has been a goal for many years, and in that duration a number of individuals and institutions have provided material and moral support. Without them, this book simply would not be, and it is a joy to record my gratitude to them.

The project began as a Ph.D. dissertation at Indiana University under the supervision of Suzanne Stetkevych, who has been an exemplary mentor and colleague. Few people outside her circle of students witness the unflagging energy and countless hours she devotes to training Arabists and cultivating in them the sensibilities of the ode (*qaṣīda*) genre, which is the backbone of the Arabic literary heritage. Her knowledge of the Arabic literary tradition in particular and classical culture in general serve as an inspiration. I have also benefited from conversations and comments from Jaroslav Stetkevych, who served as discussant on several conference panels, providing compelling suggestions and insights. It has been my good fortune to witness his avuncular wisdom and breadth of knowledge in Arabic and comparative literatures.

Research for this book was originally funded by a Fulbright-Hays Training Grant, part of the Doctoral Dissertation Research Program of the U.S. Department of Education. I am indebted to the Fulbright commissions of Egypt, Germany, and Spain for their assistance during 1998–99. An early version of chapter 4 was delivered to the Departamento de Estudios Árabes (Instituto de Filología) at the Consejo Superior de Investigaciones Científicas, Madrid, Spain, where I benefited from the comments of Heather Ecker, Howard Miller, and Manuela Marín. Later, chapter 4 was published in *Writers and Rulers,* edited by Beatrice Gruendler and Louise Marlow. I appreciate the care and acumen of the two editors and the permission of the publisher to incorporate that chapter in this book. Similarly, I thank the *Journal of Arabic Literature* for permission to republish chapter 5 and the *Journal of Arabic and Islamic Studies* for permission to use chapter 6. Likewise, many improvements were brought about in those articles because of the journals' editors and reviewers. Sections of this paper were discussed at the Working Group on Modernity and Islam at the Institute for Advanced Studies, Berlin, 2000–2001, and I appreciate the productive exchanges I had with Angelika Neuwirth, Renate Jacobi, Hilary Kilpatrick, and Friederike Pannewick.

I owe my gratitude as well to my colleagues at the Department of Middle Eastern Studies, University of Texas at Austin, who welcomed me there in fall 2001 and provided encouragement with their example and wisdom: Moh Ghanoonparvar, Adam Newton, Esther Raizen, Abe Marcus, Kamran Aghaie, Faegheh Shirazi, Keith Walters, Peter Abboud, Mohammad Mohammad, Mahmoud Al-Batal, and Kristen Brustad. I want to thank successive chairs in particular for funding support and research leave: Harold Liebowitz, Abe Marcus, Ian Manners, and Esther Raizen. All have served with such fairness and effectiveness as to create a hospitable and invigorating environment crucial for scholarship and communication. At a critical point in the writing of this book, I had the privilege of teaching an undergraduate seminar titled "Loyalty and Rebellion in Arabic Literature," where we focused on the issues of patronage and literary performance in medieval Arabic and Icelandic societies. Those seventeen students discussed, wrote, and thought along with me during fall 2005, thus enriching the book. With the support of the department and the dean of the College of Liberal Arts, I was given a research leave in 2004–5 to accept the Fulbright-Hays Faculty Research Abroad Grant. This grant, as well as that of

1998–99, not only offered the opportunity to write in peace, but to examine manuscripts at world archives. Without that funding, it would not have been feasible for a private individual to finance trips to Spain for the Real Biblioteca del Monasterio, San Lorenzo de El Escorial, Madrid; to Germany to visit the Staatsbibliothek, Berlin, and Universitätsbibliothek Leipzig, Bibliothek der Deutschen Morgenländischen Gesellschaft; to Egypt for the Manuscript Institute of the Arab League and the Egyptian National Archive in Cairo; and to Morocco to use the Madrasat Ben Yusif Library (Marrakesh), Bibliothèque Hasaniya (Rabat), and Bibliothèque Générale (Rabat). I mention this funding in name to indicate the critical role of public funds in supporting research and cultural understanding.

I am grateful as well to family and friends who have voluntarily made sacrifices for this book, and I appreciate their constant inspiration and affection. My mother and father have bestowed many advantages on their children despite never having had those advantages in their own childhoods. I gladly recognize their greatness and the example they have set for generations. May your years be filled with love and warm memories. I want to thank as well beloved Zainab, Ehab, Jackie, Camila, and Ade, whose love and support sustain me. A circle of friends in Chicago and Austin aided me with drinks along the course of the marathon. Thanks to Jihad and Sofia Shoshara, Nejd and Fauzia Alsikafi, Hans Boas, Claire Colton, Carolyn Eastman, and Sharmila Rudrappa.

Introduction

Judging by the number of American universities that have added faculty and courses in Middle Eastern and Islamic studies to their curricula since September 11, 2001, many educators have come to the realization that Middle Eastern cultures and Islamic societies ought to be part of a liberal arts education. In addition, the most foresighted among policy makers have long held the view that the United States cannot wait for disaster to demonstrate that an understanding of foreign languages and cultures is vital.[1] Fear of the foreign, the new, and the unfamiliar can itself be an alluring disaster. As the ancient Sumerian proverb describes and warns: "What I know makes everything else seem strange." The challenge to educators is this: How do we cultivate the cognitive capacity to assimilate the foreign? In particular, how do we alleviate the cultural anxieties that might hinder this process?

Edgar Allan Poe, the nineteenth century's master of anxiety, illustrated the value of these questions in his horrific rewrite of the ending of the *Thousand and One Nights*. Whereas in the original Arabic tale the heroine's verbal prowess as a raconteur triumphs over the king's brutal mania, in Poe's version, "The Thousand-and-Second Tale of Scheherazade," Shahrazad's plan to save herself and her society goes tragically awry. This one extra night of narrative becomes too much for the impetuous, dimwitted king. He is unable to apprehend or assimilate the wonders Shahrazad tells, real as they may be. At first, he fails to understand the wonders of Arabic language and culture. This presentation of the king as a xenophobe renders him—according to Poe's wry humor—analogous to nineteenth-century critics who were unable to comprehend, let alone appreciate, Poe's or Arabo-Islamic culture's achievements because of fear of the unfamiliar.

The king's unfortunate intellect fails him again as he hears and rejects the marvels of Western society in the eighteenth and nineteenth centuries: the colossal eruption at Laki, Iceland, in 1783; the Petrified Forest of North America; Maelzel's automatic chess player; Babbage's calculating machine; the daguerreotype; the Voltaic Pile; and the telegraph. Without fail, the king cannot bear to perceive or assimilate the unfamiliar; his anxiety generalizes to every discovery Shahrazad relates—whether natural, historical, aesthetic, or technological. Poe seems to be asking implicitly if we can afford to have parochial attitudes toward other cultures, for fear itself has a tragic allure.

The formation of cognitive maturity, and thus sociability, depends on one's trained capacity to see one's own reality as a single perception among a valid plurality. The study of other cultures thus opens the possibility for individuals to see beyond the centrality of their own lives, an essential rite of passage in becoming a mature and fair human. By virtue of the "smallness of our own experience," the folklorist Henry Glassie notes, "we mistake artifice for nature [and] . . . we are doomed merely to perfect our own imperfections. . . . What is becomes what is right."[2] When one engages the mind in the products and achievements of another culture and sustains an "investigation of alternatives," the process can provide a means of establishing "a second center distinct from our own."[3] Another center, with its own integrity and coherence, challenges our ideals and stimulates a multiplicity of standards for understanding and measuring human achievements.

In the mid-nineteenth century, the German folklorist Johann Gottfried Herder became so frustrated with Enlightenment hubris toward non-European cultures as to deride it: "Look! To what enlightenment, virtue, and happiness the world has ascended! And look at me! I am high atop the pendulum!"[4] Without a study of other cultures—a thoroughgoing engagement of what makes others human—great societies can bring about great acts of cruelty. Literature in particular, because of its intimate and symbolic connections to language usage, imagination, anxiety, and aspiration, can figure as a generative means of relating to cultures. As the Arabist Salma Khadra Jayyusi notes, "One of the most effective and humanizing ways that people of different cultures can have access to each other's experiences and concerns is through works of literary merit."[5] The essence of empathy relies on one's conditioned skill in conjuring up another's interests, values, customs, conditions, and priorities. I believe the stewards of liberal education in America have a responsibility to promote the ideals of empathy and plurality by ensuring the presence of world arts and literatures in their curricula.[6]

Scope and Issues

This book examines the origins, functions, and impact of literary salons (*mujālasāt;* sg. *mujālasa*) in medieval Islamic culture. *Mujālasāt* emerged in ninth-century Iraq and flourished in the tenth century, spreading from Iraq to the west, to Andalusian Spain and to North Africa. These literary salons endured as a cultural practice well into the modern era. Particularly in an age before television, *mujālasāt* were the nightly venue for witnessing the oral performance of new poetry and narrative as well as poetry that was considered "heritage." This forum for literature offered edification, entertainment, and escape for middle- and upper-rank men and women; it also served as a means of building one's public reputation, establishing one's status, expanding one's social network, and socializing the young. For these reasons the *mujālasa* surely must have held intense meaning in medieval Arabic society. Yet the field of Arabic scholarship has focused almost exclusively on the written dimensions of the tradition at the expense of the oral aspects, although both modes are interconnected in medieval sources. This emphasis has overlooked the more acoustic and social dimensions that enabled the literary tradition to endure and adapt, despite dramatic societal changes over nearly a millennium and a half.[7]

Until recently, scholars of Arabic literature have taken for granted the continuity of a literary tradition that spanned three continents and fifteen centuries—a rare feat in world history.[8] The existence and ubiquity of books transmitting this world heritage indicates their appeal, but Arabic literary studies have fallen short of explaining the reasons for that appeal. There has been little investigation into how such a long, tight-knit tradition might have remained meaningful and classical for such a surprising duration and across such a large geographic range, from Spain to Iraq. The question is more pressing when one considers the dramatic risks posed to the passing on of any tradition through the ages by boredom, apathy, famine, disease, war, or simply other distractions. Arabists, by and large overlooking the issue of appeal, might find it useful to analyze the ways in which generations of audiences, mostly amateurs, received, engaged, and reinterpreted old literature in order to breathe new life into traditional texts and forms, which can turn cold, alien, and stifling. Without an analysis of audience reception, we are left with a canon detached from the particular needs and choosy sensibilities of those who exercised the privilege of selecting texts for future transmission—or not. By focusing on the *mujālasāt,* this book investigates the chief literary forum where middle- and upper-rank members of society received the tradition and adjusted it.

By analogy, I draw parallels throughout this work with the institutions of the *marzēaḥ* (of western Asia in the Bronze Age) and the Greek *symposion* (beginning in the Geometric period, 900–700 B.C.). I review the corpus of modern scholarship that gauges these social institutions' character and impact. Judging from the rigor, vividness, and volume of the existing scholarship on the *marzēaḥ* and *symposion* since the 1960s,[9] Arabists might benefit from identifying *mujālasāt* as an institution with socio-literary implications and exploring some basic questions: How large were *mujālasāt?* What type of people attended—elders, women, children, or servants? Who spoke what, and to what degree did attendees take turns or dominate? How long did sessions last, and were they held at night or during the day? Were they held indoors or outside, and which buildings were used? For a social institution that has occupied more of a place in the daily lives of medieval men and women than television or classroom education in our own time, this gap in knowledge is grave.

I attempt to address these basic questions and take that description to the level of cultural analysis. If *mujālasāt* were prevalent and enduring, why did individuals participate? If people performed poetry and competed for prestige in *mujālasāt,* what impact did their text selection and performance in assembly have on the formation of canon, identity, community, and ideology? How did the performance of poetry and narrative shape their vision of an Arabo-Islamic past?

Outline

The book is organized in two parts that examine, respectively, the character and the impact of *mujālasāt.* Part I, composed of three chapters, addresses some of the most basic questions. Chapter 1 traces the development of the Arabic literary salon custom from its earliest origins in ancient Mesopotamian, Canaanite, and Greek cultures and its emergence in Iranian Sasanian culture, which inherited the Hellenistic tradition as part of Alexander the Great's legacy in Asia. The chapter examines the motivations for attending and participating in *mujālasāt,* including external social pressures such as sociability and the amassing of prestige (i.e., medieval networking), as well as the more cognitive and physical joys of social interplay.

Chapter 2 goes beyond fundamentals to examine one of the Gordian knots of medieval scholarship, whether European or Middle Eastern. It appears that professional and amateur littérateurs, who were seemingly honest and intelligent, fabricated narratives in *mujālasāt* that they recounted as being truthful and historical. Drawing on previous scholarship on Arabic, European, and Persian historiography and literature, I argue that littérateurs employed a set of principles for speaking in assembly that need not be reconciled with our own modern principles. If we are ever to understand the way medieval littérateurs spoke of the world (in particular, the past), we must be willing to set aside our own sensibilities and imagine another set of principles for speaking. Children in antiquity and the Middle Ages were socialized to speak and think in a figurative language that artfully encoded actual people and events with meaning. The result does not represent the actual people or events in question, of course, but the various interpretations associated with them. Chapter 2 also looks at how these principles were applied as techniques to render people, places, and events heroic and sacral. As such, the products of *mujālasāt* reflect not literal but metaphorical truths, which, if decoded, offer up a storehouse of deep-seated beliefs, attitudes, and mythology.[10]

Chapter 3 follows the journey of a single poem from ninth-century Iraq to thirteenth-century North Africa. Here I illustrate the way in which literary reception and performance in *mujālasāt* radically reframed the meaning of the poem. Although it was first delivered as a praise hymn to the court of the caliph al-Mutawakkil in Iraq, serving political functions, performers in assembly appropriated and "subverted" it into a mystical ode when thirteenth-century North African Sufis (Malamatiyya Lodge) adapted it for their own spiritual and apolitical purposes. Anecdotes of its reception and performance by the Malamatiyya show how the poem gave voice to their culturally specific ideology of renouncing this world's glories for the sake of those of the next. The ode, like a prism, refracts their intense hope—and consequent ambivalence—in God's mercy.

Part II analyzes the impact of *mujālasāt* on the formation of tradition. Chapters 4, 5, and 6 examine examples of the effect of performance in assembly on how littérateurs adjusted and transmitted specific past communal events. These chapters focus on a series of odes and narratives related to the first patricidal regicide of Islamic history in which the caliph al-Muntaṣir (d. 862) was implicated in the grisly murder of his father, the caliph al-Mutawakkil (d. 861). I look at the major poetic ceremonies staged by al-Buḥturī, the ninth-century court poet, to influence how later generations would remember this traumatic sequence of events.

Chapters 4 and 5 isolate a group of poems composed by al-Buḥturī to shape cultural memory of the patricide in perpetuity. These poems were composed and performed by this court poet in the wake of Caliph al-Mutawakkil's murder and in the era subsequent to it. More important, they were recited in *mujālasāt* for generations as canonical heritage. Together these poems constitute the last major statement by a contemporary on the subject. In chapter 6, I demonstrate how this body of poems sowed the seeds for historical narratives for some twenty generations of performers in *mujālasāt.* I argue that al-Buḥturī's odes illustrate the *determinative* role that poetic heritage can play in concert with audience reception and adjustment to form communal historical narratives that entertain and edify audiences even today.

Sources

An examination of performance in group necessitates a broad and creative use of sources because it encompasses a wide variety of issues: the training that poets and reciters require in order to become competent, the immediate demands of face-to-face performance before an audience, the ways in which audiences express their responses and judgments, and the ways in which performers might adjust their texts or styles of delivery to attract and hold an audience's attention. I address these questions without the benefit of direct observation or live recordings. Needless to say, that limitation alone poses a daunting challenge for the field of Arabic literature; it accounts in part for the reluctance among some scholars to examine the oral and sociable dimension of this literary form of communication.

It is possible, however, with the appropriate methods, to interpret the available sources with an eye for these performance issues. I have culled details and sentiments primarily from texts but also, to a lesser extent, from architectural studies revealing how physical spaces were used in the salons. Medieval texts are used in large part as ethnographies that were composed by professional or amateur littérateurs. Anthologies of poetry and prose reveal themselves as transcripts of *mujālasāt* or as mnemonic devices for learning one's lines (a feat that earned the admiration of one's friends and colleagues). These sources serve the purpose of illustrating the culture of the *mujālasāt,* audience expectations, a performer's training, norms of performance and reception, audience-performer interaction, text adjustment in performance, and even composition in performance. Most important, when these sources nonchalantly use the medium of writing to promote and ensure the oral dimensions of the tradition, they manifest certain norms of interplay between orality and writing.

I also examine prose and poetry texts that were known to have been performed in *mujālasāt* and received as heritage. That these texts were reselected for recitation and transmission—despite the vagaries of history and psychology across generations—stands as a testament to their suitability for performance. With the support of Fulbright-Hays funding (1998–99, 2004–5), I visited ten archives in Spain, Morocco, Germany, and Egypt, where I examined more than a thousand manuscript titles. For this study, I have relied on manuscripts of anthologies, historical narratives, political advice manuals, poetry texts, and personal notebooks of students to understand how performers used these books for performance. I examined these manuscripts not only for the unprinted texts they may convey, but as physical artifacts that might indicate their usage as mnemonic devices explicitly or implicitly. As a physical artifact, each manuscript provides clues that often tell a story, and I have endeavored to foreground those stories by gauging the ways the book has been bound, supplemented, and rebound, interpreting marginal notes, noting shifts in script style or ink color, and observing the many strategies that manuscript owners employed to personalize and customize tradition. In referring to these manuscripts, I have used specific archival names and reference numbers and, where available, titles. It deserves to be mentioned, however, that manuscript numbers hardly ever coincide with a single title, since a single volume will often comprise a florilegium of titles. This medieval convention confounds our print-minded notion of "book." Likewise, many works are not set "books" at all, since they served as personal notebooks composed by amateurs or as customized renditions of well-known texts. It is often difficult, therefore, to supply a neat label, let alone a title. In effect, this problem illustrates the invigorating challenges researchers face in engaging medieval manuscript culture on its own terms, apart from our contemporary idea of the stable printed book.

Methods

In the course of this exposition on *mujālasāt* and their impact, I have developed and drawn on several methodological strategies to support my thesis. First, this book demonstrates that, far from being an ideological and brainy enterprise, the Arabo-Islamic literary heritage was governed by sociability and social interaction at heart. These interactions and the underlying social need to charm and be charmed enabled odes and stories to take on pragmatic value in social exchanges that took place in the salons. Implicitly, I hope to put into question the presumption that canonicity is an a priori given and to show that a canon can be authoritative only insofar as it remains appealing and current. Second, the continuity of the Arabic tradition throughout time and across regions—over a millennium and a half, across three continents—cannot pass as an unquestioned phenomenon. Individual men and women who had the intellect and virtuosity to promote vested interests adjusted and performed inherited cultural knowledge to meet immediate demands. Thus the issue of canon formation can scarcely be divested from local interests: people transmit a canon by using it.

Third, I employ a variety of methods from folklore studies and cultural anthropology to illustrate the way in which medieval littérateurs relied on manuscripts to prepare for oral performance. As such, I join a group of researchers who argue against the so-called great divide theory—that paper-based technologies inevitably *displace* oral performance.[11] The great divide theory has the drawback of giving technology a determinative role in shaping knowledge and society, deemphasizing the agency of people who perhaps might use those technologies to serve emerging goals rooted in their specific class, age, ethnicity, gender, and ideology. This book explores the ways in which individuals and groups use both oral and written modes of communication together to achieve social and political goals.

Fourth, by tracing the impact of recited poems on historical narrative, I aim to question the rigid lines between genres and forms that were eminently combined and related in *mujālasāt* when performers alternated between them to entertain and edify their audiences. I hope to offer readers a study of medieval Arabo-Islamic *mujālasāt* that places the agency and impact of individuals and groups—whether amateurs or professionals—at the center of literary communication and canon formation. Beginning in the ninth century, these forebears created literary practices reflecting and shaping a savvy sociability that empowered and celebrated human dignity and tenacity. That heritage is now bequeathed to the world to reject or esteem.

A Note on Transliteration

Throughout this book I have employed standard abbreviations for the first and second editions of the venerable *Encyclopaedia of Islam,*

EI^1 and *EI*^{2}, common reference works in Middle Eastern studies. The transliteration system I have used is that of the *International Journal of Middle Eastern Studies.* Because this book addresses both Arabists and non-Arabists, I explain here the transliteration symbols: The macron on the vowels *ā, ī, ū* simply indicates a long vowel. Assuming a midwestern American accent, compare the short *a* in *bat* to the *ā* in *father,* the *i* in *pit* to the long *ī* phoneme in *bee,* the *u* phoneme in *took* to the *ū* in *boot.* As for the consonants, the ᵓ (as in Maᵓmūn) is merely a glottal stop (the popping of the glottis in *up*), so it can be tinted with any of the three vowels, such as in *at, it,* or *oh.* The Arabic sounds *ḍ ṣ ṭ ẓ,* are emphatic versions of the dotless *d s t z.* The ᶜ (as in the biblical name Yaᶜqūb) has no English phonemic equivalent, but once acquired, it doubles as a respectable duck call.

In conformity with convention, however, Arabic poetry has not been transliterated but rather transcribed to stress its aural dimensions. In the case of words that have entered the English language, such as *kaaba* and *hajj*, I have adopted the practice of not transliterating but using standard English spellings found in the *American Heritage Dictionary of the English Language.* Unless otherwise noted, all translations of Arabic texts are my own. An appendix of poetry texts in Arabic has been included for the reader's convenience. I have attempted to offer readable translations in idiomatic English. In balancing the needs of Arabists with non-Arabists, I have assumed that the Arabist will be able to consult the original, so the translations primarily serve to engage non-Arabists. At least, I hope so.

Part I

Literary Salons: Outlines of a Topic

one

Literary Salons

From Ancient *Symposion* to Arabic *Mujālasāt*

SALONS: HIERARCHICAL VERSUS EGALITARIAN

In the year 750, at a time when North America's redwoods and sequoias were seedlings and sprouts, a revolution was taking place seven thousand miles away in the Middle East as a new dynasty, the Abbasids, came to power. Although governed by Muslims, Abbasid society would enable Arabs and non-Arabs, as well as Muslims and non-Muslims, to interact and influence each other in unprecedented ways. Abbasid society (A.D. 750–1258), centered in Iraq, would sustain a golden age of Islamic civilization, which thereafter Muslims and Arabs would consider a model for organized communal life.[1] Not only did this era produce a canonical literature, its triumphs fostered the ideals of cultural exchange, leadership, and civic participation.

One of the primary mechanisms for forming Abbasid society and literature was the literary gathering or salon. These *mujālasāt* enabled people in new venues and ways to inherit, borrow, adjust, and share cultural knowledge. The types of knowledge that were most relevant to these *mujālasāt* were specifically in the Arabic language. Although particular literary ideas could originate from Greek, Syriac, Indian, or Armenian, they would be dubbed "Arabic" fields of knowledge (*ᶜulūm ᶜarabiyya*) if their ultimate language of composition and recitation was Arabic.[2] According to the historian Ibn Khaldūn (d. 1406), the defining feature of Arabic knowledge was not merely language, but the norm-driven imperative to perform it and teach it to the young, to learn it by heart, and to recite it *in assembly.* In contrast to Arabic knowledge, if any "foreign" fields of knowledge (*ᶜulūm ᶜajamiyya*)—which included Greek, Indian, and Persian sciences (such as philosophy, mathematics, chemistry, medicine, pharmacy, and astronomy, as well as dream interpretation)—were forgotten or became extinct, they could be rediscovered by intellect. In this way they were viewed as perennially deducible.

Arabic studies were viewed as cultural and thus set by communal convention, sentiment, attitude, and belief. The Middle East scholar George Makdisi notes, as further indication of this distinction, that foreign knowledge was sometimes referred to as "reasoned" (*ᶜilm maᶜqūl*), whereas Arabic knowledge was "personally transmitted" (*ᶜilm manqūl*).[3] In Ibn Khaldūn's view, if Arabic knowledge was lost, sheer intellect could not regain its form or substance.[4] It would die out along with the vast majority of cultural knowledge, such as family experiences, traditions, and lore, that ceases to hold meaning.

Arabic knowledge comprises two subtypes of heritage: religious knowledge (*dīn*) and humanistic knowledge (*adab*).[5] Those aspiring to good repute would learn from *dīn* the various transmissions of the Qur'an and reports by or about the Prophet Muhammad (known as Hadith) by heart. From *adab,* they would memorize classical proverbs (*amthāl*) and public speeches (*khutab*), inherited (*qadīm*) and "modern" (*muḥdath*) poetry, as well as charming or historical narratives (*akhbār*).[6] Whereas *dīn* guided the faithful to the path of God's deliverance in the hereafter, *adab* delivered a person from isolation, trauma, and grief in the here and now. Whereas *dīn* taught mortals what God expects, *adab* taught them the manners, sensitivities, and verbal arts of charm (*ẓarf*) and sociability (*muʾānasa*) that human beings expect. This humanistic knowledge—not of divine but of social salvation—is the focus of this book, along with the social practices that surround its performance in *mujālasāt.*

Mujālasāt were one of the many social institutions that promoted in varying degrees humanistic edification, which produced generations of professional and amateur humanists or littérateurs (*adīb;* pl. *udabā*ʾ). Makdisi, in his important study of the rise of humanism in medieval Islamic culture and later in Christian Europe, notes that students could acquire this knowledge in several venues. Wealthy patrons endowed institutions, the most important of which was the mosque. Beginning with the advent of the Islamic polis, master teachers, poets, and scholars used the Friday mosque (*jāmi*ᶜ) throughout urban centers and the neighborhood prayer-nook (*masjid*) for regular study circles.[7] In tenth-century Iraq, patrons established elementary and secondary schools, called *kuttāb* or *maktab,* where the young gained a foundation in foreign and Arabic knowledge. These schools often served as a gateway to higher education.[8] A century later, students could gain competence in privately endowed seminaries (*madrasa;* pl. *madāris*).[9] As early as the ninth century, scholars had the opportunity to hold study circles at independent libraries; two centuries later, when seminaries housed their own libraries, this practice was extended.[10] Makdisi observed that the government imperative to train secretaries—whether copyists, calligraphers, or epistle writers—meant that state chanceries and courts graduated actual and would-be professionals of humanistic studies. In many cases chanceries became work-study situations where graduates of endowed institutions, such as secondary schools and seminaries, could apprentice the art and craft of preparing eloquent communications for the high-stakes purposes of intelligence, diplomacy, warfare, state accounting, and tax collection.[11]

Most significant, Makdisi offers a brief but important summary of *mujālasāt* that emerged in mid-ninth-century Baghdad independent of the control of wealthy patrons or the state.[12] The *mujālasāt* were unlike other edifying circles in three ways. First, they were held in gardens, homes, and bookshops, so participation was semiprivate and relied on the health and wealth of one's social network. Attendance and participation in these self-organized *mujālasāt* counted as a marker of prestige and influence, opening doors of opportunity for income, professional advancement, and the marriage of one's children. Second, the *mujālasāt* were independent of mosques and religious institutions, which enabled non-Muslims and Muslims alike to associate, socialize, and influence each another in unprecedented ways and degrees. Although medieval urban culture enabled the social interaction of classes, professions, ethnicities, and ages, the mixing of religious identities in *mujālasāt* further stoked the fires of sociability and personal charm across religions and ethnicities, making these literary salons a vehicle of cultural integration in the Abbasid era.

Third, these gatherings were relatively intimate. Thus they were more egalitarian and more ludic than other circles, legitimizing a full range of human seriousness and play. As such, one must distinguish these collegial salons from royal salons held at courts for the amusement and edification of kings and courtiers. Such royal salons were governed by principles of royal decorum and hierarchy, ensuring that guests showed deference to the entire chain of command represented at the assembly. Drawing on Persian as well as Arabic classical sources, Brookshaw notes that royals craved an air of intimacy but not the loss of power that accompanied it:

> This "intimacy" was often only apparent, and the rules of protocol governing subordinates' relations with rulers still applied. At formal, courtly *majālis* . . . guests and performers were expected to keep to their allotted "seats" (or more commonly cushions) throughout. Positions at the *majlis,* which would often be dictated by the patron-host, were generally allotted according to social rank. Some participants were seated . . . while others . . . stood throughout.[13]

In the Berlin manuscript of *Ḥalbat al-Kumayt* (The Racing Formation of the Bay Horse/The Gathering for Bay-Colored Wine), al-Najāwī notes a palpable difference between the two salon types based on the presentation of one's bodily and psychological comfort:

> It is appropriate that one leaves behind inhibition in the literary salon, for it is said that it is good manners for a person to let go of good manners (*min al-adab tark al-adab*) around those he does not fear or dread, to see little squabbling, to be treated fairly, to be forgiven in one's drink, to be allowed to feign no answer, to remain happy, to

> relinquish the past, to ask the service of those present, to recite what comes easily, to expect others to keep one's faults private, yet to refrain from reproach or artistic enjoyment (*ṭarab*) entailing hollering and screaming, to put aside boasting of one's merit (*ḥasab*) and pedigree (*nasab*).
>
> As for those, however, that one fears and dreads, such as kings, caliphs, princes, and viziers, it [their salon] has arduous rules, strict decorum for which the heart quakes upon hearing, let alone seeing or witnessing: One must perfect his manners and stone silence—without vexation—never leaning on a cushion, nor playing with his clothes nor beard, nor showing any pain when [his foot] swells or goes numb (if it's pinched under his clothes), nor can he rub his hands together, nor crack his knuckles, nor play with his ring, nor yawn even. . . . Thus the salon of one of the merchants or commoners (*al-tujjār wal-ᶜawwām*) feels more joyful (*alṭaf dhatan*) and more literary (*akthar adaban*) than that of a king or vizier.[14]

While language does not always denote or connote practice, one finds that medieval littérateurs sometimes make a distinction in terminology between collegial and hierarchical salons. At times, they refer to the more egalitarian collegial salon as *mujālasa* (pl. *mujālasāt*), the verbal noun of the Form III *jālasa,* meaning "to sit *with someone,*" indicating reciprocity or sociability. The hierarchical salon of royalty, however, often takes the name *majlis* (pl. *majālis*), the noun of place for the Form I intransitive verb *to sit* or *to take a seat.* No reciprocity or equality is implied. When littérateurs use other labels for the collegial salon, it is usually a verbal noun modeled on the Form III verb implying reciprocity, such as *mudhākara* (the act of reminiscing with someone), *musāmara* (the act of conversing with someone late into the night), *muḥāḍara* (the act of contending with someone), or *munādama* (the act of drinking with someone).[15] Like any label flaunted by professionals and amateurs, *mujālasa* and *majlis* sometimes lose their formal distinction; however, the distinction in practice—in experience—remains evident. As the passage from *Ḥalbat al-Kumayt* explains, the operant difference between one type of salon and the other is the presence of superiors versus colleagues. In the presence of superiors, one feels dread and anxiety at the risk of being judged harshly for drawing attention to one's bodily or psychological comfort or discomfort. In the presence of peers, one can safely expect empathy between self and other, even some degree of indulgence for one's foibles (excess drinking, feigning no answer, and relief from criticism and competitive boasting). Perhaps the most serious indicator of equality in collegial salons is asking a peer the favor of his service (i.e., serving a drink, food, etc.).[16] Moreover, with such a piquant premium placed on companionability and pleasure, it should be no surprise that *mujālasāt* in homes and gardens often prompted bacchic excess: banquet foods, wine, fruits, flowers, perfumes, singing, and, of course, displays of sexuality and love.

Mujālasāt are intriguing for historical and literary reasons. On the one hand, they were a social institution valuable to understanding the everyday history of Arabo-Islamic culture and the wider diffusion of that culture to other Islamic societies. On the other hand, they were a literary pretext that framed the majority of literary anthologies. Compilers of anthologies bolstered the authority of their works by framing their literary content as having been heard or overheard in *mujālasāt*. This framing device indicates the texts were current, alive, circulating, and widely performed—thus important. So authoritative was this credential that the number of works whose titles and prefaces situate literature in *mujālasāt* was legion. For example, from the tenth century we have Abū Ḥayyān al-Tawḥīdī's (d. tenth cent.) *Book of Delight and Good Company,*[17] al-Ṣūlī's (d. 947) *Anecdotes about al-Buḥturī,*[18] al-Dīnawarī's (d. ca. 940) *Book of Literary Gathering and Jewels of Knowledge,*[19] and al-Tanūkhī's (d. 994) *Recollections of the Assembly and Anecdotes of the Salon.*[20]

This practice continues well into the late Middle Ages, with reference to "springtime" and "gardens"—favored times and places for *mujālasāt*—such as the littérateur-exegete al-Zamakhsharī's (d. 1144) *Vernal Gardens for the Virtuous and Texts of Anecdotes,*[21] which is expanded by the littérateur al-Amāsī (d. ca. 1533) as *Garden of the Best, Selected from 'Vernal Gardens for the Virtuous' on Knowledge at Literary Gatherings, and the Varieties of Discourse on Arabic Knowledge and Literary Arts.*[22] In some cases the author evokes a late-night time frame as a lyrical setting for recitation, as in a Sufi work attributed to the Sufi master Ibn al-ᶜArabī (d. 1240), *Book of Repartee with the Virtuous and Late-Night Talk with the Elect on Humanities, Sto-*

ries, and Anecdote,[23] al-Ḥanbalī's (d. 1503) *The Joy of the Late-Night Raconteur for Anecdotes about Laylā al-Akhyāliyya* and *The Joy of the Late-Night Raconteur for the Lore of Majnūn Banī ᶜĀmir,*[24] and al-Suyūṭī's (d. 1505) *Techniques for Holding Late-Night Conversations with Ancestors.*[25] Despite spanning seven centuries, these works share the framing device of presenting stories and poetry in the context of "socials," "salons," or "assemblies," where littérateurs—amateurs and professionals alike—gathered to recite *adab.* In some works the source even structures the reader's experience with each new chapter organized as a "night" of recitation. Thus this book attends to *mujālasāt* as both a social and a literary construct.

Perhaps the most famous and well-attended *mujālasa* of the Abbasid era began in the home of Yūhanna b. Māsawayh (d. 857), a littérateur, philosopher, apothecary, and physician. Known in Christian Europe as Johannes Mesuë for his manual on aromatic medicines, *Liber de Simplicibus,* Ibn Māsawayh is credited in Arabic sources with redefining and promoting the custom among the *adab* urbanites in Baghdad in the early ninth century. By many accounts, the decisive factor in this feat was the man's charm (*ẓarf*) and playful wit (*daᶜāba*), which attracted the most diverse gathering of littérateurs. He was a Nestorian physician of Persian origin who had immigrated to Baghdad with his family as a child from his natal city of Jundishapur. One of the most worldly ancient cities in western Asia, Jundishapur was home to an ancient medical school, a library, and a stronghold of Iranian Hellenism and Nestorianism.[26] The credit that Ibn Māsawayh receives in biographical sources for the emergence of the *mujālasa* in Abbasid culture points to a variety of cultural influences and salon-like precedents in the ancient Middle East. These precedents yield comparative insights, in addition to offering a plausible autochthonous history for the emergence of Abbasid *mujālasa,* situating it within the socio-religious life of the ancient Middle East.

Historical Comparisons of the *Symposion* and the *Marzēaḥ*

The *symposion* was a gathering of friends for the sake of ritual feasting, drinking, sex, and singing and can be attested in Sumerian culture before 3000 B.C. as an institution with a sacral function. In the latter part of the fourth millennium B.C., societies in the Middle East began domesticating the plants that would enable the stable production of alcoholic beverages—beer in Egypt and wine in western Asia. This period, the early part of the Bronze Age, saw the world's first use of metal tools, the first glimmers of organized urban life, and the kind of specialization of labor—farmers, bakers, merchants, priests, warriors, and kings—that would dramatically increase complexity and hierarchy in social life.

As the archaeologist Alexander H. Joffe notes, the advent and development of ritual drinking correlates with the increasing stratification of the earliest city-state and its systems of patronage; these rituals were likely intended to assuage frustration. Thus the ways in which wine and beer were produced, rated, distributed, and ritually consumed provide clues to the polities and politics of early civilizations. Although the drinking of alcoholic beverages engendered a feeling of community and well-being, their production and consumption also reflected relationships of patronage and privilege.[27] For the purposes of this book the *symposion* enables us to chart some of the major transformations in the Middle East, in particular, the ways in which the Abbasid *mujālasa* redefined an ancient cultural practice to serve new literary and social needs.

One of the most consistent dimensions of the ancient *symposion* was its elite character relative to the rest of society and the protection or support it received from high-status patrons. The earliest narrative art from western Asia depicts the *symposion* as the epitome of luxury. Many of the pictorial representations were on materials dedicated in temples, on wall decorations, or on inlaid furniture in prestigious homes. Some of these representations were also on cylinder seals, a status symbol used by men and women of prominence or office to mark their identities on property and documents. The images depicted in the narrative art show executive accomplishments, such as kings performing official duties like protecting the interests of their city or deity, worshiping, engaging in warfare, and constructing sacred buildings.

When undecorated men and women appear in these representations, they are seated under the sponsorship of a royal patron, often depicted with fans, surfeited with food supplies and music, and drinking from beakers and straws. In some instances particular royal events seem to be marked with a *symposion,* such as the scenes on the Standard of Ur, where a military victory receives commemoration with a procession of clients or subjects coming before the king and his courtier, who are seated while drinking to musical accompaniment. Gods and prominent individuals are sometimes drawn in drunken or sexual positions in *symposion* scenes, suggesting that excess was considered a recognized privilege of untouchables. Moreover, cylinder seals depicting the *symposion* are most commonly found in the graves of high-status men and women.[28]

There is remarkable continuity of themes from the third to the first millennium, from Sumerian to Neo-Assyrian culture in Mesopotamia. One of the reasons for this astonishing pattern might be the fact that *symposion* scenes were depicted on perishable objects, such as cylinder seals, textiles, and furniture, for which there would have been a continuous demand and manufacture, regardless of conditions that prevented their purchase in royal courts.[29] In the first millennium Assyrian narrative art begins to indicate that the *symposion* deserved a special room within the architecture of the home, with evidence that prestigious homes nearly always included a ceremonial room for ritual feasting and drinking, appointed with high-value furniture, such as one piece from the ninth century that depicts the *symposion* in an ivory panel. Assyrian art also evinces a new style of *symposion* that became prevalent and must have dramatically altered the ambience of the gathering. Whereas previously *symposion* attendees were shown primarily sitting and sometimes standing, Assyrian art began illustrating a type of *symposion* where attendees were reclining on couches with a raised armrest, much like a chaise longue.[30] Seemingly trivial, this innovation would endure for many millennia and meant that each individual claimed more space in the volume of the room, necessitating a new norm of fewer people being invited to the *symposion.* Smaller groups partaking in the *symposion* signaled emerging possibilities of more intimate collegial gatherings.

The "reclining *symposion*" seems to have originated outside of Mesopotamia; the Assyrians probably imported it from newly conquered regions in the eastern Mediterranean. Scholars have yet to determine the names for the *symposion* in ancient Mesopotamia, but in the Levant the regional version of the *symposion* was dubbed the *marzēaḥ* (revelry) and seems to have been in practice among the courtly and mercantile bourgeoisie of cities in Phoenicia and farther south in Palestine. Although the first records of the *marzēaḥ* are attested in Ugarit in the fourteenth century B.C., the institution spread over the course of two millennia throughout the Levant, and probably farther to Carthage with Phoenician trade. One finds it in Roman Palmyra and the Nabatean cities of Petra and Avdat (Obodat) from the first and third centuries A.D.[31]

Records are not complete about the character of the *marzēaḥ* in all localities, but in its earliest versions in Ugarit, Phoenicia, and Palestine, this cultural institution had pagan and posh overtones that put it in conflict with the developing monotheisms of the time. The *marzēaḥ* was at root set in veneration of a deity or deification of forebears, the *rephaim*. These ancestors were in particular the "heroic . . . dead warriors of elite status, who dwell in the netherworld among the lower ranks of gods and who can be summoned to partake of food and drink with the living." Most important, attendees recited ritual texts, epics, songs, and poetry to bring about mythic transformations, such as the epic of the bygone Aqhat, whose son Danel brings him back to the living with the help of Baal. The sacral protection of deities is further recorded in a Ugaritic text that mentions the *marzēaḥ* of Shatrana, Hurrian Ishtar, and Anat.[32]

The austere prophet Amos of the early first millennium railed at the practice:

> Alas for those who lie on beds of ivory, and lounge on their couches, and eat lambs from the flock, and calves from the stall;
> who sing idle songs to the sound of the harp, and like David improvise on instruments of music;
> who drink wine from bowls, and anoint themselves with the finest oils, but are not grieved over the ruin of Joseph!
> Therefore they shall now be the first to go into exile, and the revelry (*marzēaḥ*) of the loungers shall pass away.[33]

Within this philippic, Amos reveals the elegiac mood and purpose of the *marzēaḥ* and betrays the similarities that link it with its Mesopotamian precursors: drinking wine to excess, listening to music, eating ritual foods, reclining on couches paneled with ivory. These ivory panels display a constellation of placid motifs that evoke the values of kindness, protection, and sustenance—key benefits of patronage for which a client's devotion is expected in return.[34] In short, the *marzēaḥ* in the first millennium evinces the character and function of a distinctly religious, namely, pagan, ritual. Because of the power of the sacred in ancient society, it bears mention that these gatherings received the direct material and moral support of monarchs, who must have viewed them as critical to their legitimacy as sacral kings.[35]

While descriptions of the *marzēaḥ* point to its elite nature, a hierarchy can also be observed within the association itself. To be clear, membership in these regular gatherings was limited to those who could afford to acquire and display its luxuries of food, wine, and oils and all the secondary costs of flaunting such wealth. Yet the ordinary member of the *marzēaḥ* was distinguished from the administrator of the association. The regular member was called *mt. mrzḥ,* and the head was dubbed *rb. mrzḥ*. Along with this distinction in honor, there was a drastic difference in responsibility. The honor of the title *rb. mrzḥ* was sought by or fell upon wealthy elders by turns, in the hope that they would assume responsibility for the cost of the proceeding for a year at a time. The *rb. mrzḥ* also presided over the finances of the *bēt marzēaḥ,* an estate that was usually donated to the association by a ruler, which often included furnished meeting halls, farmland, vineyards, and wineries.[36] Other officers included the secretary, chef, wine steward, and additional ceremonial positions.[37] Membership in the *marzēaḥ* relied on wealth and status but apparently no particular kinship ties. Nevertheless, sons could inherit their fathers' membership, thus preserving the prestige accrued from elite associations within families.[38] By comparison, the Arabo-Islamic *mujālasāt* were largely independent of state patronage and accessible to a wider swath of society.

In Hellenic culture the *symposion,* much like the *marzēaḥ,* was prevalent as early as the ninth century B.C., in Athens, Sparta, and Crete, as a gathering of elite warriors intended to commemorate battle feats and bygone heroes. In the eighth century, however, the *symposion* began to adopt the practice of reclining as a result of Crete's regular contact with Phoenicians through trade and immigration.[39] Lyric poetry—solo elegiac song for the lyre—was the favored content for performance in the *symposion*.[40] Much has been made of reclining as an "orientalizing" shift, but perhaps the most fascinating aspect might be that Hellenic culture was conscious of the borrowing and the similarity with Phoenicia, with indications that "oriental" motifs and styles were considered status symbols among the elite.[41]

Scholarship on the Greek *symposion* offers a particularly nuanced description and analysis of the institution and provides further insights into its analogs in the Bronze Age Middle East, as well as in the Abbasid era. The *symposion* was a tripartite sequence of ritual feasting, drinking, and entertainment (consisting of games and the performance of oral literature) and is suspected to have begun as warriors' postbattle celebrations, "the feast of merit" in tribal Greece, well before 800 B.C. It persisted as a form of voluntary organization for the gentry in the first millennium B.C. Sources refer to the host of the gathering by the honorific *symposiarch,* which establishes a hierarchical distinction somewhat like that of the *marzēaḥ*. Wine was also a ceremonial component of the *symposion,* with the role of mixing the wine being highly honored and ceremonial. This role had practical effects on the gathering, as the actual proportion of water to wine (usually three to one) delivered to guests surely had a fateful effect on the course of events in any particular evening.[42]

The institution of the *symposion* influenced and was influenced by banqueting rituals in the Middle East, most notably in Phoenicia and Iran.[43] Under those influences, as early as the eighth century B.C., the *symposion* changed from a seated event to one where guests feasted, drank, and socialized while reclining, thus reducing the number of guests a host could invite and cultivating a more intimate atmosphere.[44] At the *symposion* space was used to create a feeling of exclusivity and intimacy. The Greek scholar Oswyn Murray describes the *symposion* as such:

> The guests reclined in couches around the walls of the *andron* [the men's room], which was later often especially designed, with stone benches. . . . The fact that the participants reclined, rather than sitting [*sic*], created a specific space limited *in size* by the need for all to communicate. . . . The typical . . . "men's room" held between seven and fifteen couches with two men to a couch. This "sympotic

> space" created an exclusive, internal world, centered on the loyalty of members of the group to one another, and encouraging a sense of separateness from the external world of family and *polis.*[45]

This separate realm was also a place for formally breaking the code of honor that ordered ordinary life. Thus the *symposion* was governed by its own conventions of sexuality that permitted homosexual bonds with the young male "beloved" (*eromenos*), a kind of unfettered love with companions, nubile attendants, and performers, as well as ritual exhibitionism and a display of violence at the end of the sessions.[46] This mood of "escapade" also appears in accounts, discussed elsewhere in this book, of more bacchic literary gatherings in Abbasid society.

Most important for literary studies, the *symposion* was an event at which ancestral literature was performed. Here individuals could gradually channel the course of a tradition through social practice. They could shape and reshape a canon through usage. Performers adapted the Greek traditions of epic and lyric to new audiences at the *symposion,* thus cultivating long-term patrons for each art.[47] Rather than conceive of performance as an ancillary distraction to the artistic tradition, one might see that the performance event, wherever and whenever it took place, sparked and revived the continuity of the poetic tradition in much the same way that staged theater serves drama.

Various types of *symposion* appear to have been crucial to the social life of elites before the rise of Islam and to the formation of tradition throughout the Levant and Mesopotamia over the course of at least four millennia. In Greece the *symposion* began later in the first millennium B.C. In the early part of that millennium, the already luxurious *symposion* became a reclining event with more intimate overtones. One of the most intriguing commonalities between types of *symposion* throughout the millennium and across the various regions is the overarching association with loss and mortality. In the Levant and Mesopotamia, for example, scenes of *marzēaḥ,* as well as the ivory inlaid couch, were incorporated in burial chambers.[48] In Greece the couch used for reclining had a primary use as a ceremonial deathbed and funeral bier. In a remarkably reflexive move, the deceased is often depicted as lying on the *symposion* couch-deathbed amid full *symposion* scenery, complete with food, music, attendees, and wine, though without friends and colleagues.[49] One might theorize that the seemingly inconvenient position of reclining in the actual *symposion* while eating and drinking among friends has the more redeeming quality of evoking the deathbed scene, thus enhancing the funerary associations of the *symposion* event.

Gatherings under the Moonlight

The preceding discussion describes the ancient background of the Arabic *mujālasāt* that probably influenced the emergence of the Abbasid institution indirectly, but there is one direct link that can be established. The Nestorian physician credited with establishing and promoting Abbasid salons, Yūhanna b. Māsawayh, hailed from Jundishapur. The primary agents for stoking the fires of interest and providing a model for Abbasid society were subsequent physicians from Jundishapur, and they were primarily Nestorian. Nestorian Christianity was especially influenced by Dionysian and Epicurean sensualities, which were ritually enacted in wine-merry *symposia.*[50] These influences—Jundishapur, Nestorianism, and medicine—provided Ibn Māsawayh with a trifecta for direct access to the tradition of the ancient *symposion.*

Jundishapur was the prime seat of Hellenism in the Middle East. It was located in Iran, the heartland of Alexander the Great's empire where he established a successor empire, the Seleucid dynasty, which hybridized Greek culture with local ancient cultures for some two hundred fifty years. Furthermore, in A.D. 260, King Shapur settled three thousand Roman soldiers in Jundishapur (originally Wandyu-Shapur or Shapur's Antioch), which helped to ensure the city's role as a center for Hellenized Christianity and a vortex of ancient regional traditions. Both in name and in deed the city was designed to match that other center of Hellenistic Christianity, Antioch. Shapur then founded the Academy of Jundishapur, which became a beacon of medicine and philosophy in Asia.

Physicians tended to be the stewards of Hellenism, as the Greek physician Galen was considered the ancestral founder of the profession. Physicians were assured of royal patronage because kings needed them for their own longevity. In Abbasid society non-Muslim, non-Arab physicians who sought greater assimilation into Arabo-Islamic society preferred *adab* among the Arabic fields of knowledge, which was nonreligious. They would often host gatherings in their homes, as other venues, such as mosques, were not suited for non-Muslims. According to Ibn Abī Uṣaybiᶜa, the biographer of physicians, when Ibn Māsawayh migrated to Baghdad, he began to host clinical hours after sunset in his home. While examining patients' eyes, ears, and heart, he would recite humorous stories, poetry, and song to them, in an effort to heal the body by stimulating the soul. In addition to creating a welcoming environment for guests, Ibn Māsawayh had an impeccable capacity to charm and amaze with wit and manners, not to mention the entertainment his pet monkey, Jumājim, provided.[51] These *mujālasāt* developed from primarily clinical events to literary events, ultimately spreading to the homes of nonphysician littérateurs.

References to *mujālasāt* are legion in Arabo-Islamic sources, although description of these assemblies are paradoxically rare, suggesting the degree to which classical authors took this institution for granted. One source, however, manuscript 1708 at Spain's Escorial library, offers what might be the most detailed description of setting, mood, and collegiality at *mujālasāt.* The source has the disadvantage of being from the seventeenth century, several centuries after the period in question. Nevertheless, it provides a starting point that can be modified for different times and places. Manuscript 1708, titled *Al-Maqāma al-Badīᶜiyya fī Waṣf Jamāl al-Maᶜālim al-Makkiyya* (The Wondrous Story Session Describing the Beauty of Mecca's Landmarks), was compiled by Muḥyī al-Dīn ᶜAbd al-Qādir b. Muḥammad al-Fayyūmī (d. 1614), a Hanafi law professor of little acclaim who worked in Mamluk Cairo.[52] His chief virtue for our purposes rests in his status as an amateur of humanities, thus reflecting common practice.

Al-Fayyūmī frames his collection of stories and poetry as "heard knowledge" and describes in his preface how anecdotes naturally took shape in group:

> Abū al-Ṭayy [his friend] narrated an account of how he disseminated these fresh anecdotes. He said, "I yearned to remember loved

> ones and to talk into the night with those of mind and heart. So we would sit down for late talk on moonlit nights acquiring from each other's mouths the freshest fruits of knowledge. We would not grow tired of late-night talk until daybreak. If the novelty of recent anecdotes dried up, the wittiness of old and new replenished us. Each one of us was admired for what he remembered and esteemed for what he remembered. . . . Each one began to pour out what he had in him—what exhilarated him. He would stir the attendees with the merits of his oratory."[53]

Not all texts fit the definition of performances, not even all texts recited aloud. According to the folklorist Richard Bauman, the defining moment of performance begins with the speaker's assumption of responsibility to an audience for the display of skill in communicating. As the Homerist Albert Lord noted, the performer faces the judgment of the audience moment by moment as he or she competes to attract their attention and to hold it, thus compelling the performer to respond to their cues with adjustments in text and delivery. The instability of an audience, the fact that a performer can never take their attentiveness for granted, implies that the performer has the perpetual responsibility to display competence according to the audience's expectations. The performer implicitly agrees to stand subject to the approval or disapproval of an audience, and thus external validation becomes an incentive for performing.[54]

In this light al-Fayyūmī's description provides indications of the defining features that make opening one's mouth in the *mujālasa* a stirring performance. The speaker receives the judgment of his or her peers and will be held accountable to the audience's standards and expectations. Accentuating the positive, al-Fayyūmī notes the stakes of performance: admiration and the esteem of one's peers. The goal, in his phrasing, was to stir the attendees with one's delivery. We surmise that shoddy performance would fail to earn such a response, and the performer would know or come to know.

In the Arabic literary tradition, audience response counted as a performance detail worth noting in anecdotes about performances, thus suggesting that performers craved it, sought it, esteemed it, and transformed audience response into the stuff of narrative. In one instance a poet's performance caused a caliph to lean back and kick the air (like a sacrificial animal) in rapture.[55] Another anecdote depicts a prince listening to a poet so entranced that he crawls (like an infant) along his mattress (*maṣallā*) toward the performer. The patron inches forward in three stages, each time he pleads for more (*zidnī*). In the second and third stages he is drawn off the mattress and releases a cry (*ṣayḥa*) of ecstasy (*ṭarab*).[56] In another anecdote a well-established vizier listening to the poet al-Buḥturī began to tremble in a fit of rapture in response to a favorite line.[57] The caliph al-Hadī (r. 775–85) on one occasion lost control at the end of the performance; ecstasy was the culprit. He sprang from his seat and screamed out, "By God, encore—by my very life!"[58] A contemporary of Charlemagne, the caliph Hārūn al-Rashīd (r. 786–809), is said to have leaped to his feet and kissed the performer's head.[59]

Competent performers remained attuned to forms of audience reaction such as smiles, pensive looks, cheers, sighs of Amen, encore requests, foot-stomping, and clapping. In this way they could optimize the effectiveness of their performance and reduce the risk of embarrassment.[60] As Bauman notes, performers gained influence by virtue of their skill and wielded their power onstage to subvert power relations—a phenomenon that often rendered them feared and admired.[61] Thus for professional as well as amateur performers, personal clout rested in the sustained ability to elicit validation.

In addition to the generic pressures on the performer to attract and hold the audience's attention, one cannot rule out specific demands particular to the situation. In the Andalusian love story of Bayāḍ and Riyāḍ, for example, Bayāḍ is invited to recite poetry at a garden *mujālasa* to win the heart of Riyāḍ. When Bayāḍ shows deference to the kindly matron who facilitated his courtship of Riyāḍ, she advises him to focus on his performance: "My son, I don't need this [deference] from you, rather prepare your mind, consider your speech, and sequence your utterances for your introduction to a proper lady's palace." His response conveys performance anxiety (in love and art): "If all of this, all of what you say, is as you describe, then I can't enter her palace ever."

In due course Bayāḍ impresses his audience, and the Lady of the House lauds him with the label "a poet genius and winning littérateur" (*shāʿir mufliq wa adīb arīb*) and explains the basis for her admiration: "*We* recite what we have related, memorized and overheard from others, but *you* recite what you improvise from within yourself." She does not rest, however, without raising the stakes for Bayāḍ, when she says: "We all humbly ask and suggest, show us the breadth of your soul, the freshness of your mind and your perceptiveness of poetry. We would like you to describe the garden that we are in. It will not be difficult for you." To which, Bayāḍ responds with a cock of the head and an instantaneous composition of poetry and melody, earning rousing compliments and more requests.[62]

In Andalusia and the Arab West it was fairly common for both men and women to participate in mixed *mujālasāt,* such as the example we have in the romance of Bayāḍ and Riyāḍ. In the Arab East, however, middle- and higher-ranking women tended to have separate salons. This dynamic is attested in residential architecture with a separate salon space (*qāʿa*) for men and one for women in the more private section of the house (*Ḥarīm* or *Ḥarāmlak*). Women's salons can be found in Fustat homes from the Tulunid and Fatimid periods (ninth–eleventh cent., Cairo, Egypt), as well as in Ottoman townhomes, such as Ajikbash House (eighteenth cent., Aleppo, Syria), Harrawi House (1731, Cairo, Egypt), and Suhaymi House (1648, Cairo, Egypt). In the Ottoman homes, often the women's salon is located on the second floor, and in the case of Harrawi House, it has a rooftop gallery screened by a wood-carved arabesque Mashrabiya. Interestingly, though, the gallery is accessible only via a tight service staircase, indicating that servants and slaves would have looked on to witness the lady of the house as she earned prestige and admiration in her role as host and littérateur. While textual evidence for the participation of women is scant, the fact that there was a dedicated space for *mujālasāt* in the homes of middle- and higher-status women suggests that women sought opportunities to acquire the verbal prowess and tenacity that *adab* instills.[63]

One of the most compelling examples of women's tenacity using *adab* comes from a collection of anecdotes about acts of generosity. A woman named Maria the Copt wanted the honor of playing host to the caliph al-Maʾmūn and his entourage as they passed by her village, of which she was chief (*ṣāḥibat al-qarya*). She beseeched him for the honor of hosting: "O Commander of the Faithful, you camped in every village, but you passed by my village. Other Copts will ridicule me on that account. I beseech the Commander of the Faithful to give me the honor of alighting in my village so that I and my descendants may also enjoy the privilege, and that my rivals may not lord it over me." She cried vigorously, and al-Maʾmūn took pity on her. He bent the reins of his horse toward her and dismounted. Since persuasive skill and audience impact are two of the hallmarks of *adab,* her display of *adab* is validated by the caliph's acceptance.

Though the caliph obliged her, his aristocratic contempt would occasionally flicker, much to Maria's disappointment. Nevertheless, she was undaunted in her effort to impress with a banquet of near-mythic proportions. The next morning the caliph al-Maʾmūn persisted with his arrogance but would face another surprise:

> When he awoke the next day and set out to depart, she came to him with ten servants each carrying a large dish. As he saw it from afar he mocked to his attendants, "The Coptic lady is bringing you gifts of the countryside, vinegar-sauce, salt fish and bitter aloes." When she placed them in his hands, he noticed each dish had in it a pouch of gold, and he deemed it beautiful but demanded she take it back.
>
> "No," she said, "by God I won't!" He looked at the gold pieces and he noticed that they all had the exact same mintage. He said, "By God, this is wonderful! Our treasury may very well lack something like it." She said, "O Commander of the Faithful, do not break our hearts, nor deride us." He said, "To the contrary, a fraction of what you have done would've been sufficient, and we wish not to impose. So take back your money, may God bless you."
>
> She then grabbed a clump of land, and said, "O Commander of the Faithful! This—pointing to the gold—is from this—pointing to the soil she picked up from the land—and thereafter from your justice, O Commander of the Faithful! And I have a lot of it!" He then gave the command, the gifts were accepted from her, but, he bestowed upon her farmland, and awarded her in her village, Ṭāʾ al-Naml, two hundred feddans free of kharāj-taxes. He departed amazed at the magnitude of her manliness (*murūʾa:* pun on her name) and the extent of her means.[64]

Examples of men and women using *adab* methods to charm, shame, and blandish are the staple of *adab* material about caliphs and sultans. They illustrate the ideal of influencing authority without a loss of dignity, embodied in the pithy dictum, "Teach them (*tuʿal-limahum*) as though they teach you, educate them (*tuʾaddibahum*) as though they educate you; if not, then stay as far away as possible!"[65] These techniques for public speaking and communicating with daunting authority figures could be learned in *mujālasāt* only by a steady diet of listening to and performing *adab*. Her stellar performance would have had to be an immaculate conception for Maria, if a woman of her talent did not frequent the *mujālasāt*.

In addition to romance, the *mujālasa* must have provided a proving ground for gaining earthly benefits such as sex, monetary gain, and prestige, which would have raised the stakes of the performance. With audience responses being such a prized result, one must consider the impact of ends on means. When a performer assumed responsibility for the display of skill, for attracting and holding attention, what effect might this have had on his or her text and delivery? Furthermore, because most *adab* performances purported to represent people, places, and events (mostly in the distant past) in the form of historical narrative and verse, what are the standards for evaluating the authenticity of such speech? What are the principles for producing such speech? This is the focus of chapter 2.

TWO

Adab Principles for Artistic Speech in Assembly

The Pragmatics of *Adab*

The concept of *adab* is central to Arabo-Islamic cultural analysis. It denotes, on the one hand, a corpus of varied literary knowledge (e.g., poetry, charming anecdotes, even historical narratives) that a young littérateur must know—akin to the Greek concept of *paideia.* On the other hand, *adab* refers to the constellation of courtly manners and tastes to be conditioned and exhibited. These two senses of the term have been abundantly discussed in modern Arabic scholarship.[1] Whether speaking of texts or behaviors, however, the debate over the meaning of *adab* in classical Arabic culture has widely assumed that medieval society experienced literature in the form of private reading, which is a modernist bias. Private reading was far from the norm in medieval societies globally, yet scholarship surrounding *adab* has overlooked or discounted the impact of the *mujālasāt* on literature, society, and the formation of a canon. Perhaps by examining the social dimensions—prestige, networking, intimacy—we can ask questions that help us understand how it was that teenagers and status-conscious adults throughout the ages cared so deeply for these arts, despite the intimidating challenge of gaining skills and competence in *adab.*

What made *adab* worthy of their trouble? What was appealing to people about this endeavor? The value of *adab* literature has by and large been taken for granted; thus scholarship has tended to offer tautological definitions grounded in ideals of form and content. This view discounts the documented external effects that *adab* must have produced in audiences and the equally documented methods that performers used to prepare in order to achieve exactly their intended effects.

In addition to curricula and manners, a sense of *adab* emerges in lexicons that might facilitate our endeavor to understand the motivating forces that spurred millions of novices to invest themselves in this form of education. The intransitive verb *aduba/yaʾdubu* denotes "to be well brought up, to become cultivated." The transitive verb *adaba/yaʾdibu,* with the altered middle vowel, gives us the meanings "to prepare a banquet for someone or to invite someone to a banquet." This sense yields the noun for "banquet" or "repast"—*ʾadb* or *maʾdaba.*[2] *Adab* can hold a flexible yet pragmatic definition that can accommodate inevitable local and temporal variations of curriculum and behavior: words and deeds that elicit approval in social settings. Thus to acquire or teach *adab* would entail learning or transmitting words and deeds that would accrue glory in the eyes of others and eschew embarrassment. It is telling that when al-ʿĀmirī comes to the defense of *adab* culture (under attack from pious ascetics), he says:

> Some of the pious ascetics find fault in the humanistic arts (*ādāb*) and charge that anyone who is driven to acquire them must be one of the following men: Either a man who aspires to be praised for eloquence and clarity, or a man who ornaments himself with them before the mighty and the noble to gradually gain by its [*ādāb*'s] glory a means to success and rank.[3]

Curiously, both characterizations establish an association between *adab*-type knowledge and status seeking. In the first instance the littérateur wants praise, conventionally from subordinates and peers, and in the second instance, the littérateur seeks the approval of superiors in order to gain benefits that can translate into opportunity for oneself and one's family.

The ideal of *adab* opens up semantic and cognitive associations between literal and figurative hosting and dining, raising the possibility that principles of sociability (*muʾānasa*) and charm (*ẓarf*) influence how littérateurs produced and consumed *adab* as they would a meaty repast (*maʾdaba*). If *adab* was speech and conduct that entitled one to banquet with others time after time and to earn their admiration, then perhaps we might derive a pragmatic definition to measure the quality of *adab* by its impact expressed as audience reaction.

Adab, like the modern academic terms *discipline, field,* and *school,* denotes a variety of cognitive skills and behaviors that are subject to peer evaluation. Were it not for the reality of peer validation, the procedures of one's academic "discipline" would unravel. As a safeguard of integrity, external validation prevents *adab* from becoming idiosyncratic and bizarrely subjective, while ensuring that personal innovations see the light of day in a manner that meets collective standards of merit. Banqueting and peer validation give us incentives that are fundamental to human behavior, at any age, and hence serve us well in outlining the norms that guided *adab* production and reception. It is thus not surprising that the scholar-littérateur al-Zamakhsharī, among others, included in the category of *adab* knowing how to conduct oneself in *mujālasāt*.[4]

History: A Type of *Adab*

The norms of *adab* production and reception have wide implications for the formation and presentation of the Arabo-Islamic past, as *adab* texts included historical verse and narrative that purported to depict past people and events.[5] The curriculum of *adab* could include traditional and contemporary poetry and narrative transmitted in the Arabic language, although the narrative report (*khabar;* pl. *akhbār*) itself constituted the basic unit of many genres of writing outside our modern categories of literature. This category included genealogy of tribes (*ansāb*), genealogy of horses (*ansāb al-khayl*), speeches (*khutab*), tales (*qiṣaṣ, hikāyāt*), prosopography (*ṭabaqāt*), hagiography (*ṭabaqāt al-awliyāʾ*), cosmological-natural history (*ʿajāʾib al-makhlūqāt*), geographic-archaeological lore (*ʿajāʾib al-buldān*), zoological lore (*ʿajāʾib al-ḥayawān*), battle history (*maghāzī*), biography/heroic epic (*sīra*), proverbs (*amthāl*), and periodized history (*taʾrīkh*). All these *akhbār*-based genres employed narrative patterns to elicit wonder within the audience and reward it with cultural information.

Typically, medieval Muslim historians, by virtue of their language-based training as professional jurists or littérateurs, were steeped in literary know-how. Historical works offer a panoply of *adab* materials plotted along a chronological scheme, such as the historian al-Nuwayrī's (d. ca. 1332) *Nihāyat al-Arab fī Funūn al-Adab* (The Utmost in Types of *Adab*). This thirty-three-volume history vaunts one of the most impressive displays of Arabo-Islamic cosmology, geographic lore, proverbs, tribal rituals, animal and plant folklore, Arabian legend, apropos proverbs, and poems, often in the name of "history."[6] Thus, when thinking about medieval Arabo-Islamic culture, we should bear in mind the debt that history owes to the *mujālasāt* as a forum for the performance of *adab*.

As we can see from the placement of history within *adab,* the key problem modern scholars have faced in the study of historical narrative remains the difficulty of appreciating the literary performative atmosphere in which narratives are deployed, recited, and transmitted to future generations. In the modern era we tend to think of history and historiography as a form of scholarship, whereas people in medieval Arabo-Islamic culture and indeed in most medieval cultures tended to think of historical narrative as an organic fruit of artistic performance in group. Abbasid historians—with rare exception—did not *discover* what happened in the past.[7] Consider, for example, that archaeological remains of previous eras were deemed important by historians and littérateurs because they elicited wonder and lyricism, not concrete answers about what actually happened.[8] Historians seldom if ever investigated or interpreted such "archival" documents as contracts, bills of sale, or state epistles to contradict popular perceptions.[9] (In effect, as I explain later in this chapter, educators and adults in positions of responsibility gave little credence to knowledge that was divested of a persona.) History that accurately reconstructed the past was not the sort of history that littérateurs wanted or expected.

Rather, historians saw themselves as arranging and reporting various versions of what was widely performed in *adab* gatherings, where narratives were crafted and adjusted to shape memory of the past.

In line with modern positivist views of history, however, the source-critical approach to medieval Islamic history has disapproved of the crafted nature of narratives. This view concludes that literary devices in narratives make it clear that "transmitters and collectors invented and circulated reports on a large scale." The methods employed in producing historical narrative indicate falsification of fact, "a process of compiling and systematizing, of expanding and abbreviating, or inventing the chronology and the other order of events, or omitting and creating, and through other manipulations." This inconvenient reality has yielded "grave reservations concerning both the overall historicity of the Arab-Islamic literary tradition and the view of early historians which emerges from that tradition."[10] At best, on this view, scholars can hope to sift through the falsifications to unearth "kernels of truth."

The problem with the source-critical approach, and in effect the trouble with all positivist approaches to medieval history, is a misplaced assumption that medieval audiences share with the positivists the same standards of authenticity for historical narratives—namely, scholastic positivism. I illustrate how historical narratives were viewed and practiced as a performed art in assembly. This discussion serves as an opportunity to analyze the standards of authenticity that applied to historical narrative recitations in the *mujālasāt,* which tended to emphasize performance quality and figurative truth over banal and literal audits of events and people. I argue that littérateurs employed a set of principles for speaking in assembly that need not be reconciled with today's positivist standards of historiography or the modern view that history must be a field of scholarship and not art. If we are to understand the way medieval littérateurs spoke of the world (particularly the past), we must be willing to set aside our presentist sensibilities and employ another set of principles for speaking in assembly. Arabo-Islamic culture deemed history a field of *adab,* thus a performed, recited art, along with poetry. Performance made *adab* norms and principles relevant to the production, transmission, and recitation of historical narrative.[11]

Methods of Preparation for Performance: The Interplay of Oral and Written Knowledge

Literary salons were fundamentally a forum for the transmission and display of knowledge between responsive people. Thus preparation was a means to gain credibility for one's display. Credibility was dependent on observing certain habits and norms that accredited education in the Arabo-Islamic Middle Ages. The central principle governing the culture of medieval education was the imperative to preserve the face-to-face social dimensions of knowledge delivery and reception. Knowledge was considered a social and sociable enterprise, and thus self-study did not become the norm in Arabo-Islamic personal development.[12]

Books were a vital part of learned circles of all sorts, whether in the fields of Arabic knowledge (religious or *adab*) or so-called foreign knowledge (astronomy, philosophy, medicine, and so on), beginning in the eighth century with the introduction of paper and state support for its production. The bias against self-study was scarcely a bias against books per se; rather, it was a bias against the solitary unguided use of books. There were visible exceptions to this norm, of course, such as those accredited professionals atop the arc of their careers who did not need the added credentials of guided study or those who had vested interests in the production and sale of books.[13] But in general there remained no societal mechanism for credentialing self-study, so the balance of opinion and practice favored sociable models of teaching, in which books were employed and deployed for the sake of memory and public recitation.

Rather than displace face-to-face recitation, the availability of paper in the Middle East invigorated and multiplied the social bonds and rituals deemed necessary to transmit knowledge, as well as the face-to-face performance that authenticated it. In short, people used books and paper in unprecedented ways to complement the oral dimensions of education. In medieval seminaries as early as the tenth century a system of certification (*ijāzat al-samāᶜ*) was used to accredit students for knowledge gained.[14] As the historians Pierre MacKay and George Makdisi have argued, this system authorized a student to teach not a subject but particular books within a subject, indicating that the special role of books in face-to-face education was still reliant on personal credentials.[15] This norm indicates the degree to which professionals and amateurs viewed Arabic fields of knowledge as detailed and high stakes, such as the modern professions of medicine or law. How many of us today would entrust our worries to a self-taught physician or lawyer?

The development and use of paper in Europe and the Middle East differed fundamentally. Latin Europe, before the thirteenth century, had little or no pulp paper technology, thus making education dependent on books made of vellum or parchment, both laboriously processed from animal skins.[16] This rendered books an expensive, rare commodity, as it might require the skin of some forty cows to make an average book.[17] In contrast, the Middle East followed China's lead to affordable technologies in the form of flax- and cotton-based paper, which was available in pre-Islamic Iran as early as the sixth century. In the eighth century Samarqand in Central Asia became known for the efficient production of its paper, known as *kāghid.*[18] Knowledge of paper-making techniques enabled a proliferation of manuscripts in the urban centers.[19] Abbasid Baghdad boasted a special copyists' market (*sūq al-warrāqīn*), where a hundred copyist-merchants sold and lent out manuscripts.[20]

In Arabo-Islamic culture a piece of technology such as a book could not adequately substitute for the authority of learned gifted personalities, largely because of the premium on lyricism and elegizing. For example, when the great philologist al-Mubarrad passed away, Ibn ᶜAllāf reminded colleagues in a eulogy that only one great philologist of the era remained: al-Thaᶜlab. To his students, Ibn ᶜAllāf provided these words: "My advice to you is to record his very breathing, if indeed breathing can be recorded," suggesting that the best lessons cannot be captured in writing.[21] Even in the case of the collegial *mujālasāt,* the focus was on a solemn relationship. As the scholar al-Fayyūmī noted, colleagues are referred to as those of "mind and heart," who would keep each other company nightlong, "acquiring from each other's mouths the freshest fruits of knowledge."[22] An event's finesse and sociability was as important as the quality and quantity of knowledge displayed. Forging social bonds was perhaps the most important lesson of any subject; thus education was a means of binding people together in ontological chains of being. For this reason education in the fields of Arabic knowledge received credibility chiefly from face-to-face exchanges.

Ibn Buṭlān (d. ca. 1068), a professional physician but an amateur littérateur, composed a succinct outline of the reasons against relying on books instead of people. Aptitude being equal, Ibn Buṭlān said, students learn better and easier from teachers rather than books. First, meaning transfers from like-minded to like-minded, and thus it would be simpler for a student to learn from a sentient eloquent being like himself than from an inanimate volume. Second, if a student fails to understand a technical point or an idea, a teacher can clarify with rephrasing, whereas a book can never rephrase. A teacher is more suited (*aṣlaḥ*) to the student's needs. Third, knowledge can exist only in a being that has a soul. The soul can be knowledgeable, but a book cannot retain knowledge by its soulless nature. Likewise, only a sentient being can receive knowledge.

Fourth, the form that knowledge takes is expression (*lafẓ*), and expression has three stages: The first is intimate (*qarīb*), when the mind forms an idea; the second is intermediate (*mutawassiṭ*), when the idea forms a vocal expression; the third is more distant (*ba^cīd*), when the vocal expression is written down in a book. The book, in Ibn Buṭlān's view, is thus necessarily a form of a form of a form, thrice removed from the mind that produced an idea, whereas the vocal expression is only twice removed. This greater degree of ease and intimacy facilitates learning more than do books. As a side note to this logic, Ibn Buṭlān states that the transmission of ideas through books relies on a sense that is "alien" (*ḥāssa gharība*) to vocal expression—sight. The most appropriate sense is hearing, since the expression is vocal. This dynamic of the intimacy of senses makes learning from the voice of a teacher more comfortable (*ashal*) than from the script of a book. Fifth, the student who recites a book to a teacher receives knowledge from a teacher aurally as well as from the book visually, and one of these senses is more intimate. Thus the teacher can correct his recitation if he errs, but the book's visual nature would not provide such a corrective.

Although Ibn Buṭlān's first five reasons are philosophical, suggesting deep-seated assumptions about soul, mind, and communication in education, his final reason addresses the practical design of the Arabic script system as well as the nature of writing in general. In written texts there are technical and Greek terms that are unfamiliar to the student. There are also errors in copying. Moreover, the Arabic script (*abjad*) was consonantal, up until the tenth century at the earliest, and any diacritical or vowel marks were in flux, and not widely adopted, creating a built-in ambiguity.[23] How would a student thus be able to decipher a text with confidence?[24]

Ibn Buṭlān's arguments assume a concept of knowledge dramatically different from those that might operate in postindustrial society. First, in his view knowledge is embodied in a person. There can be no knowledge outside of a person. The historian Ibn Khaldūn reaffirmed this premise: "Know that the storehouse for knowledge is the human soul."[25] One line of poetry signals the hazard of trusting paper, as opposed to people, to transmit knowledge: "He committed knowledge to paper, then lost it / Paper indeed is a bad place to keep it."[26] Knowledge therefore can only be "kept" within a person.

Second, the exchange of knowledge between people requires a relationship of trust. A relevant adage informed, "Wise men say, do not teach the dastard anything anytime; he might benefit from it and then become your enemy." One scholar was asked, "What type of knowledge would be deemed most dangerous?— That which benefits only fools." Similarly, even in the case of established authorities, further self-study outside a relationship of trust did not necessarily provide the necessary credibility to transmit knowledge. For example, the littérateur al-Ṣūlī was criticized, despite his erudition and expertise, for teaching texts he personally had never heard recited.[27] The historian Marshall G. S. Hodgson observes the importance of personal witness for historical narratives in guaranteeing the integrity of each link in a continuous human chain.[28] The historian Richard W. Bulliet likewise explains that the authority to communicate Hadith-knowledge rested in personally hearing it from someone who personally heard it in a chain going back to the Prophet himself or a companion of the Prophet.[29] A student aspiring to a career as a scholar would strive for the privilege of joining that historical chain. He would essentially become a permanent member of this ontological chain of being by witnessing the oral event, what Bulliet calls being an "ear witness," and by passing on the tradition to future generations.[30] In al-Ṣūlī's case, because his aural reception was not witnessed by others, he lacked the license to transmit this particular knowledge. One also finds suggestions that literary speech cultivated relationships of trust: "The best of speech forges bonds between hearts."[31] In these few confirmations, we see knowledge being framed as a privilege, a type of power, not to be taken but assigned and conferred in a normative manner.

Third, one senses in Ibn Buṭlān's outline the assumption that writing is a phantom of real communication in the form of speech. Within this framework speech conveys musical qualities, such as tone, volume, and cadence—subtleties that in the Arabic script would be lost in the translation from speech to writing. In a similar vein Ibn Khaldūn considered Arabic orthography a minimalist notational system for recording speech without the warm nuances of delivery that makes a text come to life.[32]

In addition to the musical dimensions of voice, the Arabic script in Islam's early centuries noted only consonantal sounds. In effect, Arabic orthography played the role of a stenographic system for recording dictations. Arabic orthography, as in other Semitic languages, does not show short vowels.[33] Vowels, and even the diacritic dots that distinguish homographs, were seldom used in the earliest epigraphic script of Islam's first century.[34] In its second century a multiplicity of idiosyncratic systems were in use, including that by the grammarian Khalīl b. Aḥmad (d. 791). One of the consequences, perhaps even an aim, of this stenographic system was to render self-study intimidating for the novice, thus generating demand for a credentialing establishment. Consider, for example, that without vowels or diacritics the word *bayt* (house) could be misread, since the consonants *bā, tā, thā, nūn,* and *yā* would all be represented by the unpointed dish, yielding *bint* (daughter), *nabāt* (plant), *nābit* (sprouting), or *thabāt* (steadfastness) or *thābit* (steadfast), just to name half a dozen of the many possibilities. In this respect this stenographic system served to prevent unauthorized access by novices to a living tradition, requiring them to seek the aid of instructors within the credentialing network.

The potential for confusing the uninitiated increases exponentially with barriers to knowledge, such as archaic terminology, neologisms, and disciplinary jargon. To make matters even more daunting, Arabic cursive script well into the tenth century would break off at the end of the line in midword at letters that do not connect to the left.[35] Implicitly, words were not written as grapheme units but as a sequence of phonetic cues.[36] The earliest Arabic cursive served as a coded stenographic system—a shorthand for interpersonal speech. After Arabic orthography was standardized, it preserved an enigmatic quality, rendering it among a category of scripts whose orthography challenged its reader with a built-in "element of interpretation."[37] To learn a text (to read, memorize, understand, and recite it), a student would thus need to seek out a teacher.

The teacher's recitation provided the necessary vowels for the student, while the written text remained a visual prompt to the spoken utterance. As late as the fourteenth century, Ibn Khaldūn advised the anxious student to break down the relationship between written sign and meaning into two links, joined by the spoken utterance. For the first link the student should dwell on the connection between the written sign (*al-kitāba al-marsūma*) and the spoken utterance (*al-alfāẓ al-maqūla*). Thereafter he or she should comprehend the connections between the spoken utterance and the desired meaning (*al-maᶜānī al-maṭlūba*).[38] It is compelling that Ibn Khaldūn preserved a vital oral component in learning and cognition that encouraged a teacher's intervention.

Because medieval educators considered self-study both impractical and unsociable, the most acceptable methods were those that would lead to face-to-face exchanges. Students were trained to memorize countless texts by heart from childhood. This was considered essential content—knowledge—to earn the admiration of audiences. Then they were trained to develop performance skills, which included thoughtful recitation verbatim, as well as improvisation when needed.[39] The methods that students learned for acquiring and performing texts suggests that rather than displacing orality, writing facilitated it in the realm of Arabic fields of knowledge.

Rather than insist that writing played a determinant role in shaping society—along the lines of the great divide theory—I would like to probe the agency of people in alternating between oral and written media. The great divide theory poses the problem of techno-determinist arguments, which give "agency" to technology without due regard for sociological factors of age, gender, race, and class. These factors of course might suggest how differing or vying groups used technology to achieve discrete interests. From a performance perspective, let us examine how groups and individuals mobilized technology (in this case, books) to hold and sustain an audience's attention. For example, the *Book of Monasteries* by the littérateur al-Shābushtī (d. 1000) is organized by chapters named after various monasteries and contains bawdy anecdotes celebrating the bacchic escapades of famous Abbasid nobles.[40]

In the margins of the Berlin manuscript an anonymous hand jotted a remark that stresses the connection between text, memory, and responsibility in performance. The note reads: "The anecdotes falling under this monastery are very delightful. The late-night raconteur (*musāmir*) must memorize them and perform them, for the soul is ennobled by the best of anecdotes."[41] The raconteur is not only encouraged to memorize, but to do so with an explicit purpose: to touch the soul of audiences. The note suggests the delicate interplay of writing and orality for the purposes of the *mujālasāt.* Interestingly, the note comments on one particular chapter in the manuscript, suggesting that a raconteur might not be bound to slavishly memorize all chapters or all anecdotes with equal rigor. In fact, sporadically on every page or so, the margins bear a note in the same raconteur's hand (*yuḥfaẓ*): "ought to be memorized."[42] A competent raconteur may well find that certain chapters are better suited for some audiences than others. A book could remain in his collection until the need arose for more narratives.

Another maxim recognizes the pitfalls of memory but simultaneously affirms the necessity of aural-oral transmission. It states: "People misrecite the best portion of what they memorize, memorize the best portion of what they write, and write the best portion of what they hear. So if you acquire knowledge (*adab*), acquire it directly from the mouths of men. You will not hear except the best—or unstrung pearls."[43] While casting doubt on all the steps between listening and performance, the anecdotes affirm first the subjective dimension of selection and second the importance of exposing oneself to the most competent educators. This maxim implies that students needed to exercise selectivity in whom to listen to, what to dictate, what to memorize, and what to recite (or misrecite). Neither orality nor writing is given a determinative role that a student must respect. Rather, a student must cultivate good judgment.

Although the preceding examples indicate interplay when possible, there are several indications that hearing trumped sight in cultural and educational value. As a measure of the centrality of oral face-to-face performance in education, one might gauge handicaps as a barometer of accommodation. Medieval education welcomed and educated untold numbers of littérateurs who were blind, including many who set standards as professional narrators or poets, such as Bashshār b. Burd and al-Maᶜarrī. Few littérateurs of note were deaf or mute, however.[44] In addition, many of the finest transmitters of poetry and lore during the Abbasid period were illiterate members of Bedouin tribes pasturing their herds in southern and western Iraq. Many Bedouins appear in anecdotes taking a seat of honor at the *mujālasāt* of urbanites in Baghdad, Basra, Kufa, and Samarra, such as ᶜUmāra b. ᶜUqayl, an illiterate Bedouin poet. Most surprisingly, al-Ṣūlī defended the poetry of Abū Tammām by illustrating the endorsement of ᶜUmāra.[45]

In effect, illiteracy or blindness had little to do with cognitive or performative display—except maybe enhancing it—as the adage proclaimed: "Silence is the mind's slumber, and speech is its awakening. There is no slumber without awakening and no awakening without slumber."[46] By the same token, that which redeems the blind and the illiterate disadvantages the mute and the deaf: the mute's mind would be deemed in perpetual slumber, and the deaf would be deemed unperceptive to the cognitive stirrings of others. Flaws in speaking or hearing were considered so serious that one Bedouin, Ibn Lisān al-Ḥummara, blasted another tribe with the following: "Among them are those who finish their utterance before their tongue starts up. Among them are those [whose] utterance[s] never reach the ears of his salon companion. Among them are those who compel the ear, but burden the ears with a heavy mental load."[47] Implicitly, his own illiteracy must have been no liability for this Bedouin poet.

There appears to be a preference for sound over sight because it embodied something lyrical by evoking that which is absent. Thus it was almost a matter of fact that hearing was closer to desire—to the heart—than vision. The Abbasid minor poet Ibn Qanbar noted, "If you are not with me, your memory/glory is with me. My heart sees you though you may be absent to my sight."[48] Similarly, the Abbasid poet Abū Qāsim ᶜAbd al-Ṣamad playfully compares sight, scent, and sound when he says, "Basil the sprig lives a day, though basil the utterance never dies. Scarcely does basil the scent impact men compared with basil of the ears."[49] These lyrical attitudes toward the vocal world of *adab* culture were consistent with the emotional states found in the *mujālasāt.*

Emotional States in Performance

Of course, emotions and moods are elicited by particular pieces of narrative and poetry, but they are also engendered by the institution of the *mujālasāt* as a tradition. The ancient *symposion* in the Middle East was essentially a means of coping with a perennial ontological crisis: mortality and the grief it aroused. The ancient *symposion* was dedicated to bygone gods and heroes, and this fundamental mood found expression in the phrasing of al-Fayyūmī: "I yearned to remember loved ones." The ancient *symposion* and the Arabic *mujālasa* were in certain ways a type of family, a community of love. Like family, they provided security against the perennial sources of vulnerability: misfortune and mortality in the short term and loss of legacy—that is, being forgotten postmortem—in the long term. There were two legitimate and mature responses to the perennial crisis of mortality. The first was to remember mortality, *memento mori,* which was the mainstay of Semitic monotheism employed to chasten and reprimand the pious. The second was the spirit of carpe diem, which had two complementary expressions in the *mujālasāt:* a tragic-elegiac mode (*nasībī*) and a comic-bacchic (*mujūn*) mode.[50] Both provided ritualized catharsis in coping with mortality in a manner that affirmed human agency.

The physician Ibn Buṭlān, for example, was said to never have married or had children, and thus he composed these verses noting the elegiac value of the *symposion* postmortem: "If I die, no one will weep my death / except my gathering (*majlis*) for medicine and books; they will weep."[51] In a similar vein, the poet al-Buḥturī composed an elegy that suggests the *mujālasāt* were nothing short of a community of love whose role it was to preserve the immortal aspect of one's being, one's legacy:

May showers bless our gathering that you made joyful,
Alas to our gathering that you left bereft.
You made our gathering by your memory lively;
You attend hereafter another forever.
Your memory is a friend to us present,
Though you yield your body to others.
Our day will relish the taste of your memory;
So, those by whom you gathered will take joy for you.[52]

In a hierarchical society, where most public and private associations were governed by the principles of patronage and clientage, the *mujālasāt* offered a kind of intimacy and equality that was inherent to the session itself. This is evidenced by al-Fayyūmī's romantic admiration for his colleagues and his mention that performers took turns, without dominating. In contrast to the impersonal interactions of society at large, interactions in the literary salon were expected to be warm and personal. Al-Buḥturī, for example, sent an invitation in seven verses, at the week's end, to the grammarian al-Mubarrad, in which he notes the sensual and emotional warmth of the gathering.

It's a Saturday, and we abound in food for
the freeman; blossoms are at hand.
Ours is a gathering (*majlis*) on the river, aromatic,
roomy. There, hearts find relief.
The passing of wine around, draws you closer to
what you desire, even if you your beloved wronged.
Come out to us, O Muḥammad Ibn Yazīd, in secret,
so sees you not a spy.
We chase away grief with three drafts, brimming of wine, in
morning, by which anguish is banished.
In wine, wane the bittersweets of love.
My pulse for the littérateur stirs.
Let not the gray of years keep you from me,
For gray years have not kept me from singing of passion.[53]

The *mujālasāt* instilled among friends the expectation of security from gossip and scandal and the assurance of joy and companionability. As al-Buḥturī suggests, these gatherings were as much an escape from the wrongs of the world as they were a coping method to address them. In a hierarchical society where self-disclosure and vulnerability could be explosive, the *mujālasāt* invited a degree of trust enabling participants to put aside rank and pretense and to reveal an inner subjectivity to confidants.[54]

As a testament to the way that performers gave personal voice to verse, the literary critic Ibn Rashīq often referred to poetry performance as singing (*ghinā*ʾ), which emphasizes a performer's responsibility to have lyrical impact by showing some degree of inner subjectivity.[55] In comparison with the ancient *symposion* of western Asia and Greece, thc Arabo-Islamic *mujālasa* enjoyed a far greater degree of intimacy, equality, and prevalence in society, thus raising questions about the socioeconomic conditions that supported this transformation. The Abbasid period, the tenth century in particular, experienced an increase in the influence of the middle strata, which included men of overlapping professions, such as merchants, absentee landlords, military personnel, and courtiers, as well as pious and literary scholars. One cannot discount those of the highest ranks who rose up from humble families.[56]

In comparison to the ancient *symposion,* where the host was a lord over his guest, receiving the state's patronage to support the festivities, the Arabo-Islamic *mujālasāt* were financially accessible to middle-ranking members of society in terms of the costs of hosting. The cost of a clay amphora of good wine, for example, was approximately one dinar, a third to a tenth of the cost of an ordinary book.[57] The most palpable barrier for the middle stratum was clearly cognitive. If one could gain credentials and competence, for which no material resources could adequately substitute, one would be admired for his charm (*ẓarf*) and his display of *adab* (including both poetry and narrative) through effective, savvy communication (*balāgha*).[58] The admiration of one's peers could be redeemed for the currency of influence in society.

The impact of one's language ability on one's personal status in part helps to explain the abundance of anthologies in the tenth century for and about *mujālasāt,* such as the work of Abū Ḥayyān al-Tawḥīdī, al-Dīnawarī, al-Ṣūlī, and al-Tanūkhī.[59] From the ninth century on, middle-ranking men had clear strategies for how to use their personal eloquence and their associations to redefine norms and ideals of selfhood, culture, and government.[60] One might characterize *mu-*

jālasāt as the "secular religion" of the Abbasid era, much like professional and amateur sports in today's era, which allows those of humble origins to circumvent the more typical status markers of wealth and lineage, thus adjusting social values to suit contemporary needs.

In Abbasid culture the *mujālasāt* of middle-ranking individuals took the royal salon (*majlis, majlis al-uns;* architecturally, *dīwān al-khāṣṣ*) as their poetic model. The *mujālasa* ritually reenacted the royal salon in which the ruler privileged his closest companions in an evening celebration within the sanctuary of the palace.[61] The royal salon had an air of privilege, even familiarity, as guests enjoyed carnal, spiritual, and intellectual delights under the sponsorship of a powerful patron. The scholar Régis Blachère notes that association with salons was considered a marker of personal and moral worth, which outside the salon translated into prestige. Blachère explains, "The life of [the royal] salon occupied an important place. No one could aspire to public admiration, if he were not also a man of the world, an agreeable conversationalist with a lively mind and prompt at repartee, skilled in creating situations which he could turn to his advantage."[62]

The royal salon was an arena for the display of skill, and therefore association with it certified one's social and verbal capacity. The royal salon was hardly the place for amateurs. Within this idyllic, even mythic, social setting master-poets came to the court to personally deliver their praise to their patron in the presence of his guests.[63] In anecdotes that depict face-to-face encounters between a poet and a king, the poet's delivery is quoted as third-person speech, using the formulaic signal "he entered, then recited" (*dakhala fa-anshada*). This reported speech is not merely a literary device; rather, it is the climactic focus of the anecdote.[64] In other words, the anecdote models not the king's actions per se but the poet's language usage in relation to the king, which emerges as the prime reason for reporting the anecdote and the action most worthy of reflection and emulation.

Al-Fayyūmī explicitly framed his moonlit *mujālasa* as a vehicle to yearn for and summon "loved ones," meaning the impressive poets and littérateurs who originated verse and narratives in royal salons. Thus his *mujālasa* relived or reenacted an archetype of some sort, where he and his colleagues identified with the personal and verbal influence of poets and littérateurs. Within the lyrical yearning of the *mujālasa,* saturated with the earnest desire to be *with* bygone heroes, one finds an analog in the ancient Greek rhapsodes who enter a state of performance by identifying with Homer as their archetype. Artistically they *are* Homer.[65] That identification of personae, complete with involuntary gestures and a loss of self, creates a riveting dramatic tension that elicits the emotional participation of audiences.[66] The wider implication of this act of identification was felt precisely by commoners and middle-ranking individuals, especially children. Those moments of identification—open to anyone with verbal aptitude or skill—served as regular rites of passage into higher degrees of confidence and influence in society.

Abbasid literary gatherings, like Greek *symposion,* prompted a mood of comic-bacchic (*mujūn*) escapade, complete with its sexual, comic, and boisterous dimensions. The historian Yāqūt al-Ḥamawī related that the Buyid minister al-Muhallabī used to host sessions for littérateurs at night and that he reserved two nights a week for ribaldry and orgy with the most respected of Abbasid men. The sensuality of flesh and the word were therein indulged simultaneously in an atmosphere of bacchanalia. This passage falls in the midst of Yāqūt's biography of the Abbasid judge Abū al-Qāsim al-Tanūkhī. Note his emphasis on the pious turning impious during these carnival events:

> He [Abū al-Qāsim al-Tanūkhī] was among those who socialized with the vizier al-Muhallabī and gathered at his house two nights a week to throw off all inhibitions and to revel in good cheer and bacchanalia (*al-tabassuṭ fil-qaṣf wal-khilāᶜa*). They were Ibn Qarīᶜa, Ibn Maᶜrūf, the Qadi al-Tanūkhī, and others. All had long and white beards, as did al-Muhallabī. When all was congenial, the *mujālasa* fun, the music pleasing, then ecstasy (*ṭarab*) swept them up, they cast off the vestments of gravitas for the sake of wine, and they let loose in the far reaches of living, between levity and levitating! A thousand-weight golden chalice was placed in each one's hand filled with wine from Quṭrbul and ᶜAkbur. Each would dip his beard into it, actually soak it in there until it had sopped up most of it, then they would proceed to splash it on each other while dancing with bi-colored garlands braided![67]

This display demonstrates the more comic-bacchic mode of *mujālasāt* conduct, at ritual times and places, enabling urbanites to socialize in seemingly nonroutine ways. One should be careful to differentiate comic-bacchic expression from a debauched way of life, however. Although there were Abbasid figures who cultivated the persona of debauchee, for most littérateurs bacchanalia was an occasioned social practice. It provided a distinct contrast and counterbalance to the boredom and banality of serious pursuits. Abū Ḥayyān al-Tawḥīdī justified his own bacchic performances in the eighteenth "night" of his work in such terms: "Perhaps, this sort of talk might elicit disapproval roundly. That, however, would not be fair, for the soul needs levity (*bishr*). I have been told that Ibn ᶜAbbās [a renowned early teacher] used to say in his gathering—after delving into the Book, the Sunna, the Law, and various issues—'Now, let's have some fun!' I think all he intended by this was to give *balance* to the soul, so that the tedium of serious things does not overtake it, so that it can borrow the fire of new energy, so that it can prepare to receive what greets it. It will then listen.'"[68] Once again, one notices a drastic contrast between indulging in bacchanalia to counterbalance more dreary pursuits, and debauchery, which precludes other pursuits. Bacchanalia did not negate other aspects of life; rather, it was a means of coping with and reexperiencing serious existence.

The depictions of bacchanalia make it not only a topic of reflection but one of convention as well. As the anthropologist Mary Douglas notes, drunkenness relaxes inhibitions according to culturally specific patterns, making the comic-bacchic expression a mode that is conditioned and learned through interpersonal communication.[69] For this same reason the modern concept of alcoholism would be completely out of place in premodern societies that did not categorize chronic drunkenness in terms of pathology.[70] In ancient Greece, for example, bacchic scenes of sexuality at the *symposion* were depicted in a formalized manner on archaic pottery.[71] Many poems were composed specifically for the *symposion,* and therefore certain scenes and poses became set motifs. There were artistic expectations of when and how men would drink. Xenophanes believed that in the *symposion* men of nobility should first praise the god with reverent tongues, only "then [they] may drink." He added other expectations: a guest must drink only "as much as a man can carry home needing no attendant." At no point is the participant freed from responsibility and the judgment of others, however. Sober or not, he must live by the special standards of the gathering. Xenophanes suggested, "Praise the man who reveals his worth while drinking, and has memory and song for virtue."[72] It would seem that the performer, however inebriated, must continue to assume responsibility to an audience of colleagues who will judge his nobility. The archaeologist Ezio Pellizer argues that the point of wine drinking in the *symposion* was precisely to discipline the soul to moderate *between* the extremes of dull sobriety and aggressive drunkenness.[73] This ideal finds an analog in the Bayāḍ and Riyāḍ romance, when the Lady of the House advises in matters of love and wine: "The best course is moderation." In the course of the romance and throughout its scenes of wine drinking, this unfolds more as a precious unlikely ideal than a practice.[74]

The bacchanalia in Arabic literary gatherings never ceases to be the object of reflection and judgment. There are no innocent or purely descriptive accounts. The earlier passage related by Yāqūt is a commentary on the indispensable nature of *impiety* for the strict pious scholars. The account is a judgment of how participants should behave. One also notes a plethora of anecdotes in *The Book of Songs, The Thousand and One Nights, Meadows of Gold,* and *The Book of Monasteries* that represent and comment on bacchic behavior.[75] Ironically, the more bacchanalia becomes an experience and a topic of speech, the more it can be standardized and evaluated for its qualities. Of course, the inverse relationship is possible also: the more it is formalized, the more it will become a topic of speech and an experience.[76] Ultimately, bacchanalia can never be a complete escape from culture; rather, it represents an alternative form of cultural expression and experience.

In attempting to understand the performance of poetry and historical narrative, one might ask how these emotional states create communicative pressures. The threat of mortality and the spirit of carpe diem in *mujālasāt* seem to engender a performer's intense desire to connect with audiences.

Adjustment in Performance for the Audience

There are two broad categories of performance adjustments: those to the text (e.g., rewording, elision, addition, or repetition) and those in delivery style (e.g., changes in voice quality, volume, eye contact, and facial and bodily gesture). The field of Arabic studies has conventionally viewed adjustments to text as by and large illegitimate changes to text or tradition, thus placing individual performance at odds with text and tradition. In this book I build on the work of Najar and Gruendler to argue the appropriateness of adjustments in performance, if and only if the adjustment earns the external validation of audience approval.[77] Drawing on performance theory and practice, I emphasize the ways in which individual performance animates and enlivens both text and tradition.[78]

Adjustments in Style

Unfortunately, one rarely comes across a discussion of delivery style in the classical sources, making it difficult to explain or analyze, but it seems to have been important. One adage explains method by effect: "Better your recitation (*inshādak*) so that the poetry comes to life in my mind." Another adage suggests tone by poetic genre: "If you recite praise (*madīḥ*) be grand, lament (*marāthī*) be grief-stricken, elegiac love (*nasīb*) be humble, lampoon (*hijāʾ*) be harsh and extreme."[79] On rare occasion one encounters an accidental description of performance style. We are told, for example, that al-Buḥturī, in his recitation (*inshād*) style, walked up and down the stage and shook his shoulders and head, pointed with his sleeves, and paused to punctuate or repeat certain lines. He also approached the audience at times.[80] Other sources of style are recorded in the margins of manuscripts as cues. Manuscripts in the Moroccan National Archive record pause markings (*qiff*) in the margins of the poetry collections of the pre-Islamic Imruʾ al-Qays, as well as in that of the Abbasid al-Mutanabbī, after especially intense lines.[81] Similar markings are placed in the Berlin manuscript margins of *The Book of Monasteries,* in the course of jokes and at strategic moments in narrative and poetry. In poetry one finds that pauses often fall for effect after the first line.[82]

As a measure of how important style of delivery was relative to text, consider the case of the Abbasid poet Abū Tammām. This poet genius had the chronic curse of a coarse voice. When the vizier Muḥammad b. Abī Duʾād, wanting to promote the poet, mentioned him to the caliph al-Muᶜtaṣim, the caliph snapped, "Isn't he the one who has that gruff voice?" Ibn Abī Duʾād parried, "But he now hires a rhapsode who recites on his behalf with a sweet voice."[83] The point of this startling anecdote stresses the power of delivery style to carry or destroy a text despite poetic form and function. Al-Muᶜtaṣim knew Abū Tammām well, as having composed and delivered one of the most triumphant and aesthetic odes of early Islam—the panegyric celebrating the Abbasid conquest of the Byzantine trophy city of Amorium—yet this was not enough to recommend the poet.

In the Andalusian romance of Bayāḍ and Riyāḍ, one forms the impression that poetry was sung but in a recitative style (monody) to enunciate the wording of verse. This did not preclude the self-accompaniment of light strumming of the mandolin (*ṭanbūr*) or the lute (*ᶜūd*) for the purpose of amplifying the tale's lyrical qualities. The manuscript of the narratives at the Vatican contains illustrations that depict the peacock-like Bayāḍ singing-strumming while leaning over his right shoulder into his audience. At other times the more frail Riyāḍ droops her head over the lute, like a withering lily.[84] Although it is not entirely clear what other delivery styles were employed besides pauses, repetition, bodily movement, and the accompaniment of strings, one might extrapolate that the normal demands of performance would require the performer to charm the audience further with changes in his or her rate of speech and inflections of voice, expressions of the face, eye contact, and hand gestures.

The one inescapable reality of performance would be audience impact. Emphasizing effect, the Abbasid secretary-governor al-Ḥasan b. Sahl wrote, "Exchanging literature with men [means] impregnating the heart" (*muḥādathat al-rijāl talqīḥ al-albāb*).[85] In that vein Bayāḍ punctuated his singing of poetry to the lute with this disarming flourish: "When he finished his turn, he kissed the lute and placed it on the carpet. He said, 'This is my utmost in singing.' "[86] The goal of impressing an audience, rewarding its divisible attention, can scarcely be achieved with a dry, artless reading, no matter how competent the verbatim text. One of the primary catalysts then for the appeal of traditional genres and texts may very well have been the personal finesse and flare that a performer brought to face-to-face performance.

Adjustments to the Text

The degree to which a text might be adjusted resides in norm-driven attitudes about the text's fixity. Al-Buḥturī was said to have arranged the wording and verse order of his elegy of al-Mutawakkil in one fashion in order to meet the short-term needs of a particular audience, but then to have opted for another, more controversial wording and verse order for the sake of perpetuity.[87] The rules for text adjustment were defined by local practice, but they deserve further inquiry by Arabists. At one end of the continuum some texts were "protected" from rewording, such as sacred texts after canonization, while other texts were considered still formative and emergent, such as literary texts even after canonization.[88] Whereas it would be appealing and credible for a performer to adjust a narrative or poem by substituting a metrically equivalent word, in a more sacred protected text such a replacement—no matter how thoughtful or artistic—would be unappealing and none too credible, if it fell outside the traditional lines of transmission.[89] These textual adjustments, instead of being deemed corruptions or adulterations, indicate serious performance demands. Whether by professional poets or amateurs in *mujālasāt,* the adjustments evince an urge to communicate, to make language a faithful messenger.

That sense of responsibility to an audience can be felt in the ways that manuscript holders personalized their copy of a work. In the Berlin manuscript of *The Announcing of News of Prophets and the History of Caliphs,* one finds textual supplements and "updates" in the margins of especially controversial narratives. They increase in frequency as the chronology approaches the scribal date of 1058.[90] In Berlin manuscript Spr. 46 the owner of the manuscript seems to have taken al-Masᶜūdī's history, *Meadows of Gold* (Murūj al-Dhahab), as a starting point for his own performance of events. The manuscript includes jarring frenzied textual adjustments in the margins for all narrative dealing with the period from pre-Islamic Arabia to the reign of the first Umayyad caliph, Muᶜāwiya—that is, the period encompassing the Prophet Muhammad's biography with the prologue and epilogue.[91] A similar example can be found in manuscript Pm. 127, in particular, the narratives dealing with the succession of Muᶜāwiya, the civil war between the sons of Hārūn al-Rashīd, al-Amīn and al-Ma^ɔmūn, which are both heavily supplemented and amended.[92]

These additions suggest that the owner conceived of the book not as a static reference but as a personal notebook to be exploited for the purposes of edification and display in group. The degree of adjustment and alteration to an author's original suggests that the manuscript owner assumed responsibility not simply for knowing the author's work, but for a recitation of narrative that would fulfill audience expectations. Note also one debate about the wording of a poem by Abū Tammām in which the issue is never what the poet actually composed but which wording was most pleasing to the ear, mind, and heart. Authorship and the "sanctity" of the original hardly matter in comparison with audience effect.

Other text adjustments in manuscripts illustrate that personalizing a text for immediate purposes could be quite drastic. Berlin manuscript We. 17 stands as a severe abridgement of al-Azraqī's *History of Honored Mecca* (Tārīkh Makka al-Mukarrama), prepared by one Yaḥyā al-Kirmānī. The manuscript has a scribal date of 1418 and seems to have been used by its composer and then passed into the hands of other amateurs who added and subtracted at will, probably in response to what would be most appealing and credible to audiences at the time. Scholars found it legitimate to tailor texts to particular purposes. Consider, for instance, al-Ṣūlī, who cites an anecdote about ʿAlī b. al-Jahm confidently and fully, only to qualify it by saying, "I don't recall exactly, and I can't find it, because I wrote it down—I think—in a book of narratives, but I heard him say . . . ."[93]

Instances of failed memory in performance rarely yielded disastrous results as long as the performer was competent. Such a performer, rather than collapse from embarrassment, would improvise with a thoughtful approximation. In one instance, even the Abbasid littérateur al-Tanūkhī (d. 994) assumed the license (because of verbal competence) to refashion the narratives of his childhood, under the aegis of restoration:

> It so happened that I attended gatherings in the City of Peace [Baghdad] in 360 [A.D. 971] after an absence of years. I found it devoid of those who made it habitable, who made it worthy and lofty with

> their gatherings. I found only vestiges of that class of elders. The gathering proceeded and I began to notice that what I remembered of these narratives was becoming extinct and what was emanating from their mouths was faulty in meaning to the extent that the raconteur—telling anecdotes we heard often—mixed them by altering and corrupting them. I saw that if every account I had forgotten had only remained in my memory, it would work well as a kind of gathering, a sort of Pleasant Conversation in Salons [the title]. So I ascertained the rest, in addition to what I long remembered. I resolved to ascertain all that I had heard in that vein, to embellish it with whatever might encourage recitation.[94]

Such improvisations or "restorations" are legion when authors cited texts from memory, thus licensing a wide latitude for readjusting the text to meet the demands of new audiences. Interestingly, al-Tanūkhī acknowledges that both he and his negative models are forgetting and altering, but what is the criteria that makes his versions valid? Certainly, not fidelity to a fixed tradition; rather, his renditions would encourage recitation. We have here an explicit recognition by a professional littérateur indicating that textual adjustments promote the appeal, authority, and continuity of tradition. If such adjustments are necessary and credible in writing, they would be more so in face-to-face performance in response to a live audience.

Historical Narratives: From Literal to Figurative Truth

Audience expectations and reactions ultimately held the performer responsible minute by minute—through hope of approval and fear of derision—for meeting certain standards of preparation and delivery, of eliciting or maintaining the assembly's appropriate emotional states, and of adjusting style and text to hold and sustain the audience's divisible attention. If these performance pressures did indeed regulate and inspire the performer, then one might find it useful to examine how these pressures influenced the tone and content of historical narratives in performance. These performative and social pressures might be instrumental to understanding how banal, literal lives and events were transmuted into the artistic, figurative truths that have greater potential to move, persuade, and inspire.

The rudimentary problem of the source-critical approach rests in the assumption that the reciters of historical narratives in early Islam share our modernist and rather scholastic standards of authenticity. If early Muslim audiences wanted and expected literal reconstructions of the past, then regardless of the innocent intent of transmitters and performers, today's scholars could conceivably examine narratives and identify "falsehood" or "deception." Every culture has its definition of fraud based on audience expectations: if material is counterfeit—not consistent with expectations of value and standards of authenticity—then that would certainly be fraud. But such evaluations depend on a thorough understanding of an audience's standards of authenticity. In principle, no evaluation can be made based on universal standards, because none seem to exist across cultures. Consider, for example, the conventions of today's capitalist advertising, when copywriters use alluring symbolism to implicitly promise consumers the illusory prospect of fun, joy, or even happiness with the purchase of a car or a sandwich—does that constitute fraud? To understand the effect of these advertisements and how audiences are lured into the fantasy of the product, would it not be wise to explore the standards of authenticity that audiences employ when interpreting (i.e., enjoying) this capitalist art form?[95]

Several historians of the medieval Middle East have responded precisely to the misplaced assumptions of the source-critical method by examining the artistic character of historical narratives, which implicitly recategorizes audience expectations. This move has aptly placed historical narrative in its original context of *adab,* offering generations of researchers the invitation to reexamine history as an art form and to credit the medieval historian with the skill of an artist who inspires thought and behavior with the use of sophisticated literary devices.

On the surface the classical historian al-Ṭabarī (d. 923) gives the impression of an objective collector who did not wish to comment or interpret. Partisan devices in narration are deemed "rather naïve and rather easily surprised," making it simple to detect rare instances of propaganda. In most cases it would appear that "the objectivity of Arabic historiography is remarkable."[96] Marshall Hodgson, however, notes that al-Ṭabarī's method of selecting and arranging verbatim reports can seem deceptively inert. He explains al-Ṭabarī's sophistication in sequencing and arranging narrative details: "He is like the detective who would give in immaculate detail every piece of evidence which he has found relevant to his own private conclusions about a case[,] . . . leaving you to draw your own conclusions from the evidence. . . . Unless you have something of the mind of a detective yourself, you are likely to miss the point." Readers may be led, so to speak, to water, but they are never compelled to drink: "If they are not prepared to face certain problems, the writer is not forcing them to do so; but if they are prepared, the writer gives them the leads they require; thus every reader is satisfied at his own level." Al-Ṭabarī could thereby hope to please a wide audience, maintaining his uncommitted public stance as a historian and limiting the potential that he will inadvertently impose divisive issues on the community.[97]

In addition to arrangement, though, the Islamic historian Tayeb El-Hibri points out that al-Ṭabarī shows a strategic use of complex rhetorical devices. Historiography in the Abbasid era was a contentious forum, too important to obviate the need for persuasive skill. El-Hibri demonstrates that even historiographers such as al-Ṭabarī, narrating contemporary events, disseminated narratives not to "tell facts, but rather to provide commentary on a certain political, religious, social, or cultural issue that *may* have derived from a real and controversial historical episode."[98]

There were, of course, political questions about the moral legitimacy of Alids (supporters of Ali, the son-in-law and a cousin of the Prophet) against the political might of the Abbasids, the relations between kings and their upstart courtiers, and succession. But there were more pressing existential considerations that lingered, one crisis after the next. El-Hibri notes there were questions about "the relation between morality and politics, the religious significance of historical change, the nature of divine judgment, and the complexity of issues related to fate and destiny."[99] Al-Ṭabarī thus plays host to the reader's contemplation of divine responses to human need, the cosmic plan, the effectiveness of human speech, and the perennial cycles of temptation, fall, and redemption. Many of these political and existential issues were invoked during the civil war (811–13) between the caliph Hārūn al-Rashīd's sons, al-Amīn and al-Ma'mūn, and before that in two civil wars (656–61 and 683–92) that locked the noblest of Muhammad's followers in tragic conflict. To reopen these issues publicly would risk the danger of reopening the wounds of a traumatized community, reawakening bitterness and promoting divisiveness. However, these were real questions that remained pertinent to government officials, scholars, littérateurs, and many other members of the urban middle class. El-Hibri reasons that narrative was used to address sensitive issues discreetly and to persuade readers to new moral and political views.[100]

There are two principal occasions for enhancing narratives with rhetorical devices: when a source close to the court (the reporter) recounts his narrative at a literary gathering and when he orally transmits it to the historian, who may then record and arrange it in written form. El-Hibri notes that by and large, during the reigns of al-Rashīd, al-Ma'mūn, and al-Mutawakkil, reporters were in demand because of their insider knowledge of the court. They were often eyewitnesses to internal conflicts and thus had opinions and reflections on the outward display of the court. Moreover, the courts that employed them were venues for the exercise of verbal power, especially through the persuasive force of ceremonial poetry. Reporters, wanting their stories to take root, perfected the "literary form of the *qiṣṣah* or *khabar* [narrative report], often with the intention of discussing the controversial results of a political, social, or moral point." There were, one should recall, numerous current issues open to opinion: relations between Abbasids and Alids, between Khurasan and Baghdad, and between kings and their lowborn viziers, as well as questions of succession and religious policies.[101]

Given a milieu in which courtiers and others want to communicate their perspectives and shape public opinion, one might envision a procedure for the emergence of historical narratives in *mujālasāt,* when a performer seeks to inspire and persuade his audience. In particular, literary gatherings offered raconteurs a safe and intimate opportunity to recount palace incidents, intrigue, ceremonies, and communications in a manner that would be deemed by listeners appealing and convincing. A raconteur would need to assume responsibility for all dimensions of his performance in the face of his audience. He would vouch for the text and the authority of his source (if mentioned). In addition, he would assent to standards of performance, which entailed adequate preparation for the act of communicating, adjustment in performance to attract and hold attention, and respecting the assembly's emotional tone informed by the reality of mortality. In the context of a social event, a literary gathering, the raconteur assumed the pressure of not only besting other storytellers in a spirit of sociable competition but also convincing auditors to take up his views and the version of the past it might entail.

Face-to-face performance would then call on interested parties to employ complex rhetorical and social strategies that would enhance the appeal of their verbal art, making it more memorable and more worthy of repetition by others in subsequent performances. To that end, the performer might use two licensed devices, among many others—embellishment and sheer artifice—for the sake of conveying a figurative truth. These devices helped the artist break from referential reality and mark his performance as an artistic endeavor. As the folklorist Richard Bauman notes, "The aesthetic considerations of artistic performance may demand the embellishment or manipulation—if not the sacrifice—of the literal truth in the interests of greater dynamic tension, formal elegance, surprise value, contrast, or other elements that contribute to excellence in performance in [a] subculture."[102]

Performers also may have elected to shape their narratives according to desirable and familiar literary or archetypal patterns. No doubt, these devices were not particular to the performance situation, as writers also used them. However, in the literary gathering communication is synchronous, so they would have been employed to achieve results that were immediate: attracting and maintaining the audience's attention, as well as besting other raconteurs. In some cases writers produced literary texts that they hoped would be memorized and delivered, but in a memorized performance the raconteur assumed responsibility for transforming the memorized text into a skillful rendition. This organically emergent and collective process enabled the raconteur to transmute banal lives and events into figurative truths that commented on pressing social and existential issues. Through his narrative the performer left audiences with a new, value-laden narrative that influenced collective visions of the past, thus promoting interested beliefs, sentiments, and sensibilities.

No doubt, some performances may have been so impressive and memorable that they inspired reperformance at other literary gatherings. The line of performers in this case thereby contributed not only to an immediate social event but also, in an appreciable way, to the formation of cultural memory. This performative approach to the emergence of historical narrative helps us to theorize the process by which memory becomes canonical and collective, because it enables us to contemplate how parties employed historical reports for discrete ends. If speakers vouched for the value of their narrative, on their authority or someone else's, then we can also begin to perceive how interested social beings vied to define exactly what should be remembered and how. Through performance people perpetually *participated* in refashioning cultural memory.

Al-Ṭabarī, in this regard, was thus one of many participants in a process of shaping the past. Reporters frequently had the upper hand in dealing with historians, because they often had unique perspectives yielding narratives that were important *and* impossible to dispute. The historian Tarif Khalidi notes that for al-Ṭabarī the practice of historiography was radically unlike his other expertise, exegesis, where deduction and inference were possible and necessary. Historiography suggested no clear procedure for sifting the "true" from the "false," implying the more important criteria of transmission and circulation. Al-Ṭabarī was cognizant of this new landscape: "Knowledge of the past cannot be deduced or inferred; it can only be transmitted."[103]

Al-Ṭabarī did express his interest in the overall scheme of his history. He assembled verbatim narratives into a sacral history spanning some fourteen thousand years, originating with and guided by God. As a pious scholar, it would have been irresponsible to remain "descriptive."[104] For example, Al-Ṭabarī piques his readers' interest in the concept of history by disclosing the sort of questions he asks of mythic Time and answers: "What is it? And how long is it? When is the first of its Beginning and the last of its End? Was there anything before God on High created it? Is it transient? Is there anything after its passing beside the Face of the Glorious Creator?"[105] The formation of history was far too controversial to obviate the use of style. Al-Ṭabarī's history was rooted in a Qur'anic concept of history, the primary function of which was didactic: "To warn, to remind, to authenticate the past."[106] Khalidi notes, "Scholars believed they were transmitters rather than creators. But the process of transmission became, as so often in the history of cultures, creation through transmission."[107] A historian's merit thus rested on his creative ability to "plot human history."[108]

Al-Ṭabarī was the earliest Islamic historian to arrange and plot "a vision of history inspired by the regular rhythms of Qur'anic narrative."[109] In practice, that rhythm fostered a type of moral symmetry between actions and outcomes. The major figures of this sacral history were subjected to earthly judgment in order to construct moral examples for the community. In the case of bygone caliphs, viziers, and military heroes, readers wanted to evaluate "how they dealt with a range of ethical, political, and historical challenges."[110] Al-Ṭabarī himself declared his consciousness of God and the pious imperative to judge powerful parties. He said, "I mention in this my book the kings of every age . . . who among them has been ungrateful for His blessings, and then He sapped them of the blessings He initiated toward them and hastened their punishment . . . or let them dally in blessings until their death and demise."[111] Moral judgment could come in the form of actions that prefigure consequences decades or centuries later. El-Hibri takes the course, therefore, not of attempting to reconstruct yet another picture of the Abbasid era or to establish the veracity of reports, but of positing "a literary-critical approach to reading the sources."[112] The fruit of this endeavor is not a license to dismiss Abbasid history as a forgery; it is rather to gauge "broader systems of historical interpretation that are anchored in the vital issues of the time."[113]

The European medievalist Ruth Morse treats similar issues in European historiography of the Middle Ages and argues for a reconception of the issue of fraud or deception in the use of embellishment or even sheer artifice. She contends that literary devices, rather than being a veil that shrouded the literal truth, enhanced the appeal of narratives.[114] An elegant narrative was memorable; thus its lessons would remain alive in generations of recitation. Conversely, an inelegant but literal narrative would neither survive nor educate across generations. The principle of memorability can be witnessed in al-Masᶜūdī's choice of narrative patterns. He craftily "staged" a nerve-wracking narrative depicting the betrayal and murder of the caliph al-Mutawakkil, and then when he released the audience from the grips of the narrative, he finally said—conscious of his rhetorical charm—"And we mention here only a smidgen of what we mentioned [in other works]. This is what we select for now, since it is the most eloquent expression and the easiest to memorize."[115] The historian precisely at this point seems to be self-conscious of his audience impact, wanting the text to be eloquent, that is, easy to memorize. Eloquent patterning is to narrative what melody is to music.

What Morse ultimately describes are shared habits of interpretation between raconteurs and their audiences, which train novices to think figuratively and allegorically: "On the assumption that something very like this might be thought to have happened, how are we to understand the event?" Morse observes, "They were neither stupid nor credulous, but considered that the historian's right of invention did not invalidate the truth of what he wrote." In most cases, then, the modern researcher might want to take these accounts of the past as medieval readers did and judge them on literary grounds, not factual ones.[116]

If understood for what they are, as opposed to what we in the modern period think they should be, these narratives convey much about the beliefs and attitudes of those who transmitted them. In a spirit of emic appreciation, Morse warns against condemning medieval modes of communication or even attempting to "salvage" those rare kernels of literal truth: "Importing our own motives into past societies can bring serious misinterpretations in its wake. Castigating those societies for not feeling what we feel, not writing as we write, imports a 'developmental' view of the history of writing which judges in terms of leaps of realism, and elevates a few unusual texts as the only 'true' biographies in an age dominated by stale and stifling conventions. . . . [T]hey were not 'failing' to write what we might have preferred them to have written."[117] Nevertheless, if we acknowledge that certain inventions in representing the past are legitimate, then which inventions are not so? What are the community standards that audiences might have employed for determining authenticity and appeal?[118]

Standards of Authenticity: Beneficial Lies versus Divisive Truths

One of the most intriguing themes that frame the work of El-Hibri, Khalidi, and Morse is how these scholars respond to the issue of invention, which would include embellishment and sheer artifice. On the one hand, the source-critical method seeks to identify and purge invention in order to "credibly" reconstruct history. On the other hand, El-Hibri, Khalidi, and Morse would accept the invention in medieval historiography as integral to the cultural production of history as *adab*. One learns from El-Hibri, Khalidi, and Morse that these medieval historians and their informants felt a need to convince audiences to take up lines of action or beliefs with narratives that serve broad moral and political or otherwise ideological goals.

Khalidi is less direct about the issue of invention but certainly recognizes the value of history as a form of moral guidance and the pressures for performers to use it as a persuasive strategy to edify or promote views. Khalidi illustrates the power of subtle invention in the massive synthesis that al-Ṭabarī undertakes in his opus *The History of Prophets and Kings*. In the pre-Islamic section of the history al-Ṭabarī prefigures Abbasid Islam with two traditions of authority: biblical prophecy and Persian kingship. The Persians are chosen because they enjoy a tradition of "unbroken" kingship, and biblical prophecy embodies God's concern for humanity and his willingness to intervene. The historian's accomplishment is no less than magnificent: God's guidance begins with Adam down to the Israelite and Arab line of prophets. He then weaves a thread of Persian kingship into the fabric, which gives way to the Prophet's tribe, Quraysh, and the stunning Muslim conquest of Mesopotamia. Al-Ṭabarī, though, weaves together more than a new history. He composes a grand narrative that authenticates a new Abbasid identity that can safely merge the heritage of both the conquering and the conquered peoples. As Khalidi notes, "The *umma* [community] was . . . shown to be the prophetic heir of the biblical tradition and the temporal heir of Persian dominion." Al-Ṭabarī's most discreet historical invention was no doubt his grandest. He re-presents a history that provides a vision of the pre-Islamic past that authenticates the Islamic imperial present.[119]

Morse notes that while achieving the goal of teaching and instructing, narrators may have used a palette of inventive strategies, such as putting arguments in the mouth of a likable personality or enriching a narrative with literary details.[120] At root, invention may have taken the form of embellishment or outright artifice, which can best be appreciated in the context of social interaction at the performance event. In a setting of sociability, one can better apprehend the pressures to attract and hold the attention of an audience and to compete with colleagues in a show of verbal skill. Most important, invention was licensed according to certain principles and conventions of persuasion. What these scholars implicitly emphasize is the benefit of invention—not to an individual person, but to a community.

The communal criteria for invention can be found in a short Hadith, in which lying is made legitimate by the good results it brings to people. The Prophet's daughter Umm Kulthūm said she heard the Prophet say, "A liar is not one who reconciles people, nor one who speaks beneficently (*khayr*) and cultivates beneficence."[121] Speech here is conceived of as persuasion, and if spoken words reduce hostility and bring about reconciliation, then lying is categorically valid. In an addendum, as reported in *Ṣaḥīḥ Muslim,* the Hadith continues with one of the transmitters, Ibn Shihāb, elaborating, "I have not heard anything permitted that people would say by way of lies except in three [cases]: war [i.e., deceiving the enemy], reconciling people, and the sweet talk of a man to his wife or a woman to her husband."[122] Lying is expanded now in the addendum to include persuasive speech in the context of war and relationships, where the speaker would have to assume responsibility for his or her elocution. Again if the aim of persuasion is beneficial, then invention is sanctioned.

From the Persian literary tradition, one also finds not only the category of "beneficial lie" but of "divisive truth." Because community and sociability stand supreme as an arbiter of ethics, the category of divisive truth applies to those truths that can only lead to grave harm. Here we witness ethics governed by effects and results. In the *Gulistān* of the Persian littérateur Saᶜdī (d. 1291), a narrative is told that illustrates this principle. Note, in particular, that the "liar" and the "truth teller" are judged on moral effects:

> I heard of a King who signaled the execution of a prisoner. The helpless fellow, in a state of desperation, took to cursing the King and reviling him. . . . The King asked, "What is he saying?" One of the viziers of good counsel said, "Lord, he says, 'and those who temper anger and forgive people' [Qur'an 3:134 in favor of clemency]." The King had mercy and spared his life.
>
> Another vizier opposed to him said, "It is not fitting for men of our stature to speak other than the truth in the presence of the King: This fellow no doubt cursed the King and swore."
>
> The King frowned at these words and said, "I approve more of that 'lie' than this 'truth' you say. The former was for kindness and the latter vileness."
>
> The sages say, "A beneficial lie is better than a divisive truth."[123]

There are several points to observe to help explain the conventions of "beneficial lying." First, the king judges and evaluates not only rhetorical methods but also whether the aim is "kindness" or "vileness." Second, the king categorically dismisses the speech of the desperate man when he discovers it. Although his words are heartfelt, sincerity counts for little if impertinent. A person who "gives up hope of living" can hardly be expected to assent to more evaluation. The king then is left to decide between a person who lies for the sake of kindly intercession and a person who tells "the truth" to prevent intercession. One is artful, employing a quote from the Qur'an to deceive and diffuse the situation; the other is obvious and referential, showing no self-restraint or style. The king's final judgment praises lying for benefits and condemns truth for divisiveness. The aims of persuasion, not the means, prove critical in assessing the morality of lying.

Conversely, when it comes to light that the goal of one's invention (i.e., lying) is simply self-service, the action is deemed shameful. Consider, for example, an anecdote in which al-Buḥturī fails to contain his boredom and displeasure in the presence of singers hosted by the caliph al-Muᶜtazz. The caliph confronts him and censures him in two ways: first, for failing to dissemble out of kindness to the artists and the audience, and second, for lying to al-Muᶜtazz simply to deny his boredom and save face before the caliph. This is how al-Ṣūlī tells the story:

> Sawār b. Abī Shurāᶜa told me that al-Buḥturī said: I have never seen a caliph sharper in thinking or gentler in nature [than al-Muᶜtazz]. We were before al-Muᶜtazz one day and in the gathering were the singing maidens Shāriya and ᶜArīb and other talented singers.
>
> Al-Muᶜtazz said, "Let the singers from Khurasan begin." They sang for hours on end, and I said to myself, "What *is* this selection?!"
>
> Al-Muᶜtazz caught me with his glance *just* as I was thinking it, and he surmised what occurred in my heart. He summoned me. He said, "O Buḥturī, do you have in your homeland [Syria] anything like these Khurasanians?"
>
> I said, "We have something like it, but of *their* talent, not at all!"
>
> He said, "Then the soul is bored with what is best and entertained with what is worse?!—Do not criticize my selection. Were it not for the variety of appetites (*taṣarruf al-shahawāt*), people would not busy their stomachs except with the best of foods and leave the rest. *Pretend* that you are now in your homeland listening to this."
>
> I said, "My master (*sayyidī*), nothing of that sort came across my mind."
>
> He said, "That's enough. I understood you. Go back to your place." By God, he was not mistaken about what rested in my soul.[124]

Interestingly, al-Buḥturī admires the caliph for his perceptiveness and his use of authority. But more important, we are reminded that speakers are responsible *to* their audiences, and if the listener is a peer or a superior, the speaker may elicit disapproval for violating the principle of communal benefit. In the context of face-to-face interaction, the effects of persuasion can readily be verified and thus the moral value of speech assessed. There are discernible principles to be followed, and the result ought to be a recognizable benefit. In fact, cold truth would be immoral if the effect were harmful to others.

The *adab* principles derived here have largely stressed how they govern the performance of narrative. The other, stronger component of *adab,* however, is poetry, since it has the potential for wider distribution and influence than narrative because of its infectious musicality and structure to the accustomed ear. These generic features make it more memorable, repeatable, and durable as cultural ware. A question remains, however, about the criteria for invention in poetry.

Principles of Authenticity for Poetry: Freedom from Objective Truth

In these medieval narratives, invention is justified by desirable aims and implications; morality and even sociability figure as a lower priority than audience impact. Several medieval theories of poetry advise poets to use embellishment, artifice, or any other rhetorical device to achieve the much-desired effect of reframing perceptions of reality. The poet is thus permitted to invent to transcend the obviousness of objective truth.

There were two aphorisms that were emblematic of medieval poetic criticism. One stated, "The best poetry is the most truthful (*khayru al-shᶜiri aṣdaquhu*)." The other stated, "The best poetry is the most mendacious (*ashᶜaru ash-shiᶜri akdhabuhu*)." According to the literary critic ᶜAbd al-Qāhir al-Jurjānī (d. 1081?), truthful poetry had the advantage of being intellectually cogent and readily validated by reason.[125] Literal truth, however, had the drawback of not being open to reinvention or refashioning; it was constant, subject only to perception and confirmation. Truth, therefore, was too obvious for the poetic profession, and the whole realm of truth was constrained by the finitude of material reality. The second view permitted comparatively more inventive power (*ṣanᶜa*) in the poet. Invented meanings were multifaceted, reflective, refractive, and, most important, boundless. Moreover, invention is a mark of perception and intelligence on the part of the poet and his audience, so long as the audience acquires the interpretive skills conditioned by tradition to understand the poet's figurative idiom.[126]

Even when the poet goes to the furthest extreme of meaning in his artful lies, he is held to standards of aesthetics. The license to be mendacious does not permit him to plainly say to a watchman that he has the virtues of the caliph or to tell a humble fellow that he is the prince of Basra or Kufa. Rather, the license to invent, even to lie, "demands much effort, and scrutiny of meaning (*tadqīq fī 'l-maᶜānī*) which requires subtle acumen (*fiṭna laṭīfa*), keen perception (*fahm thāqib*) and rigorous exploration (*ghawṣ shadīd*)."[127] In short, invention was an open arena for the poet to display his perception and rhetorical skill.

Inventiveness also delivers the poet from the conformism of pious truth, and he can better distinguish his art from religion. The linguist and poetry anthologist al-Aṣmaᶜī (d. ca. 828), in particular, argued in favor of an absolute separation between poetry and religion, which appears to have been a productive civilizational theme.[128] If poetry tries to be good or pious, it loses its teeth and therefore its bite. "If goodness creeps in," he said, "it becomes soft (*lāna*)," and "soft" in his diction meant the poet was "hoping for rewards in the Afterlife."[129] Reaffirming the separation, the literary critic Abū Hilāl al-ᶜAskarī (d. 1005) placed the responsibility for interpretation on the audience, when he said, "A philosopher was once told: 'So-and-so lies in his poem.' To which he answered: 'One expects from poets a beautiful discourse; truthfulness is expected from prophets.'"[130] Whereas the Prophet and his revelation distinguish between black and white, the poet can and should blur those distinctions to reformulate stale perceptions.[131]

The Andalusian writer and anthologist Ibn ᶜAbd Rabbih (d. 940), for example, explained that freedom from objectivity is one of the merits of great poets: "He who can present what is false under the appearance of truth, and what is true under the appearance of falsehood, through the charm . . . of an appealing expression, in such a way that he may be able to deface the most perfect beauty and to embellish even utter ugliness."[132] We should be forewarned, according to poetic standards, that court poets will eschew pious morality. If morality creeps into poetry, it will undermine the poet's independence and credibility in perception. This, however, does not imply that poetry proffers no persuasive guidance, but that one should beware that such guidance is not the morality of heavenly answers and delayed rewards but that of earthly (unanswerable) questions and immediate triumph. Al-Buḥturī's poems in chapter 4 of this book illustrate the prevailing concern for earthly, perennial questions.

Lying also served the poet by shifting greater emphasis on his verbal skills and poetic "perception." Ibn Rashīq (d. 1078) observed that the poet, almost by definition, was expected to perceive and express meaning: "A poet (*shāᶜir*) is called this because he perceives (*shaᶜara*) what others do not. For if the poet did not form a concept or invent one, or did not embellish an expression or give it an original twist, or did not expand the concepts others treated clumsily, or shorten the expressions others made excessively long, or use a concept in a different way than it had been used before, then the name of poet would be given to him in a figurative sense and not in a real one, and he would not possess *any merit* other than that of metre, which in my opinion is no merit at all."[133]

Most notable here is what Ibn Rashīq considered a poet's "perception": invention, embellishment, expanding a phrase or contracting it. These stylistic manipulations, not truth-value, show that he perceives what others do not. The poet capitalizes on stylistic and rhetorical opportunities to demonstrate his acumen. Without that ability, he is as limited as ordinary people. The Arabist Johann Christoph Bürgel goes as far as characterizing the poet as a model man who exemplifies a kind of verbal licit magic. By marrying fantasy and reality, the poet can make the inanimate come to life and the mute speak.[134] In short, he can modify perceptions of and perspectives on everyday existence. The poet's capacity also enables him to crystallize historical events that are familiar to audiences through the historiographic tradition.[135] Bürgel notes that the "label of licit magic meant much more than mere word juggling, mere display of rhetorical devices. It meant, at least for those who used it, transmuting reality."[136] When the poet composes what others yearn to hear, remember, and recite, he in effect brings into the world an idea, a concept, an image that people believe in and assimilate. The poet is charged not with imitating what already exists but with bringing into society something that never before existed.

Adab and Children: Rite of Passage

In his *Anecdotes about al-Buḥturī,* al-Ṣūlī recounted the story of "first-encounter" when he was fifteen and the poet seventy-one.[137] He reported that he was at the educational circle of al-Mubarrad the Basran grammarian (d. 898) when an elderly long-bearded man greeted al-Mubarrad. The teacher stopped dictating to the class, and older students rose, hovered around the visitor, and asked him if they could recite his poetry to him so that he could confirm its authenticity. The celebrity indulged the adoring students and listened to their poetry recitations. Soon al-Ṣūlī realized it was al-Buḥturī himself but had no memorized poetry to recite to him. Al-Mubarrad consoled him, saying he could find the poet later at a certain place. Al-Ṣūlī seized the opportunity. Al-Ṣūlī the teenager worked with a friend to memorize some poetry, then checked his retrieval in the presence of a seasoned elder. Later he found the poet at a literary gathering. When the occasion arose, he recited what he knew and finally received al-Buḥturī's blessings. At the end of the anecdote al-Ṣūlī notes that in a single evening, students performed twelve full odes in the presence of the poet.[138] Al-Ṣūlī begins his collection of anecdotes about al-Buḥturī with a testament to the risk of embarrassment for incompetence in *adab* recitation. It is also a personal testament to the potential of *adab* performance to redeem and transform the neophyte.

The most humorous manuscript I encountered in Berlin was Spr. 1242, scribal date 1820, which is bound at the top like a stenographer's notebook. The script was not just amateur but wild and unpracticed, leading me to suspect it belonged to a juvenile, probably a teenager. The youth would alternate between poetic descriptions of a horse by the pre-Islamic genius Imruʾ al-Qays followed by "and this is my description of a horse to match it!" Again, with wholehearted bravado, he would mention lines by Abū Nuwās about wine, followed by "and this is my description of wine to match it!" Displaying a mix of naïveté and machismo, charming only in a youngster, he would seek to engage and outdo the best of the classical *adab* tradition. This notebook illustrates the pride and dignity that children found in learning and communicating *adab,* linking them to a chain of novices before them.

Likewise, children must have experimented and played with adult uses of *adab* in their everyday lives. In a comic work titled *Anecdotes about Idiots and Fools,* the littérateur Ibn al-Jawzī (d. 1201) regaled his audience with an anecdote by al-Ṣūlī about a boy who was especially mischievous:

> Muḥammad b. al-Ḥasan had a son. He said [to his father], "I have some poetry."
> "Well, recite it to me."
> "If I do well, will you bestow a slave-girl or -boy on me?"
> "I'll give both to you!"

So he sang [in parody]:
The abodes like a phantom have
stirred up sorrows that had passed.
They made me weep for my mischief
and rendered my neck and head all the same [i.e., getting smacked on both].

He said, "Son, by God, you deserve neither slave-girl nor -boy! And your mother is divorced three times [i.e., irrevocably] if she gives birth to another [rascal] like you![139]

For children throughout Arabo-Islamic culture, *adab* (both poetry and narratives) was a means of gaining recognition as adults.[140] The Arabic language offers an etymological link between mental and physical maturity (*bulūgh; mablagh al-rijāl*) and rhetorical proficiency (*ba - lāgha*), which appears in discussions of pedagogy and child rearing.[141] More important, in practice, public displays of oratory served as a ritual to mark the passage of a boy to manhood. For example, when al-Mutawakkil held a celebration for his son al-Muᶜtazz's coming-of-age, the father prepared a gem-studded pulpit for him, which the initiate had to mount to deliver an oration (*fa-ṣaᶜada wa khaṭaba ᶜalayhi*).[142] Ibn Khaldūn's *Muqaddima* and other sources indicate the paramount importance of teaching prepubescent boys to memorize ancestral poetry (*shiᶜr*) and lore (*akhbār*) for the sake of performance.[143]

The key piece of advice enjoins parents to start early with a steady diet of poetry and narrative. Ibn Khaldūn advised parents and teachers to encourage children to commit classical poetry and anecdotes to memory, so that a "loom" forms in their minds that enables them to "weave" speech like that of the Bedouins.[144] He applauded the people of Andalusia and the Arab West for the custom of introducing poetry to children early in their education, even *before* the Qur'an and Hadith. He admitted that children are more receptive in this manner than learning and comprehending the revelation later in their education.[145] The caliph Muᶜāwiya, for example, is said to have advised, "A man has a duty to educate (*taʾdīb*) his son, and poetry is the highest rank of *adab*."[146] Another saying suggests, "Have your children listen to poetry. It unties the tongue-tied. It emboldens the heart of the timid. It opens the hand of the stingy. It inspires beautiful traits."[147] Based on these directives, failure to raise a child to be eloquent and generous would be tantamount to parental neglect in middle- and upper-ranking society.

An early start had other advantages as well, since child littérateurs could transmit contemporary poetry well beyond one generation. For example, al-Buḥturī, unlike, for example ᶜAlī b. al-Jahm, was fortunate to have gained the following of a young reciter, ᶜAlī b. Ḥamza al-Iṣbahānī (d. 985), who is said to have lived eighty-eight years after the poet was gone.[148] Al-Iṣbahānī's life and work perpetuated the legacy of al-Buḥturī deep into the tenth century. If artists and aficionados desired the perpetuation of their art well into the third and fourth generations, it would stand to reason that young boys attended literary gatherings as part of their poetic apprenticeship and adult socialization.

In this chapter I have placed sociability and performance at the center of *adab* education, production, and transmission. By contemplating how littérateurs learned to speak in assembly, what standards they were expected to achieve before their audiences, and how they were held to account for those standards, we can better understand the social and performative norms that shaped perceptions of the Arabo-Islamic past. Such an understanding will serve us well in chapter 3, when I examine how the Malamatiya Sufi Order radically reframed the legacy of a highly political court poet, ᶜAlī b. al-Jahm. Social and performative forces enabled them to subordinate his legacy and poetry in the *mujālasāt* in order to articulate deeply spiritual ambivalences about the nature of power, especially divine power.

Three

Poetry Performance and the Reinterpreting of Tradition

The Puzzle

The Abbasid court poet ʿAlī b. al-Jahm (d. 863) is most famous for his *Ruṣāfiyya* ode extolling the virtues of his generous patron, the caliph al-Mutawakkil (d. 861).[1] The original functions of his praise verse were to give legitimacy to the caliph and his dynasty. However, one of the most entertaining anecdotes about Ibn al-Jahm comes to us in the anthology *Muḥāḍarat al-Abrār* (Conversing with the Virtuous), attributed to the Sufi master Muḥyī al-Dīn b. al-ʿArabī (d. 1240). He regales his audience with an account of the first encounter between Ibn al-Jahm and al-Mutawakkil. In this anecdote Ibn al-Jahm comes to the court as a simple Bedouin bumpkin bearing the gift of praise for his desired patron.[2] He tries to woo the ruler with his poetic offering, only to fail miserably. Ibn al-Jahm naively says, "You are like a *dog* in maintaining your loyalty. You are like a *billy goat* in confronting your challenges! / You are like a *hide-bucket*—may we never do without you as a bucket—one of the biggest buckets! Great in size!"[3]

According to court protocol, Ibn al-Jahm's gauche utterances to the king might have put his life in danger.[4] The king, however, is not insulted. To the contrary, he sees promise in Ibn al-Jahm and takes him under his wing. After six months of living under the auspices of the caliph in the metropolis of Baghdad, Ibn al-Jahm returns to the court and delivers a monumental tribute to his patient sponsor. The poem would become his most famous, taking its name, *al-Ruṣāfiyya,* from a point on the city's breezy riverfront, al-Ruṣāfa.[5]

The anecdote is curious first because courtly material is re-presented by a Sufi master; surprisingly, nearly all of Ibn al-Jahm's extant poetry has come down to us through the Sufi tradition. Second, Ibn al-ᶜArabī's anthology stands as the *only* known source to report the anecdote. Most anecdotes about poets in the Arabic tradition are corroborated and repeated in other sources, but no other source remotely echoes this bumpkin-in-Baghdad narrative. In effect, earlier sources of biography sketch another persona altogether. They depict Ibn al-Jahm as being of Arab stock but born in Baghdad or Marv, Khurasan (Central Asia), where his family originated. In either case he grew up in Baghdad, so these sources imply that Ibn al-Jahm was neither Bedouin nor provincial.

To the contrary, the reports tell us that Ibn al-Jahm's family were Baghdad insiders. His father, al-Jahm b. Badr, was an officer in the administrations of the caliphs al-Maᵓmūn (r. 813–33) and al-Wāthiq (r. 842–47). His elder brother, Muḥammad, was on close terms with the caliphs al-Maᵓmūn and al-Muᶜtaṣim (r. 833–42). Muḥammad was an accomplished littérateur in his own right.[6] Regardless of banal facticity, it is important to note that the earlier sources do establish a common knowledge, and Ibn al-ᶜArabī's anecdote seems to countervail it for reasons hitherto unknown. In effect, Ibn al-ᶜArabī seems to disseminate a narrative about the court that has currency and appeal as Sufi lore. The issue of appeal is far more salient in this case, since the narrative went uncorroborated, because appeal would seem to be the primary source of credibility.

Moreover, it appears that the legacy of Ibn al-Jahm had special importance to Sufis. Nearly all of the extant fragments of Ibn al-Jahm's poetic corpus were preserved in devotional handbooks used by Sufis of the Maghrib. Whereas the culture of the Abbasid court was saturated in earthly glory and luxury, Sufis rejected the same in favor of austerity and the glory of God. One can only wonder how Sufis identified with Ibn al-Jahm and his courtly legacy. How does Ibn al-Jahm's legacy become so immanently Sufi? What about this anecdote was appealing and authentic to this otherworldly audience? From a performance perspective the *mujālasāt* provide the artistic event, with social and symbolic dimensions, that enable us to examine the ways in which a social group might customize *adab* according to a group's specific subcultural needs and patterns. Just as the Arabist Suzanne Stetkevych shows a semiotic and exegetical relationship between odes and their anecdotes, I suggest a relationship forged in performance between Ibn al-Jahm's legacy in manuscript handbooks and the identity of the speakers who perform that legacy in *mujālasāt.*[7]

The task of this analysis is to embed the *Ruṣāfiyya* and the legacy of Ibn al-Jahm in an ethnology of local Maghribi Sufi tradition. To do so, I must venture an interpretation of the *Ruṣāfiyya* on its debut performance in ninth-century Samarra in honor of the caliph al-Mutawakkil. Then I shift to its reception in *mujālasāt* in the late-medieval Maghrib, evidenced in devotional handbooks that are still in manuscript form. With a clearer understanding of performance in Abbasid culture, it is finally possible to resituate the anecdote about Ibn al-Jahm and his patron in a performance tradition and to investigate some of the ways in which the performance inspires the performer to relate and respond to his audience's interests and aesthetics.

Supplicant: The Mythic Role of the Poet

The *Ruṣāfiyya* falls within a subgenre of Arabic odes (*qaṣīda*) in which the poet offers (usually in person) a praise hymn (*madīḥ*) in honor of a place or a thing, most commonly to a patron in order to valorize him as a model in the eyes of his public and especially his clients. The patron may be of humble means (e.g., an onion or eggplant merchant), of middle rank (e.g., a chancery employee), or of high-profile (e.g., a vizier or caliph).[8] In principle, every living thing on earth—past, present, and future—deserves praise for its solemn role in the cosmos, from the plants and the ants to the caliph and God. Often these shows of gratitude were extended to places, such as personified lands and cities. Praise hymns were a staple of the *mujālasāt.*

Despite their apparent appeal and meaning to premodern audiences, however, praise hymns have posed special problems for modern scholars. Perhaps this is because the praise was trafficked as a commodity or perhaps because of the asymmetry present at times in the power dynamic between patron and poet. Both reasons seem unconducive to a romantic image of heartfelt admiration.[9] Thus scholars have recently turned their attention to social functions. Scholars have made major endeavors to reframe the issue of sincerity, to posit practical functions for praise in the context of the court and society. The Arabist-Persianist Julie Scott Meisami, for example, illustrates how the praise poem can instruct and guide the patron.[10] Beatrice Gruendler argues that the poet could shape the terms of patronage itself.[11] Stefan Sperl views praise as a liturgical expression to the king.[12] Suzanne Stetkevych examines the praise hymn as a kind of rite of passage, entailing a change in social condition ratified by a ritual exchange. Stetkevych's most recent work explores the praise hymn as a supplication to the patron in assembly, which can effectively shame, coax, blandish, and otherwise entrap the patron before a watchful audience.[13] These theories are fundamental to a savvy understanding of the praise hymn as more than an expression of feeling. Because the ancient prophetic dictum of "speaking truth to power" would have been both naive and counterproductive, these theories point to the praise hymn as the prime guidance apparatus that made Islamic government function.

I extend Stetkevych's conclusions about the supplicatory grip that the poet commanded by placing that image in relationship to the near-absolute power that the caliph enjoyed. The pressure points of this tension help to elucidate the value of Ibn al-Jahm and his ode in the *mujālasāt* of the Malamatiyya order. Neither the poet's nor the caliph's power can be minimized, which creates a dramatic tension between the mythic roles that rivet an audience's attention in court performance and outside the court in *mujālasāt.* This encounter quite bluntly places the power of word and sword in a relationship not of confrontation but of engaged resistance, which can be phrased as the classic theme of artifice against brute force. In modern parlance the praise hymn was functionally a traditional Arabo-Islamic form of nonviolent resistance to power, wherein the ostensibly weaker party customarily gained influence by implicitly appealing to a public for moral legitimacy, although the manner of achieving that goal relied on specific Arabo-Islamic cultural patterns.

The instrumentality of poetry has been well recognized by the North African literary critic al-Ḥasan b. Rashīq al-Qayrawānī. He explains that by serving state secretaries (*kuttāb*), poets enjoyed the opportunity to show their strength. He observes, "Some object that poets perennially serve secretaries, but that we never find state secretaries serving poets. They [the critics] are, however, unaware of certain facts (*anbā*ᵓ). It happens to be this way only because the poet relies on his *own* devices. With what he wields, he can *overpower* (*mudillun*) the secretary and even the king. He [the poet] demands what they possess! And he can *take* it! As for the secretary, with what instrument (*ālah*) does he appeal to (*yaqṣudu*) the poet and supplicate (*yarjū*) him for what he possesses?"[14]

Implicit in these comments is a notion of supplication that gives the poet unexpected power as he asks his patron for favors. The favor may entail a direct gift to the poet, but Ibn Rashīq is careful to give several examples of poets who supplicate their patron on behalf of others.[15] That is, he shows us the poet playing a mythic role as an intercessor or redeemer (*shafī*ᶜ) before a fearsome authority. One such example is the role that ᶜAlqama b. ᶜAbada played in redeeming his brother (or some say nephew) who was held prisoner by the Ghassānid king al-Ḥārith. In this case the praise poem served as an offering in a ritual gift exchange, namely, as a ransom bid, that the king would value more than a languishing prisoner.[16] Alternatively, the case of the fugitive Kaᶜb b. Zuhayr illustrates that the poet could present a gift of praise in order to redeem himself and essentially buy back his (renewed) life.[17] When the poet showed himself as redeemer or intercessor by the use of the praise hymn, he courted power. Nevertheless, he vividly proved his own rhetorical power in effecting the results that he desired. The praise hymn as performative speech ultimately glorified the poet. The Abbasid poet al-Buḥturī concurred when he said of his own poetry, "And praise hymns cannot spread far and wide / unless glory is the glory of the poet."[18]

The theory that the praise hymn could serve as an instrument, even a weapon, in the face of authority rests fundamentally on the power of supplication before an assembly, which only gains persuasive force by the sanction of tradition. The supplicant, in a stylized sense, recognizes his vulnerability and need in the face of his superior, yet he calls on his patron's benevolence and power to relieve him of privation. In this encounter the prospects of mercy and violence coexist.[19] The supplicant, however, could appeal to the superior in a manner that aligned him with a long tradition of urgent needs, thus inviting the superior to enjoy allegorically the moral authority that previous benefactors have enjoyed.[20] As Stetkevych proposes, what Kevin Crotty observes for Homeric epic equally applies to supplication scenes at the Abbasid court.[21] Because supplication calls on parallel situations in group memory whose characters and roles are familiar, it "enables the participants to experience victory, shame, memory, pity in an especially compelling way and to apprehend and configure them anew."[22]

The Abbasid court poet derived a large measure of his power not only from the aesthetic (memorable) quality of his work but also from appealing to a relationship sanctioned by tradition, putatively between a reverential client and a beneficent patron. Within this rapport the poet could elegantly employ strategies that helped to achieve his interests, which categorically benefited society at large by providing an alluring model of persuasive skill, to say nothing of tenacity in the face of potentially fearsome authority. In the autumn of his life, al-Buḥturī could thus take stock of his career and admire his patrons and the influence he had on them. The poet was well aware of his interests:

> Whether I live on or die, I dealt the things
> that fed the hearts of my friends and foes.
> I gained the amity of caliphs, minding
> my glory and for them my joys are sweet.
> I plead to them in one mighty matter
> after another, and they let my requests prevail.
> I worked among the Arabs masterpieces
> as gifts for the needy and redemption for the slave.[23]

For al-Buḥturī, "influence" constitutes a capacity to reach the hearts of allies and enemies, to make and express a culture that Arabs will want to celebrate, and, most important for this discussion, to pierce through the armor of kingship—to ask for and receive concessions—tactfully yet efficiently, yielding results without marring the dignity of the office of the king. The number of poets who ultimately exercised this magnitude of communicative power might only have been an elite among society, but their productions constitute a substantial share of the Arab poetic heritage. Their work was taken as an enchanting model of persuasion and reenacted for more than a millennium, from the Atlas Mountains to Mesopotamia, in *mujālasāt.*

Poets exercised certain prerogatives that traditionally marked their social power. Tradition gave them a license to praise themselves and thus amplify their reputation without opprobrium. No other class had that option, not even kings.[24] As part of a ritual exchange, poets had the means to give patrons what they needed most, glory, in return for satisfying the moral-archetypal expectations of beneficence toward the weak. The authority of patrons, most of all rulers, was in part dependent on crowd-pleasing conduct, but it was the memorable broadcasts of the poet that translated temporal deeds into timeless glory. Poets in their praise hymns made the patron's deeds and aspirations newsworthy and memorable to an audience whose goodwill was to be courted.

As mentioned in chapter 1, the joyful reaction of caliphs to live poetry performance demonstrates that they allowed themselves to express abject helplessness in the face of stirring performance. Often, performers were both admired and feared for their capacity to stimulate their audience's emotional participation and thereby influence the emergence of advantageous relations.[25] Tradition gave poets a degree of privilege by virtue of their vocation, and they could also acquire distinction in the performance situation by exercising persuasive skill. The necessary precondition to this persuasion was for the poet—or any courtier, for that matter—to speak in a coded figurative manner.[26] According to one adage quoted as courtiers' advice, the Umayyad court adviser Khālid b. Ṣafwān (d. 752) counseled aspiring courtiers to be cautious but purposeful with kings: it is wise to "teach them (*tuᶜallimahum*) as though they teach you, educate them (*tuʾaddibahum*) as though they educate you; if not, then stay as far away as possible!"[27]

Hero: The Mythic Role of the Patron

The power that the poet faced was a daunting force believed to be in principle sacral and thus legitimate, yet the legitimacy of this sacral being paradoxically depended heavily on ceremonial displays of responsiveness to human need. At the Abbasid court one finds that the smooth face of ceremony belies a conflict of interests in the elegant dance of courtly interchange. The praise hymn enabled the poet to exploit the vanity of privilege and the need for prestige in order to exact concessions from his patron. In effect, he calibrated the terms of devotion and legitimacy. To set the stage for the contest between poet and patron, one might bear in mind customs for the initial performance of the praise hymn. Courtly praise was typically performed live at the court. As the Ibn al-Jahm anecdote described earlier suggests, poets would make their entrance before the caliph in order to deliver their offering of praise, in recognition of the virtue, greatness, and achievement that adhered to his office, if not to his person. Kings expressed their position at the pinnacle of the social pyramid with various outward displays, such as donning rings, seals, fine clothing, and special headgear; hosting grand banquets, polo games, and hunts; and requiring certain decorum and ceremony.[28] Abbasid etiquette called on courtiers to display deference befitting their rank and closeness to the king.

The organization of the Abbasid court, as with society in general, was hierarchical and centripetal.[29] In practice, this meant that etiquette served two primary purposes: for the majority of supplicants and courtiers, it provided a safe distance from the throne; for an elect set, it modulated an intimate rapport with the king. Proximity to the king was therefore a formal privilege for which the visitor needed to display gratitude in the form of deference. The closer one approached the king's throne, the greater the deference one had to display. Exhibitions of deference were relative to one's rank in society, however. The higher one's rank, the less submission one needed to show relative to others in the court hierarchy. The intimate would submit himself before the master, and the master might honor him with tokens of intimacy, such as a touch or an invitation to approach. From the subject's perspective every token of honor from the king required him to further return the gesture (and thus subordinate himself even more). The Ayyubid poet-secretary Abū al-Faḍl Jaᶜfar b. Shams al-Khilāfa Mujidd al-Mulk (d. 1225) advised, "If he gives you honor, give him majesty. If he makes you a son, make him a master. If he makes you a brother, make him a father. If he makes you a father, make him a lord (*rabban*)."[30] Because proximity meant intimacy and intimacy conferred honor on the subordinate, the king reserved for the most dignified subjects the most physical tokens of closeness—kissing his feet, stirrups, hem, or hands.[31]

Kissing a subject's head was almost an inversion of the hierarchy. In one anecdote the historian Muḥammad b. al-ᶜImrānī (d. 1543) depicts the enthronement of Jaᶜfar al-Mutawakkil after the death of al-Wāthiq, his brother. Chief Judge Aḥmad b. Abī Duʾād, who was a fixture of the court since al-Mutawakkil's birth, dressed the new caliph in ceremonial black, crowned him with the customary turban, seated him on the throne, and then stepped back. He approached al-Mutawakkil once again, kissed him between the eyes, and pronounced his new title: "Peace be upon you, Commander of the Faithful, and the mercy and blessings of God."[32] Only a man of his temper, proven to be a kingmaker, could enjoy the privilege of such closeness.

On the whole, etiquette was not a restraint to intimacy but a means of managing it. What the anthropologist Abdellah Hammoudi observes for kingship in modern Morocco also applies to the Abbasid court: "The existence of a full-fledged royal etiquette is not incompatible with the prince's . . . intimate attitudes and styles in the presence of his visitors."[33] On rare occasion the king could answer the request of a close vizier, commander, or nobleman to pay him a visit at home on a particularly sad or joyous occasion. Such requests had the express purpose of drawing public attention to the social standing of the person visited.[34] Theoretically, the king may also have elected to visit "one of his men" simply to exalt him in the eyes of others. Such visits, we are reminded, "do not occur by request or by the will of the visited, since it is not in the etiquette of a vizier or a nobleman (*sharīf*) to tell the king, 'Visit me in order to exalt me, in order to elevate my name and might in the eyes of the people.' "[35]

A person proudly arriving at the palace on horseback would most likely reduce himself by dismounting at the first gate or archway, and at subsequent thresholds he would bow and then prostrate himself. The last gesture might have involved kissing the threshold to the throne room and, if intimacy permitted, kissing the ground (*arḍ*) or carpet (*bisāṭ*) at the king's feet.[36] Standing, bowing, and prostrating oneself were considered formal gestures of supplication that paralleled the ritual prayer appropriated by the pious Islamic tradition in the worship of Allāhu Taᶜālā (God on High).[37] The transfer of these perennial gestures indicates their capacity, in new religious contexts, to evoke a "timeless" tradition of human vulnerability and appeal to the "timeless" beneficence of a sacral authority.[38] They perpetuate a means of persuasion that could be reapplied to other spheres of authority outside the court.

The king's claims to authority and his subject's deference were rooted in presumptions of power that reenacted mythic precedents. Without a positive mythology the acts would unravel out of entropy, as artificial, tedious, and senseless.[39] In particular, there were two important media meant to convince subjects of the king's mythic role. The ruler commissioned palaces and praise hymns, which complemented each other to raise expectations that he would be a beneficent patron, a cosmic hero who sympathizes with humanity. In this chapter I focus more on poetry (I return to the subject of architecture in chapter 4), but here I will briefly note that the construction of palaces in the Abbasid era at Samarra would sprawl into the size of towns.[40] In addition to the business of state, the king and his courtiers lived and perpetuated an "enviable" bacchic life evocative of Hellenic divinity and ancient Persian kingship. The art historian Robert Hillenbrand acutely notes, "Immured within their colossal palaces . . . their lifestyle expressed in the most extreme form the ancient Near Eastern concept of the king as god, even though such a belief was utterly incompatible with [pious] Islam."[41]

In addition to architecture, the king's mythic role was corroborated by the poet in his declamations of praise. Although the panegyrist was an interested party, there are some indications that rulers at times sought to shield themselves from the poet's words by ordering the chamberlain to deny access.[42] Patrons enjoyed certain aspects of the praise hymn but were entrapped by it all the same. By convention, praise entitled the poet to assume an air of closeness with the ruler. Unlike any creature who faced the king, the poet could call him by his first name, identify him by his mother's name, and address him with the familiar second-person singular—"as he would the least of the king's subjects."[43] Whereas no human should think himself worthy of praying for, consoling, or blessing the king, the poet could and did.[44] The poet would personally offer his gift of praise to the king before an assembly of high-profile guests and openly insinuate or name a favor in return.[45] If the declamation of praise was a scheduled event with a prestigious poet, full ceremony accompanied the praise celebration. The praise might occur on a special day marking a joyful occasion for the patron, such as his wedding, the birth or circumcision of a son, victory at battle, return from hajj, a holiday, recovery from illness,[46] or the erection of a new palace.[47]

One such occasion was al-Mutawakkil's "covenant of succession," which officially broke with Abbasid practice when al-Mutawakkil appointed his three heirs and determined their order of succession.[48] The covenant was grossly unfair to the youngest son, al-Muᶜtazz, who was favored by many at the court, including al-Buḥturī. The covenant was celebrated with a day of state festivities on the Tigris, making it one of the most extravagant galas in Islamic history. Al-Buḥturī exercised the privilege of withholding his praise services, however, thus forcing the caliph to resort to poets of lesser rank.[49]

Poets gave their endorsement through verse at other state events of equal grandeur, such as the coming-of-age celebration for al-Muᶜtazz.[50] That occasion marked the prince's newfound manhood and fertility with the construction of a new palace for him, as well as the debut of a mythopolitical poem from al-Buḥturī, which honored the father for recognizing the son's merits.[51] This increased the likelihood that people would begin to favor al-Muᶜtazz as the most legitimate heir. Al-Buḥturī's support for al-Muᶜtazz, signaled in his endorsement of the coming-of-age celebration and the lack thereof for the earlier covenant of succession that favored the older son, illustrates the strategic decision making that poets must have exercised at times to promote perceived communal interests.

Panegyrists offered their patrons legitimation that no other profession could provide. The constant demand for praise hymns suggests that brute force was not sufficient for a patron but that a rhetorical procedure was needed to convince the poet and others that triumph was justly deserved. Praise hymns, in this sense, justified privilege and can be said to have served as a kind of public relations or image building to counter the insinuations of rivals and rumormongers. For this reason the praise hymn was "almost always polemical."[52] A cadenced poem was viral, penetrating even the camp of a foe. Al-Buḥturī boasted of his poetry along these lines to his patron Muḥammad b. ʿAlī al-Qummī: "The chanting of [this] broadcast verse will recur continuously, / so, for its beauty, even *rivals* chant it."[53]

Patrons, especially rulers, desired a reputation as someone whom poets would supplicate. The poet's gesture toward the ruler counted as a public "act of allegiance."[54] The poet's performance was "part of the iconography of power."[55] As confirmation of his generosity and charisma, a king would bestow on the artist a material gift of some sort—money, domestic servants, horses, jewels, scented oils, or perhaps even land. Nothing was secretive about the exchange of praise for goods; the praise ceremony was intended to be known. In *The Book of the Crown on the King's Etiquette,* for example, al-Jāḥiẓ advised the king to bestow all honors to some extent openly:

> It is king's etiquette that he bestow robes of honor on whoever brings him joy privately or affirms his sovereignty publicly. If the joy is to and for him [the king], then he must claim the *privilege* of bestowing robes of honors on him [the subject] within the comfort of his palace, in the *presence* of his coterie and entourage. If it [the joy] affirms his sovereignty, then he must claim the *privilege* of honoring him [the subject] in the *presence* of the masses, in order thus to spread his reputation and enhance the story (*al-uḥdūtha*). Consequently, all that will revitalize goodwill, and he will instill the desire to affirm his sovereignty and shore up its foundations.[56]

The rationale presented here illustrates the transparency of gift politics as a means of shoring up public support, which could neither be ignored nor taken for granted.

The poet's benefit in this arrangement exceeded mere material gain. Namely, the poet exercised a power, recognized by others, to make culture and identity; he reconfigured the community's values, aspirations, anxieties, and ideals by projecting a coveted model of nobility. The ninth-century poet Abū Tammām (d. 842) declared the socioverbal power of his trade when he said, "Were it not for a tradition *modeled* by poetry, men seeking / greatness would know not whence to attain virtue."[57] Abū Tammām seems to touch on the anxiety of a system in which men compete for honor and recognition. Praise stems from the anxiety of not knowing *what* to do to gain respectability. The poet therefore guided others by setting a standard for the nobility that patrons covet. Court poets hoped that their alluring models would cultivate virtues of honor and honor virtues that are cultivated. Al-Buḥturī, an apprentice to Abū Tammām, appropriated this idea in praising his pupil, the caliph Ibn al-Muᶜtazz: "When we circulate poetry in his honor, his virtues grow, / cultivated as they are by poetry."[58]

Because men sought the admiration of others, as Meisami notes, praise was an impetus for excellence: "The poet does not merely record the noble deeds of his patron, he creates the motivation for them."[59] All in all, while granting patrons certain privileges, praise poetry enabled poets and later generations of devotees to shape the standard of excellence. Both praiser and praised, client and patron, thus emerge as winners, at the very least because one gains favors and the other prestige. In fact, al-Jāḥiẓ quotes a folk adage that presumes that the praiser-praised relationship stands as the framework for mutual sacrifice and benefit. In this adage the victim of a bad sale makes fruitless sacrifices and counts neither as praiser nor praised: "He who is cheated in a sale is neither the subject of praise (*mamdūḥ*) nor the object of bounty (*maʾjūr*)."[60] In other words, he who allows himself to be cheated makes sacrifices without honor, whereas patrons and clients make the proverbial sacrifices (to one another) that improve their social and moral standing.

In the analysis of the *Ruṣāfiyya* that follows, the discussion focuses on two life-saving powers of heroism that have become landmarks of Arabo-Islamic authority: being the protector against the ravages of personified Fate (the loss of loved ones, a natural disaster, etc.) and being the munificent benefactor in times of privation. If we are framing engaged resistance here as a relational, ongoing struggle, rather than as an abrupt break, then each party in a poet-patron rapport might see these images as strategies to his advantage. The patron views such images as justifying and celebrating his triumphs, whereas the poet views them as a means of modeling the obligations of nobility. Alternatively, the patron is gratified to exact the allegiance of others, and the poet is confident he is exacting the beneficence of his patron. In contrast, we now turn the discussion to the Sufi *mujālasāt,* to examine how these political connotations were reframed for spiritual purposes.

Hero against Fate in the *Ruṣāfiyya*

The poem that Ibn al-Jahm presented to al-Mutawakkil follows a tripartite organization typical of the praise ode: elegiac prelude (*nasīb*), transitional section (*raḥīl*), and triumphant tribute (*madīḥ*). The elegiac beginning in this case is lines 1–27; the transitional middle, lines 28–31; and the triumphant ending, lines 32–62. The excitement of the tripartite form derives from a transformation in the poet akin to the rite of passage paradigm developed by the French folklorist Arnold van Gennep and applied to the *qaṣīda* by Suzanne Stetkevych. The paradigm begins with themes of separation and detachment from community, followed by a transitional liminal state out of community, and concluding with reaggregation to the community.[61] This tripartite structure is fundamentally teleological and parallels other types of development that are typically labeled progress and maturation, such as human growth from childhood to adulthood or a hero's attainment of skill and knowledge through personal quest.[62] In the context of court performance, the ode structure therefore implicitly worked toward the patron and marked the poet's tribute to him as the culmination of maturity and knowledge.

The *Ruṣāfiyya* begins with a failed supplication to a romantic beloved, which leads the poet to rejection and spurs him to his courtly benefactor. Sufi performance introduces another dimension, however, which opens a frame of interpretation that essentially subverts the glory of the court. In either frame of performance the ode begins with intense vulnerability, a flight into lyricism, at the sight of the beloved's eyes:[63]

Doe's eyes—between *Ruṣāfa* and *Jisr*—
    import passion from where I know and I know not where.
They bring back old ardor in me—I hadn't
    recovered—adding embers to embers.
They are unharmed, but trounce hearts,
    as if spiked by the tips of fire-hardened spears.
They say to us, "We are crescents who light the path for him
    stealing through the night to us. Though we never rightly host."
No gift is there, but what the eye supplies,
    nor love, but from a phantom that steals.

If, when they shook the heart from its calm
　　and stoked what lies within my heart and bosom,
they had only refused as a wine drinker who
　　contents himself not to sip for fear of insobriety.
If only they forebode of ill news at first, before
　　my frosty locks had appeared, or hinted of perfidy.
If they were to dissolve or deny a tie we shared,
　　it is neither new for freewomen nor unbelievable.
But alas, youth is cut short, and
　　oryx are chased between youth and one's prime.
Let passion suffice as folly, and frosty locks as chide.
　　If only passion would subside with a chide!
By my hoary head, were it not that it scares them off, many a time
　　would they thrive lying in bed from dawn to daybreak,
and would we while away the night, despite rumormongers,
　　as if we were a mix of drizzle and wine.
My friends, how sweet is passion! How bitter!
　　How knowing am I of its sweet and bitter!
By all that is sacred between us, friends, have you seen
　　aught more delicate than a lover's plea?
　　or harsher than departure?
and aught more divulging of a lover's secret than his eye—
　　but more so if it frees a tear in stream?
Come what may, I shall not forget *in-Justine* and her words[64]
　　to her girlfriend, "How fierce is the love of a freeman!"
The latter said to her, "How come our friend aches?
　　In killing him, do you have a cause?
"Let him be; perhaps your union will quicken him.
　　Know that the prisoner of love is in the staunchest prison."
She said, "I will beguile my people about him, though rarely is love
　　sweet but the veil is torn."[65]
They make well sure that I hear *that,* then cry out,
　　"Who's the visitor stealing toward us, without our knowledge?"
I said, "A man! If you wish, he will contain passion.
　　But if not, he throws off the bridle and restraint
"—though he protests *in-Justine* for her paltry way
　　of giving him kindness and cheer."

She said, "We are *defamed!*" I said, "Some
of what you say is true. Perhaps though fire fights fire."

She said, "As if I'm infamous through verse:
they go out toward one town and come back from another."

I said, "You have me all wrong! I am no poet,
though my heart swells with poetry at times.

"Be my love and ask whomever you wish; he will tell you
that I am, come what may, the best keeper of secrets.

"Poetry is not the kind I seek for shade,
neither does it raise nor lower me in status.

"I'm not one whose fame is spread by poetry,
rather it's my fame that spreads my poetry.

"Poetry has many devotees, though I've been
a devotee of poetry in neither hard times nor ease.

"Not all who ride steeds master them,
and not all who are made to sprint are dubbed sprinters.

"Rather, it's the beneficence of the Caliph Jaᶜfar [al-Mutawakkil]
that bids me to convey what I say of him in poetry.

"It travels the path of the sun in every land
and stirs like wind over land and sea.

"If any lord is above thanks for a favor,
the Commander of the Faithful is surely above thanks.

"He is a man! Eyes are pleased to see the beauty of his face,
as are hands pleased to receive his beneficence.

"Islam with him is safe from every heretic.
Divine punishment befalls the wayward folk.

"Guide to guidance! He reveals true religion after
its partisans were rivaled by the partisans of disbelief.

"His liberal hand scatters his gathered wealth,
and thus an excellent reputation adheres to him.

"When he ponders an issue, his thinking attends to
mysteries that occur not to mind or thought.

"He gathers not wealth except to sacrifice it,
as a ritual offering is not led but to proper slaughter.

"What aim might a poet have in praising him, though he be
Zuhayr, al-Aᶜshā or Imruʾ al-Qays of Ḥujr?[66]

"Is it not when one likens his face to the sun or round moon,
we say, 'One fears for the sun and moon?'

"Whoever says, 'The sea and rain are like his
bounty,' then he brings glory to sea and rain!
"For if seven seas are added to the sea,
they wouldn't approach the bounty of his ten fingertips.
"If the glory of yore is mentioned, he recounts to us
stories already revealed in scriptures.
"If Jaᶜfar grows reliant upon God [Mutawakkilan ᶜalal-lāh]
in matters private and public,
"then, God thanks the Caliph Ja'far
and blesses him with a kind that does not wither eternally.
"The heirs apparent for the Muslims are three:
They are greeted with Aid, Might, and Victory.[67]
"Is there more than the Book of God,
O Abbasids, that you want as witness, beyond your glory
and honor?
"It suffices that God entrusts His affairs to you
and ordained that 'you must obey those in authority.'[68]
"The Prophet Muhammad asked people not for payment
but to love his closest kin.
"So, faith alone is unacceptable without real love for you.
Does God accept ritual prayer without ritual purity?
"There are those of dubious estates,
but your domain is between al-Ḥajūn and al-Ḥijr.
"The House of God remains among your houses.
You defend it with Indian swords, sharp-edged.
"Abū Naḍla, ᶜAmr al-ᶜUlā—he is Hāshim [Breaker of Bread]—your
forefather. Is there among men any more honorable than ᶜAmr?[69]
"And the libation bearer for the pilgrims after him is
the grandfather of praise. He is the Father of Ḥārith.[70]
He bequeaths to you the highest honor.
"You [Abbasids] drank and gave drink. Your blessings are superior
to others' like the blessings of loyalty over betrayal.
"The faces of Abbasid kings adorn a line of kingship as
shining stars adorn the heavens.
"Kingship does not commence to shine but by the right kin.
Are not months made of days?
"Islam did not rise, but while your kin, Sons of Hāshim,
stood amidst the *Milky Way* and *Aquila*.

"Salute the Sons of ʿAbbās with greetings wafting
upon the days like a sweet scent!
"When recited, it cheers your heirs with privilege
And serves as divine punishment for the wayward folk."

The poet's opening line erupts as he mingles both desert and city imagery: "Doe's eyes—between *Ruṣāfa* and *Jisr*—import passion from where I know and I know not where." The doe's eyes are visualized as those of the female Arabian (white) oryx (*al-mahā; Oryx leucoryx*). English translations often render the image "wild cow," although that translation falls short of capturing the appropriate zoological or symbolic associations. The oryx is biologically a type of antelope (family Bovidae, order Artiodactyla). The female is distinguished by an ivory-white coat, a black patch on the forehead, and two long straight horns.[71] Use of the oryx in poetry has evoked a lyrical delicacy commonly associated in American culture with the deer. Most important, the oryx's eyes are smoky and almond-shaped—a perennial substitute for the eyes of the beloved.[72] Alongside his Bedouin evocations, Ibn al-Jahm's ode calls up two landmarks of Baghdad's cityscape. The eyes of the oryx appear to him between two points: Ruṣāfa and Jisr. In the case of the *Ruṣāfiyya* one observes the poet reframing a lonely pastoral dream with markers of urban design that liberate his images from their referential context and project them as literary, symbolic devices. The ode's opening thus debanalizes language and invites the audience to participate in a compelling artistic experience.

The fixed place-names the poet uses are laden with symbolic charge. Ruṣāfa itself was a vibrant neighborhood built on a masonry embankment by the same name flanking the Tigris, just north of the medieval city center.[73] The neighborhood was an emblem of the Abbasid metropolis, and the Arabic root *r-ṣ-f* connotes stability and solidity, as well as "the compactness and firmness of stone." The firm embankment gives way to the lapping of waters, which separate it from another bank, flanking the river on the other side.[74] Water divides the river valley but paradoxically joins the two sides in a symmetrical relationship—one bank yearning for the other. Lexically implicit in Ruṣāfa is the idea of a counterpart across the distance, like a port opening onto the sea. Ports are symbolically similar to and interconnected with their counterparts, although necessarily removed from them as well. Just as Ruṣāfa implies its counterpart, the word *jisr* connotes a *ruṣāfa*. *Ruṣāfa* can mean an "embankment" or "dam" as well as a bridge that joins one bank to another.[75] The two words thus allude to one another. Removed from their specific denotation, Ruṣāfa and Jisr adumbrate each other as one riverbank implies another. The poet's own passions arrive from unknown points, amid these abiding points, affirming the delicacy of love within the urban structure.

In the first hemistich of his first line (just six words), Ibn al-Jahm used the taut Arabic poetics of the *nasīb* to signal a remarkably syncretic poem that launched him on a path toward the beneficence of his patron. The first hemistich in effect demonstrates not a total break with his Bedouin culture but a reframing of the Bedouin within the urban. A traditional view of "Bedouinness" and its perceived opposite—urbanity—underpins Ibn al-Jahm's transformation. Nomadic herders of Arabia—as opposed to merchants, craftsmen, and oasis farmers—were believed to be coarse, rough, and a bit boorish as a result of their harsh way of life.[76] Although their roughness was a point of criticism (as in the anecdote described at the outset of the chapter), the effeteness of city dwellers was deemed even more dangerous.

The scholar ᶜAlī b. ᶜAbd al-ᶜAzīz al-Jurjānī (d. 1002) lamented how Bedouin immigrants to the city lost their rustic manner of expression because of the new "softness of their civilization and the laxity of their moral character." In the metropolis the mix of languages and Arabic dialects forced speakers to take on "affectation" and "artificiality" in the process of assimilation.[77] It was a theme of medieval culture that when Bedouins settled, their natural parlance faded, never entirely to be regained. Bedouins were thus considered an idealized order of humanity; it was said they were closer to a lyrical "primeval" nature.[78] City dwellers, worried about their children's linguistic (and moral) well-being, would send their babies to nurse with Bedouin milk-mothers and to absorb so-called male ideals of honor and self-defense.[79] In one poem a completely urbanized poet, Abū Tammām, sought to effect some Bedouinness by using a "primitive" register believed to strike elegance without artifice, only to have his artifice exposed.[80] In Ibn al-Jahm's case his patron did not want to suppress his former state completely but rather to meld it with a cosmopolitan aesthetic.[81] In the end his patron confirmed the value of both when he said, "I almost feared that he might lose his charm and subtlety."[82]

Although much is innovative in the first hemistich, Ibn al-Jahm achieves movement toward his patron in ways that are typical of the established tradition. The eyes of the oryx are a substitute for the eyes of the beloved. Although she is desirable, she remains unattainable. In the world of the *nasīb* the oryx is a solitary animal, the *Einzelgänger.*[83] In the elegiac prelude she is prototypically the female "other," not allied with the poet. Ultimately she does not provide any relief for his psychic angst, so she introduces "images of heightened lyrical delicacy."[84] Her image recalls an archetypal agonistic tension between the needy and the needed. Yet for the vulnerable poet there is no end in sight for his privation. The eyes trounce upon his heart (line 3); they tease but do not satisfy (line 4). The beloved's eyes abandon him, leaving him with little hope of new love (lines 8 and 9). The fledgling love suffers the hostilities of Fate.

When Fate torments humanity in praise hymns, there is a generic expectation that the patron will come to the rescue. This expectation prepares the audience for the poet's progression from romantic love to political allegiance. The caliph is thus portrayed as the cosmic hero who saves humanity from the malice of Fate (*al-dahr, al-manāyā, al-layālī, al-zamān*). The arrows of Fate have many forms in praise hymns, ranging from poverty, lost love, and homeland to mortality itself. Chief among Fate's cruelties is the dispassion and disloyalty of women. Sperl observes that Fate is "master over life and death, generation and decay, but its rule is chaotic and arbitrary, amoral and hostile to human society."[85] In contrast, the king is the protagonist who protects humanity. Sperl writes, "The Caliph's rule . . . is not arbitrary but in accordance with virtue, justice and divine will. His accession to the throne marks the defeat of fate."[86] Sperl describes the structure of the praise ode as a liturgy to the sacral king. The poet in this scheme is "the prime victim of fate's power. By defeating fate, the Caliph saves the poet from his afflictions."[87] In this vein, when Ibn al-Jahm pleads with his beloved, he "protests *in-Justine* for her paltry way of giving him kindness and cheer" (line 23). In contrast, the caliph is beneficent and responsive—the personification of justice.

To illustrate how the king's benevolence foils the unkind hand of Fate, consider a short praise poem that the poet and musician Isḥāq al-Mawṣilī performed in honor of the caliph Hārūn al-Rashīd. Showing his patron exactly where his allegiance lies, Isḥāq complained of his beloved to al-Rashīd:

> I replied to my ungenerous belle, "save it,
> for that is something that leads nowhere."
>
> . . . .
>
> "My gifts have been those of a generous man giving graciously,
> yet, what I hold as you know is little.
> "But how, after all, can I fear poverty or be deprived of riches,
> when the wisdom of the Commander of the Faithful is well?"[88]

"How indeed?" cried the king, needing to be seen as the savior, and ordered a reward of 100,000 dirhams (a standard prize).[89] The poet's supplication could not fall on deaf ears; the king had to respond to human needs.

In Hellenic and Hellenistic society a preference existed for the king as a near god over other distant authorities. Calvin McEwan notes, "One might believe vaguely in the power and glory of the Olympians, but he could see and feel the glory of the power of the Diadochs. The local god fed nobody in times of famine, but the king could and did." Athenians sang to Demetrius, "The king comes, light-hearted as befits a god. . . . Hail! Child of mighty Poseidon and of Aphrodite. The other gods are a long way off, or have no ears, or no existence, or take no care of us; but thee we see face to face—a *true god,* not of wood or stone."[90]

Abbasid pleas were more veiled, but literary sources record supplications to the king that are in manner and content highly emotional. Consider, for example, the rhapsodic supplications of Mu ḥammad b. Ṣāliḥ al-ᶜAlawī in *The Book of Songs.* He was a poet and renegade who sought to change al-Mutawakkil's cruel policies toward the Alids (the descendants of Fatima, the daughter of the Prophet, and Ali, the Prophet's cousin—the precursors to modern Shia).[91] Note especially his rhapsodic apotheosis addressed to the king:

> You have joined the bonds of the Caliphate with Guidance.
> When you ascended, you calmed the eyes of the sleepless.
>
> . . . .

I supplicated you (*daᶜawtuka*) and you answered (*f-astajabta*)
my supplications,
when death was but a hand-span away from me.
You pulled me out from the bottom of the trough of demise
safely, and you did not give credence to the claims of my critics.
You unbound my fetters when disaster was fated.
You set the limbs of a man who had no bone-setter.
You took pity on your blood-kin by which you
aspire to the proximity of the Sovereign the Mighty.
I seek refuge in the grace of your forgiveness (*aᶜūdhu bi-faḍli ᶜafwika*)
that one might meet my aim at your door, to offset back-breaking ordeals.[92]

One can scarcely know what Muhammad the rebel felt inwardly toward al-Mutawakkil, but no one can retrieve these public words once issued: "I supplicated you and you answered." The term *duᶜāʾ* (supplication) implies that the object of supplication has force sufficiently cosmic to change Fate, such as God. One Hadith states, "Nothing changes Fate except supplication [to God]."[93] Although supplication is a drastic measure born of desperation, the supplicant expects benefits in the end. In this light one can better understand why an Alid renegade would praise the tormentor of his people. Using praise hymns as supplication is implicitly or explicitly a form of engaged resistance cloaked in elegant ceremony. The renegade says, "You pulled me out . . . safely" and "I seek refuge in the grace of your forgiveness."[94]

In a literal sense one might dismiss such statements as desperation, but within the traditions of supplication they transform a relationship of victor and conquered to one of patron and client, with benefits for both parties. The client vividly evokes the significance of the patron's "own love for those dearest to him and of his love for his own life as something uniquely precious—sentiments that he as a ruler is constrained to deny."[95] The ruler then has the chance to appear beneficent, to show that he seeks more than blood and conquest, that he appreciates the most sacred aspects of human life. The supplicant not only begs; he conspicuously draws attention to the fact that he is begging. He so urgently appeals to the superior not "to press to the hilt the power he enjoys" that he, in effect, increases the likelihood that the superior will feel some pity or risk losing face before his assembly.[96] One adage warned authority figures that a lack of shame with the weak decreases a man's status: "The weakest of the weak, for God, is a strong man who weakens the weak."[97] Supplication thus gives the patron a golden opportunity to play the role of a savior.

Women become a source of angst and fear in the *nasīb,* as the poet blames them for rejection and heartbreak, one of the many vagaries of Fate. In the world of the *qaṣīda,* if women are the problem, the patron is the solution. Ibn al-Jahm's poem sets up the agonizing situation exquisitely. Lines 17–27 present an escalating dialogue between the poet's beloved and her handmaiden, then another dialogue directly between Ibn al-Jahm and his beloved, echoing the verse of the early Islamic love poet ᶜUmar b. Abī Rabīᶜa (d. 711), renowned for his romantic dialogues. She toys with his expectations, however, alternatively giving and withdrawing hope. The beloved finally rescinds her approval of Ibn al-Jahm, blaming him for scandalizing her with even the mention of her name: "As if I'm infamous through verse: they go out toward one town and come back from another" (line 25). Line 26 begins Ibn al-Jahm's self-vindicating soliloquy, which reveals a bond to his beloved that is increasingly tenuous. He tries to reverse the decline with his claim, "You have me all wrong! I am no poet, though my heart swells with poetry at times." He calls her to an affair necessarily beyond the public eye: "Be my love . . . I am, come what may, the best keeper of secrets" (line 27). In the end, though, private love for the female gives way to public love for the male superior. The heart surrenders to the self-evident path to male honor. Ibn al-Jahm says, "It's the beneficence of the Caliph Jaᶜfar that bids me to convey what I say of him in poetry" (line 32). The poet has chosen to defer to authority at the expense of amorous desire and has used the language of desire to legitimate the gesture.

The anthropologist Lila Abu-Lughod, in her contemporary ethnography of the Awlad Ali Bedouins of Egypt, describes deference behavior as "honor of the weak" in the face of superiors.[98] As in Bedouin society, a patron at the court must appear to earn the respect of the weak, not by his force, but by virtue. Those, then, who are dependent on him for status and material sustenance can seek honor (save face) by subordinating themselves voluntarily. Abu-Lughod notes, "What is voluntary is by nature free and is thus a sign of independence." One must underline her observation that deferential behavior applies not just to women, but to any party exposed to his or her superior.[99] Women in Bedouin society may find themselves in such situations more often than men, but weaker males also defer to more powerful men and to older, stronger women—a mother or a superior's wife, for example.[100] In the end the strategies of deference are similar among men and women when exposed to authority. They amount to restraining one's desire (i.e., ceasing to eat, drink, recline, or laugh in the presence of the superior), as well as assuming a formal rigid posture, observing silence, and casting a downward gaze. All are ways of masking self-assertions.[101]

In Ibn al-Jahm's praise hymn the transmission of poetry provides the vehicle for shifting from private desire to public obligation without loss of face. The poet's "locomotive" words are responsible for promoting his reputation (line 29), as well as that of the patron. News of the king's generosity "travels the path of the sun in every land and stirs like wind over land and sea" (line 33). To the extent that Ibn al-Jahm can voluntarily bow to authority, he preserves his dignity and gains status as client.

The Generous Hero in the *Ruṣāfiyya*

In praise hymns the patron relied on the poet to corroborate and enhance his public appearance as the cosmic hero. The poet could then pressure him to prove his nobility with a sign of generosity. Only when the patron parts with his resources openly—actually making a sacrifice to the poet—does he publicly verify his rank. In material terms the poet's "reward for panegyric confirms its veracity" in the audience's eyes.[102] Although the poet may recognize other virtues, such as noble lineage, courage, might, and justice, generosity is the one most immediately verifiable. When generosity is thus proven, other virtues appear all the more dazzling and convincing.[103] The key to mana for the patron, especially a ruler, was therefore his capacity to seize on the praise hymn as an opportunity to make ostentatious sacrifices to the poet.

Recent work on Muslim kingship argues that royal power in Islamic cultures was sacral or allied with the sacral, which also meant it was absolutist, hubristic, and untamable.[104] Although it is necessary to link Muslim monarchy with earlier forms of kingship in the Middle East, the theory that royal power was expressed without palpable resistance in the court overlooks the role of poets in cultivating the ruler's addictive need for poetic glory. No doubt, the caliph's centrality to the Muslim community deserves to be accentuated, in particular for his official role as the supreme being on earth who sacralizes the community's daily life.

As Benedict Anderson observes, the classical religious communities of antiquity and the Middle Ages "conceived of themselves as cosmically central, through the medium of a sacred language linked to a supernatural order of power."[105] That order of power had earthly form in the figure of prophets and kings who demonstrated to the community their intimate bond with heaven. Anderson's notion reincarnates the formulation of Arthur Lovejoy, who argued that medieval society in Europe viewed the universe as a "Great Chain of Being." In this view every being, from the simplest existence to the most complex, was hierarchically ordered and linked to the grade of existence above it until reaching the most perfect being.[106] Lovejoy's theory does not account for competition, but one can introduce that dynamic and only enhance his basic position: all beings, from gnats to God, were thus linked in an unbroken chain; placement on the chain relied on distinctions of perfection (and thus sacrality). In the Abbasid realm the caliph categorically represented the highest manifestation of sacrality on earth, approximating the status of the Prophet Muhammad and emulating the functions of God on earth.[107] Given the dependence of the universe on the caliph's sacral functions, Aziz Al-Azmeh has some footing for claiming that "the peoples over whom kings preside are wholly subsumed in the king, and have no independent existence."[108]

Anderson notes that, alongside the king's sacral power, however, the other medium for sacralizing the world was language.[109] Its perfection was a means of inducting the uninitiated and marking a stratum of littérateurs, who were cosmologically linked in a hierarchy culminating in the caliph and God.[110] Sacred language, in the hands of poets, could then be used as an instrument for engaging the king and his delegates in the hierarchy. Members of the hierarchy were perennially in need of poets to boost their public reputation, especially in terms of their generosity. One courtly advice manual turned the self-interested practice into an obligation: "Patronizing poets is the duty of rulers."[111]

Generosity was the crux of earthly authority. When set against the threat of wrath, it was a veritable factory for charisma, without which power had no justification. Generosity was the material and ideological basis for the patron-client relationship and thus for nearly all relationships of dependency in society. As one adage warned, "Stinginess is the canker of politics."[112] That is, he who risks economizing with his subordinates risks rebellion and disgrace.[113] One maxim even mocked the would-be miser: "The most stingy with his money is the most spendthrift with his honor."[114] The importance of generosity is a matter of consensus in Arabo-Islamic culture, and some scholars have conceived of it as the mother of all virtues.[115] A man who gives generously, the reasoning goes, knows the social value of a gift. All virtues of character are gifts to society; therefore, a man who is generous is by nature virtuous. The littérateur ʿAlī b. ʿAbd al-Raḥmān b. Hudhayl relates, "Generosity (*karam*) is a term applied to every sort of virtue. It is a term that includes the meaning of forgiveness and munificence. Every trait that is good, every innate quality that is kind . . . falls under the term generosity."[116] Of course, the author plays up the double meaning of *karam,* which can mean either "generosity" or "nobility."

Displays of munificence satisfied expectations of mythic authority. To be generous to subordinates was to play the role of sacral hero, to take on characteristics of divine perfection.[117] Having and dispensing wealth was considered godly: "Wealth is better than poverty, because wealth is a trait of God while poverty is a trait of created beings."[118] Another author advised in unequivocal terms, "If you give, you will be happy. . . . God is generous, so you be generous."[119] Statements such as these rarefy the act of giving and lend credibility to sacral interpretations of authority and its techniques. Generosity was a self-conscious ideology in Arabo-Islamic culture and underpinned relations of inequality. Men of authority (altruistic or not) could countenance sacrificing wealth because it vested them with the worthwhile returns of mana. In effect, generosity fostered a mutually convenient dependency based on a principle of gratitude, as the lord would make sacrifices to the poet and thus expect long-term allegiance. As one unnamed poet advised, "Be generous to people—you will enslave their hearts. O, how often people are enslaved by generosity."[120]

It is to be expected that privileged patrons would see themselves as "buying" allegiance from supplicants, but from the perspective of poets this is no less than the vanity of privilege, which poets are all too happy to exploit. Al-Buḥturī had the standing to spell it out to his patron's face: "He is inebriated. He revels in supplication, *as if* the starved man / sings of him, or a worshipper."[121] The patron desires a song that celebrates his glory. The poet, however, persuades him to pay a price. The poet coaxes a concession for himself or others as a trophy, which shows that the patron's veil of intimidation is penetrable. One seasoned courtier related, "Supplicating a generous man mingles you with him and draws you near him and lifts the veil of timidity between you and him."[122] Needless to say, the supplicant would bear full responsibility for the quality of his oration: "If you supplicate a man of authority for something, make your supplication aesthetic."[123] On the surface the poet proclaimed his gratitude, and the patron paid him for it. Below the surface, however, there was a complex game of strategies and counterstrategies. Neither the king nor the supplicant could afford to play a truly submissive role. If the poet succeeded, if he could break through the king's veil, he not only departed with a reward but also evinced once more that his patron could be overpowered.

The praise section (*madīḥ*) of the *Ruṣāfiyya* is precisely where the poet showed his rhetorical skill in persuading the patron to make sacrifices. The poet commanded a repertoire of strategies that he might use to entrap his patron by appealing to the patron's sense of shame, pity, or vanity. As the poet turns the screws, pressuring the caliph, he might even be rightly accused of employing a sort of symbolic violence against the patron. This supplication is an anxious confrontation between two interested parties. If we take praise hymns as a discourse of Arabo-Islamic authority, the encounter between poet and patron coincides with the philosopher Michel Foucault's view that discourses are a means to social action, not an end in themselves, and therefore can be "a hindrance, a stumbling-block, a point of resistance and a starting point for an opposing strategy."[124] In examining the praise section (lines 32–62) of Ibn al-Jahm's *Ruṣāfiyya,* my goal is to illustrate how the praise hymn becomes a means of resisting royal authority for the poet and for the Sufis who recite the text in group.

The praise-filled verses of the poem (lines 32–62) are basically of two complementary types. In lines 32–48 the poet vouches for the king's personal virtues, whereas lines 49–62 celebrate his legitimacy as an Abbasid monarch, descending from the Hashimite line of Quraysh (as opposed to the Umayyad line). The first theme to emerge in the praise section is, of course, generosity, increasing pressure on the patron in this public document. Making the exchange perfectly clear, the poet also alludes to the power of his verse to broadcast glory. Lines 32–35 read:

"Rather, it's the beneficence of the Caliph Jaᶜfar
    that bids me to convey what I say of him in poetry.
"It travels the path of the sun in every land
    and stirs like wind over land and sea.
"If any lord is above thanks for a favor,
    the Commander of the Faithful is surely above thanks.
"He is a man! Eyes are pleased to see the beauty of his face,
    as are hands pleased to receive his beneficence."

Line 35 is stressful for the patron. The poet places his patron's manhood in the balance, if he refuses to please others with his countenance and gifts. Lines 36–37 introduce a theme that recurs in other forms, namely, defining the patron's religious decrees as Islamic orthodoxy. Here one observes a common preoccupation of Abbasid caliphs and their poets: convincing their audiences that contenders (such as the Alids, Ulema, Qarmatians, and Kharajites) in the Islamic domain lacked divine sanction to determine true religion.[125] The Abbasid caliph jealously guarded certain regalia inherited from the Prophet, all intended to prove divine election and favor and thus the prerogative of speaking for God as his chosen agent on earth.[126] Al-Buḥturī, for example, foregrounds the divine sanction of one caliph: "The Leader (*imām*) al-Muᶜtazz bi-llāh [Made Mighty by God] is / the Hashimite most deserving of victory and support." This is followed by, "He is heir of the Mantle and Staff [of the Prophet] and / the Authority of God above every leader and follower."[127]

In the *Ruṣāfiyya,* therefore, opponents of the caliph al-Mutawakkil are not only traitors but apostates as well: "Islam with him is safe from every heretic. / Divine punishment befalls the wayward folk" (line 36). Then, the caliph alone exercises the power of explicating the religion: "Guide to guidance! He reveals true religion after / its partisans were rivaled by the partisans of disbelief" (line 37). His capacity to enlighten the world, both literally and figuratively, thus outshines the sun and moon (line 42), the traditional touchstones of moral and physical radiance.

The poet then raises the issue of generosity again and the sacrifices he expects from his patron (lines 43–44). Measuring the hero's munificence in cosmic terms, the poet proposes that seas and rain are no match for his bounty (line 43). In the next line, the poet expands the image of bounty—"if seven seas are added to the sea"—but localizes it in his patron's fingertips. The demand, like a spike, is further hammered in line 40, noting that the patron does enjoy an income of riches but that enjoyment is made licit by his benefactions. The obligation to give is made holy when the poet likens it to dedicating and slaughtering an animal sacrifice. At this point the poet has maneuvered his patron into an awkward position. If the patron were to fail to make concessions to him, the offense would not simply be personal and public; it would be religious. If he decides wisely to make sacrifices, however, he may enjoy all the honors of the poem, including a reputation for munificence. In praise hymns when the poet verifies his patron's generosity, the verification activates the other honors of the poem![128] If we or al-Mutawakkil have any doubts about the contingency of a good reputation on generosity, Ibn al-Jahm spells it out adoringly, insistently: "His liberal hand scatters his gathered wealth, / and thus an excellent reputation adheres to him" (line 38). The causal relationship is clear: "If you want the glory, concede my requests publicly!" The poet's case gains strength in public performance, but he is not finished showing his prowess.

Line 49 opens a new type of praise that persuades audiences to obey al-Mutawakkil as an article of communal faith. In the Abbasid period, allegiance to the caliph was often conceived as a precondition of Muslim salvation.[129] In effect, before the Prophet became the model man, the Abbasid caliph served that function.[130] Believers were expected to take his wishes as commands. The article of faith is first rooted in the "Book of God," which is said to bear witness to the Abbasid right of sovereignty (line 49) by demanding that believers obey God, the Prophet, and, after him, "those in authority" (line 50).[131] The Abbasid claim is also authenticated by the Prophet, whom the poet insists asked followers to love his clan (the Hashimites) in return for his guidance and sacrifices (line 51). That prophetic demand culminates in a verse that renders love of the Abbasids a condition for true faith, just as ritual purity (*ṭuhr*) is a precondition for worship (line 52): "So, faith alone is unacceptable without real love for you. / Does God accept ritual prayer without ritual purity?"

The Abbasid insistence on a bond of love, not just loyalty, is paralleled in a praise hymn by the early Abbasid poet Abū al-ᶜAtāhiya, who depicts the relationship between the caliph and the Muslim polity using a metaphor of concubinage.[132] Poets, of course, preserve the aura of domination, while one poet after another places demands on the caliph that he may ignore at risk to his public image. Despite the fact that the Abbasids were mythologized, demands of love seemed overweening or absurd. One scribe produced a manuscript that dispensed with the phrase *ḥubbikum* (love for you) in favor of *ḥukmikum* (rule by you).[133] The latter phrase apparently was more palatable.

Lines 53–56 are encoded with proper nouns that were well known to Abbasid Muslims. They invoke pre-Islamic Qurayshi lore that celebrates the nobility of Hāshim b. ᶜAbd Manāf (the Prophet's great-grandfather) and Hāshim's son, ᶜAbd al-Muṭṭalib (the Prophet's grandfather and foster father). The ninth-century littérateur Abū al-Walīd al-Azraqī recorded a corpus of Qurayshi lore in his *Lore of Mecca.* He transcribed an oral tradition in midcourse; most of the narratives were told to him by his father and grandfather, as well as other men close to the family.[134] After al-Azraqī, later generations of readers continued to add narratives they had heard, increasing the size of the volume considerably.

Al-Azraqī's *Lore of Mecca* reflects the liveliness of oral narrative tradition and helps to further explicate the mythology behind two important toponyms in the ode. In line 53 the poet names two places, al-Ḥajūn and al-Ḥijr, as marking the distinguished domain of the Abbasids. On the day of Muhammad's conquest of Mecca in 622, the Prophet stood at al-Ḥajūn, a pre-Islamic burial ground atop a mount near Mecca where his first wife, Khadija, was buried. From there he looked toward the holy shrine, where Ḥijr Ismāᶜīl (the grave of Ishmael) is located. He then reconsecrated this mythic space. The moment was an intense one for the Prophet, at a site that was evocative of his early struggle, his sudden flight from Mecca, and the bitter loss of his wife and first believer. He looked down on the sanctuary in the valley and said, "By God, you are the best of God's land and the most loved of God's land. If I were not forced to leave, I would not have left. It is not the right of anyone before me, nor is it the right of anyone after me. Verily, it is mine by right for an hour of the day and from this my hour of the day forward."[135]

This site was appropriated by the Abbasids and recognized in this poem honoring al-Mutawakkil. However, there is a polemical dimension that allows the verses to stand as a warning to internal competitors and critics (such as the Alids, Ulema, Qarmatians, and Kharijites) who do not control the sanctuary: "There are those of dubious estates, / but your domain is between al-Ḥajūn and al-Ḥijr" (line 53). The idea is expressed a line later more forcefully: "The House of God remains among *your* houses. / You defend it with Indian swords, sharp-edged" (line 54, emphasis mine). In courtly parlance, though, might requires right: power must be clothed in verbally constructed moral legitimacy. Here the effect is achieved with a Hashimite version of the past. Lines 55–57 index a corpus of Meccan lore surrounding the legendary personae of Hāshim and ᶜAbd al-Muṭṭalib, a father-and-son pair who would influence world history by instituting a Qurayshi brand of monotheism that culminated in the message of their descendant, Muhammad. Their legacy was common knowledge to Abbasid Muslims, especially those who had endured a pilgrimage to Mecca, hearing them firsthand from proud Meccan descendants. In lines 55 and 56 of the ode they are invoked as part of a communal memory:

"Abū Naḍla, ᶜAmr al-ᶜUlā—he is Hāshim—your
forefather. Is there among men any more honorable than ᶜAmr?
"And the libation bearer for the pilgrims after him is
the grandfather of praise. He is the Father of Ḥārith.
He bequeaths to you the highest honor."

Both the Umayyad and Abbasid dynasties traced their lineage not to the Prophet himself, for he had no male heirs, but to his tribal forebears: his grand-uncle (Umayya b. ᶜAbd al-Shams) and his uncle (ᶜAbbās b. ᶜAbd al-Muṭṭalib), who were patriarchs of the tribe of Quraysh. The historical lore of Quraysh, as formulated in Abbasid sources, projects backward a nascent imperial vision for the tribe that had taken form well before Muhammad. The tribe fulfilled the vision of late antiquity, best formulated by Emperor Constantine: "religious self-propagation with the political, military, and economic expansion of empire."[136]

The historian Khalīl ᶜAbd al-Karīm, in his study of the rise of Quraysh, argues that the glory that culminated in Muhammad's expansionist message was the upshot of a tribal enterprise that began some five generations earlier with his fourth grandfather, Quṣayy b. Kilāb.[137] It was he who laid the foundations of a new era when he wrested the ill-used sanctuary of the Kaaba at Mecca from the tribe of Khuzāᶜa by marrying into it and waging a fight for the keys. Quraysh rallied around him, inspired by the prospect of wealth and fame in hosting the services of the sanctuary. Most important, the founders of the proto-polity — Quṣayy and his son ᶜAbd Manāf and his son Hāshim and his son ᶜAbd al-Muṭṭalib — promoted the Dār al-Nadwa (Assembly Building) at the shrine. It was their center of administration, used as a chamber for deciding war, peace, and trade pacts, as well as for local rites of passage (such as the puberty rites of boys and girls).[138] Certainly one can see in these sources the historical formation of a monotheistic religion, but ideologically for the Abbasids they lend credibility to a sacral communal history by planting the seeds of Islam well before the Prophet; these narratives cast the pre-Islamic as proto-Islamic.[139]

The heroes of Quraysh echoed the merits of older Semitic prophets and established daunting precedents for Abbasid rulers. Grandfather ᶜAbd al-Muṭṭalib was an Abraham-like figure, raised in childhood among the Jews of Yathrib (later named Medina), who served as priest (*kāhin:* cohen), received dream revelations, and preached the oneness of God and the severing of a thief's hand. He also forbade idolatry and female infanticide.[140] Hāshim in particular left a memorable legacy in folklore as a servant of the holy shrine. In the course of discharging his duties, Hāshim dug wells so that pilgrims could find fresh water. In Christ-like fashion he fed a mass of pilgrims during a famine with a miracle meal of freshly slaughtered meat, along with bread and flour he had imported from Syria, an incident that won him his name Hāshim (Breaker of Bread). Hāshim ᶜAmr al-ᶜUlā more than once saved the pilgrims from suffering. He established a festal meal that would become the touchstone of legitimacy for some three centuries, well into the Abbasid period. For generations people would sing their gratitude to Hāshim. As one poem recounted, "ᶜAmr al-ᶜUlā ground (*hashama*) the flour for people who were / in Mecca destitute and hungry."[141]

The legendary heroes, Hāshim and ᶜAbd al-Muṭṭalib, were prophet-like men whose reputations were synonymous with proto-Islamic nobility and the calendrical rituals of the hajj. The "Hashimite" legacy of service and charity was precisely the sort of legacy the Abbasids needed to identify with in order to give legitimacy to their rule, as well as their administration of the Meccan sanctuary and the hajj. The ending of the ode (lines 57–62) proclaims Abbasid preeminence and warns contenders simultaneously that the Abbasids are the "right kin" who inherit the prestige and merits of their ancestors.

The irony of this praise hymn is that the patron provides the funds for its artistic production, even though he is only one of many subjects. The poet supplicates, and thus he draws attention to himself and his capacity to pierce through the patron's aura of intimidation, effectively pressuring him into making concessions. In the original performance two interested parties encounter one another. The poet, by exposing the limits of caliphal prowess, in effect proves his own.

Ibn al-ᶜArabī's anthology reframes the ode by presenting it as memorized knowledge for Sufi gatherings. The key to reframing rests in a performance situation, imagined or actual, in which men recite the text as part of an evening's edification. When performed, oral communication gives the speaker added authority by enabling him to re-enact the poet's dramatic delivery. The Sufi speaker has the opportunity to identify with the verbal prowess of the court poet. Needless to say, al-Buḥturī expressed this ideal when he declared that in courtly praise hymns, glory is the glory of the poet![142] The poet exhibited his capacity to exert pressure, elicit reactions, and in the end exact the patron's beneficence as a trophy. He is the ultimate hero whose skill in supplicating both earthly and heavenly patrons is in evidence. As the rhapsode identifies with the verbal heroism of Homer, so too the Sufi performer with ᶜAlī b. al-Jahm.[143] Whether his name appears as ᶜAlī b. al-Jahīm or Abū ᶜAlāᵓ al-Maᶜarrī, the archetypal power of the poet for the Sufi performer remains an impressive model. The Sufi performer inherits a tradition of enacting the poet's resourcefulness. The bumpkin-in-Baghdad anecdote frames the *Ruṣāfiyya* as Sufi literature by inventing a narrative that stitches together a sequence of events: encounter and failure, then encounter and redemption. The manuscripts that transmit the *Ruṣāfiyya* indicate an equally active endeavor to frame the praise hymn in ways that redirect its hegemonic impact, *causing* the poetic persona to abandon the patronage of al-Mutawakkil for that of God. Even before the Creator, the poetic persona continues to provide a model of supplication.

From the speaker's perspective the appeal of supplication lies in a seeming reduction of the self, while exercising a persuasive force that can make the mighty patron *feel* such intense and socially complex emotions as shame and pity. While patrons, especially rulers, may exercise the privilege of giving life and death and cultivating an aura of awe and fascination, eloquent speech provided a means of scrutinizing privilege. In short, the speaker's supplication was recognized for its effect on feelings and social structures when the speaker gained admiration and control for his show of communicative skill.[144] In this vein Arabic eloquence, chiefly poetry, was deemed a kind of "licit magic" that could be exercised by nearly anyone who could acquire the skill.[145] A magical effect was achieved primarily through the power of the speaker to rearrange the value of things in society, so as to question the social demarcations of beauty and grotesquerie, truth and falsehood, and honor and stigma.[146] The Prophet Muhammad is made to concur with this capacity in a saying, "Eloquent speech is magic; poetry is authority (*inna min al-bayāni la-siḥran; inna min al-shiᶜri la-ḥukman*)."[147]

The overwhelming sacrality of the ruler described in Al-Azmeh's work appears to be only one side of a dialectical relationship. The sacrality of the community was achieved not only through the hubristic power of the divine ruler but also through the sacrality of language.[148]

The authority of language under the control of a skillful speaker could counterbalance the authority of rulership. This connection is noted not to minimize the terrible power of the ruler but to suggest that through supplication speakers could compete, struggle, and often win concessions that proved the patron's need for approval. When the supplicant identifies his unfortunate situation with "a long tradition of urgent need,"[149] the patron is then invited, sometimes forced, to do as legendary heroes do when they restrain their wrath and display clemency. There is a savory irony to supplication. The "subordinate" speaker exhibits the verbal capacity to influence how he is perceived, treated, and finally judged. That exhibition of skill at the court and in other sectors of society has served as an alluring model of individual tenacity in the face of authority.

THE *RUṢĀFIYYA* IN SUFI GATHERINGS

The poem-and-anecdote extract presented in Ibn al-ᶜArabī's anthology represents one example of the literary reception that ᶜAlī b. al-Jahm received in Sufi circles. Further investigation, however, shows that Maghribi Sufis in particular were chiefly responsible for preserving the poetic heritage of Ibn al-Jahm. His poetry is transmitted almost exclusively in Sufi manuals directed at disciples, with his signature poem, the *Ruṣāfiyya,* towering above the rest as a favorite. Nine known manuscripts housed in Berlin and Madrid archives convey the works of Ibn al-Jahm. Seven of them are Sufi devotional manuals. All told, some 90 percent of his poetry survives because of the Sufis' interest. Were it not for the support of Sufis in the late-medieval period, the first and only modern edition of his *dīwān,* published by Khalīl Mardam in 1949 (reprinted 1996), would have been impracticable.[150]

Ibn al-Jahm's legacy, especially his depiction as the bumpkin in Baghdad, illustrates a phenomenon of performance that poses particularly interesting questions. A court poet's legacy has somehow been reframed for a Sufi audience. His devotion to the king is appropriated for the sake of devotion to the Sufi master and God. Although he made his living at the Abbasid court by praising the caliph al-Mutawakkil, giving him homage, and receiving his protection, Ibn al-Jahm's legacy and performances are delivered to a new audience, thus opening a new "interpretive frame."[151] The new frame draws attention to the court ode as an artistic, symbolic event in the context of Sufi aesthetics. To address this issue, it will be worthwhile to examine neighboring texts in the manuscripts that transmit Ibn al-Jahm's poetry. These texts come to us in handbook form and were likely used to prepare for performance in Sufi *mujālasāt,* and they give structure and function to the legacy of Ibn al-Jahm in the lives of those who used the handbooks. These texts performed in a group constitute what Bauman calls a "culturally patterned use of language as an element and instrument of social life."[152]

The first hints to orient a performance analysis are found in an assortment of devotional manuscripts that transmit Ibn al-Jahm's persona and poetry in the context of other devotional texts. They provide the only material link to spoken communication. The personae of the poet and the patron are often deconcretized, laying greater emphasis on the archetypal poet and king—that is, the mythic roles of supplicant and hero. In Berlin manuscript Spr. 1242 (scr. ca. 1820), the poet is Ibn al-Jahm ᶜAlī, in manuscript Spr. 1142 (scr. ca. 1688) he is ᶜAlī b. al-Jahīm, and in manuscript We. 183 (scr. ca. 1650), the poet becomes Abū al-Alāᵓ al-Maᶜarrī (d. 1057), a poet renowned for his *resistance* to praise hymns and patronage. The patron is also conceived of as a type: he can be the caliph al-Manṣūr (see manuscript Pet. 39; scr. ca. 1800), or al-Muᶜtaṣim (see manuscript Esc. 369; scr. ca. 1593). This latitude in naming the supplicant and the hero reaffirms the importance of each as perennial archetypal roles.

The bumpkin-in-Baghdad anecdote forms essentially a rite of passage narrative, in which the passenger (Ibn al-Jahm) moves from buffoon to refined courtier. The preoccupation with self-mortification and buffoonery, which the king understands and redeems, is far from a coincidence and had particular relevance to the Maghribi Sufis of the Malamatiyya branch, or the Path of Shame. Sufism in general subordinates the appetites, especially the ego's craving for glory, deferring to God's glory. In the early years of proto-Sufi thought, in the eighth and ninth centuries, the mainstream deemed this path somewhat ludicrous, for it countered a culture that valued men and women who performed glorious deeds and a social hierarchy that rewarded valor. In the formative period of proto-Sufism the entire premise of rejecting glory was blameworthy in the sense that it subverted, rather perverted, the key principles of patronage culture. By the tenth century, however, Sufism had gained credibility and become surprisingly a means of gaining esteem and glory in the eyes of earthly subordinates and superiors alike. In seeming contradiction to renouncing the glory of men, a state chancery employee named Abū ᶜAlī Hārūn b. ᶜAbd al-ᶜAzīz accepted a rousing praise hymn from the tenth-century poet Abū al-Ṭayyib al-Mutanabbī, although the civil servant had Sufi leanings.[153]

Here we find a conspicuous example of how early Sufism was unable to escape worldly commerce of glory and patronage, thus placing the inner motives of followers in doubt. The innovation of the Malamatiyya was to teach followers never to let on that they were remotely Sufi, as that would earn glory in the eyes of some. At the time of its earliest beginnings in Nishapur (Central Asia), followers were encouraged to identify themselves in public by worldly markers, if they must, such as their profession (*ṣanᶜa, ḥirfa*) or their chivalry (*futuwwa*), so as to preserve the sanctity and integrity of their service to God as Sufis. The idea was to shroud oneself in a worldly base identity, to avoid any worldly status-seeking via the Sufi identity. In time the Malamatiyya, like most other Sufi branches, transgressed regional and continental boundaries, reaching as far as Andalusia and North Africa. By the twelfth century, renowned Malamatiyya saints such as Moulay Bouazza (d. 1177) had emerged and helped to spread new methods of hiding Sufi honor (in the eyes of God) from the public by consciously adopting distressing self-styled shamefulness, including public self-humiliation, sin, scandal, and buffoonery. Moulay Bouazza gained sainthood and a following by violating socio-religious norms with acts of cross-dressing, self-inflicted slavery, and eating the Wanalgut plant that sprouted out of trash heaps—thus his nickname, Abu Wanalgut. In concrete terms the Malamatiyya paid for their dignity before God by selling their dignity before men. In a culture of glory and patronage these acts had the effect of being deeply disturbing and puzzling to nonmembers, which was precisely the intention.[154]

Thus the bumpkin-in-Baghdad anecdote gently alludes to a transformation from uncouth buffoon to urbane courtier, embodied in the resounding success of the *Ruṣāfiyya,* socially and artistically. In the *Ruṣāfiyya* ode the poet symbolically forgoes the romantic feminine beloved for the political beloved in the person of al-Mutawakkil. When Sufi brothers assume *responsibility* for representing the legacy of Ibn al-Jahm to one another, however, court triumphalism gives way to a further transformation that radically reframes the *Ruṣāfiyya* transition from earthly buffoon to spiritual buffoon.[155] Ibn al-ᶜArabī in his *mujālasāt* playfully figures the *Ruṣāfiyya* as simply the first (most naive) stage of a long journey to divine knowledge. Ibn al-Jahm now "repents" of having expressed allegiance to the caliph al-Mutawakkil and rededicates himself to the ultimate patron, God. As with the Beloved and the King, God too requires sole allegiance from his clients. One Hadith says, "There is no one more jealous than God." Another states, "No one likes praise (*madḥ*) more than God."[156]

In pious terms praise was a form of glory that was sinful, unless reserved for the only true deity. In his *mujālasāt* Ibn al-ᶜArabī narrated a short epilogue that depicts Ibn al-Jahm "returning to God on High" after a prodigal career of praising earthly patrons. He "repents," yielding to whatever Fate might bring. He finally declares, "We have placed trust in the Lord of Heaven. / We have surrendered to the Courses of Fate (*asbābi-l-qaḍāʾi*) / And we are at home with the Rancor of Nights (*al-layālī;* i.e, Fate) / With souls that, after pride, now soften. / The doors of kings are sealed shut, / But the door to God is wide open (*mabdhūlu-l-fanāʾ*)."[157] A seasoned court personality bears witness from experience that there is no worthy patron except the one ultimate patron whose doors stand wide open for supplication.

However glorious the patronage of God may be, supplication to him provides no guarantee against the dangers of Fate, traditionally personified as a malevolent force. As always, supplication can result in tenderness or cruelty. The concept of God as deity can never be fully denatured from its earthly model. Not only does God's court have doors, but he, like earthly kings, might see fit not to gratify a supplicant to test his loyalty (*imtiḥān* or *ibtilāʾ*). He might even send catastrophe in his direction for the same purpose. Ibn al-Jahm's repentance is not free from anxiety and ambivalence about what will happen to him in the hands of God. In one sentence he says, "We have placed trust in the Lord of Heaven," but in another that trust is tantamount to surrendering dangerously to "the Courses of Fate" and the "Rancor of Nights." On the one hand, God's patronage is infinitely accessible and glorious; on the other, his patronage makes no promise of safety from the vagaries of Fate, which traditionally include loss of life or loved ones, natural disasters, and poverty. To submit to God's patronage was therefore tantamount to voluntarily yielding to what Fate might bring. In Sufi parlance this was the epitome of martyrdom—that is, self-sacrifice for a worthy patron (God).

Divested of its courtly framework, the *Ruṣāfiyya* survives in Sufi manuals, surrounded by supplications to God and his Messenger. More notably, the poem is framed by the theme of death and martyrdom. For example, one manuscript presenting Ibn al-Jahm's ode (Pet. 39) begins with a section spelling out what counts as martyrdom. The essay is titled *Doors of Felicity on the Causes of Martyrdom* (Abwāb al-Saᶜāda fī Asbāb al-Shahāda). The work proposes a broad definition of martyrdom that includes death in any catastrophe (flood, drought, fire, earthquake, etc.) and under any pain (hunger, thirst, disease, sorrow, grief, lovesickness, etc.), always reinforcing the notion that a victim may enjoy the glory of a martyr if he surrenders voluntarily to the designs of the ultimate patron, God.

Another manuscript (Spr. 1239) ends with a chain of birth and death notices that successive owners had apparently penned in; many are quite personal, like diary entries, referring to sons, fathers, and brothers by name, and in some cases death follows birth by only a few years. These pages are of a distinctly heavier stock, making it look as though they were *added* by design when the book was rebound. It appears that owners wanted to universalize their personal joy and grief by having it ride on the coattails of this manuscript.

Within the theme of martyrdom and mortality, one can begin to appreciate Ibn al-Jahm's poetic missive to al-Mutawakkil in which he expresses frustration with the false promises of earthly patronage. Most shockingly, he again resigns himself to the vagaries of Fate. Apparently having nothing more to lose, he chants the following nine lines to sever his ties for good:

Fate (*al-dahr*) recedes and advances.
　　One condition (*ḥāl*) follows another.
He who befriends Days (*al-ayyām*) is forgetful,
　　but for Days there is no forgetting.

A man is characterized by his actions.
People are stories and parables.
You there, who expresses his hopes,
before your hopes [come true] there is death.
How often does life put us to trial with suffering, then restore us?
How often does it put us to trial, then deceive us?
How sweet is patience! Especially for the nobleman,
when his conditions constrain him?
My rivals will bear witness that I know
well how to sever and build ties.
Adversity controls not my resolve,
nor do glory and wealth agitate me.
Notify (*balligh*) the Commander of the Faithful,
who is well-advised and competent![158]

His renunciation of al-Mutawakkil in these verses is encoded but effective nevertheless. He forgoes the articulation of hopes (supplication) and the power of anyone to motivate him with glory or wealth, preferring to suffer rather than supplicate. These subtle shifts are fundamentally a rejection of the underpinnings of courtly patronage, which would have appealed to Sufi and especially Malamatiyya audiences, giving purpose to their worldly self-sacrifices.

The topic of death and martyrdom also takes form in a fresh supplication to God Almighty. In one case the supplicant journeys toward the archetypal hero:

They climb toward an elevation. The road to it seemed appealing,
as though sweet waters (*ᶜadhb*) were derived from murky ones (*ᶜadhab*).
To You I direct my hopes and they were not denied access
to the doors of Your generosity. Lack of access is real death!
I have supplicated You. I beseech a favor from You.
Far be it! Far be it for You that I supplicate and You not answer.[159]

There is almost an air of entitlement in this supplication, demonstrating how a time-honored ritual procedure can embolden the heart of the supplicant when he gains access to the countenance of his benefactor.

In manuscript Esc. 369, however, the audience encounters the abject dimensions of supplication, where fears (not hopes) come true. A vivid example illustrates the inherent drama of supplication—a confrontation of interests that can conclude in gentleness or violence. The martyr in this poem is likened to a flickering candle doomed in the breeze. Antagonistic forces are simultaneously likened to the King, the romantic Beloved, and God as archetypal authorities. The candle is "slender like one of the King's boon-companions, / Pale like an infirm lover. / He dances with the dark, when the dark dances with him. / He loses all and is lost at once."[160]

The archetypal hero is sometimes ungenerous and whimsical; the supplicant can preserve dignity and gain status as a martyr by relinquishing all attachments voluntarily. In manuscript Escorial 369, for example, these lines provide a fretful preamble to the *Ruṣāfiyya*. In effect, Ibn al-Jahm's personal testimony to patronage, the *Ruṣāfiyya,* is countervailed in the Sufi context with sobering reminders of death and martyrdom for a *higher* patron. The loss is all-consuming absolute reality that sublimates the victim. In Sufi gatherings God's patronage frames momentary supplications to the Beloved (in the *nasīb*) and to the King (in the *madīḥ*), and the latter is proven no less a delusion than the former. In short, the *Ruṣāfiyya* is preceded by death and martyrdom as a device that foreshadows the false promises of the world (in the Beloved and King archetypes), compared with God's permanent albeit delayed bounties.

In Sufi *mujālasāt* these three archetypes are presented as progressions in stages. Each is vested with sacral authority by the Arabo-Islamic poetic tradition and demands exclusive allegiance, creating a crisis for a believer who must live in this world in order to prepare for the next. In each case allegiance not only affirms the service of the supplicant; it also validates the preeminence of the authority figure.[161]

This chapter began with a question about how a piece of the courtly canon extolling the caliph's grandeur became appealing and meaningful to those who would categorically reject such a conceit. I have proposed implicitly and explicitly that the process that sublimated the *Ruṣāfiyya* and the legacy of ʿAlī b. al-Jahm was animated by the artistic and social dimensions of face-to-face performance in *mujālasāt*. In an era that rejected or distrusted the false intimacy of written modes of educating and communicating, the *mujālasa* would have been the probable venue for receiving, adjusting, and re-presenting inherited knowledge. The probability or even the possibility that the sociability of the *mujālasa* could empower individuals to radically reframe tradition points to new avenues of thought about how the *mujālasa* might have influenced the way that individuals and groups enjoyed, adapted, and formed their enduring literary canon.

Part II

THE *MUJĀLASĀT* AS FORUM FOR LITERARY RECEPTION

FOUR

The Poetics of Sin and Redemption

Performing Value and Canonicity

THE PROBLEM OF CONTRADICTION AND LITERARY VALUE

The caliph al-Mutawakkil ᶜalā llāh reigned for fourteen years (r. 847–61) as head of the Abbasid state. In winter 861 he unexpectedly withdrew his approval from the heir apparent, al-Muntaṣir billāh (d. 862), in favor of his youngest son, al-Muᶜtazz billāh (r. 866–69). Shortly thereafter, al-Mutawakkil was murdered in his palace by his personal guards, in a plot that implicated al-Muntaṣir. Al-Mutawakkil's court poet, Abū ᶜUbāda al-Walīd b. ᶜUbayd al-Buḥturī (d. 897), rose to the occasion by voicing his loyalty to al-Mutawakkil and his outrage about the assassination. In a vehement elegy (*rithāʾ*) al-Buḥturī extolled his late patron, cursed and accused al-Mutawakkil's son of patricide, and vowed vengeance—according to one version of the historical events.[1] The poet not only stigmatized al-Muntaṣir; he also urged members of the court to support a worthier candidate for the caliphate (in lines 32–33 of the elegy).[2] The court did not follow the poet's political guidance, however. In effect the new caliph was stigmatized and damaged.

Abbasid literary sources indicate that al-Buḥturī then left Samarra for the hajj, and two months later he returned to praise none other than al-Muntaṣir.[3] In a second poem, a praise hymn, the poet now salutes al-Muntaṣir as the hero who thwarted disaster and renewed the majesty of the caliphate.[4] The two poems have elicited admiration from medieval scholars in both literary and historical sources, but the odes stand in puzzling contradiction.[5] In the first poem the poet stigmatizes the heir; in the second he valorizes him. At first al-Buḥturī clearly withholds his support, but later he finds it plausible to reverse this stance.

Despite the major strides that Meisami, Gruendler, Sperl, and S. Stetkevych make to reframe the simplistic issue of sincerity, by positing practical functions for praise in a social context, al-Buḥturī's two odes remain a puzzle because they stand at cross-purposes.[6] Putting aside the question of sincerity, if al-Buḥturī is effective in the first ode, how can he be effective in the second ode? Recently, critics have attempted to address this question but have ascribed evaluations (in this case, negative) intrinsic to the poet and the text. Their analyses have disregarded the pair of odes by attributing them to frantic opportunism.[7] What is at stake here is not whether one's evaluations are favorable or unfavorable but whether one's method of evaluation rests in the pragmatics of social reception or in putatively universal, unpragmatic (usually ideological) qualities or properties inhering to the poet or the text universally.

According to Shawqī Ḍayf, for example, the poet created a problem for himself by criticizing al-Muntaṣir and thus needed to excuse himself.[8] Attitudes that dismiss poetry and poets in this way bring scholarly investigation to a dead end, for they fail to explain the value of these poems *as art* to their immediate audiences and their canonicity for generations. If Ḍayf can dismiss these odes, he ignores the rousing reception they received. One would still have to ask, why would these odes be appealing at the time and canonical for generations?

The issue of appeal and canonicity rests on the emotional and aesthetic effects of these odes *on people,* as well as long-term use and benefit *to society.* One cannot presume that al-Buḥturī presented the praise hymn to al-Muntaṣir solely to compensate for an "error," because even a preliminary reading of the text shows the absence of any formal features of apology or self-redemption.[9] To the contrary, al-Muntaṣir himself treats the poem as a needed favor. He reciprocates with an extraordinary prize sum, a completely uncharacteristic act.[10] Whatever function the praise might have served, it did more than turn a profit or appease an angry patron. The most problematic aspect of Ḍayf's approach, however, is his assumption that court poets were in effect weaklings. This assumption underestimates the pride with which many medieval scholars and littérateurs viewed the verbal and thus political power of al-Buḥturī.

This "poet's greed" theory also falls short of explaining the value of these poems, especially when one examines their impact and reception. Less than a generation after the event, the littérateur Abū Bakr b. Yaḥyā al-Ṣūlī registered the poet's effect in restoring al-Muntaṣir's battered public image.[11] Likewise, a tenth-century historian, Abū al-Ḥasan al-Masᶜūdī, took note of al-Buḥturī's cleansing of al-Muntaṣir's reputation.[12] Al-Buḥturī's poems were in fact transmitted for eleven centuries, so that ten of fifteen extant poetry collection (*dīwān*) manuscripts record them. Despite the instabilities of court patronage, the more persistent question is one of poetic function and value, which invites a pragmatic approach of judging utility, readjustment, appeal, and canonicity.

I address both the political and mythic effects of al-Buḥturī's words, building on the proposition of this book that performers assumed responsibility for a text before audiences in face-to-face performance. I focus on how al-Buḥturī moved and inspired others in a moment of state crisis and how, thereafter, the text of his odes were adjusted in order to extend their value and ensure canonicity. I wish to deploy the literary and social construct of the *mujālasāt* as a pragmatic testing ground for literary value. The literary critic Barbara Herrnstein Smith formulates a theory of valuation based on the analogy of market dynamics. Smith argues that when human beings evaluate their experience of cultural products (e.g., verbal texts, performances), this is not a discrete behavior punctuating experience but intrinsic to existence and cognition itself: "For a responsive creature, to exist is to evaluate. We are always calculating how things 'figure' for us—always pricing them, so to speak, in relation to the total economy of our personal universe."[13] Things that are deemed "good" compete for our attention, our resources, so in order to experience one needs to evaluate which of the good is most worthy of those resources. Moreover, Smith employs a Darwinian model to gauge how literature is put to the test: in a literary survival of the fittest, texts that are backed by their supporters take on a life of their own, figuratively. They must be made to adapt to new environments and compete for attention with other texts. One of the uses of the *mujālasāt* as a social and literary construct would be to envision how that competitive proving ground for texts might influence the ways that poets and performers frame and adjust texts in order to frame the very reception they anticipate.

I argue that the two odes functioned on both political and mythic levels, thus having short- and long-term effects. At the moment of crisis, in the short term, the dyad served as a memorable ritual for the "transfer of allegiance" between patrons.[14] Initially, al-Buḥturī's elegy for al-Mutawakkil withheld al-Muntaṣir's much-needed endorsement, but his praise hymn to al-Muntaṣir granted it, thus emphasizing the poet's prerogative to unmake and make authority. However, the poet's choice of Mecca as the goal of his journey, and the hajj as the ritual of atonement, suggests a mythmaking redemptive ritual that resonated far beyond the moment in cultural memory. Group performance in salons gives a likely venue where the two odes could be received and transmitted as a dyad forming a ritual redemption for the Abbasid dynasty.

The phenomenon of framing and adjustment in the *mujālasāt* is especially relevant because it poses an intriguing contrast to our contemporary experience of print literature. Whereas the natural selection of modern printed literature limits the possibility that individuals and groups will adjust the text to suit their needs—thus the media curtails reception in the form of adjustment—the media of face-to-face performance in the *mujālasāt* validates and facilitates the option of textual adjustment in order to preserve the durability, survivability of a text in the long term.

Verbal Art and the Power of the Poet

The argument I pose here assumes that the poet possessed a high degree of verbal influence. This approach is predicated on the critical proposition that artistic communication both creates and expresses the authority of the speaker. Performers of verbal art were both admired and feared for their capacity to stimulate the emotional participation of their audiences and thereby influence the emergence of new relations of power and privilege.[15] In addition to literary theory, Abbasid sources themselves confirm the poet's power to move his audience publicly and demonstrate his influence in the face of royal authority. Al-Buḥturī, in particular, played a special role for the Abbasid dynasty. More than any other contemporary, he used his personal stature as a poet-hero simultaneously to vent discontent and to uphold the public image of the Abbasids as sacred, legitimate, and generous rulers. In the Samarran era he endured as caliphs were made and unmade, serving six of them. In the autumn of his life, al-Buḥturī had reason to boast of his verbal prowess and the concessions he wrested from caliphs, benefiting himself, others, and society at large.[16]

Extending the findings examined in chapter 3, I propose that al-Buḥturī possessed the privileges of his mythic role as poet, in addition to particular powers of charm, based on the way he presented himself to his audiences, the way his audiences received his work, and various modern theoretical formulations about verbal prowess. I recognize the poet's role as not only politically influential but also mythic by virtue of al-Buḥturī's capacity to assume convincingly the role of supplicant or redeemer in the face of awesome authority. In doing so, he invoked time-honored beliefs and attitudes about the vulnerability of life, the prospects of renewal, and the need for cosmic order. Based on the power that supplication gave a poet in his patron's eyes, one might give due weight to the drama of the courtly encounter by viewing caliphal praise hymns as a show of verbal charm in the face of royal authority.

While the caliphal patron had an interest in preserving a public image of munificence, the poet safeguarded his privilege of verbal effectiveness as measured by favors granted. Within this rapport the poet could be expected to employ strategies wisely that might help him achieve his interests. These interests would categorically benefit society at large by providing a model of how subordinates could gain surprising leverage through oratory in the face of authority. Most important, poets served as models of tenacity. One should not presume, however, that resistance inevitably led to victory or revolution. Rather, there were no clear winners or losers, and in an Arab courtly context it would be counterproductive for the poet to mar the dignity of the caliph's office. If we read praise hymns as an Arabo-Islamic discourse on power and patronage, the exchange between poet and patron can be viewed as an exchange of messages that are not an end in themselves but a means of defining and adjusting a relationship. They can therefore be "a hindrance, a stumbling-block, a point of resistance and a starting point for an opposing strategy."[17] In short, the discourse between poets and patrons demonstrates that interaction was possible between these two interested roles, despite the layers of intimidation a monarch employed.

In tandem with a discursive approach, there is a need to expand our concept of artistic communication to encompass verbal as well as nonverbal art (such as material culture) in a community and to realize the dialectical relationships among diverse art forms.[18] In this case the poet communicated most notably in verse, but his artistic expressions responded to symbols the king used, most visibly here in the monumental symbolism of the palace. This approach follows the folklorists Richard Bauman's and Charles Briggs's contention that artistic expressions act as modes of persuasion, enabling interested parties in a cultural setting to communicate and compete for privilege and recognition.[19] Thus the poet's role herein stood in a dialectical tension with the king's. In relation to the poet, the monarch used architectural symbolism to evoke and claim the mythic role of sacral king. In the face of the caliph's absolute power, embodied in the palace, the poet had the task—daunting as it might have been—of convincing his audience of his own verbal prowess.

Spatial Symbolism and the Power of the King

The caliph al-Mu^ctaṣim (r. 833–42) is credited with moving the capital from Baghdad to Samarra within a year of his ascension to the throne.[20] His intention was to end the persistent friction between his Turkish troops and Baghdad's civilian population.[21] Samarra remained the capital until the caliph al-Mu^ctamid decreed a return to Baghdad in 892.[22] Literary and architectural remains document that Abbasid caliphs commissioned palaces, which projected their cosmic centrality and simultaneously their putative control over the cosmos. Of the scores of palaces that were erected in Samarra, a few have been excavated, and some plans have been drawn and studied at least partially. The common theme of Samarran palaces appears to have been their titanic size,[23] which obliquely but forcefully suggested the mythic stature of their owners.[24] Al-Mutawakkil, for example, built a residence called al-Jawsaq al-Khāqānī in 836, which covered 432 acres, an area that took researchers twenty years to excavate.[25] Planners designed the palace complex with enormous courtyards, wide gardens and parks, open-air fountains, canals, game preserves, and polo grounds.

Several reflections in classical literary sources believe that al-Mutawakkil intended to evoke a cosmos with his palaces, as if he possessed and controlled a mythic realm. This idea crystallized in anecdotes and the very naming of some of his structures. In reference to the royal palace, al-Jawsaq al-Khāqānī, *The Book of Monasteries* reports that al-Mutawakkil asked Abū l-ᶜAynāᵓ, a courtier famous for his quick wit and sharp tongue, "What do you think of my residence here?" He replied, "I see people building homes in the world, but you build the world in your home."[26] Thus in its size and complexity al-Mutawakkil's creation "contained" the creation of God.

Other anecdotes reveal a perception that the caliph projected his centrality in architecture. When Jaᶜfar al-Mutawakkil completed a new palace city just north of Samarra, he identified it explicitly with himself: he named it al-Jaᶜfariyya, called its chief palace al-Jaᶜfarī (constructed ca. 859–61), and requested that on his death the edifice be his sepulcher.[27] According to the Abbasid historian Aḥmad b. Abī Yaᶜqūb al-Yaᶜqūbī (d. 897), al-Mutawakkil held audience and said, "Now I know that I am indeed a king, for I have built myself a city and live in it."[28] In a double overlay of meaning, the palace was thus an extension of the caliph's person and a thumbprint of the cosmos.

The king's centrality was further embodied in the throne room of his palaces. In the palaces of Bulkuwārā (ca. 849–59), Iṣṭabulāt (ca. 847–50), and al-Jawsaq al-Khāqānī, the throne room was accentuated by a dome, a novel architectural feature in the ninth century.[29] The first two palaces also elaborated the symbolism by extending the throne chamber into four pavilions (sg. *īwān*) in a cruciform shape. The pavilions intersected exactly above the throne. In the Near East the cruciform, along with the circle and the ark, evoked associations of salvation. Qaṣr al-Jiṣṣ (ca. 877–82), the latest known Samarran palace, exploited those connotations further by expanding the cruciform over the entire structure and dividing the palace space into four quadrants that intersected at the center, above the throne chamber.[30] The palace architecture thus intimated an ideology of cosmic centrality and control, which was consistent with the king's long-established mythic role in the Near East.

To gain access to this central figure, a visitor to the Samarran palaces (usually a member of the nobility) had to traverse interminably long corridors of procession. To endure adversity implied deference to the king and was thus inscribed in bodily practices. In Bulkuwārā the corridor measured some 575 meters, that of Iṣṭabulāt was 1,000 meters, and the earliest and longest corridor was at al-Jawsaq al-Khāqānī with a procession of 1,400 meters, or nearly one mile.[31] In addition, the axes of procession were often designed with built-in stages, suggesting a drama of self-transformation resembling cultic initiation rites. Samarran architects contrasted vast open courtyards (sensory overload) with tightly knit warrens (sensory deprivation), which enabled them sufficiently to awe visitors by physically and psychologically shocking them with the extreme contrasts of space usage, lighting, and, in the summer, blistering temperatures. Because in every palace the main axis was also processional, one might associate the protracted discomfort of traversing the sun-baked courtyard (*fināʾ*) with the rite of passage reflected in many ceremonial poems.[32] The rite of passage in the ode genre has been well documented as a formula of composition and as an artistic transformation.[33] The parataxis of triumphant arches and vast courtyards offered the visitor a walk, sure to remind him of his smallness as he pondered his host's majesty and to produce the proper frame of mind—fear of the caliph's wrath and hope for his beneficence.

Caliphs were convinced of their own power and centrality, and they were jealous of competing localities that might be recognized as empowering and central to others. Of the palaces that have been excavated and studied thus far, three at Samarra were oriented in opposition to the holiest site in Islam, the Kaaba (which indicated the *qibla* direction used for Muslim daily prayer, proper burial, and pilgrimage).

At least three Samarran palaces— Qaṣr al-Jiṣṣ, Iṣṭabulāt, and Qaṣr al-ᶜĀshiq (ca. 877–82)—are oriented with the processional axis pointing northeast. The use of the anti-*qibla* axis enabled the caliph to face the Kaaba as God's sole vicar on earth.

This plan must have created a problem for visitors of the Muslim nobility. If a visitor were to give his backside to the caliph, this would constitute a vulgar gesture to the court. When the visitor departed, propriety demanded that he exit the throne room by walking backward.[34] In the case of three known palaces, the anti-*qibla* processional axis forced the visitor to honor the caliph ceremonially with his front and desecrate the *qibla* with his back as he moved, bowed, and prostrated in fulfillment of court protocol. For pious Muslims the *qibla* is the most symbolic of bodily orientations, so the medieval subject had to either figuratively offend God or the caliph, creating a hierarchical conflict between God and his first officer.

In Baghdad, bodily orientation and architecture were used even more explicitly to entrap subjects. The city's palace abutted on the mosque so that in the palace subordinates had to turn their back on the Holy Shrine (the pious center) and in the mosque they did the same to the throne chamber (the caliph's center).[35] Hodgson notes that the ruler's appetite for conspicuous displays of submission provoked the anger of pious men and true believers.[36] From their perspective the caliph did not have the right to create any ceremony that resembled divine worship. In what was surely an affront to pious sensibilities, palace architecture was designed to draw the subordinate into a space beyond his control and force him to recognize royal authority as a goal of bodily ceremony, at the expense of Mecca. This is not to suggest that the subject was barred from the mosque space; instead, the tension was meant to be tacit and covert. By sanctioning this pitting in opposition, caliphs fostered a conflict of loyalties to subtly deflate potentially legitimate pious rivals and critics among the Alids, Qarmatians, Kharijites, and other men of religion who preferred to take their orders directly from God.[37] In the Abbasid realm Mecca thus represented an opposite center of power, the symbols of which caliphs sought to manipulate and mitigate. It is thus poetically significant that al-Buḥturī had to venture to the palace's counter-center to acquire the power of redemption.

The Poet-Hero as Redeemer

Owing to the imposed centrality of the king figure, his demise posed a catastrophe, which was potentially cathartic in both Semitic and Iranian cultures. In ancient Persia the king was the personification of law that guided and protected his subjects. Calvin McEwan explains that when the king died, law ceased for five days. He notes further, "The king was the state and its animate constitution."[38] But the death of the king, to be sure, was not simply a tragedy for the court; it was a catastrophe that affected the entire commonwealth. Sperl observed the notion that "when the king, as secular and religious pivot of society, is killed or harmed the whole world order may collapse; diseases and destruction may afflict the land."[39]

In lower ancient Mesopotamia the king's death was also deemed a woeful omen for the land's fertility, causing drought and low crop yields.[40] In the same vein, though employing pastoral imagery, the sixth-century poet al-Nābigha al-Dhubyānī warned in one poem, "If King Abū Qābūs perishes, the vernal camps of all / people and their sacred month perish with him."[41] In Bedouin life "vernal camps" denoted the mildest season at a place where water and pasturage were sufficient to sustain a gathering of kin, young and old, a festive event among Bedouins.[42] As a topos, however, it connoted an idyllic habitation, one that was cosmologically "primal."[43] The loss of vernal camps and the accompanying sacred months (for pilgrimage, slaughter, and feasting) marked a collapse of tribal joys and customs.[44]

Al-Mutawakkil's death posed graver problems still because he did not quietly pass away; rather, he was assassinated in his home. This patricide threw the court into a moral and political conflict because of a clash of imperatives. Courtiers who felt loyalty to the Abbasid caliphate—presumably all but a small faction—found themselves in a double bind. On the one hand, they had the duty to avenge or at least grieve for the dead king. On the other hand, they had to greet the ambitious successor. Under the circumstances the one deserving welcome also deserved wrath. Fulfilling both duties was impossible, and failing to do so was dishonorable. A general feeling of shame thus prevailed at the court for not being able—out of fear—to act honorably. The court needed a redeemer.

A literary parallel can be found in the Greek tragedy of Orestes' vengeance. Abbasid sources provide only fragments of poetry and narrative that structure the court's pathos, but these coincide with ancient Greek literary patterns of trauma, blood sacrifice, and redemption. The Orestes tragedy illustrates this emotional double bind, for it presents a clash between a son's duties to his unavenged father and those to his guilty mother. Orestes' father, Agamemnon, is away at war as the tragedy opens. His mother, Clytaemnestra, plots the murder of her husband upon his homecoming, to conceal her affair with Aegisthus.[45] Once Agamemnon is killed, the adulterers celebrate their new reign over the House of Atreus and their rule over Argos. The boy Orestes is sent away, and no hero remains to right the wrongs. Lesser members of the House of Atreus live in fear but cannot forget the unavenged blood of Agamemnon. Orestes' sisters, Electra and Chrysothemis, are powerless to avenge their father's blood themselves, but they reject their culpable mother and her lover by castigating them in public and frequenting their father's grave.[46]

In *The Libation Bearers,* Electra visits the grave of "godlike Agamemnon" and unleashes her grievances:

> I . . . call upon my father: Pity me;
> pity your own Orestes. How shall we be lords
> in our house? We have been sold, and go as wanderers
> because our mother bought herself, for us, a man,
> Aegisthus, he who helped her hand to cut you down.
> Now I am what a slave is, and Orestes lives
> outcast from his great properties, while they go proud
> in the high style and luxury of what you worked
> to win. By some good fortune let Orestes come
> back home. Such is my prayer, my father. Hear me; hear.[47]

The supplication reveals not only Electra's anguish after the regicide but also her vision of a hero to rid the House of Atreus of wrongdoing and infamy—namely, Orestes.

While away, Orestes is haunted by spirits to avenge Agamemnon's blood and warned by Apollo and Zeus that if he fails he will suffer an outcast's fate, debarred from temple and sacrifice and afflicted with leprosy. To fulfill this imperative, Orestes risks angering the furies, however: avenging his father means matricide. According to the classicist Robert Graves, the boy who once drew milk from his mother's bosom must now, as a man, draw blood. Aegisthus, in the meantime, lives in fear of Clytaemnestra's son, but when he is drunk he becomes contemptuous. On one occasion he dances on Agamemnon's grave and pelts the headstone with rocks, singing, "Come Orestes, come and defend your own!"[48] The villain is tempting Fate, and the hero is burning to oblige him.

Although different in detail, the situation at the Abbasid court is roughly analogous, for the narrative of the regicide is highly stylized to suit literary convention. Regicide narratives—such as those in the tragedies of Oedipus, Julius Caesar, Hamlet, Macbeth, and the slaying of Ḥujr, the father of Imruʾ al-Qays—share the motif of treachery at the hands of kin or allies, whence they derive their "primordial horror."[49] Along with the horror, treachery evokes shame in those who are helpless to thwart or redress it. For example, Electra complains that she and her brother "have been sold, and go as wanderers because our mother bought herself, for us, a man." The mother's woeful "sale" brings about a new, vulnerable condition for her children. Electra says, "Now I am what a slave is, and Orestes lives outcast from his great properties."[50] From once occupying a place of pride and status, she and her brother are cast out because of their lack of power to prevent or remedy the situation.

A similar sense of shame can be found at the Abbasid court. We read in the *Book of Songs* about a poetess named Faḍl (d. ca. 871) who composed an elegy for al-Mutawakkil (echoing Electra and the chorus). Conflicting imperatives immobilize her. She is conscious of the demands on her but tragically torn. Faḍl is asked on the morning after al-Mutawakkil's murder, "What befell you yesterday?" She sings through tears, "Time demands revenge from us / But how unmindful we are, how heedless! / What does Fate want from me, that I have become its target? / What does Fate want from me? Would that Fate existed not."[51] The poet Diᶜbil al-Khuzāᶜī (d. 860) also sensed that courtiers could neither fully grieve the father nor salute the ascension of the son. They were thus trapped: "A caliph died for whom no one grieves, / and another rose for whom no one rejoices."[52] ᶜAlī b. al-

Jahm (d. 863), furthermore, exacerbated the collective shame by voicing his disbelief: "Was Jaᶜfar [al-Mutawakkil] carefully killed in the caliphate's residence, / while away from allies, and you all stood by? / And is there no one to avenge him, upon his death, nor / anyone to defend his life from those who want it?"[53]

The historian al-Masᶜūdī's narrative stressed the cowardice of those present when the crime occurred. Except for al-Fatḥ b. Khāqān, the caliph's familiar and vizier, all attendees failed to stand and fight. Al-Masᶜūdī reported that the Turkish guards stormed the chamber; then "when the slave-boys and those present among the attendees (*julasāʾ*) and boon companions (*nudamāʾ*) saw them, they ran away helter-skelter (*ᶜalā wujūhihim*)."[54] The caliph's courtiers are still ridiculed seven centuries after the murder: Ibn al-ᶜImrānī reported that the lion-hearted al-Fatḥ threw himself before the caliph to shield him and cried: "There is no life without you, O Commander of the Faithful." In contrast, an effete courtier ran for the door, screaming: "A thousand lives without you, O Commander of the Faithful."[55]

Narratives close to the event, however, convey no humor. Honor required the son to slay the murderers, but they were his co-conspirators. Who, then, could rise up against him and remedy such a loathsome situation? Marwān b. Abī al-Janūb (the Younger) (d. after 861) in particular invoked the pulpit as an emblem of caliphal authority, proclaiming that if the son does not avenge his father, the pulpit "will never cease to weep for him [the father]."[56] In effect, Ibn Abī al-Janūb issued a reminder to the heir that the pulpit would testify against him. In the wake of the son's inaction, another person was to redress the crisis.

Mandate for Sacrifice

The pre-Islamic elegy (*rithāʾ*) calling for vengeance (*thaʾr*) follows a ritual pattern, namely, that of the rite of sacrifice. In poems and anecdotes blood vengeance functions as a sacrifice for the deceased and evinces a particular tripartite structure. In this respect al-Buḥturī's elegy evokes a pre-Islamic tradition of poetic vengeance and proposes a renewal by shifting from "the profane to the sacred and from the sacred back to the profane." It has also been observed that this structure brings about a new status for the poet in that the tripartite form of the rite of sacrifice coincides with Arnold van Gennep's formulation of the rite of passage. In this regard blood vengeance is a religious act that modifies the moral and social condition of the avenger when he offers up a victim and shoulders the burden of avenging his slain kinsman.[57]

In the case of al-Buḥturī's blood vengeance, the dynamics hark back to ancient Arab tribal precedents. The poet's ambit of influence, as a redeemer, is expanded to reflect the changes he effects for an imperial, not tribal, community. Although the poet relies on precedent and tradition, these verbal procedures are neither hackneyed nor invariably convincing. From a performance perspective it is necessary to illustrate how the poet sustains the emotional involvement of his immediate audience, for that inspires generations of performers to impress their respective audiences in *mujālasāt.* If al-Buḥturī could do this, he would ascend to new heights in his profession.

Al-Ṭabarī suggested that after the assassination public pressure mounted on the court to take swift action to fend off a state of crisis. He reported that some twenty thousand horsemen offered to avenge al-Mutawakkil, among them even vagabonds and gangsters.[58] The narrative implies that even lowly men knew their duty to avenge a slain leader. The poet's solution was neither to deny the tragedy nor to take up the sword himself but to attempt to galvanize court opinion to avenge al-Mutawakkil and to install a suitable heir.

Al-Buḥturī first uses his elegy to move from the profane to the sacred, consistent with the rites of blood vengeance.[59] In the elegy he affirms the court's anguish, shoulders the brunt of that burden, and vows to draw blood. The opening of an elegy does not usually include a *nasīb* (prelude to the ode), with its bittersweet themes of lost love, people, and places. The critic al-Ḥasan b. Rashīq al-Qayrawānī explains that the poet in a state of shock and mourning preoccupied himself with the heavy business of conveying sad news.[60] He elaborates that an excellent elegy "evinces distress and conveys sorrow, mingling grief, sadness, and the magnitude [of the moment]."[61] In other words, the specific losses of the day are framed in an elegiac idiom used to express distress and sorrow universally. In the opening of al-Buḥturī's elegy the specifics of the moment are lifted to the level of the universal. The ode escalates in intensity as the poet faults those present and absent, then, dramatically, himself. At this point (in line 25) he forswears wine until blood vengeance is achieved:[62]

A halting place on the Qāṭūl, its fading [traces] have worn away;
like an army, the calamities of Fate attacked it repeatedly,
As if the east wind is fulfilling its pledges, when it unfurls,
lagging gusts blow evening and morning.
Many a gentle era, over here; the selvages of those years
were delicate and their foliage was budding.
The beauty of the Ja^{c}farī palace turned and so its pleasant company;
the Ja^{c}farī collapsed both within and without.
Those who dwelt there left abruptly; its abodes
and graves became alike.
When we visit it, our grief is renewed, while before
this day, the visitor would delight.
I cannot forget the gloom of the palace when its herds
were frightened, and its fawns and calves were terrified,
and when departure was announced, and covers and
curtains were hastily torn down,
nor its desolation, as if no kind soul ever lived there
and no scene ever delighted the eye.
As if the caliphate never slumbered there with its carefree mien
nor did kingship ever rise with a bright complexion.
[And as if] the world had not gathered there its splendor and radiance,
nor were [the twigs of] life, when broken, sappy and tender within.
Where are the forbidding curtains,
the doors and chambers that were impregnable?
And where is the pillar of the people when disaster strikes?
Where is the man among them who forbids and commands Fate?
His assassins lay in wait for him covertly—
it would have been more worthy for his assassin to come openly!
His guards did not fight back death,
nor did his wealth and stores defend him.
The one hoped-for failed to help the "Mighty" [al-Mu^{c}tazz];
the truly mighty among his tribe is he whose helper is mighty.[63]
Death appeared to his *Fatḥ* [Help],
and his *Ṭāhir* [Pure] was away in Khurasan.[64]

If the dead one had lived or the distant one been near, the cycles of
fortune would have turned away from disaster.
If ᶜUbaydallāh [b. Yaḥyā b. Khāqān] had had support against them,
coming [out] would have been difficult for those
going [in] to the affair.[65]
Passion misled reason; an age came to an end;
death was urged on by the fates.
The family of the victim violated by murder was not to be feared;
its pegs and ropes were not respected.
He is a slain man from whom swords sought the last breath of life,
which he bestowed generously while death's talons turned red.
I was trying to defend him with my two hands, but one man cannot
deter the many enemies at night without arms and armor.
If my sword had been in my hand at the time of fighting,
the swift murderer would have learned how I attack.
Forbidden to me is wine after [your murder], until I see blood
for [your] blood streaming on the ground.
Shall I hope that an avenger will seek blood vengeance ever,
while [your] avenger is the slayer himself?
Did the heir apparent harbor betrayal? Then how strange that
his betrayer was appointed heir!
May the survivor never enjoy the legacy of him who died;
may his mosque pulpits not bear benedictions for him.
May the suspect never find refuge; may he who drew the sword in
treason not escape from the sword, nor he who pointed it.
How excellent is the blood you shed on Jaᶜfar's night,
during a part of the night as black as pitch.
[You act] as if you do not know, under the whetted blades,
who is his heir, his mourner, and avenger.
I surely hope that the rule over you reverts to
a scion of his character who does not betray him.
To one who ponders ideas, whose equanimity is dreaded,
when the hasty fool is dreaded for his whims.

The *qaṣīda* (ode) can be divided into four sections: opening lament (lines 1–11), accusation of the court (lines 12–25) and the successor (lines 26–29), and denial of allegiance (lines 30–33). The first line, however subtly, conveys the announcement of death (*na*ᶜ*y*). As it circulates it artfully sends a warning and serves as a message within the elegy.[66] Al-Buḥturī announces the death only by insinuating it. The caliph is neither named nor mentioned. His official dwelling is alluded to as "a halting place" (*maḥall*) located on the Qāṭūl channel (line 1). The poet plies a partial pun (*jinās*) in the name of the waterway (Qāṭūl) and the word "murderer" (*qatūl*), thereby piquing the listener's curiosity and prefiguring the news to come. A suggestion of betrayal is contained in his reference to calamities attacking the traces "like an army," since Turkish troops were a hallmark of the palace. The lack of literalism places greater emphasis on the symbolic, archetypal significance of losing a leader.

Al-Buḥturī not only conveys news in the first line; he uses the lyrical idiom of the *nasīb* to transfigure a temporal, localized crisis into a cataclysm of mythic proportions. Although he comments on actual events outside the artistic frame of the ode, they are expressed through the symbolic, evocative, and universal world of the *nasīb*.[67] The ode's opening employs lexically charged words typical of the *nasīb:* the place is *dāthir* (line 1), wearing or fading away like traces of human habitation in the sand; Fate (*dahr*) shows itself as an enemy of organized social life (line 1); the gentle east wind (*al-ṣabā*) ends abruptly (line 2). There is a pervasive elegiac mood as the poet expresses the ominous deprivation felt in the present, in contrast to the glorious past al-Mutawakkil cultivated (lines 3–11).

The lament concludes with acutely lyrical phrasing that exemplifies the inventive (*badī*ᶜ) style that characterized much of the Abbasid period with its "intentional, conscious encoding of abstract meaning into metaphor."[68] In line 3 the mood is constructed with a borrowing from the Abbasid poet Abū Tammām: "the selvages (*ḥawāshī*) of those years."[69] Here, sweet memories are metaphorically depicted as a garment, whose selvages are soft and delicate. Al-Buḥturī also heightens the loss of life (and innocence) by using the metaphor of broken twigs (*makāsir*) filled with sap (line 11). This metaphor, likewise taken from Abū Tammām, paints al-Mutawakkil's reign in ideal terms as fresh, pliant, moist, and thus, by extension, young and full of life.[70] The use of *makāsir* metaphorically suggests a life cut down in its prime. Centuries after al-Buḥturī's lifetime, this elegy impressed the poet-warrior

Usāma b. Munqidh (d. 1188), who recalled it as a touchstone for the loss of idyllic places.[71]

In the second section of the ode (lines 12–25), the poet hints at al-Fatḥ's heroism but denounces all other members of the court for their criminal actions or omissions as he works toward his own assumption of responsibility. After nine lines that lament the end of a golden era, the weight of al-Buḥturī's censure falls heavily on those who actively or passively contributed to the late caliph's demise. The list is extensive and includes chamberlains (line 12), army personnel (line 13), the assassins themselves (line 14), personal guards (line 15), the caliph's "good" son al-Muᶜtazz (line 16), the Khurasanian ally Ṭāhir b. ᶜAbdalla (line 17), and the vizier ᶜUbaydallāh b. Yaḥyā (line 19). The poet then widens the stigma of inaction to the entire court, when he states in line 21 what is obvious yet unspeakable: "The family of the victim violated by murder was not to be feared; / its pegs and ropes were not respected." A group that is unable to fight off aggression has little hope of security. The murder lays open the bitter reality that the dynasty has waned in might and grandeur. The poet admits that the Abbasids and their entourage have suffered a decline followed by a new, more vulnerable status. Al-Buḥturī's sentiment echoes Electra's admission at Agamemnon's grave.[72]

As the list of recriminations grows in the ode, al-Buḥturī claims the ultimate burden as one of the men closest to the deceased caliph, in terms of both proximity and rapport. The assumption of responsibility, it would seem, is critical to the persuasive effectiveness of his atonement procedure. The philologist-anthropologist W. Robertson Smith notes that a precondition of sin-offering in Semitic culture is that the "priest" represents the sinner "or bears his sin."[73] In lines 23 and 24 the poet's admission of fault enables him to shoulder the court's burdens, including those of the heir, to perform the ritual sacrifice. He marks his resolve with a graphic vow, in line 25: "Forbidden to me is wine after [your murder], until I see blood / for [your] blood streaming on the ground."

In the arena of politics al-Buḥturī's hope was to delegitimize al-Muntaṣir so that courtiers would then support the official heir, al-Muᶜtazz. His oath and call to vengeance thus underscore the crime's horror and the heir's guilt. In this vein the remainder of the poem, particularly the rebuke (lines 27–29), serves the public function of denying allegiance to a false caliph. Generations later, however, the political exigencies of the crisis become secondary to the ritual pattern formed by the juxtaposition of the two odes with the intervening hajj journey. At the mythic level the end of the elegy would be recognized as a preparatory phase for a communal ritual of atonement. The convention of forswearing women, meat, ointment, wine, and the joys of communal life until blood has been spilled "amounts to excommunication or anathema and entry into the liminal or sacrificial phase."[74] Almost paradoxically, the poet must exit the community to redress its traumas. The sacred or taboo phase of his rite ends only when he slaughters the sacrificial victim (i.e., when he fulfills the obligation to take blood vengeance).[75]

In the third component of the elegy (lines 26–29), the poet directs accusations particularly to the ousted heir apparent and inflicts a series of shocking curses (lines 28–29). These are probably the biting verses that prompted the littérateur Muḥammad b. ᶜImrān al-Marzubānī to consider this poem invective (*hijāʾ*).[76] However, within the poetics of this elegy al-Buḥturī by his vow assumes a sacred and highly symbolic state. Moreover, he is ritually at this point a representative of the group. His first words (in lines 26–27) are consistent with his liminal condition: "Shall I hope that an avenger will seek blood vengeance ever, / while [your] avenger is the slayer himself? / Did the heir apparent harbor betrayal? Then how strange that / his betrayer was appointed heir!"[77] Lines 26 and 27 express a pair of antitheses (*ṭibāq*), the lines between which have been blurred, producing an abomination. In the first instance the poet concedes that the distinction between murderer (*wātir*) and avenger (*mawtūrun bi-l-dami*) has faded. In the second instance the distinction is lost between trust and betrayal, since the heir apparent (*walīyyu l-ᶜahdi,* lit., "entrusted with the covenant [of succession]") concealed betrayal (*ghadra*). The community's moral structure relies on clear categories of membership and exclusion as reflected in these antitheses. When these distinctions break down, so too does the social order.

The praise hymn by convention ends with a benediction for the patron. These well-wishes often invoke God or other concepts that are sacred and serve the function of endorsing the social order.[78] Al-

Buḥturī accomplishes the opposite with his curses, however. In particular, in lines 28 and 29 he profanes the successor, al-Muntaṣir, denying him even the slightest legitimacy: "May the survivor never enjoy the legacy of him who died; / may his mosque pulpits not bear benedictions for him. / May the suspect never find refuge; may he who drew the sword in / treason not escape from the sword, nor he who pointed it." Whereas the praise hymn typically expresses or confirms allegiance and corroborates the caliph's claims to authority, invective (*hijāʾ*) amounts to "the substitution of an act of sedition for an act of . . . submission."[79] The Abbasid poet draws on well-established cultural precedents in pre-Islamic Arabia, in a manner that might be termed shamanistic, using curses and invective as a form of magic. The poet's curses are made all the more frightening by these links to the world of jinn and satans.[80] Not only does al-Buḥturī publicly refuse to pledge his allegiance, but he also invites others to rebel against the man now labeled a traitor.[81] In the last four lines, lines 30–33, he recaps the principal message and calls for a revolt:

> How excellent is the blood you shed on Jaᶜfar's night,
> during a part of the night as black as pitch.
> [You act] as if you do not know, under the whetted blades,
> who is his heir, his mourner, and avenger.
> I surely hope that rule over you reverts to
> a scion of his character who does not betray him.
> To one who ponders ideas, whose equanimity is dreaded,
> when the hasty fool is dreaded for his whims.

In these lines al-Buḥturī, who has so far been speaking in the first person, addresses the second-person plural, thereby directing his message collectively to those who aided the false heir. This audience is accused of failing to recognize which scion could genuinely serve as heir, mourner, and avenger to al-Mutawakkil. Moreover, al-Buḥturī admonishes them (and the umma as a whole) not to let the community be ruled by a renegade (lines 32–33). Naturally, for al-Buḥturī the only advisable alternative is the ascension of another heir, namely, al-Muᶜtazz. But al-Muntaṣir persists as caliph. Nevertheless, the ritual value of these verses also persists. Al-Muntaṣir's political troubles exacerbate his battered image while the poet's verbal prowess is enhanced.

The Pragmatics of Value: Adjustment and Reception

A poet in performance is faced with the demands of attracting and holding the attention of an unstable audience.[82] Nevertheless, what we witness in this ode goes beyond that because of a series of textual adjustments. The poet or later performers assumed responsibility for influencing the anticipated reception. Recalling Barbara Herrnstein Smith's theory of literary valuation, one can observe textual adjustments meant to ensure the durability and survivability of the ode, thus enhancing its appeal and the chances of reproducing value for generations.[83] One anecdote in particular indicates that some littérateurs held that the text of the elegy was adjusted after the initial crisis. That is, the sociopolitical pressures of the court put the short- and long-term appeal of the ode into mutual conflict. The compromise, it is believed, was a succession of textual adjustments in *different* performance settings. Al-Ṣūlī reports that al-Buḥturī added lines 27, 28, and 30 of the ode—three of the eight lines of rebuke—later, during the reign of al-Muᶜtazz, in order to court his favor. Al-Ṣūlī says, "I asked ᶜAbd Allāh b. al-Muᶜtazz, Did al-Buḥturī [really] dare to say, when al-Mutawakkil was killed on the day of al-Muntaṣir, 'How excellent is the blood. . . . May the mosque pulpits not bear benedictions for him' [al-Ṣayrafī's lines 30, 27, 28 (in this order)]."[84] Ibn al-Muᶜtazz replied, "He composed the lines during the reign of al-Muᶜtazz to ingratiate himself to him thereby (*yataqarrabu bihā ilayhi*)." According to the anecdote, al-Buḥturī responded to the diverging expectations of two audiences. At the time of the murder he issued a slightly milder rebuke of al-Muntaṣir, because the outcome of the succession struggle was still uncertain. For al-Muntaṣir's sibling and successor, al-Muᶜtazz, the poet later amplified the onus on al-Muntaṣir, giving subsequent generations further dramatic tension in the atonement rite. This anecdote suggests not only the poet's capacity and willingness to adjust the texts in response to changing conditions but also the readiness of subsequent generations to rate the ode not by historical veracity but by artistic impact and ultimately persuasiveness in *mujālasāt* performances.

Al-Buḥturī's readapted and weaponized rebuke of al-Muntaṣir earned rousing literary reception and circulation in several historical and literary sources. Al-Masᶜūdī, in narrating the story of the murder, recalled lines 27 and 28, both full of condemnation.[85] Similarly, the littérateur Abū Isḥāq al-Ḥuṣrī al-Qayrawānī (d. 1022), in *Blossoms of Humanistic Arts and Fruits of the Heart,* cites eleven lines of the poem, including lines 26 and 28.[86] He quotes Abū l-ᶜAbbās Thaᶜlab as commenting, "No better Hāshimite [ode] was ever said. [Al-Buḥturī] spoke in it the truth, like someone whom misfortune has distracted from fearing the consequences." These indications suggest that the elegy's textual adjustments sustained audiences' attention over nearly two centuries and maintained its appeal as an ode confirming the burden of those involved. One might also speculate that the adjustments were not the poet's invention but that of later generations of performers who sought to sharpen the poem for maximum rhetorical effect in *mujālasāt.* In either case al-Buḥturī or his performers shouldered the responsibility of communicating with audiences to ensure valuation in perpetuity.

The Court's Redeemer

After composing the shocking elegy, al-Buḥturī is said to have performed hajj.[87] The Syrian poet and writer Abū al-ᶜAlāᵓ al-Maᶜarrī (d. 1057) sensed al-Buḥturī's artifice when he characterized the pilgrimage as the proverbial hajj for reasons other than religious piety: "Our friend performed pilgrimage without piety / as did my brother from Buḥtur the year of al-Muntaṣir."[88] Al-Ṣūlī gives the impression that a mood of anticipation prevailed until al-Buḥturī's return. Al-Muntaṣir initiated a series of pro-ᶜAlid policies, but no poet dared celebrate this development.[89] Al-Buḥturī had created a ritual tension, and he was to be the sole bearer of dispensation, which would come in the form of a praise hymn dedicated to al-Muntaṣir upon the poet's return. This praise hymn follows the pattern *nasīb-raḥīl-madīḥ:* elegiac prelude (lines 1–10), journey transition (lines 12–13), and triumphant praise (lines 14–36). The tripartite form mimics the experience of rite of passage. Like the rite of passage, the ode brings about new social conditions.[90] The ode and the rite of passage both begin with themes of detachment from the community, followed by a transitional liminal state outside the community, and they conclude with reaggregation into the community. The rite of passage effectively "modifies the condition of the moral person who accomplishes it."[91] The poet, as group representative, brings about an atonement to avert civil strife, but he undergoes a passage as poet as well. If successful, the praise hymn enables him to prove his verbal prowess in playing the role of redeemer.

His bid is most prominently insinuated in the hajj-*raḥīl* section, which stands as a rejoinder to the spatial strategies of the Abbasid caliphs. Let us recall that courtiers were essentially forced to desecrate the Kaaba as they turned their backs on the Holy Shrine in order to face and bow toward the throne. Bodily orientation was consciously prescribed and circumscribed within these grandiose palaces. No doubt, these hubristic designs were sanctioned by caliphs in their bid for control over their subjects. Al-Buḥturī was able to covertly tap into resentment to the caliph by journeying beyond the court and to its "opposing" center. This proves to be more than a ritual creation of a new order for the court. The poet thus challenges authority by giving voice to the audience's sentiments.

According to the poem's literary lore, al-Muntaṣir wanted al-Buḥturī to broadcast his new policies. He began his reign with goodwill gestures toward the Alids, whom his father had persecuted.[92] In contrast, al-Muntaṣir appointed several Alids to important and ceremonial positions and initiated a policy of distributing charity to them, which confirmed their bonds of kinship to the Abbasids and their status as protected subjects. He wanted to publicize his new policy toward the Alids and implicitly contrast the cruelty of his predecessor with his more compassionate stance. Al-Buḥturī, on his return from the hajj, as the story goes, sensed the caliph's hopes and seized the opportunity. Using an eerie *nasīb* opening, al-Buḥturī stepped into the caliph's audience hall and said:[93]

1 She smirks with teeth, white and serrated
    and gazes with eyes, dark and languid.
She sways like the bough of an Arak-tree
    swept from the side by cool zephyrs.
(Among the scenes that stir the heart of a staid man
    are a graceful figure and a languid gaze.)
Though I forget, I will not forget the years
    of youth and ʿAlwa when old age rebuked me.

Stars of gray cling to [black locks of] youth
and diminished its beauty that once was plentiful.
And I have found—do not deny it—
the black of passion in locks of gray.
One must renounce, no doubt, one of two things:
youth or long life.
Have you ever seen how lightning unfurls?
And how the phantom of an unkind beloved flashes by?
Her apparition approached from Siwā, while we were
praying by night at Baṭn Marr.
What does she want with pilgrims (*al-muḥrimūn*),
dragging at midnight their ample garbs?
They hastened by night to run to al-Ṣafā,
stone the Herms [at Minā], and touch the Stone.
We performed the hajj to the House out of gratitude to
God for what He gave us in al-Muntaṣir:
Forbearance when forbearance waned,
and resolve when resolution crumbled.
He bestows justice when he judges.
He lavishes pardon when he decrees.
He remains constant in character:
sufficient unto himself, of majestic rank.
He does not endeavor to rule as a man
who begins with good but follows with evil.[94]
Nor is he fickle, conferring benefits in the evening
and doling harm in the morning.
Rather, he is as pure as the waters of stormclouds;
their first drops are as sweet as their last.
He restored his subjects after a civil strife
whose black night cast them in gloom.
And when its darkness reached its blackest,
he shone in it and became the moon
With a resolve that lifts darkness and blindness,
and with a purpose that sets straight pouting and
smirking [faces].
By right, you wove on that day the ties
of the caliphate until they were firm.

By might, you established yourself atop
the shoulders of the realm until it was steady.
Had it been another man, he would not have risen to this task—
nor would he have been able.
You redressed injustices and your hands
restored the rights of the oppressed:
The family of Abū Ṭālib [the Alids]—after their herd
was seized and scattered,
And the closest of kin received treatment so cruel
the sky well-nigh cracked open because of it!—
You joined the bonds of their kinship,
when the ties were nearly severed.
For you put their share, once far, within reach,
and made their drinking water, once murky, pure.
How lofty are you [Abbasids] compared to them [Alids]?
Though their rank is neither distant nor remote.
[They are] your kin, no, rather full brothers and clansmen,
beyond all humankind.
Though, who are they, when yours are the two hands of victory,
two edges of a sword, gleaming of old.
Your precedence is chanted in the Book
and your virtues are recited in suras.
No doubt, ᶜAlī is more worthy and free of sin
in your eyes than ᶜUmar.
Every [steed] has its merits, when vying in excellence,
while anklets are beneath blazes on foreheads.
May you live on, Imām of guidance, for guidance's sake
to renew its paths that has faded away.

The *nasīb,* in general, serves the critical purpose of gaining an audience's sympathetic attention, as would an exordium.[95] This *nasīb* in particular (lines 1–10) constitutes the poet's first words to al-Muntaṣir since the murder and their estrangement and thus carries the added burden of attaining the sympathy of the desired patron. The poet achieves this aim with three motifs, the first of which is the shapely, delicate beloved likened to a doe. Following *nasīb* conventions, the beloved exhibits serrated teeth—implying youth and immaturity—gentle gaze (line 1), and swaying bough-like stature (line 2), images traditionally deployed to stir passion and yearning for ideal love, although they expose an undercurrent of apprehension at the beloved's immaturity.[96] These emotions are confirmed when al-Buḥturī conveys the perspective of an otherwise collected man whose heart is moved (line 3) by the youthful beloved.

The second motif is *al-shakwā min al-shayb,* the lament of gray hair (lines 4–7), which offers the poet the opportunity to draw attention to himself as a victim of Fate's afflictions. Having gained his audience's attention with the opening motif, he can now solicit empathy, in particular, from the patron he courts. The lament-of-the-gray-hair motif touches a sensitive chord, for it expresses fears of mortality and the finality of life. In line 4 rebukes are now directed against him as old age forces him to part with youth and a former beloved, ʿAlwa. He now suffers the stigma of graying locks that are slowly diminishing his handsome appearance (line 5). In line 6, however, the poet admits his reluctance to forgo youth and passion completely. But the only means of holding on to youth is to forsake a full and long life (line 7).

The third and last motif of the *nasīb* depicts the phantom of the beloved who appears unexpectedly (line 8) and, in formal terms, very late in the *nasīb* section. Here it would seem that the phantom represents a former attachment, which suggests it might be an allusion to his former patron, al-Mutawakkil. In Abū al-Ṭayyib al-Mutanabbī's first ode to the tenth-century sultan of Egypt, Kāfūr, the poet abrogates his allegiance to the sultan of Syria, Sayf al-Dawla, by poetically substituting him with a former beloved in the *nasīb*.[97] By detaching himself from the beloved and reattaching himself to the patron, the poet simultaneously declares his commitment to this new patron. Al-Buḥturī similarly seizes the opportunity to dispel any lingering doubts about where his new loyalties reside. When the beloved's phantom approaches him (lines 9–10), he does not reciprocate: "Her apparition approached from Siwā, while we were / praying by night at Baṭn Marr. / What does she want with the pilgrims (*al-muḥrimūn*), / dragging at midnight their ample garbs?"

The poet is preoccupied with a ritual: holy acts performed in special garb at appointed times in sacred places. At this point in the ode it is not clear whether he fulfills these obligations in the name of the new patron, but certainly he does not do so out of longing for a bygone era. In short, Al-Buḥturī makes it clear that he does not welcome this bond, but new ties are yet undetermined. His hesitation is not merely a matter of political exigency. In this *nasīb,* the most subjective section of the ode, he acknowledges the erstwhile value of past allegiances, yet signals his readiness to move forward. The phantom's visit to the pilgrims makes the transition to the *raḥīl* (journey section). In the following couplet, the poet now reinterprets the rites of the hajj as a service performed specifically for the new caliph. His activities at pilgrimage will gradually increase the pressure on the patron to show gratitude for this service.

RITES AND RESTORATION AFTER CRISIS

The *raḥīl* conventionally involves physical movement on a vehicle such as a camel mare, horse, or ship, but here al-Buḥturī adapts the paradigm to the social and mythic context that surrounds the poem (lines 12–13). The journey is the physical and psychological transition of the hajj. Motion is philologically indicated by the verb *sarā/ yasrī* (line 11), meaning "to journey or travel by night."[98] Al-Buḥturī alludes to three common hajj rites at the point of transition from a former allegiance (to al-Mutawakkil) to a new one (to al-Muntaṣir). Line 11 constitutes the pivot for the praise hymn, as an expression of allegiance and, on the mythic level, as a rite of atonement. The mythic and political drama revolves around three verbal nouns and their direct objects (*maf*ᶜ*ūl bihi*): *li-sa*ᶜ*yi l-Ṣafā*, *ramyi l-jimāri, wa masḥi l-ḥajar,* meaning "to run to al-Ṣafā, to stone the Herms [at Minā], and to anoint the Stone."

In the first rite al-Buḥturī refers topographically to the Ṣafā hill in the vicinity of the Kaaba. Traditionally, pilgrims run along the *mas*ᶜ*ā* (course) between the two hills al-Ṣafā and al-Marwa.[99] In addition to running, the verb *sa*ᶜ*ā/yas*ᶜ*ā* conveys the idea of striving or applying oneself assiduously, which of course hints at the poet's troubles for his new patron.[100] The second rite demands of pilgrims that they collect seven pebbles for stoning (*rajm*) each of the three herms (*jimār* or *jamarāt*) that represent devils. Finally, the poet relies on the rite of anointing the Black Stone of the Kaaba with the blood of the animal sacrifice.[101] According to legend, the stone was completely white in ancient times and became black over the generations when pilgrims anointed it with the blood of their sin-offering to supplicate forgiveness.[102] This explanation, legendary as it may be, calls attention to the Black Stone as a communal perennial well for redemption. The verb *masaḥa/yamsaḥu* is used idiomatically to convey atonement as in *masaḥa llāhu ᶜanka mā bika* (lit., "may God wipe away your sins").[103] Al-Buḥturī thus integrates three rites evocative of atonement and renewal in Muslim communal life.

The need for legitimacy was most urgent for al-Muntaṣir. He was haunted by the burden of complicity in al-Mutawakkil's murder. In conversations the twenty-four-year-old caliph would become self-conscious at any mention of the regicide.[104] He was also tormented by anxiety dreams, guilt, and the taunts of hecklers.[105] In line 12 the poet redresses the traumas of the caliph and the community. The object of the poet's new allegiance and the purpose of his hajj-*raḥīl* become evident in lines 12 and 13: "We performed the hajj to the House out of gratitude to / God for what He gave us in al-Muntaṣir: / Forbearance when forbearance waned, / and resolve when resolution crumbled."

In this brief phrasing, the poet celebrates a restoration of order after *fitna,* a moment of crisis for the community, surely to be remembered along with the internecine wars of early Islamic history.[106] On a personal level, though, *fitna* denotes a trial of faith or loyalty, a temptation to defect. The English scholar James Garrison observes that one of the principal functions of praise hymns in premodern societies was to herald a national reconciliation after a period of instability.[107] In particular, the seventeenth-century praise hymns of John Dryden addressed the needs of two audiences: they reminded the ruler of his duty to respect societal values, and they exhorted the subjects to offer the ruler obedience and loyalty.[108] The poet thus effects a restoration of order by publicizing the terms of a delicate relationship.

In line 12 the poet's gratitude gives credence to a theme of collective renewal. He casts his performance of the hajj as an act of thanksgiving for a state of well-being. Indirectly, one learns that God now sanctions al-Muntaṣir, though implicit in this sanction is a balance of obligations. The community can expect their leader to be firm and forbearing; the leader can expect the community to accept his virtues as a divine "gift" that implies thereafter the duty to repay God's gift with submission to his deputy.[109] On the mythic level the poet who had stigmatized the "false" heir now returns from the hajj with deliverance.

The poet's invocation of the gift-exchange ritual heralds the return of life's normal rhythms.

The brief hajj-*raḥīl* syntactically connects to the following *madīḥ* (praise section). In line 14 the poet draws on the invocative dimensions of the praise hymn to coax his patron to virtuous behavior. The speaker protects himself by the broadcast potential of his text. He valorizes pardon and justice as two tokens of al-Muntaṣir's powers, committing him to clemency as a means to glory: "He bestows justice when he judges. / He lavishes pardon when he decrees." Moreover, al-Buḥturī solicits his own security by addressing in line 15 the theme of moral consistency. Using his new patron's thirst for power, the poet lures him into an unwavering course of action: "He remains constant in character: / sufficient unto himself, of majestic rank."

Praise can sometimes prove surprisingly critical to shaping human conduct. Caton, in his study of Yemeni tribal poetry, argues that praise poetry at weddings in honor of the groom commits the young tribesman to an image of himself that is desirable to the community.[110] Using the anthropologist George Herbert Mead's model of the self, Caton notes that the self emerges in society reflexively, through communication and interaction with others. The self responds to affirmations of speech and gesture. Formal praise in honor of the groom, then, reminds the young man of "who he must become." The mirror of manhood is held up to the young tribesman precisely before marriage obligations.[111] In al-Muntaṣir's case al-Buḥturī sees the opportunity to publicly commit the caliph to an image that rewards consistency. In lines 16–18 he holds to the caliph a mirror of manhood that society would sanction: "He does not endeavor to rule as a man / who begins with good but follows with evil. / Nor is he fickle, conferring benefits in the evening / and doling harm in the morning. / Rather, he is as pure as the waters of stormclouds; / their first drops are as sweet as their last."

The adjective *muṣaffan* (pure) produces a few semantic associations. The verb *ṣaffā* can mean "to clear, settle" (of debts) or "to clarify, filter" (of water: sediment).[112] Moreover, the adjective *muṣaffan* can serve as the passive participle (*ism al-mafʿūl*), place noun (*ism al-makān*), and time period noun (*ism al-zamān*).[113] Thus, referring to al-Muntaṣir, the line can read, "He is [a debt] cleared" or "He is pure." In reference to the court or the era, the line can read, "Its [debts] are cleared" or "It is pure."

One might object to the "[debt] cleared" reading on the grounds that it does not seem to suit the rest of the line. The heaviest debt is the duty to avenge the blood of fallen kin, however, and the rain imagery is consistent with themes of blood vengeance. The motifs of bloodshed and rainfall are both rejuvenating and common in elegies (*rithāʾ*).[114] One might consider also that the particle *ka-* in Arabic can govern a noun or a manner of action, meaning "as" or "like." In that view one might read the line, referring to al-Muntaṣir: "He has cleared [debts] like the waters of stormclouds [i.e., he has avenged spilt blood]. Their first drops are as sweet as the last." On returning from the hajj, the poet thus pronounces the atonement ritual complete.

The next six lines (19–24) valorize al-Muntaṣir as the victor who restores order and saves the community from factionalism. The crisis is depicted as a full-fledged *fitna* that plunged the umma into darkness and fear (line 19). The poet celebrates the caliph's power to dispel the gloom (lines 20–21), restore calm (line 20), and discipline his critics (line 21). There is an acknowledgment of the extreme measures the caliph took to accomplish his purpose (lines 22–23), but the poet also emphasizes the caliph's individual agency by turning to the second-person singular. Caliphal praise hymns commonly reflect the Islamic tenet that God appoints only one caliph over the umma, and divine sanction is proven with executive power. The poet thus attests that no other person would have the sanction or the power to act.[115]

Lines 25–35 commemorate al-Muntaṣir's new policy of showing mercy to the Alids.[116] This policy, in contrast to al-Mutawakkil's earlier harshness, was meant to demonstrate the caliph's legitimacy.[117] It betrays the caliph's need to defuse the criticism of his challengers. Al-Buḥturī memorialized this policy in the midst of his praise hymn. In a manner that is consistent with his theme of reconciliation, the poet recognizes the wrongs that the Alids suffered under the former caliph (lines 25–28):

You redressed injustices and your hands
    restored the rights of the oppressed:
The family of Abū Ṭālib [the Alids]—after their herd
    was seized and scattered,

And the closest of kin received treatment so cruel
the sky well-nigh cracked open because of it!—
You joined the bonds of their kinship,
when the ties were nearly severed.

The cracking open of the sky, as found in the Qur'an, is a sign of the final *fitna* in Islamic eschatology—the apocalypse—and connotes its sense of upheaval.[118] The Qur'anic text describes a cataclysmic rupture: "When skies are cracked open / When stars are scattered / When seas are vented / When graves are disgorged / Every soul will realize what it has done and not done."[119] The caliph as champion of his people thus prevents cataclysm. His kind policies toward the Alids enact one of his mythic duties, namely, to preserve order and stay Fate's destructiveness.[120]

The Alids, however, are assigned a delicate position in the new hierarchy. The poet makes rank an issue with his apostrophe concerning the loftiness of the Abbasids in relation to the Alids, although he is sure to mention that the latter do not lag far behind (lines 30–31). The two Hāshimite lines, once competitors, now complement one another like two sword blades and two hands for the sake of victory (line 32). Lines 33–35 clarify, however, the Abbasids' precedence in the new order. Al-Buḥturī concludes his praise hymn (in line 36) with a benediction that asks for divine wisdom and guidance at the hands of the new caliph: "May you live on, Imām of guidance, for guidance's sake / to renew its path that has faded away."

Sperl notes that "imam of guidance" (*imām al-hudā*) is one of the epithets of divine grace and power.[121] Yet al-Buḥturī adds another degree with "*for guidance's sake.*" The young caliph must now take up the honor of being *imām,* as well as the protector of guidance. In Garrison's terms, the poet here intervenes between the king and society.[122] Al-Buḥturī's use of the title *imām* reminds the caliph of his duties and exhorts the umma to obey his lead. The caliph is further advised, after a period of crisis, actively to "renew the path" of guidance. The use of the verb *dathara* resonates with the first line of al-Buḥturī's elegy to al-Mutawakkil. There he had employed the word *dāthiruh* ("its fading [traces]"), referring to the era's bygone glory. Al-Buḥturī's present closure thus salutes al-Muntaṣir as one who has renewed a legacy. The parallel between the first line of one poem and the last line of the second also links them to one whole cycle: the first stigmatizes the court; the second redeems it. The poet thus demonstrates his capacity to restore the community after trauma.

At the end of the ceremony al-Ṣūlī signals the weight of al-Buḥturi's service to the caliphate. To be sure, he figuratively indicates that the poem was received not as an apology or a peace offering, as Shawqī Ḍayf contends, but as a favor.[123] The text lacks the typical indications of an apology as established in such odes as those by al-Nābigha al-Dhubyānī and Kaᶜb b. Zuhayr, which require the poet to note the charges, deny their veracity, then redirect blame to foes and calumniators (*aᶜdāʾ, wushāh*).[124] Although al-Buḥturī hints at caliphal justice and mercy, his praise hymn offers no self-defense, because no defense is warranted. In the eyes of society the poet acts within his traditional mythic role. The patron, by contrast, is guilty of patricide in the public eye, and no poet yet dared lift the stigma cast on him by al-Buḥturi. All things considered, al-Muntaṣir was fortunate to receive al-Buḥturi's defense.

Al-Ṣūlī says of the caliph, "He gave him [the poet] a lavish reward, though he rarely rewarded poets at all (*fa-waṣalahu wa-ajzala, wa-lam yakun yaṣilu l-shuᶜarāʾa illā qalīlan*)."[125] The extraordinary award recognizes the perfect redemption, and to highlight this, al-Ṣūlī shows another poet capitalizing on al-Buḥturī's success. As if breaking a ritual fast, the Abbasid poet Yazīd al-Muhallabī for the first time composed verse celebrating al-Muntaṣir's pro-Alid policies. Al-Buḥturī's ritual effect thereby becomes a public reality that others could sense and celebrate. The dyad is so effective at redeeming both father and son that typically neither al-Mutawakkil nor al-Muntaṣir has been wholly condemned or criticized throughout the ages.

Al-Buḥturī's Dyad in the *Mujālasāt*

In the absence of an imminent state crisis, subsequent performers in *mujālasāt* enjoy the liberty of accentuating the mythic universal dimensions of al-Buḥturī's dyad. The *mujālasa* performer is faced with the social and artistic demands of holding and maintaining the attention of his or her audience. In a patronage culture, the dyad would give voice to a wide array of brooding impulses—rebellion, betrayal, rage against patriarchs and patriarchy—while providing a socially sanctioned means of redeeming them by affirming values that preserve the social order: honor, munificence, and loyalty.

The performance of this ritual before an audience may not dramatize a dualistic struggle for order *against* disorder but rather the immolation of one order for the sake of a new one.[126] Moving beyond the reiterative nature of ritual, Victor Turner emphasizes the emergent, unpredictable, and emotional dimensions that give ritual accomplishments dramatic appeal.[127] In al-Buḥturī's case it is precisely ritual that gives his accomplishments the necessary appeal to elicit and reproduce value in perpetuity. So long as members of society feel that need for atonement individually or collectively, the ode will serve a ritual and aesthetic purpose. In the atonement rite, animal sacrifice represents, as it were, the dismembering of an old system and prefigures the "re-membering" of a new one. In this sense ritual itself serves a paradigmatic function and confirms to a society its capacity to bring about "creative modifications." Quite apart from the merits of one order (or leader) over another, it would seem that by upholding values and ideals in ritual, society can foster hope. In the elegy one notices that before line 25 the poet chants of tragic failures (line 24)—that is, failures to meet societal values. In response to the dissonance between actions and values, the poet abandons one path and vows to take another. His vow is the first step in a bid to reassert the Abbasid values.

To the reader of these odes, eleven and a half centuries after their premiere, the ritual might seem distant and foreign. These odes, in the way they starkly contradict one another on the surface, caution us against evaluating court poetry by the standards of modern historiographic representation. The critic Northrop Frye notes that, unlike the historian, the poet uses the language of poetry to comment on existence: "The poet makes no specific statements of fact, and hence is not judged by the truth or falsehood of what he says. The poet has no external model for his imitation, and is judged by the integrity or consistency of his verbal structure. The reason is that he imitates the universal, not the particular; he is concerned not with what happened but with what happens."[128] Although it remains to be seen how readers today will receive or value al-Buḥturī, in large part the aim of this chapter has been to identify and apply a pragmatic method of gauging the functions of the ode at the time. In addition, the *mujālasāt* provide us with a forum for putting literature to the test, thus helping us to envision how and why poets and performers adjusted texts to ensure their survival across the generations. Chapter 5 examines further the pragmatic uses of the *mujālasāt* as a social and literary construct.

FIVE

Al-Buḥturī's Īwān Kisrā Ode

Canonic Value and Folk Literacy in the *Mujālasāt*

AN ANTI-IMPERIAL ODE?

The murder of Caliph al-Mutawakkil in winter 861 figured as the first patricidal regicide of Islamic history and forced the umma—ostensibly sacred—to recall the profaning traumas of the first and second civil wars (*fitan;* sg. *fitna*).[1] Sometime later, during the post-Mutawakkil period, the court poet al-Buḥturī (d. 897) composed an unusual but intense poem.[2] In it he left behind haughty patrons and the urban setting of Samarra and ventured out to the ruins of a Sasanian palace at Ctesiphon, twenty-four miles south of Baghdad, famed for its sole remaining ruin—Khosrow's Arched Hall, or Īwān Kisrā.

The poem is unusual in several ways. First, unlike most of al-Buḥturī's poetry, which is addressed to a named benefactor or at least a recipient, the Īwān Kisrā poem is not meant to be a communication to a specific person. This otherwise audience-oriented poet was addressing no one in particular. Second, in contrast to his long poetic practice, al-Buḥturī in this ode does not follow the conventional tripartite pattern of the ode, composed of elegiac prelude (*nasīb*), journey section (*raḥīl*), and a third communal theme, such as praise (*madīḥ*) or lampoon (*hijāʾ*). Neither is the ode of the bipartite variety that elides the *raḥīl*. Instead, the poet begins with expressions of indignation and disappointment (roughly lines 1–10), channeled into a short camel journey (roughly lines 11–13), and then a tribute to the Sasanian palace (lines 14–56). The tribute is saturated with a mood not of triumph but ultimately of lyricism, for these are not current but former glories. The more glorious the Sasanian achievements, the more wistful the poet becomes. In effect, the "praise section" in this ode is unexpectedly like the elegiac *nasīb*. Instead of triumphant closure, this poem gives us perpetual tears and yearning dedicated to the glory of the Sasanian period.

Several modern scholars have taken al-Buḥturī's grief and praise for the Sasanian ruins as a veiled critique of the Abbasid dynasty and its cultural or poetic conventions. They note that al-Buḥturī's indignant tone resembles that of the brigand poet (*suᶜlūk*) of pre-Islamic times. As part of al-Buḥturī's protest, the poet lambastes the "vilest of the vile" and a "cousin," which some scholars have taken to refer to specific people.[3] Richard Serrano argues that the poet's choice of Persian abodes over the classical Bedouin sort suggests a harsh criticism not only of the Abbasids but also of traditional Arab poetics and culture.[4] This theory assumes that al-Buḥturī became disappointed in the Abbasids (and their culture) and lost faith, and thus composed an anti-imperial ode. To date, this anti-imperial theory has not been challenged and stands uncontested as conventional wisdom in Arabic literary scholarship.

The anti-imperial reading generates irreducible problems, though. Al-Buḥturī meticulously developed a career that would protect his chief personal interests throughout his life: his professional reputation as a poet in Iraq and his property in Syria.[5] As for the property interest, we are told that he owned land in his hometown of Manbij, Syria, in the environs of Aleppo, and thus visited Manbij repeatedly while living in Iraq. There al-Buḥturī petitioned the governor (*wālī*) of Manbij in order to protect his property interests.[6] This deep attachment—whether material, social, or emotional—was symbolized and privatized in his ghazals to his legendary first love ᶜAlwa (or ᶜAlw) bint Zurayqa of Syria.

As for the interest in maintaining his professional reputation, the anti-imperial reading would stand as anathema to al-Buḥturī's public persona as court poet, as he specialized in praise hymns that aimed to build the public image of men of state. He is reputed to have shown an interest in this profession early, as a teenager, when he would traipse about the local mosque in Manbij reciting poetry and declaiming his first praise hymns by leaning out of the mosque to praise humble onion and eggplant merchants.[7] These stories—regardless of their facticity—indicate a public reputation for composing praise hymns (i.e., the business of magnifying Abbasid men from humblest origins on up). In his early twenties (the 840s) al-Buḥturī judiciously scaled the Abbasid hierarchy one patron at a time—focusing on Ṭaʾīs and Syrians like himself—to reach the most defining moment of his career: in 847, when he delivered his first Abbasid caliphal ode at the Jawsaq al-Khāqānī palace in Samarra.[8]

Al-Buḥturī went on to serve a total of six rulers: the caliphs al-Mutawakkil (r. 847–61), al-Muntaṣir (r. 861–62), al-Mustaᶜīn (r. 862–66), al-Muᶜtazz (r. 866–69), al-Muhtadī (r. 869–70), and al-Muᶜtamid (r. 870–92). He also served their viziers, commanders, judges, secretaries, and so on.[9] He gave to generations a *dīwān* larger than those of the poets Abū Tammām and al-Mutanabbī combined, chiefly because of his verbal endorsements of the Abbasid empire.[10] Even al-Muhtadī, known for his asceticism and dislike of poets, had to concede al-Buḥturī's triumph in promoting the Abbasid dynasty, despite the throes of time, calling him "the orator of our family and the poet of our dynasty."[11] If we take 821 to be al-Buḥturī's year of birth, he was forty when al-Mutawakkil's murder occurred, but he continued to work at the Abbasid court another twenty-nine years.[12] I propose that the arc of al-Buḥturī's career was not propelled by faith in the Abbasids but rather by the understandable bourgeois interests of reputation and property.

One might counterargue that al-Buḥturī finally became disappointed with the Abbasids, when he transferred his allegiance to the Tulunids of Cairo in 890. A closer look at the Īwān Kisrā ode and its context, however, shows that he redirected his praise services just when Syria came under the property tax control of Khumarawayh b. Aḥmad b. Tūlūn.[13] This suggests that al-Buḥturī's transfer of allegiance was motivated by his property interests in Manbij. To safeguard his interests, the poet remained particularly loyal to Tughja b. Juff, a military commander who rose to the governorship of Syria. In a modern antimonarchical era it may seem an alluring prospect to identify a court poet who finally denounced the ideology of his patrons, but these are modern attitudes imported into a medieval subject driven by the romantic dogma of poetic sincerity. Al-Buḥturī was the consummate poet of the empire. Why would he jeopardize his life interests? Even this cursory examination suggests that his pragmatic goals, not faith in the Abbasids, spurred him to protect their reputation (and then that of the Tulunids) during their reign, as well as their legacy for generations thereafter.

Moreover, it appears that the poet systematically avoided methods of resistance employing direct confrontation. Given the caliph's executive power and the neo-Sasanian imperative of preserving the dignity of the monarch, the method of resistance that courtiers generally found effective was change through engagement—as well as a measure of artifice. This principle of engaged resistance was captured in courtly advice manuals. In dealing with caliphs and sultans, let us recall that these manuals said, if you are a courtier you must "teach them (*tuʿallimahum*) as though they teach you, educate them (*tuʾaddibahum*) as though they educate you; if not, then stay as far away as possible!"[14] The aim was to blandish, coax, nudge, guilt, or even shame the ruler into action using verbal artifice to preserve the dignity of the office. With respect to al-Buḥturī, we can note several examples where he used his skill and prestige as a state poet in order to influence caliphal policy.[15]

The Īwān Kisrā Ode and Semantic Interplay with Abbasid Folklore

Literature is categorically indeterminate in meaning, and in this analysis of the Īwān Kisrā, I suggest an alternative to the anti-imperial interpretation, based on a broader understanding of value and canonicity that presumes, strangely enough, an audience that was literate in current folklore. To the point, this ode was composed, delivered, and transmitted in a performance culture rich in folklore about Sasanian princes rebelling against their monarchical fathers. Al-Buḥturī names two such fathers in the ode, creating curious semantic links between establishment and folk literature. Whereas one might *assume* a divide between folk and canonic literature, Sabra Webber notes, "One of the canonical measures of good verbal artistry . . . is [the poet's] ability to make use of as many social and cultural, situational 'found objects' as possible in constructing his or her masterpiece, such as the literacy of the audience."[16] I propose to employ the *mujālasāt* as a socio-literary forum where performers could summon the folk literacy of audiences. By doing so, al-Buḥturī's odes reverberate with significance across socioeconomic strata, further enhancing the appeal and value of his work.

The folklore source I rely on to interpret the Īwān Kisrā ode is *The Long Lore,* a collection of lore about the pre- and early Islamic eras that was current in the Abbasid period, compiled by the littérateur Abū Ḥanīfa Aḥmad al-Dīnawarī (d. ca. 895). I show direct allegorical parallels between Abbasid and Sasanian kings, which render the Īwān Kisrā ode not a critique but a redemption for the troubled Abbasids created by a poet who was deeply invested in the institution he served. Furthermore, the poet's strategic reliance on an audience that is literate in current folklore implies that some *mujālasāt* did provide a venue for the face-to-face exchange and validation of establishment and folk literature. Here, I include a translation of the ode.[17] By venturing to the ruins of the Sasanians in Ctesiphon and employing the persona of the anti-establishment brigand, the poet presents audiences with an interplay of old and new centers of power, as well as folk and canonic literatures:

1 I saved myself from what defiles my self
 and rose above the largess of every craven coward.
I endured when Time shook me,
 seeking misery and reversal for me.
Mere subsistence from the dregs of life have I.
 Days have rationed it inadequately.
Stark is the difference between him who drinks at will twice a day
 and him who drinks every fourth day.

As if Time's inclinations are
predicated on the vilest of the vile.
My purchase of Iraq was a swindler's ploy,
after my sale of Syria, a trickster's sale.
Do not test me endlessly about my knowledge
of these ordeals to deny my misfortunes.
You once knew me as a man of qualities,
disdaining petty matters, undaunted.
But the scorn of my cousin,
after heartfelt kindness and amity, disturbs me.
When I am scorned, I am likely
to be seen rising not where I spent the night.
Sorrows attend my saddle. I direct
my stout she-camel to Madāʾin [Ctesiphon].
I console myself for such luck
and find solace in a site for the Sasanians, ruined.
Perpetual misfortune reminds me of them;
misfortune makes one remember and forget.
They live the good life, shaded by guarded peaks,
which tire and baffle the gaze.
Its gates, on Qabq Mountain, are secure, extending to the
uplands of Khilāṭ and Muks.[18]
The abodes are unlike the ruins of Suʿdā,[19]
in a wasteland, bare and plantless.
Heroic feats—were it not for my partiality—the
feats of ʿAns and ʿAbs would not surpass them.[20]
Time despoiled their era of vitality. It
devolved into worn-out rags.
As if the Arched Hall, for lack of humanity, and sheer abandonment,
is a grave's edifice.
If you saw it, you would know that the nights
are holding a funeral in it after a wedding.
It would inform you of a troop's marvels,
their record does not gray with obscurity.
When you see a panel of the Battle at Antioch,
you tremble among Byzantines and Persians.
The Fates stand still, while Anūshīrvān
leads the ranks onward under the banner

In a deep green robe over yellow.
It appears dyed in saffron.
Men in combat are under his command.
Some are quiet and hushed.
Some are intense, rushing forward with spear-points.
Others are cautious of them, using shields.
The eye depicts them very much alive:
they have between them speechless signs.
My wonder about them boils till
my hand explores them with a touch.
Abū al-Ghawth [poet's son] had poured me a drink without stinting,
for the two armies, a draft
of wine. You would think it a star
lighting the night or sun's luscious kiss.
You see, when it renews joy and
contentment for the drinker, one sip after the other,
That it was poured into glasses—into every heart.
It is beloved to every soul.
I fancied Khosrow Aparvīz handing me
a drink and al-Balahbadh [king's minstrel] my companion.
A dream that closes my eye to doubt?
Or desire that alters my fancy and guesses?
As if the Arched Hall, by its wondrous craftsmanship,
were hollowed in the cliff of a mountain side.
It would be thought, from its sadness—
to the eyes of morning and evening visitors—
Distraught like a man torn from the company of loved ones,
or distressed by the breaking of nuptials.
Nights have reversed its luck. There, Jupiter
whiled the night but as a star of misfortune.
It shows hardiness, but the cruel weight of Time
is fixed upon it.
It's no stigma that it was ravished of
silken carpets, stripped of damask drapes.
Towering, its ramparts rise high,
It looms over the summits of Raḍwā and Quds.
Donning white clouds, you do not
glimpse of them but cotton tunics.

It is not quite known: Is it the work of humans for jinn
to live in or the work of jinn for humans?
Yet, as I gaze upon it, it attests
its builder is among kings not the least a cipher.
As though I see generals and troops,
as far as the eye can see.
As though foreign embassies suffer in the sun.
They are dismayed standing behind crowds, kept waiting.
As though minstrels in the Hall's center
croon lyrics between plum-like lips.
As though the gathering were the day before yesterday
and the hurry of departure just yesterday.
As though the seeker of their trail could hope
to catch up with them the morning of the fifth day.
It was built up for joy forever, but
their domain is for condolence and consolation now.
It deserves that I lend it my tears,
tears committed to affection, devoted.
I feel this, though the abode is not my abode
—by blood—nor this race my race.
Beyond their graces toward my people,
they seeded, out of their goodness, fine sprouts.
They backed our dominion and buttressed its might
with warriors under armor, zealous.
They helped against Aryāṭ's regiment
by stabbing chests and spearing.
I find myself thereafter completely enamored
by noble men of every race and origin.

Channeling the Brigand: Redemption from Trauma

The opening of the Īwān Kisrā ode achieves perhaps the most important transition in the ode: The poet is able to move himself and the audiences from the fury and indignation of the brigand (*su*ʿ*lūk*) to redemptive tones that equate the tragedies of the ruling Abbasids and the bygone Sasanians. By creating a parallel between the Abbasid and Sasanian patricides, al-Buḥturī deems both tragic yet blameless, in order to prevent schism (*fitna*) in a community already traumatized by civil wars.

At the outset the poem's unusual features—there is no single recipient, nor is a typical structure used—link it to the well-known but archaic Bedouin verse of the *suᶜlūk* poet. And this association is rhetorically important since the brigand denotes the unforgiven outlaw type, with class connotations of deprivation and disempowerment. This marginal character—miserable but rascally—would have been a key staple in folklore performances. As a literary type, the brigand poet was haunted by his crimes, unable to trust no one.[21] His ethic is not that of tribal loyalty and duty but of antisocial rebellious individualism. At root the brigand poet is alone against the world, relying on ruses and flight for survival, and he identifies ultimately with beasts of prey.[22] It would appear that al-Buḥturī's opening appeals to the marginal, the liminal, and the disempowered.

The voice of the brigand poet echoes when one compares al-Buḥturī's tone with that of the pre-Islamic brigand al-Shanfarā in lines 10 and 11 of his renowned *Ode of the Arabs Ending in Lām*: "To recompense the loss of those who do not requite my kindness, / . . . / I have three companions—an emboldened heart, / a white polished sword, / a slender yellow bow."[23] As his ode opens, al-Buḥturī conveys a spirit similar to the brigand poet who is haunted by his past, who perpetually feels betrayed. It is not totally surprising that some scholars have presumed that the poem was composed in 861, immediately after al-Mutawakkil's murder, rendering it a kind of "pilgrimage" that enabled the poet to recover from trauma.[24] Here one can see the rhetorical effect of his brigand-like themes, which give the artful impression of a poet cast out from society, anathematized. However, whereas "brigandhood" is artistically a permanent state, pilgrimage is temporary and purposeful. The impression of pilgrimage, albeit illusory, gives context and meaning to the poem. It indicates a valid perception that there is something ultimately goal oriented about the extra-societal interim. Ḍayf hints at this issue when he says that al-Buḥturī composed the poem to "weep thereby his worry and grief at the murder of al-Mutawakkil."[25] More, however, is at stake than the murder of a single caliph or the poet's inward feelings. Unlike the brigand, whose problems are individual and whose solutions are antisocial, al-Buḥturī channels his anger and progresses beyond that.

The poet's thematic progression is arduous, though. Al-Buḥturī not only utters his intention to move toward his destination, but he must justify this to himself (lines 11–12). In line 13 he is once again driven to elaborate on his reasons. The Abbasids, although Muslim and linguistically Arab, were the ideological successors of the Sasanian dynasty in adopting its principles of monarchy.[26] In artistic terms al-Buḥturī is summoning the misfortunes of Abbasid culture on the cusp of his transition to the ruins. Specifically, these are the ruins of a "parent" civilization that Abbasids both cherished and plundered.[27] The poet's journey thus redresses oedipal anxiety about succession on the familial, dynastic, and civilizational levels.

Al-Buḥturī's first words of glory for the Sasanians express open kindness and charity (lines 14–15). Though the Arab poet shows goodwill toward them, he draws attention not only to their prosperous realm but also to their guarded northern frontiers along the Caucasus. That border is presented in the ode as mythically inviolable, tiring and baffling the human gaze. The phrasing evokes Qur'anic diction describing the effect of God's craftsmanship on any gaze that might attempt to find flaws. It is He "who created the Seven Heavens in layers. In the Creation of the Compassionate, you do not see any flaws? Look again, do you see a single breach? Look again and again, your gaze will fall, tired and baffled."[28] The Sasanians' level of perfection is, like God's, not in vain.

Al-Buḥturī's reference to the frontiers raises a key theme he later develops: security of family, dynasty, and civilization. He rekindles the memory of a Sasanian realm whose prosperity is guarded by pragmatic, presumably iron-clad, defenses. In lines 16 and 17 the guarded prosperity of that empire stands antithetical to a vulnerable barren terrain. The verses, of course, establish an antithesis between the august heritage of the Sasanians and the "simple" abodes of Bedouins. It might even tempt one to consider al-Buḥturī's subsequent verse as a veiled critique of Arab culture and of old Bedouin poetics.[29] Certainly this would be likely if al-Buḥturī had continued with the voice of the defiant brigand. However, line 16 in particular distinguishes him thematically and poetically from the brigand, who would opt precisely for the antisocial wasteland. Al-Buḥturī effectively disassociates himself from the voice of the brigand when he discloses a deep attachment to imperial heritage. As al-Buḥturī develops the themes of his ode at the "grave" of the Sasanian, it becomes clearer that his commentary serves as an allegory for something more mythic and perennial.

After contrasting desert wilderness with imperial glory, the impermanence of that glory takes precedence, and al-Buḥturī reframes the topic with a prominent use of the perfect tense. To compound the elegiac mood, the first subject of the verb is Time (i.e., Fate) itself (lines 18–20). The mighty are not immune from the vicissitudes of Time. As a villain, Time ensures decay, echoing the lamentations of the conventional *nasīb,* where Fate and its metonymies (Time, Death, Days or Nights) victimize innocent life perennially.[30] The poet for a moment dwells on the erstwhile glory of the Sasanians. Their bustling structures become fallen shells, reminiscent of tombs. The poet does not bear the weight alone, however. He finds solace in the company of remembered kings, such as Anūshīrvān (lines 21–23).

Allegory and the Folk Literacy of the Audience

At first it appears that the poet is surrendering to reverie, but in effect he alludes to circulating folklore of the Abbasid period. This simple allusion dignifies the folk literacy of audiences with a nuanced allegory. According to al-Dīnawarī's collection of tenth-century folklore, Anūshīrvān Khosrow I (r. 530–79) fought back the Byzantines in the celebrated battle of 540, wherein he seized Antioch, one of the enemy's most prized cities.[31] He was a model king for the Abbasids, but his legacy is framed by tragedy.[32] Or rather, al-Dīnawarī's narratives insinuate that Anūshīrvān could repel the mighty Byzantines, but he could not avert oedipal strife at home.[33] Knowledge of Sasanian lore thus enables us to see more clearly al-Buḥturī's theme of civilizational security as it is shaken by family trauma.

Although Anūshīrvān's martial might was incomparable and his northern borders stretched securely between the Caspian and Black Seas, he could hardly remain immune from domestic upheaval. We are told that he had a son by a woman of exceptional beauty who was

Christian. Anūshīrvān wanted her to convert to Zoroastrianism as a gesture of her love for him, but she refused. The son, standing in solidarity with his mother, also refused to convert, which provoked the father's anger, who in return imprisoned the prince. While Anūshīrvān was at the frontier fighting the Byzantines, he fell ill to a deadly disease. When the son received the news, he escaped from prison, assembled his allies, and captured a city for its financial resources. When the intelligence network delivered that news to the father, he declared the son an enemy of the state.

Without regard for familial sentiment, Anūshīrvān ordered the prince killed. The father miraculously recovered from his illness, hunted the son down, and had him killed without pause or clemency. Crisis was averted for the state, only to underscore the tension of oedipal replacement in the context of the family. Furthermore, al-Dīnawarī hinted at the futility of attempting to avert Fate. He ominously foreshadowed in his narrative the fated replacement of the Sasanians by another younger civilizational system: "The Prophet . . . was born at the end of the reign of Anūshīrvān."[34] On both the rhetorical and symbolic levels the oedipal threat to Anūshīrvān was artistically and psychologically linked to the threat of Muhammad's new order. Al-Buḥturī thus seems to allude to layers of oedipal strife that are familial, dynastic, and civilizational. The allegory leaves one with a folkloric pattern of generational replacement: Son against Anūshīrvān, Prophet's umma against the ancient empires of the region, and al-Muntaṣir against al-Mutawakkil.

The poem continues with glory on the surface, betraying darker layers of inter-reference from folklore (lines 24–26). The man (in the poem) who could command his soldiers' motions stands in contrast to the man (in lore) whose overweening manner provoked domestic rebellion. The poet, however, pulls his audience closer to the source of his description. For the first time he draws attention to the panel depicting the battle of Antioch. Most important, he focuses on the psychic-artistic gaps between his verbal description, the actual panel, and the viewer's eye (lines 27–28).[35] The viewer is not only invited to experience the panel visually, but to explore the panel vicariously with touch. One is enticed by a rich layering of artistry: the poet's, the panel's, and one's own imagination of sight and touch. The poet appeals to the senses to draw his audience into his poetic experience.

At a critical moment we are in effect invited to identify with the poet. The identification helps to transfigure the theme of imperial security to one of individual security—that is, mortality.

Precisely at the moment when we are welcomed into the poet's experience, al-Buḥturī introduces his son. Abū al-Ghawth makes an appearance as the libation bearer (lines 29–30). In a haze of reverie Anūshīrvān the Sasanian father becomes Abū al-Ghawth the Arab son. These libations of wine are part of the iconography of immortality.[36] Here the life-giving liquid does not flow from the ancients; rather, the poet dreams of his son serving him the wine of everlasting bliss out of loyalty. This idyllic image stands conspicuously in tension with Anūshīrvān's own strife with his son, and al-Mutawakkil's with his. The poet implicitly questions the gap between ideals and realities, dream state and wakefulness. It is a question he asks explicitly. In the meantime al-Buḥturī's wine appears to be a promising liquid in times of tension (lines 31–32). The poet's resort to wine displaces tensions and evokes an image of reconciliation. In pre-Islamic times the shedding of both wine and blood was associated with immortality,[37] but al-Buḥturī, in the wake of references to bloodshed, promotes instead restoration and contentment by wine. The beverage therefore directly affects the heart. At last an elite assembly of otherwise vying men gather in a mythic garden in a spirit of camaraderie and graciously share the drink of everlasting life.[38]

In this garden scene the next persona to join the gathering (in line 33) is Khosrow II Aparvīz (r. 591–628), along with his prized minstrel, al-Balahbadh. Aparvīz is the last of the Sasanian royalty to partake in the communal wine, but again al-Buḥturī calls on the folk literacy of his audiences to interpret the allegory. Al-Dīnawarī relates that though he was born the son of a competent and scrupulous king, Hurmizd IV, Aparvīz himself became a plague upon the land. He was unsuccessful in battle and unjust to nobles under his command. The nobility effectively dethroned him and gave his son, Shīrūya (r. 628–29), an ultimatum forcing the young man to order the execution of his corrupt father and replace him immediately.[39] Shīrūya asked for one day to contemplate the matter.

The next morning Shīrūya drafted a letter of execution to be sent to Aparvīz. The son rose up against the "tyrannical" father and wrote a long, shocking document that began with these words: "What will befall you is a punishment from God for the legacy of your misdeeds!"[40] Both at the level of family and dynasty, the son/successor had replaced the father/predecessor and seized the symbols of his authority. On a civilizational level al-Dīnawarī continues to synchronize the oedipal coup with the Islamic rise to glory and the Arab conquest of Mesopotamia: "It was in the ninth year of the Prophet's migration."[41] Once again, ancient cycles of oedipal replacement are employed to interpret the Abbasid patricide. It is telling, however, that the only audiences who would arrive at this allegorical interpretation would be those accustomed to folk narratives. In a sense, al-Buḥturī embeds in the ode allegory that privileges their knowledge base. Within *mujālasāt* gatherings, audiences with this folk literacy would earn a measure of dignity from their peers. In this one instance, folk and canonic literacy would be hermeneutically interdependent.

Despite his Arab lineage, al-Buḥturī's own attitude in the ode toward the Sasanian downfall is never less than sympathetic. Anūshīrvān and Aparvīz sowed the seeds of their own tragedy, but al-Buḥturī voices their praise compassionately and offers them the bliss of wine and the joy of camaraderie. Although he is an Arab, he promotes their memory in reconciliation. Perhaps the most unsettling line (line 34) of al-Buḥturī's poem is when he begins to question the possibility of reconciliation in reality: "A dream that closes my eye to doubt? / Or desire that alters my fancy and guesses?" These questions remain unanswered in the poem. Thus, for the remainder, he undertakes an extended effort to memorialize the Sasanians with implications for Abbasid social memory.

The rest of the poem (lines 35–56) rigorously eschews questions about conflict. Al-Buḥturī launches a focused elegy of the Sasanians. The lyrical mood in this section enables the poet to maximize yearning and sympathy for the Sasanians. In this manner he proposes a series of "recollections" in order for his audience to come to terms with the House of Sāsān and by extension with the House of ᶜAbbās. The significance of al-Buḥturī's words to the Sasanians is profound. As a luminary of Arab culture, he can implicitly make amends like no other orator for the violence that supplanted the House of Sāsān. The sight of the desolate building prompts him to voice the distress and sadness that Time brought upon it (lines 36–37). Any suggestion of blame remains implicit, because the ultimate culprit is Time, the *nasībic* enemy of all organized human life. In lines 39 and 40 the weight of Time is presented as an immovable beast on the site.

Al-Buḥturī's manner of recollection carefully evokes not blame but grief, because axiomatically the tragic turns of Fate are universally outside the realm of human control. The language of Fate and tragedy shifts attention away from human (Arab) culpability but nonetheless offers the bygone Sasanians the veneration due to them as predecessors of the Arabs in Mesopotamia. In the formula of elegy the greater the glory of the deceased, the greater the offering of blood or tears must be to placate the haunting claims of the dead. After admitting the injustice of plunder committed on the Sasanian Arch by Time in line 40, al-Buḥturī proceeds to celebrate the height of the ramparts and mountains that defend it (lines 41–42), the vastness of the Sasanian armies (line 45), the size of crowds made to wait for an audience (line 46), and the talent of court minstrels (line 47). In a critical moment the poet's recollection technique reclaims these bygone wonders from the distant (alien) past. He brings them into the recent (Arab) past (lines 48–49). The poetic practice of nostalgia thus refurbishes Abbasid cultural memory of the Sasanian. The military divide between Arab and Sasanian, conqueror and conquered, is overturned in favor of a project to assimilate their heritage and credit them. As al-Buḥturī suggests, the past seems closer than one might think.

In the next two lines al-Buḥturī fulfills the obligations of a loyal poet grieving his deceased kin. Note here, however, that he cannot call for vengeance against the killers (Arabs) in the classical heroic mode, and thus he offers libations of tears, implicitly renouncing armed heroism (lines 50–51). Although his tears and commemoration serve important social functions in Abbasid society, al-Buḥturī's choice of tears instead of blood as an oblation deserves notice. S. Stetkevych notes that pre-Islamic poetry of elegy is predominantly chanted for fallen kinsmen in battle.[42] The heroic, manly ideal of tribal society was to protect the sanctity of a warrior's blood by memorializing vengeance sought and achieved. As a counterpart to elegy composed by men, calls for vengeance composed by women do not offer libations of blood but of tears.[43] One can sense, then, in al-Buḥturī's decision to offer tears that he opts out of the external violence of bloodshed and instead subordinates himself to demands that are consistent with Abbasid imperial interests. If his ode to the Sasanians stands allegorically for the Abbasids, one can be sure that he offers tears and remembrance, not blood and vengeance, to the two families, dynasties, and civilizations. What we have are tears sublimated into a token of self-redemption. The poem that began with the voice of the bitter brigand now concludes with renewed resolve to recollect the estranged past.

In lines 52–55 al-Buḥturī recognizes the claims of the Sasanians on him through a bond of kinship not by birth but by "favor" (i.e., cultural influence). He nostalgically recalls the intervention of the Sasanians in pre-Islamic Arabia, although this event is commonly reported as a mixed blessing. Al-Buḥturī's recollection reinvents a checkered event in order to honor Persian culture. According to Abbasid narrative, the Sasanian occupation of Yemen replaced an occupation by the Christian Aksumite commander Aryāṭ and his successor, Abraha. Al-Buḥturī's first embellishment is to reinvent legend and lore, which indicate that the Sasanian armies faced Abraha, not Aryāṭ; actually, according to Abbasid folklore, Aryāṭ was dealt his fatal blow not by the Sasanians but by his successor, Abraha.[44]

The second embellishment: according to Abbasid sources, Anūshīrvān sent Sasanian forces to expel Abraha's army from Yemen, but the Sasanians exploited Yemen as a satrapy, and Anūshīrvān ordered a series of massacres during Yemen's thirty-year occupation until the last Persian ruler converted to Islam in 628.[45] Allowing a sweet innovation to triumph over a bitter memory, al-Buḥturī seems to accentuate the positive by casting the Sasanians as the liberators and allies of the Arab race. There is some basis for this new artifice, however, since Aryāṭ and Abraha launched massacres of Jews in Yemen, and Abraha menaced the Holy House at Mecca in 570 because it rivaled his own in Sana'a.[46] The Sasanians were loathed in Yemen, but from Mecca's perspective, the Persian occupation thwarted further attacks on the Holy House. In a spirit of lyricism al-Buḥturī records the Sasanian occupation as an unequivocal "liberation" that supported pre-Islamic and early Islamic Arab dominion.

The ultimate verse opens into a final expression of goodwill, based on this "positive" cultural experience with the Persians (line 56). Al-

Buḥturī's openness to other races, to be sure, needs to be seen in the context of Arabo-Muslim sacral history. Benedict Anderson notes that the great sacral communities of the premodern world—whether Christian, Buddhist, or Muslim—were imaginable first and foremost because they embodied superordinate principles that gave their followers a feeling of being at the center cosmically, regardless of the specific community's ethnic composition.[47] The sacredness of the leader, history, and, above all, language gave community members a sense of cosmic privilege and, most important, an impulse to domesticate people of wide-ranging ethnicity.[48] Indeed, conversion "to Islam" in the medieval period in most cases was not predicated on a change of heart; joining a new religion meant, above all, joining a new community.[49]

The equation of religious and communal identity, the historian Devin DeWeese explains, actually encouraged the expectation that people would come into the fold of their new religion not as individuals but, often, as groups of kin or locality.[50] From the perspective of the sacral community, such conversions were not baseless. The sacral efficacy of the community, by means of its leader, its history, and its language, promoted a tireless belief in the community's power to redeem newcomers, who were not viewed as pariahs but instead as fertile new ground for communal growth.[51] One can imagine that al-Buḥturī's openness to other races, after a splendid tribute to one of them, gave this poem an exceptional appeal among Muslims who were non-Arab. In effect, this perspective validated their ethnic origin, whatever it may have been, and conferred on them the privilege of membership in a vast sacral community.

Privileging Folk Literacy in the *Mujālasāt*

From the outset of the patricide, the greatest threat to Abbasid society was civil strife caused by the communal angst of experiencing a profaning abhorrent trauma. Al-Buḥturī's task was to redeem not only the legacy of the Abbasid family, but the entire society. The Īwān Kisrā ode plays with several lines of demographic and ideological division in order to validate the constituents of society and reconstitute the umma. Consider, for example, the major issues of the time, which would have been debated in the *mujālasāt:* the split between the Shuᶜūbiyya (proponents of Persian culture) and the ᶜUrūbiyya (proponents of Arabic culture),[52] the competition between young and old prompted by the symbolic effect of the Abbasid patricide, not to mention the divide between folk and elite culture, between the center and the margins. Overtly, the ode validates all parties, castigating only Fate as the perennial villain sowing tragedy within community. But perhaps the most stunning reconciliation is that between folk (margins) and elite (center), where al-Buḥturī embeds in this canonical ode allusions that would only be comprehensible to those with folk literacy, thus validating and dignifying those who would consider themselves off-center, or "folk." One might imagine that moment of face-to-face exchange in the *mujālasāt* where folk and canonic literacy embodied in competent performers meet; for a moment it becomes evident that they are interdependent. Likewise, the Abbasid center must rely on the goodwill of the folk to avert civil strife, as if al-Buḥturī elaborately plies the motif of the mouse aiding the lion. For folk audiences in the *mujālasāt,* the poet's nod is a dignifying gesture; for courtly audiences, his ode is a test of humility.

SIX

Singing Samarra (861–956)

Poetry, Reception, and the Reproduction of Literary Value in Historical Narrative

THE UNWRITTEN RECORD

In the century after the patricide of Caliph al-Mutawakkil (d. 861), historiography of the event evolved in written form from an early stage of simple description to a more influential one of mythohistorical narrative. El-Hibri's important analysis of Abū Jaᶜfar al-Ṭabarī's (d. 923) narrative demonstrates this latter stage well. He argues that despite the implication of the heir al-Muntaṣir (d. 862) in the murder, literary devices were used to illustrate the fatal flaws of father, then son, as well as key virtues that ultimately redeemed them both.[1] In a figurative idiom drawing on the Arabic poetic tradition, al-Ṭabarī addressed several questions about the injustice of fate, the assigning of blame, and the impermanence of power.[2] This artful ledger of sins and graces betrayed a preoccupation with the patricide as an event of mythic importance for Abbasid society. This was not the case in the beginning, however.

Abū Muḥammad ᶜAbd Allāh b. Muslim b. Qutayba (d. 889) was the closest historian to the murder, yet his narrative conveys the least information. He does not even mention the involvement of a son or the guards, merely saying, "He was killed in the year 247 [A.D. 861], three days after the Fitr [holiday]."[3] Ibn Qutayba makes no mention of the setting, the possible perpetrators, or al-Fatḥ b. Khāqān's presence or simultaneous murder, all of which are amplified in later historiographies. It seems conspicuous that a public event of the Abbasid era, not to mention the first regicide of the Abbasid epoch, would receive such short shrift from a leading historian and littérateur of that era. Ibn Qutayba's single sentence to posterity should be counted as revealing compared with his contemporary, Abū Ḥanīfa Aḥmad al-Dīnawarī (d. 895), however, who remains absolutely silent on the matter. In short, the situation poses a conundrum: Could it be that in the earliest phases there was no public knowledge of the event? It is difficult to imagine, with scores of courtiers employed in the palace—indeed, a number who may have even witnessed the regicide firsthand—that there was a dearth of informants or "leaked" information. To the contrary, there was probably ample incentive for informants to take their place in history by talking. Why do we have so little information in the written records closest to the event?

The historian Aḥmad b. Abī Yaᶜqūb al-Yaᶜqūbī's (d. 897) text, with more gumption than al-Dīnawarī and Ibn Qutayba, provides a bit more detail, bordering on a "plot" but still in the realm of "story" because it omits any meaningful sense of causality.[4] Al-Yaᶜqūbī does not reveal informants, though. Given the conventions of transmission, this would have diminished his credibility somewhat. Perhaps for this reason he holds himself to the details most believable to his audience: "Al-Mutawakkil had mistreated his son, Muḥammad al-Muntaṣir, so they [the Turks] incited him [the son], and plotted to attack him [the father]. When it was Tuesday, the third of Shawwal the year 247 [A.D. December 861], a band of Turks entered . . . while he was in a private gathering and attacked him. They killed him with their swords. And they killed al-Fatḥ b. Khāqān along with him."[5]

Al-Yaᶜqūbī's sparsely detailed report is a quantum leap from Ibn Qutayba's single sentence, but the account still does not spell out the causes or the motives of the caliphal guard, who are solemnly sworn to die for their master. Rather, one receives a cryptic reference to the son's "mistreatment" but nothing to justify blood vengeance. The relationship between events has yet to crystallize into a full-blown plot. More important, no literary devices are used to comment on moral, existential, and communal issues. What begins with Ibn Qutayba and al-Yaᶜqūbī in the late ninth century as a cryptic palace scandal develops a few decades later, in the early tenth century, into a mythic narrative about glory, tragedy, and redemption. In this chapter I draw on El-Hibri's theory that historical narratives answer deep-seated societal questions. I propose a determinant role for poets in defining the existential questions that historical reports need to address.[6]

I examine al-Buḥturī's poetic role, in particular, as a catalyst for cultivating sympathy for the Samarran tragedy. His poems after the patricide, broadcast from within the palace, spread news of the incident and helped to mythologize events that might otherwise have remained the painful facts of a palace scandal, which profane an ostensibly sacral community already torn by two civil wars. I argue that al-Buḥturī's intense activity sowed seeds in the form of archetypal questions that later elicited a response in the form of rhetorically rich narratives that burgeoned and diversified to address these questions. In addition, I suggest that the *mujālasāt* were the likely forum where the performance of poetry could influence the literary invention of narrative. Because the written tradition is largely dependent on oral informants, this formulation contributes to an understanding of how written narratives burgeoned from 861 to the first half of the tenth century, when al-Ṭabarī died.

The fertile soil for those poetic seeds, however, was the *mujālasāt*. There, poetic ideas are received and evaluated, and the production of historical narrative can be taken as a measure of that reception. In order to analyze the issue of reception and evaluation, I draw once again on Barbara Herrnstein Smith's pragmatic approach of literary value. Smith argues not only that people judge experience seamlessly as an ongoing act of cognition, but also that valuation is fundamentally social. Individuals seek and share valuations, in the form of advice, anecdotes, recommendations, curricula, reading lists, and gifts. All these forms of communication give explicit or implicit judgments about which products and objects are worth experiencing, given the scarcity of time, resources, and attention. Smith argues further that evaluation is so fundamental to our experience of things that we evaluate the evaluations we receive based on prior experience with the evaluator and his or her reputation in evaluating. Moreover, Smith draws attention to the authority of institutions that endorse certain titles, the authority of valuations from past generations, the recommendations of persons who have power over us or who enjoy a measure of prestige in society, such as teachers, employers, and patrons, not to mention fads, fashions, and seeming consensus. In other words, because evaluations of textual experience are social and reciprocal, individuals and groups often rely on preevaluation, which they may or may not test with their own judgment.[7] The most important observation to note with respect to the *mujālasāt* is this: There is no means for the state or any central authority to control them because they are ad hoc, in homes, informal, and responsive to the needs of hosts and immediate guests. As such, they become a pragmatic testing ground for the literary response, value, and the reproduction of value across generations. I argue here that the delay in the burgeoning of historical narrative—attested in al-Dīnawarī, Ibn Qutayba, and even al-Yaᶜqūbī—illustrates the delayed but pragmatic response from the *mujālasāt* in the form of thoughtful, mythically rich historical narrative. While the historical narratives were in their formative (mostly oral) stage, it would have been pointless to record them.

The Poet's Business

Despite al-Buḥturī's impressive influence with the Abbasid monarchs he served, the post-patricide era was an ordeal for him and the rest of the Abbasid entourage. The caliph's murder was merely the inauguration of an era of decline. Al-Muntaṣir himself reigned for only six months, but the tumult at the court continued long after. Later historiography judged the Turkic guards as traitors who began their mischief as early as al-Mutawakkil's ascension, when they appointed the caliph essentially irrespective of the Abbasid royal family[8] and indeed intimidated their master, forcing him to flee abortively to Damascus.[9] When they succeeded in co-opting al-Muntaṣir against his father, the crisis was more than a single crime. The event propelled the palatine guards to a new level of temerity. Al-Mutawakkil's death ended a golden era and initiated one of intense horror and insecurity.

In the nine years after al-Mutawakkil's regicide, four caliphs suffered overthrows or violent deaths: al-Muntaṣir (r. 861–62), al-Mustaᶜīn (r. 862–66), al-Muᶜtazz (r. 866–69), and al-Muhtadī (r. 869–70).[10] A new beginning was thought to have arrived with the next caliph, al-Muᶜtamid. He was named "al-Saffāḥ II," after the founder of the Abbasid dynasty.[11] Al-Muᶜtamid reigned for twenty-two years, despite Turkic threats at home and the fierce Zanj revolt in the southern marshland.[12] His success was bolstered by his Herculean brother al-Muwaffaq, dubbed "al-Manṣūr II" for his legendary courage, strength, and acumen.[13]

Modern historians note that the "recovery" of the caliphate still suffered from a basic weakness that was never overcome.[14] As Hugh Kennedy notes, the relative stability did not come about because an Abbasid caliph "defeated and humiliated the Turks . . . but rather [because] they were assured a place in a new regime and integrated once more into the structures of the state."[15] For al-Buḥturī and other courtiers, the post-Mutawakkil period (861–92) stood in sharp contrast to the golden era before it. Al-Buḥturī mythologized the Samarran era, both its blissful and its mortifying stages, through an intense program to shape public perception. This move had major consequences in Abbasid society by appealing to mythic sensibilities about human cycles of glory, sin, and redemption. He sublimated the Samarran era into a myth, translating Samarran memories into the poetic idiom of nostalgia as found in the elegiac *nasīb,* the opening section of the classical ode (*qaṣīda*).

Al-Buḥturī accomplished this aim with two complementary poetic endeavors. The first was a single poem discussed in the previous chapter in which he poetically traveled to the ruined Sasanian palace at Ctesiphon, Īwān Kisrā, and thereby redeemed Abbasid society. The second was an ongoing practice of allegorically embedding both the archetypal joys and horrors of Samarra in his *nasīb.*[16] In this chapter I focus on a series of Samarran odes written before the Īwān Kisrā, which further indicates al-Buḥturī's long-term project to redeem the Abbasids after the patricide of al-Mutawakkil. The Abbasid era was thereby transfigured into the archetypal ruined abode, a kind of pre-lapsarian paradise, with redemptive overtones. Samarra in particular became the *nasībic* ruined abode, evoking a deep yearning for security and glory. The past and the present are juxtaposed in al-Buḥturī's *nasīb* to project a range of tragic sentiments—from bittersweet memories of an ideal past to endless estrangement from a gruesome present.

Joy and Horror at Samarra

The Arabic place-name "Samarra" is contracted from two possibilities: the first is *surra man raʾā* (whoever sees it delights), and the second is *sāʾ man raʾā* (whoever sees it grieves).[17] As the chief poet of the time, al-Buḥturī was largely responsible for instilling the sense that Samarra, the secluded haunt of kings, had reverted to haunt secluded kings. The primary vehicle for mythologizing Samarra was the *nasīb,* the prototypical moment in the classical ode for lamenting the absolute loss of Love, Youth, and Happiness while bewailing the ravages of Fate and the tyranny of Death.

This *nasībic* mode of communication in Arabic culture is archetypal. Specific historical loss and yearning become an emblem of *all* losses and yearnings. The Arabist Jaroslav Stetkevych notes that the poetic idiom enables historical denotative allusions to "open up to new ever different poetic uses." The human experience of grief and yearning—under the theme of barren ruins, traitorous lovers, and lost abodes—reverberates between the specific and the universal to "express the full weight of contemporary events." For example, almost two centuries after al-Buḥturī's lifetime, a poet-knight named Usāma b. Munqidh (d. 1188) would suffer great losses when his family and birthplace were destroyed in Syria's earthquake of 1157. The poetic language he would use, though, as a messenger of his grief, would be that of the *nasīb,* with its antiquarian but evocative idiom of effaced campsites and ghostly traces of bygone life. The poet "converted tangible things of measurable time into transcendent poetic symbols." The power of the *nasīb* to express human sorrow is made infinite by the innumerable users of that mode of expression. One can trace a common denominator, if not a genealogy, of sociocultural heartache; it "contains a whole people's historical reservoir of sorrow, loss, yearning."[18]

There are several post-Mutawakkil poems by al-Buḥturī that implicitly or explicitly render Samarra a *nasībic* ruin.[19] Perhaps the most poignant of the group is a poem that was delivered to Caliph al-Muᶜtazz, himself a protégé of al-Buḥturī, after a faction of Turkic guards challenged the caliphate in 867. The coup was narrowly averted when the faction leader, Bughā al-Ṣaghīr al-Shirābī, was defeated.[20] In the opening lines of the *nasīb,* al-Buḥturī unloads his heavy burden with an escape to recollection. From al-Buḥturī's poem 771:

> Will Time ever retrieve for me my days in
> white palaces and courtyards?
> There's no union with them momentarily,
> nor do they have a minute for a visit.
> A moment of merriment is not renewed in memory
> without renewing my ardor for them.
> A yearning, among many, left me awake at night
> as if it were one malady among many.[21]

In these lines al-Buḥturī adheres to a pattern of time-consciousness, both measured time and Time acting as a fateful force antagonizing delicate human life. Although the coup in the background was averted, al-Buḥturī draws attention to this event as an exception to a rule: the glory of the past is irretrievably lost, and Time isolates people from their beloved forebears. Descendants thus remain alone to fend off the horrors of Fate; the more the poet recalls the dead, the more it increases his ardor. The throes of Fate will continue unhampered. In that vein the defeat of Bughā al-Shirābī receives recognition as an exception: "Fate to me has one grace to be thanked. It quelled what lies in the heart as enmity."[22]

It was conventional wisdom of the time, as historians narrate it, that a caliph could not adequately achieve victory in any struggle without backing from one or another faction of Turkic guards. Put more bluntly, Turkic factions manipulated caliphs against other factions.[23] Even the most cunning rulers found themselves allied with opportunistic guards, who were only nominally "protecting" them while jockeying for advantage against rivals. Alliances at the court were characterized by sudden betrayals. In the *nasīb* of another ode to al-Muᶜtazz, the poet uses the elegiac idiom to foreground the potential treachery of allies. The motif here is that of the elusive Ganymede. From al-Buḥturī's poem 262:

He altered and broke his promise,
    and fancied faithlessness but would not show it.
Better than most, he will let the heart
    be captivated by his frolic and earnest.
Magic sparkles in his eye
    and flowers are plucked from his cheek.
He soothes the heart, though he makes the mind
    a liar and betrays his promise,
with a face rivaling the moon in beauty
    and a frame molded as a bough in form.[24]

The motif of the elusive beloved, absolutely self-interested, allows al-Buḥturī to impress on the nobility yet another dimension of the horrors at Samarra. Like the faction that propped al-Muᶜtazz, the Ganymede lures and taunts his victim, fully conscious of his appeal, yet fully capable of betrayal.

There is also an important effect in the architectural appearance of Samarra that must have lent credence to al-Buḥturī's project in perpetuity. Although not necessarily of the architects' intent, it became part of the effect. In brief, the city's palaces were shaped with material that was readily available in Mesopotamia, meaning that mud brick (not stone) was preferable. Unlike stone, mud brick provided the convenience of quick construction.[25] Another consequence, however, was quick destruction. Mud brick, unlike baked brick or stone, was particularly susceptible to seasonal fluctuations in temperature and moisture.

In the construction of the palace Bulkuwārā (849–60?), it seems that architects were toying with the properties of various materials. The palace is built using three types of brick, varying in degrees of vulnerability. The most delicate material, stamped earth or *pisé,* was used for the outer wall; then mud brick was used for the two courtyards; but baked brick was reserved for the innermost courtyard and throne chamber.[26] Over the years this meant that the palace took on the look of a ruin in a choreographed manner. The outer walls would crumble before the two courtyards, and the very last to fall would be the inner courtyard and throne chamber, the site of the caliphal sepulcher. For other palaces that were built completely with mud brick, the appearance of the ruin would hardly be as controlled; nevertheless, there was a guarantee that it would give the appearance of ruin in a matter of years, not centuries.

Most important, the palace city was designed to become a gargantuan graveyard in consonance with *nasībic* mood and imagery. Al-Muᶜtaṣim founded the palace city in the first half of the ninth century, and al-Muᶜtaḍiḍ (r. 892–902) moved the court back to Baghdad in the second half. Most caliphs were buried in the caliphal city.[27] It is reported, though, that most caliphs were buried in unmarked graves within their palaces.[28] In effect, this would render the entire city a precinct hallowed in the lyrical idiom of the *nasīb*. One anonymous poet fused his impression of Samarra with the prototypical *nasīb* of the pre-Islamic poet Imruᵓ al-Qays. His ode begins: "Whoever-Sees-It-Delights became ruined; what a pity. / Halt you both, let us weep for the memory of beloved and campsite."[29]

In his geographic work the littérateur Yāqūt (d. 1229) expressed the *nasībic* effect of Samarra after it was abandoned: the once-splendid city had become "a ruin, a wasteland, at the sight of which the viewer takes fright. Beforehand, there was nothing on earth more beautiful."[30] It would seem that Samarra had become an uncanny fulfillment of the Abbasid poet Abū al-ᶜAtāhiya's (d. 825) adage, "Get sons for death; build houses for decay."[31] In short, Samarra had become the perceived graveyard of an Abbasid dream.

The city that was once called "whoever sees it delights" was thus transfigured into "whoever sees it grieves." Raised to the level of mythology, the tragedies at Samarra become prototypical of human impermanence and frailty, despite bygone greatness and glory. Problems and crises that belonged properly to the court alone could take on a universal relevance, prompting generations to ask plaintively what happened and why. If al-Buḥturī's poetic practice in the *nasīb* were not enough, he gives us another single poetic instance in his Īwān Kisrā poem, which seals this transformation.

Mythologizing in Narrative

This chapter began with the question of how historiography on the patricide evolved from a stage of sketchy description to mythohistorical narrative. I have shown how al-Buḥturī generated sympathy for oedipal tensions while summoning visions of reconciliation. But how did these archetypal issues seep into the narrative tradition? In order to answer this question, I propose the *mujālasa* as a likely socio-literary venue for receiving this al-Buḥturī poetry and responding to it with historical narrative that both validates and interprets it.

First, I demonstrate that al-Buḥturī's poetry was not marginal but widely memorized and recited by littérateurs (*udabāʾ*). Second, there are several indicators that al-Buḥturī became *the* expert on the patricide because of his perspective as court poet and eyewitness. Although some resent his association with the momentous event, other historians, such as Abū al-Ḥasan al-Masᶜūdī (d. ca. 956), provide an outlet for al-Buḥturī's narratives, despite the reputed mendacity of poets.[32] Finally, I argue that written knowledge of the past categorically relied on the face-to-face performance of those texts from memory in assembly.

Al-Buḥturī was a celebrity in his own lifetime, making his poetry worth memorizing and performing. His *dīwān* and lore collector, Abū Bakr al-Ṣūlī (d. 947), portrays the prestige of the poet in an anecdote of "first-encounter," which I mention in chapter 2.[33] It is worth recounting again: Al-Ṣūlī reported that he was at the educational circle (*majlis*) of the Basran grammarian al-Mubarrad (d. 898) when an elderly long-bearded man greeted the grammarian. The teacher stopped dictating to the class, and older students rose, hovered around the visitor, and asked him if they could recite poetry to him. The celebrity indulged the adoring students and listened to their poetry recitations. In doing so, he verified the memory of each student. Soon al-Ṣūlī realized it was al-Buḥturī himself, but the young student had no memorized poetry to recite to him. Al-Mubarrad consoled al-Ṣūlī, saying he could find the poet later that day at a certain place. As a teenager, al-Ṣūlī seized the opportunity and worked with a friend to memorize some poetry, then checked his retrieval in the presence of a seasoned elder. Later, al-Ṣūlī found al-Buḥturī at a *mujālasa.* When the occasion arose, he recited what he knew and finally received al-Buḥturī's blessings. At the end of the anecdote al-Ṣūlī noted that in a single evening, students performed a marathon of twelve full odes in the presence of the poet.[34]

Key features have been embedded in this piece of lore to make it appealing and believable. First, poetry is shown to be the currency of social interaction: competition, peer pressure, embarrassment, honor, and self-recovery. They all factor into the value of poetry in society. Second, the anecdote illustrates that within this competitive environment, memorized poetry allowed al-Ṣūlī to participate in a historic transfer of knowledge and thereby become one of an elite who will serve as curators of al-Buḥturī's corpus on his death. At the age of physical maturation (*bulūgh*), al-Ṣūlī is acquiring verbal proficiency (*balāgha*). Poetry, memorized and delivered, qualifies him to become a transmitter of cultural texts that will remain important in perpetuity. Third, al-Ṣūlī's anecdote reflects the place of honor that al-Buḥturī occupied in Abbasid society. The poet is someone for whom the grammarian would interrupt class, and al-Mubarrad was famed for his arrogance.[35] The poet is someone around whom devotees flutter, anxious to win approval. Most important, the protagonist, al-Ṣūlī, goes to great lengths after his initial failure to seek the poet's blessings.

After his death al-Buḥturī continued to be a cultural icon. His work and legacy were promoted by seven reciters of high standing in Abbasid culture, the youngest of whom, ᶜAlī b. Ḥamza al-Iṣbahānī (d. 985), is said to have lived eighty-eight years after al-Buḥturī's death. Al-Ṣūlī collected the poet's verse and organized it according to the end-rhyme. Al-Iṣbahānī did the same but organized the verses according to themes (*aghrāḍ*).[36] Moreover, his poetry was considered part of the classical canon that was memorized by would-be scholars for centuries. The historian Ibn al-Athīr (d. 1239) adds to his own credentials when he declares that al-Buḥturī's poetry was a cornerstone of his early learning.[37] After memorizing the Qur'an and Hadith by heart, he focused on memorizing poetry, in particular, that of Abū Tammām (d. 842), al-Mutanabbī (d. 965), and al-Buḥturī.[38] Likewise, the scholar ᶜAbd al-Karīm al-Samᶜānī (d. 1166) reports that he memorized "more than a thousand lines" of al-Buḥturī's work. He notes that in his day al-Buḥturī's *dīwān* was "famous" (*mashhūr*).[39]

At literary gatherings it is thus likely that the mention of al-Buḥturī elicited a repertoire of anecdotes about the patricide, and these narratives indexed his poetry on the topic. The two were culturally and mentally linked. Al-Buḥturī was in fact widely believed to be a witness to the murder, a belief promoted by his elegy to al-Mutawakkil in which he describes the attack in the first person.[40] This poem gave him the needed credentials to speak on the subject as an expert witness. When the historian Abū al-ᶜAbbās b. Khallikān (d. 1282) describes al-Buḥturī's long-standing rapport with al-Mutawakkil and the vizier al-Fatḥ b. Khāqān, he casually notes that "he is famous in what happened to them (*fī amrihimā*)."[41] The striking point here is that Ibn Khallikān, writing long after the incident, associates the poet with the murder. Similarly, al-Buḥturī's rivals resented his fame and association, but even they could not ignore the cultural link. They could, however, mock him, as the poet Abū al-ᶜAnbas al-Ṣaymarī (d. 888) does when he laments Jaᶜfar al-Mutawakkil and the absence of anyone to avenge him:

> How grieved is this world over Jaᶜfar,
> over the hero, the bright-faced king!
> Over a slain man from the clan of Hāshim
> who lived between the throne and the pulpit.
> By God, Lord of the House and pilgrimage rites,
> by God, if even al-Buḥturī were slain,
> An avenger from Syria would surely rise to avenge him,
> One of a thousand bastards from the Clan of Biting Crap
> Led by every one of his base brothers,
> each riding an old one-eyed ass.[42]

The antithesis in this piece is not only humorous but revealing. The leader of an empire remains unavenged, whereas the resented poet would be duly avenged by a band of brothers mounted on one-eyed asses. The august Hashimite finds no one to avenge him, but for the poet, the "crap biters" display their machismo. No doubt, these juxtapositions do not flatter al-Buḥturī, but they illustrate the inextricable association between the poet and the patricide.

Among the alluring narratives most likely recited about the patricide was al-Buḥturī's putatively eyewitness account. The first written register is found in a historical work by al-Masᶜūdī, *Meadows of Gold,* from the tenth century, nearly a century after the event. This narrative seems to have traveled far. A variation reappears in the Arab West in a book by the Andalusian littérateur Abū al-Ḥasan ᶜAlī b. Bassām al-

Shantarīnī (d. 1147), in *Treasure of the Virtues of the (Iberian) Peninsula's People.*[43] Not only does it find an audience far from Iraq, but it does so some two hundred years after al-Masᶜūdī's lifetime.

The narrative also reappears in works by historians who followed the Masᶜūdī tradition. A version of the narrative is retold in *Mirrors of the Ages* by Yūsuf b. Qizughlī Sibṭ b. al-Jawzī (d. 1257) and in *The History of Islam* by Muḥammad b. Aḥmad al-Dhahabī (d. 1347).[44] Al-Masᶜūdī's narrative illustrates the rippling effect of al-Buḥturī's message throughout the centuries. The narrative itself answers in literary detail moral, existential, and communal questions about the cruelty of Fate, the impermanence of human greatness, and the instability of allegiance. All three issues are treated by the sequencing of events and the use of literary devices. The most striking claim is the one never mentioned: the wayward heir, al-Muntaṣir, receives no blame. Despite the premium on a son's obedience in patronage cultures, the narrative echoes a deep sympathy for all the Abbasids promoted in al-Buḥturī's Īwān Kisrā ode, which transforms an otherwise sordid palace scandal into a mythic tragedy with widespread perennial appeal. The only unredeemable culprit is "fate."[45]

Let us consider for a moment the impact of these valuations: al-Buḥturī composes a series of odes about the tragedies of Abbasid society, which spur performers in the *mujālasāt* to posit narratives that explain what happened, how and why; then al-Masᶜūdī relates such narratives and implicitly recommends that audiences perform these narratives; then later littérateurs, performers, and scribes hear similar narratives and recommend the reproduction of value in the form of further performance. We have a chain reaction of valuations, driven by the need to seek and share evaluations of worthy experience, but what is at the core? What is at stake for performers and audiences, which propels them to seek and share evaluation? While there can be no central controlling power like the state, al-Buḥturī himself inspires the chain reaction with a series of implicit archetypal questions that demand answers. Namely, how could these tragedies—the patricide, the decline of the Abbasids, the rise of the Turkic guards—have happened to a sacral community protected ostensibly by the caliph and God? Who is at fault? Who deserves to be the target of vengeance or at least anger? And ultimately, for a society founded on patron-client trust, how can patrons protect themselves from homicidal betrayal? These are the restless questions that reverberate and redouble for more than a millennia of narrative.

The most prominent rhetorical strategy, and the one introduced first, is reliance on the authority of the poet, a persona known for transforming a sordid palace scandal into a meaningful tragedy. The narrative in al-Masᶜūdī's text announces its beginning with the phrase, "al-Buḥturī relates a narrative, saying (*haddatha al-Buḥturī qāla*)."[46] *Adab* principles of speaking would recommend not a historical or literal person as the voice but an archetypal or figurative persona. After all, there is no ethical or artistic principle that would prevent performers from assuming the voice of al-Buḥturī, and in a sense it would be too appropriate rhetorically to leave untapped. Moreover, there is a pietistic tendency in these narratives to censure al-Mutawakkil and loyal courtiers, which diverges from al-Buḥturī's tendency, suggesting a mingling of popular religious voices. All in all, the primordial questions are collective, which suggests the hand of collective composition and adjustment.

This technique serves to feature the poet as the man with privileged intelligence, echoing an older meaning of the term *khabar* (report).[47] The poet's authority resurfaces in the narrative when the historian punctuates the presentation with such reminders as "al-Buḥturī said" and "he said."[48] Al-Masᶜūdī uses these narrative techniques in the first instance to distance himself from the narration, but in the second instance the distance allows him to assume another even more literary voice. In fact, after al-Masᶜūdī releases the audience from the literary grips of the narrative, he finally says—conscious of his rhetorical charm—"And we mention here only a smidgen of what we mentioned [in other works]. This is what we selected for now, since it is the most eloquent expression and the easiest to memorize."[49] At this point the historian precisely seems to be self-conscious of his literary impact. Moreover, if he aims to induce memorized performance, his source is probably also memorized performance, hinting at a prewritten life of the narrative in the *mujālasāt*.

It seems that later generations of littérateurs appreciated the importance of the poet's voice and accentuated it for ease of memory and performance. In the Berlin manuscript, dated 1673, the scribe also recognized the significance of the phrase "al-Buḥturī relates a narrative, saying," by setting it apart from the rest of the text, using three markers: a new script style (*naskh*), a new color (red), and a new size (double proportion).[50] The result is an eye-catching heading, relative to the surrounding text. The look of the manuscript enhances its mnemonic value in concordance with al-Masᶜūdī's desire to make the narrative eloquent for the sake of easy learning by heart.

In answer to al-Buḥturī's poetic question about blame and anger, the beginning of the narrative deflects responsibility from al-Muntaṣir by blaming Fate, the caliph's misjudgments, and the palatine guards.[51] While the son is spared, the narrative places blame at the feet of the father by focusing on al-Mutawakkil's violations of established conventions, indeed of good judgment. By his own will, the caliph brought danger into his immediate proximity. Moreover, there is strong commentary in this tenth-century narrative about his overreliance on guards in matters that should be entrusted to no one but the most tested and competent personnel. These implicit criticisms, El-Hibri notes, can also be seen in al-Ṭabarī's ninth-century narratives. The vizier al-Fatḥ, a parvenu who rose from slavery by luck, suffers reproach for unwise counsel and dangerous adulation.[52]

Furthermore, al-Mutawakkil's dependence on Turkic guards is viewed in retrospect as foolish and ominous. Their use of force during the Samarran period is roundly censured. As El-Hibri notes, in contrast to Persian rebellions that had potentially noble causes, the palatines "do not rebel in order to restore a moral, pietistic, or social ideal, but merely to realize immediately material and political gains."[53] These soldiers, with rare exception, are figured into narratives as the quintessential traitors. The royal family is technically dependent on them for protection, but in reality they serve no practical purpose but to sow discord and sap the state's resources.[54]

The narrative doles out sharp criticism when the narrator portrays the caliph vainly purchasing the murder weapon and recklessly handing over his life to an untested guard. About a century after al-Ṭabarī's lifetime and the dreadful event, the depiction must have seemed to audiences the epitome of caliphal tragedy: a powerful ruler in need of aid but surrounded by strangers. The narrative indicates that realization, as the caliph senses the Fate he brought on himself. In the second half of the narrative, the reproach of al-Mutawakkil escalates, depicting him as inverting the normal order of things.[55] He essentially abdicates by doing what is anathema to a sacred king: putting his face in contact with the dust in front of his subordinates. Typically, caliphs conspicuously exhaust resources to evince privilege in ceremony. The will to hold and exercise power is an a priori condition of the caliphate. In this instance, however, he reduces himself with a conventional gesture of humility, even mourning, essentially giving up the will to be king and thus to live. The al-Buḥturī of the narrative is alarmed, taking the display as a voluntary step toward death. The king relinquishes what makes him unique and sovereign. The next omen stems from another odd response from al-Mutawakkil. In the face of song and music, he does not rejoice but turns inward and weeps.

The last omen seals al-Mutawakkil's fate. He receives an exquisite present from his wife. However, the standard practice for rulers in courtly anecdotes is to ask one of the poets present to compose a piece (*qit^{c}a*) that would forever capture the sublime moment and travel back to the gentle ears of the gift giver. This practice reciprocates delight with delight in perfect social symmetry. Instead, what ensues is an antisocial, almost grotesque response that absolutely precludes delight. Al-Mutawakkil receives two gifts, a red coat (*darrā^{c}a*) and a red silk gown (*miṭraf* or *muṭraf*). The first is clearly designated as a ceremonial coat (*khil^{c}a*)—not to be worn outside the proper occasion. The *khil^{c}a* was usually finely brocaded, embroidered with gold and in the front studded with rubies. The second gift, a red silk gown, was usually made of an oversized piece of cloth used as a wrap with bold borders that are embroidered. The gown was used for any dignified visit, whereas the coat was reserved exclusively for high ceremonial occasions; thus the latter denoted a more auspicious occasion.[56] In essence, al-Mutawakkil makes a mockery of Abbasid sartorial conventions, which he himself instituted. Now he wears the ceremonial coat without ceremony and drapes over it another, *less* prestigious outer garment. Al-Buḥturī is sure to stress the point to the audience: "He wore the coat on the *inside* and then wrapped himself in the gown."

The situation devolves further. We are also told that al-Mutawakkil heedlessly allowed the gown to rip while moving about. An object snags the gown, which coils and tightens around him (note the metaphor), pulls him, and finally tears. With cinematic effect the coil-and-rip scene encodes the interplay of misjudgment and Fate. Al-Mutawakkil makes an aberrant, incomprehensible choice of attire, and then Fate seemingly snags him, causing the whole outfit to coil and constrict him. The outfit, symbolic of his persona, is rent graphically "end to end." The incident prefigures his demise, enabling him to face his destiny and visualize his burial. A gown for high-class living is therefore transformed into one of burial.

In other narratives the garment became such a locus of cultural attention that it appeared in al-Ṭabarī's version in the more paradisiacal color green, often used on the tombs of heroes.[57] Likewise, Ibn al-Jawzī (d. 1201) readjusts the prop as the gift of his mother, adding a rhetorical twist[58]—the one who gave him life would give him the symbol of his death.[59] After the ripping of the gown, the cruelest event in the sequence is his instruction to Qabīḥa's servant. The wife gives him a beautiful gift meant to bring him joy, but he sends the destroyed fabric back with gloomy anticipations of his own destruction. Al-Buḥturī reacts to the disturbing scene with a formulaic phrase used on hearing news of someone's death. Symbolically, the caliph has met his fate.

Thereafter al-Mutawakkil became severely drunk. The drinking scene seems to have been an important element that was preserved in subsequent retellings of the same and variant narratives.[60] The intoxication scene redeems the hubristic father by creating the impression of an artful, peaceful death despite fatal flaws. Along these lines one poet captures al-Mutawakkil's redemptive death in verse: "This is how the death of a nobleman should be, / among pipes, guitars and wine. / Among two cups that quench his thirst completely, / one cup for his joy and another for his Fate."[61]

From Mythopoetic to Mythohistoric

Lest one assume that al-Buḥturī stands uncontested in the *mujālasāt*, it would appear that the narrative diverges from al-Buḥturī's initial purposes while ironically employing his voice as narrator. Al-Buḥturī's odes for the Abbasid family and society over the course of decades redeem the entire family from stigma, placing blame only at the feet of

Turkic guards. In the narrative virtually everyone involved endures censure, except the wayward son, al-Muntaṣir. Whereas al-Buḥturī's ode vindicates the family by holding Fate as the villain, the narrative holds the father and others accountable for deliberately walking into their fate foolishly. Ultimately, the narrative holds characters accountable for their poor judgment. As literary reception, these narratives respond to al-Buḥturī with alternative, more pious, theories about what happened and what went wrong.

One can witness, for example, al-Masᶜūdī's own agenda in his homiletic use of death and betrayal as the quintessential equalizer of patrons and clients. After al-Mutawakkil's death scene he says, "Who therefore is deluded by this world and trusts it and thinks he is safe from betrayal and catastrophe, except a fool? . . . Not even the careful soul is safe."[62] For al-Masᶜūdī the glory of God is affirmed by the impermanence of the Abbasids or any other mortals. While it is clear that al-Buḥturī succeeded in making a sordid palace scandal into a locus of deep-seated questioning, the narrative answers to those questions diverge. Nevertheless, since the *mujālasāt* remained outside the control of any central authority, participants enjoyed a sense of security and intimacy necessary to ponder alternate theories and communicate them in narrative.

Conclusion

This book began in response to the need to place Arabic literature in conversation with the humanities, to make each more relevant to the other. From academics in the humanities (and from the educated public), I have at times encountered a dismissal of Arabic literature's value to learning and self-cultivation. Usually, however, academics and the educated public seek out Arabists to make the case for that value. More than a century and a half ago, Alexis de Tocqueville affirmed this impulse in American society. In his *Democracy in America* he argues that bustling democracies cannot abide the predictability of overly familiar forms, themes, and genres, noting in effect the link between aesthetics and power.[1] While not dismissing the comforts of the familiar, de Tocqueville argues that democratic societies by their structure and character crave the novel, the new, the foreign, for these challenge expectations and sensibilities, thus questioning established powers and the order of the day and enabling new forms of influence and order to emerge in response to immediate demands.

De Tocqueville was elaborating on an ongoing, nineteenth-century fascination in Europe and America with the *Rubaiyat* of Omar Khayyam, the *Thousand and One Nights,* and the *Gulistān* of Saᶜdī, as part of "the West's" discovery of "the Orient," which included astonishing new discoveries of antiquities from Ancient Egypt, Palestine, and Mesopotamia. New ideas and forms from "the East," however orientalized, stylized, and performed, breathed new influence into an increasingly more cosmopolitan "West," emerging since the late medieval period from regional isolation.

In the following century, the same need for the unfamiliar spurred a hunger for the works of Kahlil Gibran and, most recently, the spiritual poetry of Rumi. Words from these literary masterpieces still adorn public buildings in the West and, in book form, continue to serve as gifts for graduation and other coming-of-age milestones. According to the editors of *Grape Leaves: A Century of Arab-American Poetry*, Gibran's *The Prophet* was a bestseller during the twentieth century in America, second only to the Bible, and was the mainstay of its publisher, Alfred A. Knopf.[2] The popularity of these works today suggests America's continued need to reach out to the unknown and assimilate it. An argument can be made that the people and humanities of the Middle East have become an inextricable thread in the fiber of Western culture. Beyond reasons such as the romance of "the other" or the simple utility of language, Middle Eastern literatures give students access to nearly 450 million speakers, a booming youth culture, an emerging middle class and its markets, traditions of religious thought and practice, and, most relevant here, centuries of cultural heritage.

It appears that the humanities in America and the self-cultivating public remain receptive to Middle Eastern literatures and scholarship. One challenge for scholars of the Middle East is certainly to support demand and to justify our value to our institutions or to society, but more important, our challenge is how to present and teach these cultures in a way that promotes an engagement with the other. My own response to that question in teaching and researching premodern Arabic literature is to employ methods of analysis from the broader humanities that already enjoy credibility and circulation, such as those from anthropology, folklore, Homeric studies, and performance theory. The aim is not to be trendy but to draw on those principles of analysis, as well as their currency (and familiarity) in academia, to make Arabic literature more accessible and engaging to a broader public.

I interpret Edgar Allan Poe's short story "The Thousand-and-Second Tale of Scheherazade," mentioned in the Introduction, as an example of how *not* to teach or analyze literature. Poe presents a comic-horrific alternate ending for Shahrazad, where the king dismisses every single wonder presented by her with an annoying degree of nit-picking that enables him to avoid considering wonders altogether. Parodying an orientalist conceit of his time, Poe wryly presents the source of his newly discovered ending: Lo and behold, it is an "Oriental" text "scarcely known at all, even in Europe" called the *Tellmenow Isitsoörnot.*[3] And the king echoes a false dichotomy between the true and the wondrous, as he refuses to consider the broader significance of the scientific as well as the figurative marvels of his age. Poe knows full well how to parody his literary critics, but his story also critiques a nineteenth-century modernist preoccupation with literal truths at the expense of tropes, figures, and metaphors, as embodied in the wondrous, the "Oriental," which he and many others saw as the West's necessary complement.

In this book I have chosen methods and texts precisely to move beyond a literal reading of cultural memory to a more figurative one, using multidisciplinary methods. The central aim has been to show the impact of a little-studied but pervasive social institution (the *mujālasāt*). I suggest ways that it influenced the appeal and formation of Arabo-Islamic cultural memory. It stands to reason that if medieval audiences came together to perform inherited and new literature, then both the social gathering and the texts received validation of their appeal in social practice, and those practices invigorated and perpetuated the texts and the gatherings. My method has been to use original sources wherever possible to document the *mujālasāt* and their impact, and to draw on the work of scholars such as Bencheikh, Gruendler, and others who have worked on the less egalitarian royal *majlis*. In the absence of textual sources, I have drawn on literary critical and cultural theory, as well as comparisons from other literary traditions, to help pose and answer critical questions and to provide plausible insights about the *mujālasāt* and their impact on literature and society.[4]

The arguments along the way have not been incredible, especially in light of performance theory and comparisons from other contexts. First, I make a distinction between the royal Abbasid *majlis* and earlier permutations of literary gatherings in antiquity, such as the Greek *symposion* and the Near Eastern *marzēaḥ,* and illustrate by contrast the character and function of the Abbasid *mujālasāt.* The *mujālasāt* tended to be comparatively egalitarian. They proliferated in the ninth century, enabling more littérateurs to cultivate the *adab* skills needed to participate, socialize, and gain personal influence. Second, I argue that face-to-face performance impacted *adab*-type speaking in assembly, since speaking in a group is largely motivated by an artistic imperative to impress one's audience, in fidelity to shared standards of competence. Calling on theories of performance and the "ethnography of speaking," I use *adab* sources to redefine *adab* as a social, pragmatic, performative process, not merely a set of elegant texts and behaviors, and suggest principles based on *adab* sources. Those principles indicate audience expectations (what will impress or not), thus cultivating a figurative manner of speech and text presentation in the group. At the moment of performance, a performer assumes responsibility for attracting and holding the attention of an audience, which allows, even requires, adjustment in style and text in order to meet the demands, not of fact-based truth, but of performance. Fidelity to cultural memory overrides banal "facticity" and literal truth, which are in effect standards for performing the past that did not proliferate until the modern era, and which are far from universal. In this light, poetry or narrative performance produces an artistically rich figurative truth that gives meaning to bygone people, places, and events.

In confronting *adab* performance on its own terms, without importing our modernist biases and sensibilities, we can observe how written sources of and about the *mujālasāt* offered littérateurs a communal face-to-face venue for engaging and adjusting the literary canon. Performers and audiences could use and enjoy the advantages of bimodal oral-written performance, discussed in the field of Arabic literature by Gruendler, Sprenger, Schoeler, and Toorawa. This scholarship supports the proposition that the goal of presentation was performance and display, not a mere rehearsal of bygone facts. This performative sense of *adab* requires us to recognize the role of men and women who participated in literary production and consumption on a nonremunerative basis. In short, they were *amateurs* who liked the literature and the gatherings. The vast majority of those who participated in *mujālasāt* must have been amateurs, since the terms of participation in assembly required no particular rank or credentials, but only sociability (*muʾānsa*), charm (*ẓarf*), and cultivation in *adab* (*taʾaddub*). In addition to the subjective pleasures of the text, I suggest that other motivators were at stake, such as prestige, conviviality, and love, as well as a widening of one's base of friends and associates.

In the course of this book, I also extend and apply the *mujālasāt* in chapter 3 as an interpretive tool by offering an example of how performance in a group could reframe and even subvert the aims of an ode at its debut, so that a courtly patronage ode could express values, sensibilities, and ethics particular to the culture of a Sufi brotherhood that rejected courtliness and caliphal patronage. Here, I examine manuscripts of performance handbooks that transmit the courtly ode to suggest how mystical poetry, on other pages of the same manuscript handbooks, reframes and subverts courtly materials.

If one accepts the *mujālasāt* as a venue for the reception of new and traditional literature, how might that framework help us understand the ways that bygone generations of littérateurs used and engaged their literary tradition? Chapter 4 mobilizes the framework of the *mujālasāt* to examine how an ode dyad composed by al-Buḥturī might have functioned at its time and might have been retooled for generations in the *mujālasāt*. In its immediate niche, the ode dyad redressed arguably the most horrific incident of the Abbasid era: the patricide-regicide of al-Mutawakkil, which profaned a sacral community established by the Prophet Muhammad with the murder of one of his divinely appointed successors. In chapters 4 and 5, I show that al-Buḥturī's poetic service helped to heal a communal rift that had the potential of degenerating into civil war. In subsequent generations, the *mujālasāt* offered the prime venue for selecting, evaluating, and performing these odes in order to shape and adjust communal memory of the event and to give meaning to trauma. By deploying B. H. Smith's theory of valuation and canonicity, one can appreciate anew the durability and adaptability of these redemptive odes in gaining the attention of audiences. Moreover, one can sense how these odes elicited the emotional participation of audiences, who in all likelihood found in them insight, redemption, and forgiveness for the transgressions of both the wayward father and son, echoing perennial tensions in systems of patriarchy and patronage.

Chapter 6 examines the literary aftermath of al-Mutawakkil's murder, as seen in the burgeoning of historical narratives. The sources and texts examined give narrative patterning to the storied caliph, al-Mutawakkil, his court, and his sordid patricide. Narrative patterning served the primary purpose of showing guilt or innocence via subtle praise or blame. For instance, Ya^{c}qūbī's early example of narrating the murder of al-Mutawakkil seems like a simple list of events, with no apparent cohesion. Yet on closer inspection, one finds that he posits that the father and son had a clash (no reason given) and that the Turkic guards killed the father. Even a list can have exculpatory value: the clash, without reasons, piques curiosity about motives, while the actions of the Turkic guards summarily vindicate the son of direct involvement. Although it was likely that oral narratives were performed to supply much needed "information" about the perceived events and their meaning, Ya^{c}qūbī's tantalizing tidbits actually spur performers to supply a motive for the son's rancor and details about the treacherous guards. In short, during the formative phase, narratives seem to respond directly to each generation of unanswered questions.

As the first patricide of Islamic history, the death of al-Mutawakkil was a quintessential episode in need of performance to sublimate raw trauma into edifying drama. In performance at *mujālasāt,* successive generations were able to shape opinion about hierarchical oedipal tensions and betrayals from within, which were perennial anxieties in the patronage cultures of the Middle Ages. At this distance in time, it is virtually impossible to determine *Isitsoörnot* (as Poe would call it) or the "facts of history," because such literal sources do not exist, as Poe reminds us with his parody. Such a stark admission might seem disappointing to some scholars, since it is often believed that Islam is the first world religion to emerge in the light of world history, based on the developmentalist assumption that writing and paper production were sufficiently "advanced" for early Muslims to document their own history. However, that assumption swells from a presentist and positivistic sensibility. The groundbreaking work of Robinson, El-Hibri, Waldman, Meisami, Morse, Khalidi, and others would indicate that premodern historiography and cultural memory deserve to be understood on their own terms, not ours; that stories about the past were highly literary in pattern; and that importing our reductive modernist sense of history serves no interpretive purpose. Rather, the driving motive of *adab* performers was artistic quality in order to create meaningful memory that would edify and inspire immediate as well as imagined audiences. Thus, to read and interpret such memory requires literary analysis.

Let us consider for a moment traumatic events of our own culture in recent history as an analogy for the processes of contentious historiography. The assassinations of John F. Kennedy, Martin Luther King, and Malcolm X and the attacks of September 11, 2001, just to name a few, engaged America's communal psyche because they were primordially disturbing and shook America's sense of itself to the core. They were fundamentally signs that cast doubt on what it meant "to be American." America is still at a loss to find satisfying answers to the most basic questions of what happened and who did what and why. In the absence of satisfying answers—and out of grief—society provides answers in the form of theories, blockbuster movies, top-40 songs, and best-selling novels. Even as evidence emerges, it hardly redresses the core vulnerability, which only meaning and sense can assuage through the collective artistic process of making cultural memory. By analogy, if we consider the murder of al-Mutawakkil, the primordial issues are not those surrounding the person per se, any more than the losses of September 11 were about life or property alone. Something more perennial and primordial is at stake. How do Americans reconcile their positive self-image with the trauma of an attack? How does one regain a sense of communal trust and national security (especially with Arab-looking types in the midst), while honoring long-established ideals framed in founding documents about openness and equality?

Abbasid society, too, projected its own ideals about the cascading benevolence of patronage systems and the sanctity of heroes trusted to fulfill their sacred roles, which gave Abbasid society an ontological sense of being. The murder of the caliph tore at the very fabric of those ideals, and the trauma, performed and rethought, brought about new ideals of decentralized governance, egalitarianism, and social mobility. In post-patricide historical narratives, one finds questions being raised about the nature of fate and human power, of generational tensions and frustrations, as well as deeper aspirations for a more stable system for generating order and meaning in post-patricide Abbasid society.

From a pragmatic performance perspective, the *adab* humanities call on scholars to pose literary questions of both poetry and narrative and to analyze them as an art of memory. That enterprise offers an invaluable opportunity in the classroom to teach *adab* humanities by challenging our students to manage the cognitive complexities of uncertainty and fear of the unfamiliar, as well as the indeterminacy of meaning and of diverging perspectives on bygone people and events.

Appendix of Arabic Poetry

p. 47

[قال البحتري من الكامل]

سَقياً لِمَجلِسِنا الّذي آنَستَهُ　　　واهاً لِمَجلِسِنا الّذي أوحَشتَهُ
صَيّرتَ مَجلِسَنا بِذِكرِكَ عامِراً　　　وَحَضَرتَ آخَرَ غَيرَهُ فَعَمَرتَهُ
فَالذِكرُ مِنكَ لَنا نَديمٌ حاضِرٌ　　　وَالشَخصُ مِنكَ لِغَيرِنا صَيّرتَهُ
فَلَيَنعَمَنّ بِطيبِ ذِكرِكَ يَومُنا　　　وَلَيَأنَسَنّ بِكَ الّذي جالَستَهُ

p. 47

[قال البحتري من الخفيف]

يَومُ سَبتٍ وَعِندَنا ما كَفى الحُرّ　　　وَطَعامٌ وَالوَردُ مِنّا قَريبُ
وَلَنا مَجلِسٌ عَلى النَهرِ فَيّا　　　حٌ فَسيحٌ تَرتاحُ فيهِ القُلوبُ
وَدَوامُ المُدامِ يُدنيكَ مِمّن　　　كُنتَ تَهوى وَإن جَفاكَ الحَبيبُ
فَأتِنا يا مُحَمّد بنِ يَزيدٍ　　　في اِستِتارٍ كَي لا يَراكَ الرَقيبُ
نَطرُدِ الهَمّ بِاِصطِباحِ ثَلاثٍ　　　مُترَعاتٍ تُنفى بِهِنّ الكُروبُ
إِنّ في الراحِ راحَةً مِن جَوى الحُبْ　　　بِ وَقَلبي إِلى الأَديبِ طَروبُ
لا يَرعكَ المَشيبُ مِنّي فَإِنّي　　　ما ثَناني عَنِ النَصابي المَشيبُ

p. 80

[قال البحتري من الكامل]

إِنْ أَبْقَ أَو أَهْلَكْ فَقَد نُلْتُ الّتي   مَلأَت صُدورَ أَصادِقي وَعُداتي
وَغَنِيْتُ نَدْمانَ الخَلائِفِ نابِهاً   ذِكرِي وَناعِمَةً بِهِم نَشَواتي
وَشَفَعْتُ في الأمرِ الجَليلِ إِلَيهِمِ   بَعدَ الجَليلِ فَأَنجَحوا طَلَباتي
وَصَنَعْتُ في العَرَبِ الصَنائِعَ عِندَهُم   مِن رِفدِ طُلاّبٍ وَفَكِّ عُناةِ

p. 86

[قال أبو تمّام من الطويل]

وَلَولا سُنَنٌ سَنّها الشِعْرُ ما دَرى   بُغاة العُلى مِنْ أَيْنَ تُؤْتى المَكارِمُ

pp. 88–92

[قال علي بن الجهم من الطويل]

عُيونُ المَها بَينَ الرُصافَةِ وَالجِسرِ   جَلَبْنَ الهَوى مِن حَيثُ أَدري وَلا أَدْرِي
أَعَدْنَ لي الشوق القديمِ ولم أكنْ   سلوتُ ولكن زدنَ جمراً على جَمْرِ
سَلِمْنَ وَأَسلَمنَ القُلوبَ كَأَنّما   تُشَكّ بِأَطرافِ المُثَقّفَةِ السُمْرِ
وَقُلنَ لَنا نَحنُ الأَهِلّةُ إِنّما   نُضيءُ لِمَن يَسري إِلينا وَلا نَقْرِي
فَلا بَذلَ إِلاّ ما تَزَوّدَ ناظِرٌ   وَلا وَصلَ إِلاّ بِالخَيالِ الّذي يَسْرِي
أَحينَ أُزلنَ القَلبِ عَن مُستَقَرّهِ   وَأَلهَبنَ ما بَينَ الجَوانِحِ وَالصَدْرِ
صددن صدود الشاربِ الخمرَ عندما   روى نفسَهُ عن شربها خيفةَ السكرِ
أَلا قَبلَ أَن يَبدو المَشيبُ بَدَأنَني   بِيَأسٍ مُبينٍ أَو جَنَحنَ إِلى غَدْرِ
فَإِن حُلْنَ أَو أَنكَرنَ عَهداً عَهِدنَهُ   فَغَيرُ بَديعٍ لِلغَواني وَلا نُكْرِ
وَلَكِنّهُ أَودى الشَبابُ وَإِنّما   تُصادُ المَها بَينَ الشَبيبَةِ وَالوَفْرِ
كَفى بِالهَوى غَيّاً وَبِالشَيبِ زاجِراً   لَوَ اَنّ الهَوى مِمّا يُنَهْنَهُ بِالزَجْرِ
أَمَا وَمَشيبٍ راعَهُنّ لَرُبّما   عَمِرْنَ نَياناً بَينَ سَحرٍ إِلى نَحْرِ
وَبِتنا عَلى رَغمِ الحسود كَأَنّنا   خَليطانِ مِن ماءِ الغَمامَةِ وَالخَمْرِ
خَليلَيّ ما أَحلى الهَوى وَأَمَرّهُ   وَأَعلَمَني بِالحُلوِ مِنهُ وَبِالمُرِّ
بِما بَينَنا مِن حُرمَةٍ هَل رَأَيتُما   أَرَقّ مِنَ الشَكوى وَأَقسى مِنَ الهَجْرِ
وَأَفضَحَ مِن عَينِ المُحِبّ لِسِرّهِ   وَلا سِيّما إِن أَطلَقَتْ عَبرَةً تَجْرِي

وَما أَنسَ لا أَنسَ ظَلومَ وقَولَها   لِجارَتِها ما أَولَعَ الحُبّ بِالحُرِّ
فَقالَت لَها الأُخرى فَما لِصَديقِنا   مُعَنّىً وَهَل في قَتلِهِ لَكِ مِن عُذْرِ
عِديهِ لَعَلّ الوَصلَ يُحيِيهِ وَاعلَمي   بِأَنّ أَسيرَ الحُبِّ في أَوثَقِ الأَسْرِ
فَقالَت أُداري الناسَ عَنهُ وَقَلّما   يَطيبُ الهَوى إِلاّ لِمُنهَتِكِ السِتْرِ
وَأَيقَنَتا أَنْ قَد سَمِعتُ فَقالَتا   مَنِ الطارِقُ الساري إِلَينا وَلا نَدْرِ
فَقُلتُ فَتىً إِن شِئتُما سَتَرَ الهَوى   وَإِلاّ فَخَلاّعُ الأَعِنَّةِ وَالعُذْرِ
عَلى أَنّهُ يَشكو ظَلومَ وَبُخلَها   عَلَيهِ بِتَسليمِ البَشاشَةِ وَالبِشْرِ
فَقالَت هُجينا قُلتُ قَد كانَ بَعضُ ما   ذَكَرتِ لَعَلّ الشَرّ يُدفَعُ بِالشَرِّ
فَقالَت كَأَنّا بِالقَوافي سَوائِراً   يَرِدنَ بِنا مِصراً وَيَصدُرْنَ عَن مِصْرِ
فَقُلتُ أَسَأتِ الظَنّ بي لَستُ شاعِراً   وَإِن كانَ أَحياناً يَجيشُ بِهِ صَدْرِي
صِلي وَاِسأَلي مَن شِئتِ يُخْبِرْكِ أَنّني   عَلى كُلِّ حالٍ نِعمَ مُستَودَعُ السِرِّ
وَما الشِعرُ مِمّا أَستَظِلّ بِظِلّهِ   وَلا زادَني قَدْراً وَلا حَطّ مِن قَدْرِي
وَما أَنا مِمّن سَيّرَ الشِعرُ ذِكرَهُ   وَلَكِنّ أَشعاري يُسَيِّرُها ذِكْرِي
وَلِلشِعرِ أَتباعٌ كَثيرٌ وَلَم أَكُن   لَهُ تابِعاً في حالِ عُسرٍ وَلا يُسرِ
وَما كُلّ مَن قادَ الجِيادَ يَسوسُها   وَلا كُلّ مَن أُجرى يُقالُ لَهُ مُجْرِي
وَلَكِنّ إِحسانَ الخَليفَةِ جَعفَرٍ   دَعاني إِلى ما قُلتُ فيهِ مِنَ الشِّعْرِ
فَسارَ مَسيرَ الشَمسِ في كُلّ بَلدَةٍ   وَهَبَّ هُبوبَ الريحِ في البَرِّ وَالبَحْرِ
وَلَو جَلّ عَن شُكرِ الصَنيعَةِ مُنعِمٌ   لَجَلّ أَميرُ المُؤمِنينَ عَنِ الشُكْرِ
فَتىً تَسعَدُ الأَبصارُ في حُسنِ وَجهِهِ   كَما تَسعَدُ الأَيدي بِنائِلِهِ الغَمْرِ
بِهِ سَلِمَ الإِسلامُ مِن كُلّ مُلحِدٍ   وَحَلّ بِأَهلِ الزَيغِ قاصِمَةُ الظَهْرِ
إِمامُ هُدىً جَلّى عَنِ الدينِ بَعدَما   تَعادَت عَلى أَشياعِهِ شِيَعُ الكُفْرِ
وَفَرّقَ شَملَ المالِ جودُ يَمينِهِ   عَلى أَنّهُ أَبْقى لَهُ أَجمَلَ الذِكْرِ
إِذا ما أَجالَ الرَأيَ أَدرَكَ فِكرُهُ   غَرائِبَ لَم تَخطُر بِبالٍ وَلا فِكْرِ
وَلا يَجمَعُ الأَموالَ إِلاّ لِبَذلِها   كَما لا يُساقُ الهَديُ إِلاّ إِلى النَحْرِ
وَما غايَةُ المُثني عَلَيهِ لَو أَنّهُ   زُهَيرٌ وَأَعشى وَامرُؤُ القَيسِ مِن حُجْرِ

ألَيس إذا ما قاسَ بالشمس وجهَهُ … وبالبدر قلنا خاف لِلشَمسِ وَالبَدْرِ
وَإن قالَ إنّ البَحرَ وَالقَطرَ أشبَها … نَداهُ فَقَد أثنى عَلى البَحرِ وَالقَطْرِ
وَلَو قُرِنَت بِالبَحرِ سَبعَةُ أبحُرٍ … لَما أدركت جَدوى أنامِلِهِ العَشْرِ
وَإن نُكِرَ المَجدُ القَديمُ فَإنّما … يَقُصّ عَلَينا ما تَنَزّلَ في الزُبْرِ
فإن كان أمسى جعفرٌ متوكلاً … على اللَهِ في سرِّ الأمورِ وفي الجهرِ
لقد شكر اللَهُ الخليفة جعفراً … وأعطاه مما لا يبيدُ على الدهرِ
وولّى عهودَ المسلمينَ ثلاثةً … يُحَيّونَ بالتأييدِ والعزِّ والنصرِ
أغَيرَ كِتابِ اللَهِ تَبغونَ شاهِداً … لَكُم يا بَني العَبّاسِ والمَجدِ وَالفَخْرِ
كَفاكُم بِأنّ اللَهَ فَوّضَ أمرَهُ … إلَيكُم وَأوحى أن أطيعوا أولي الأمْرِ
وَلَم يَسألِ الناسَ النَبِيّ مُحَمّدٌ … سِوى وُدِّ ذي القُربى القَريبَةِ مِن أجْرِ
وَلَنْ يُقبَلَ الإيمانُ إلاّ بِحُبِّكُم … وَهَل يَقبَلُ اللَهُ الصَلاةَ بِلا طُهْرِ
وَمَن كانَ مَجهولَ المَكانِ فَإنّما … مَنازِلُكُم بَينَ الحَجونِ إلى الحِجْرِ
وَما زالَ بَيتُ اللَهِ بَينَ بُيوتِكُم … تَذُبّونَ عَنهُ بِالمُهَنّدَةِ البُتْرِ
أبو نَضلَةٍ عَمرو العُلى وَهوَ هاشِمٌ … أبوكُم وَهَل في الناسِ أشرَفُ مِن عَمْرِو
وَساقي الحَجيجِ شَيبَةُ الحَمدِ بَعدَهُ … أبو الحارِثِ المُبقي لَكُم غايَةَ الفَخْرِ
سَقَيتُم وَأسقَيتُم وَما زالَ فَضلُكُم … عَلى غَيرِكُم فَضلَ الوَفاءِ عَلى الغَدْرِ
وُجوهُ بَني العَبّاسِ لِلمُلكِ زينَةٌ … كَما زينَتِ الأفلاكُ بِالأنجُمِ الزُهْرِ
وَلا يَستَهِلّ المُلكُ إلاّ بِأهلِهِ … وَلا تَرجَعُ الأيّامُ إلاّ إلى الشَهْرِ
وما ظهر الأسلام إلا وجاركم … بني هاشم بين المجرّةِ والنَسْرِ
فَحَيّوا بَني العَبّاسِ فيها تَحِيّةً … تَسيرُ عَلى الأيّامِ طَيبَةَ النَشْرِ
إذا أُنشدَت زادت وليّكَ غبطةً … وكانت لأهل الزيغ قاصمةَ الظهرِ

p. 95

[قال إسحاق الموصلي من الطويل]

وآمرة بالبخل قلت لها اقصري … فذلك شيء ما إليه سبيل

. . .

عطائي عطاء المكثرين تكرما   وما لي كما قد تعلمين قليل

وكيف أخاف الفقر أو أحرم الغنى   ورأي أمير المؤمنين جميل

pp. 95–96

[قال محمد بن صالح العلوي من الكامل]

ووصلتَ أسبابَ الخلافة بالهُدَى   إذ نِلْتها وأنمتَ عين الساهرِ

. . .

إني دعوتُك فاستجبتَ لدعوتي   والموتُ مني قيدُ شِبْر الشابرِ

فانتشتَني من قَعْر مَوْرِدة الردَى   أمنا ولم تسمع مقالةَ زاجرِ

وفككتَ أسري والبلاءُ موكل   وجبرت كسراً ما له من جابرِ

وعطفت بالرحم التي ترجو بها   قرب المحل من المليك القادرِ

وأنا أعوذ بفضل عفوك أن أُرَى   غَرَضاً ببابك للملم الفاقرِ

pp. 113–14

[قال علي بن الجهم من السريع]

لِلدّهرِ إِدبارٌ وَإِقبالُ   وَكُلّ حالٍ بَعدَها حالُ

وَصاحِبُ الأَيّامِ في غَفلَةٍ   وَلَيسَ لِلأَيّامِ إِغفالُ

وَالمَرءُ مَنسوبٌ إِلى فِعلِهِ   وَالناسُ أَخبارٌ وَأَمثالُ

يا أَيّها المُطلِقُ آمالَهُ   مِن دونِ آمالِكَ آجالُ

كَم أَبلَتِ الدُنيا وَكَم جَدّدَت   مِنّا وَكَم تُبلي وَتَغتالُ

ما أَحسَنَ الصَبرَ وَلا سِيّما   بِالحُرّ إِن ضاقَت بِهِ الحالُ

يَشهَدُ أَعدائي بِأَنّي فَتىً   قَطّاعُ أَسبابٍ وَوَصّالُ

لا تَملِكُ الشِدّةُ عَزمي وَلا   يُبطِرُني جاهٌ وَلا مالُ

بَلِّغ أَميرَ المُؤمِنينَ الّذي   لَم آلُهُ نُصحاً وَلا آلو

p. 114

[من البسيط]

يَسْعَوْنَ نَحْوَ هِضابٍ طابَ مَوْرِدُها　　كأنّما العَذْبُ مُشْتَقٌّ مِنَ العَذَبِ
إليْكَ وَجّهْتُ آمالي فلا حُجِبَتْ　　عَنْ باب جُودِكَ انّ المَوْتَ في الحُجُبِ
وَقَدْ دَعَوْتُكَ أرْجو مِنْكَ مَكْرَمَةً　　حاشاك حاشاك أنْ أدْعو ولَمْ تُجِبِ

p. 115

[من المتقارب]

وَهَيْفاءَ مِنْ نُدَماءِ المُلو　　كِ صَفْراءَ كالعاشِقِ المُدْنَفِ
تَكِيدُ الظّلامَ كَما كادَها　　فَتَفْنى وتُفْنِيهِ في مَوْقِفِ

p. 128

[قال النابغة الذبياني من الوافر]

فإن يهلك أبو قابوس يهلك　　ربيع الناس والشهر الحرام

p. 130

[قالت فضل من البسيط]

إنّ الزّمانَ بذحلٍ كان يَطْلُبُنا　　ما كان أغفلنا عنه وأسهانا
مالي وللدهر قد أصبحت همته　　مالي وللدهر ما للدهر لا كانا

[قال دعبل الخزاعي من البسيط]

خليفة مات لم يأسف له أحد　　وقد قام آخر لم يفرح له أحد

p. 131

[قال علي بن الجهم من الطويل]

أيُقْتَلُ في دارِ الخِلافَةِ جعفرٌ　　على فُرْقَةٍ صبرًا وأنتم شهودُها

pp. 133–34

[قال البحتري من الطويل]

مَحَلٌ عَلى القاطولِ أَخلَقَ داثِرُه	وَعادَت صُروفُ الدَهرِ جَيشاً تُغاوِرُهْ
كَأَنّ الصَبا توفي نُذوراً إِذا انبَرَت	تُراوِحُهُ أَذيالَها وَتُباكِرُهْ
وَرُبّ زَمانٍ ناعِمٍ ثَمّ عَهدُهُ	تَرِقّ حَواشيهِ وَيُونِقُ ناضِرُهْ
تَغَيّرَ حُسنُ الجَعفَرِيّ وَأُنسُهُ	وَقُوّضَ بادي الجَعفَرِيِّ وَحاضِرُهْ
تَحَمّلَ عَنهُ ساكِنوهُ فُجاءَةً	فَعادَت سَواءً دُورُهُ وَمَقابِرُهْ
إِذا نَحنُ زُرناهُ أَجَدّ لَنا الأَسى	وَقَد كانَ قَبلَ اليَومِ يَبهَجُ زائِرُهْ
وَلَم أَنسَ وَحشَ القَصرِ إِذ ريعَ سِربُهُ	وَإِذ ذُعِرَت أَطلاؤُهُ وَجَآذِرُهْ
وَإِذ صيحَ فيهِ بِالرَحيلِ فَهُتِّكَت	عَلى عَجَلٍ أَستارُهُ وَسَتائِرُهْ
وَوَحْشَتَهُ حتّى كَأَنْ لَمْ يُقِمْ بِهِ	أَنيسٌ وَلَمْ تَحْسُنْ لِعَيْنٍ مَناظِرُهْ
كَأَن لَم تَبِتْ فيهِ الخِلافَةُ تَلقَةً	بَشاشَتُها وَالمُلكُ يُشرِقُ زاهِرُهْ
وَلَم تَجمَعِ الدُنيا إِلَيهِ بَهاءَها	وَبَهجَتَها وَالعَيشُ غَضٌ مَكاسِرُهْ
فَأَينَ الحِجابُ الصَعبُ حَيثُ تَمَنّعَت	بِهَيبَتِها أَبوابُهُ وَمَقاصِرُهْ
وَأَينَ عَميدُ الناسِ في كُلِّ نَوبَةٍ	تَنوبُ وَناهي الدَهرِ فيهِم وَآمِرُهْ
تَخَفّى لَهُ مُغتالُهُ تَحتَ غِرّةٍ	وَأَولى لِمَن يَغتالُهُ لَو يُجاهِرُهْ
فَما قاتَلَت عَنهُ المَنونَ جُنودُهُ	وَلا دافَعَت أَملاكُهُ وَذَخائِرُهْ
وَلا نَصَرَ المُعتَزّ مَن كانَ يُرتَجى	لَهُ وَعَزيزُ القَومِ مَن عَزّ ناصِرُهْ
تَعَرّضَ رَيْبُ الدّهْرِ مِن دُونِ فَتْحِهِ	وَغُيّبَ عَنْهُ في خُراسانَ طاهِرُهْ
وَلَو عاشَ مَيتٌ أَو تَقَرّبَ نازِحٌ	لَدارَت مِنَ المَكروهِ ثَمّ دَوائِرُهْ
وَلَو لِعُبَيدِ اللَهِ عَونٍ عَلَيهِمِ	لَضاقَت عَلى وُرّادِ أَمرٍ مَصادِرُهْ
حُلُومٌ أَضَلّتْها الأَماني وَمُدّةٌ	تَناهَتْ وَحَتْفٌ أَوْشَكَتْهُ مَقادِرُهْ
وَمُغتَصِبٌ لِلقَتلِ لَم يُخشَ رَهطُهُ	وَلَم يُحتَشَم أَسبابُهُ وَأَواصِرُهْ

صَريعٌ تَقاضاهُ السُيوفُ حُشاشَةً   يَجودُ بِها وَالمَوتُ حُمرٌ أَظافِرُهْ
أُدافِعُ عَنهُ بِاليَدَينِ وَلَم يَكُن   لِيَثني الأَعادي أَعزَلُ اللَيلِ حاسِرُهْ
وَلَو كانَ سَيفي ساعَةَ القَتلِ في يَدي   دَرى القاتِلُ العَجلانُ كَيفَ أُساوِرُهْ
حَرامٌ عَلَيَّ الراحُ بَعدَكَ أَو أَرى   دَماً بِدَمٍ يَجري عَلى الأَرضِ مائِرُهْ
وَهَل أَرتَجي أَن يَطلُبَ الدَمَ واتِرٌ   يَدَ الدَهرِ وَالمَوتورُ بِالدَمِ واتِرُهْ
أَكانَ وَلِيُّ العَهدِ أَضمَرَ غَدرَةً   فَمِن عَجَبٍ أَن وُلِّيَ العَهدَ غادِرُهْ
فَلا مُلِّيَ الباقي تُراثَ الَّذي مَضى   وَلا حَمَلَت ذاكَ الدُعاءَ مَنابِرُهْ
وَلا وَأَلَ المَشكوكُ فيهِ وَلا نَجا   مِنَ السَيفِ ناضي السَيفِ غَدراً وَشاهِرُهْ
لَنِعمَ الدَمُ المَسفوحُ لَيلَةَ جَعفَرٍ   هَرَقتُم وَجُنحُ اللَيلِ سودٌ دَياجِرُهْ
كَأَنَّكُمْ لَمْ تَعْلَموا مَنْ وَلِيُّهِ   وَناعِيهِ تحت المُرْهَفاتِ وَثائِرُهْ
وَإِنّي لَأَرجو أَن تُرَدَّ أُمورُكُم   إِلى خَلَفٍ مِن شَخصِهِ لا يُغادِرُهْ
مُقَلِّبِ آراءٍ تَخافُ أَناتُهُ   إِذا الأَخرَقُ العَجلانُ خيفَت بَوادِرُهْ

pp. 141–43

[قال البحتري من المتقارب]

تَبَسَّمُ عَن واضِحٍ ذي أُشُر   وَتَنظُرُ مِن فاتِرٍ ذي حَوَرْ
وَتَهتَزُّ هِزَّةَ غُصنِ الأَرا   كِ عارَضَهُ نَشرُ ريحٍ خَصِرْ
وَمِمّا يُبَدِّدُ لُبَّ الحَليمِ   حُسنُ القَوامِ وَفَترُ النَظَرْ
وَما أَنسَ لا أَنسَ عَهدَ الشَبا   بِ وَعَلوَةَ إِذ عَيَّرَتني الكِبَرْ
كَواكِبُ شَيبٍ عَلِقنَ الصِبا   فَقَلَّلنَ مِن حُسنِهِ ما كَثُرْ
وَإِنّي وَجَدتُ فَلا تَكذِبَنّ   سَوادَ الهَوى في بَياضِ الشَعَرْ
وَلا بُدَّ مِن تَركِ إِحدى اثنَتَيـ   ـنِ إِمّا الشَبابِ وَإِمّا العُمُرْ
أَلَم تَرَ لِلبَرقِ كَيفَ انبَرى   وَطَيفِ البَخيلَةِ كَيفَ احتَضَرْ
خَيالٌ أَلَمَّ بِها مِن سِوىً   وَنَحنُ هُجودٌ عَلى بَطنِ مَرّ
وَماذا أَرادَت إِلى مُحرِمِيـ   ـنَ يَجُرّونَ وَهناً فُضولَ الأُزُرْ

سَرَوْا موجِفينَ لِسَعيِ الصَفا   وَرَمي الجِمارِ وَمَسحِ الحَجَرْ
حَجَجنا البَنِيّةَ شُكراً لِما   حَبانا بِهِ اللّهُ في المُنتَصِرْ
مِنَ الحِلمِ عِندَ انتِقاصِ الحُلو   مِ وَالحَزمِ عِندَ انتِقاضِ المِرَرْ
تَطَوّلَ بِالعَدلِ لَمّا قَضى   وَأَجمَلَ في العَفوِ لَمّا قَدَرْ
وَدامَ عَلى خُلُقٍ واحِدٍ   عَظيمَ الغَناءِ جَليلَ الخَطَرْ
وَلَم يَسعَ في المُلكِ سَعيَ اِمرِئٍ   تَبَدّى بِخَيرٍ وَثَنّى بِشَرّ
وَلا كانَ مُختَلَفِ الحالَتَينِ   يَروحُ بِنَفعٍ وَيَغدو بِضَرّ
وَلَكِن مُصَفّى كَماءِ الغَما   مِ طابَت أَوائِلُهُ وَالأُخَرْ
تَلافى الرَعِيّةَ مِن فِتنَةٍ   أَظَلّهُمُ لَيلُها المُعتَكِرْ
وَلَمّا اِدلَهَمّت دَياجيرُها   تَبَلّجَ فيها فَكانَ القَمَرْ
بِحَزْمٍ يُخَلّي الدُجى والعَمى   وعَزْمٍ يُقِيمُ الصّغا والصّعَرْ
سَدادٌ فَتَلتَ بِهِ يَومَ ذا   كَ حَبلَ الخِلافَةِ حَتّى اِستَمَرْ
وَسَطوٌ ثَبَتّ بِهِ قائِماً   عَلى كاهِلِ المُلكِ حَتّى اِستَقَرْ
وَلَو كانَ غَيرُكَ لَم يَنتَهِض   بِتِلكَ الخُطوبِ وَلَم يَقتَدِرْ
رَدَدْتَ المَظالِمَ وَاستَرجَعَتْ   يَداكَ الحُقوقَ لِمَن قَد قُهِرْ
وَآلُ أَبي طالِبٍ بَعدَما   أُذيعَ بِسِربِهِمِ فَابذَعَرْ
وَنالَت أَدانيهُمُ جَفوَةٌ   تَكادُ السَماءُ لَها تَنفَطِرْ
وَصَلتَ شَوابِكَ أَرحامِهِم   وَقَد أَوشَكَ الحَبلُ أَن يَنبَتِرْ
فَقَرّبتَ مِن حَظّهِم ما نَأى   وَصَفّيتَ مِن شُربِهِم ما كَدِرْ
وَأَينَ بِكُم عَنهُمُ وَاللِقاءُ   لا عَن تَناءٍ وَلا عَن عُفُرْ
قَرابَتُكُم بَل أَشِقّاؤُكُم   وَإِخوَتُكُم دونَ هَذا البَشَرْ
ومَنْ هُمْ وأنْتُمْ يَدا نُصْرَةٍ   وحَدّا حُسامٍ قديمِ الأُثُرْ
يُشادُ بِتَقديمِكُم في الكِتابِ   وَتُتْلى فَضائِلُكُم في السُوَرْ
وَإِنّ عَلِيّاً لأَولى بِكُم   وَأَزكى يَداً عِندَكُم مِن عُمَرْ
وَكُلٌّ لَهُ فَضلُهُ وَالحُجو   لُ يَومَ التَفاضُلِ دونَ الغُرَرْ
بَقِيتَ إِمامَ الهُدى لِلهُدى   تُجَدِّدُ مِن نَهجِهِ ما دَثَرْ

pp. 157–60

[قال البحتري من الخفيف]

صُنْتُ نَفسي عَمّا يُدَنِّسُ نَفسي   وَتَرَفَّعتُ عَن جَدا كُلِّ جِبسِ
وَتَماسَكتُ حينَ زَعزَعَني الدَهـ   ـرُ إِلتِماساً مِنهُ لِتَعسي وَنَكسي
بُلَغٌ مِن صُبابَةِ العَيشِ عِندي   طَفَّفَتها الأَيّامُ تَطفيفَ بَخسِ
وَبَعيدٌ مابَينَ وارِدِ رِفَهٍ   عَلَلٍ شُربُهُ وَوارِدِ خِمسِ
وَكَأَنَّ الزَمانَ أَصبَحَ مَحمو   لاً هَواهُ مَعَ الأَخَسِّ الأَخَسِّ
وَاشتِرائي العِراقَ خُطَّةُ غَبْنٍ   بَعدَ بَيعي الشَآمَ بَيْعَةَ وَكسِ
لاتَرُزني مُزاوِلاً لِإِختِباري   بَعدَ هَذي البَلوى فَتُنكِرَ مَسّي
وَقَديماً عَهِدتَني ذا هَناتٍ   آبِياتٍ عَلى الدَنِيّاتِ شُمسِ
وَلَقَد رابَني اِبنُ عَمّي   بَعدَ لينٍ مِن جانِبَيهِ وَأُنسِ
وَإِذا ماجُفيتُ كُنتُ جَديراً   أَن أَرى غَيرَ مُصبِحٍ حَيثُ أُمسي
حَضَرَت رَحلِيَ الهُمومُ فَوَجَّهـ   ـتُ إِلى أَبيَضَ المَدائِنِ عَنسي
أَتَسَلّى عَنِ الحُظوظِ وَآسى   لِمَحَلٍّ مِن آلِ ساسانَ دَرسِ
أَذكَرَتنيهِمُ الخُطوبُ التَوالي   وَلَقَد تُذكِرُ الخُطوبُ وَتُنسي
وَهُمُ خافِضونَ في ظِلِّ عالٍ   مُشرِفٍ يَحسِرُ العُيونَ وَيُخسي
مُغلَقٍ بابُهُ عَلى جَبَلِ القَبـ   ـقِ إِلى دارَتَي خِلاطَ وَمُكسِ
حِلَلٌ لَم تَكُن كَأَطلالِ سُعدى   في قِفارٍ مِنَ البَسابِسِ مُلسِ
وَمَساعٍ لَولا المُحاباةُ مِنّي   لَم تُطِقها مَسعاةُ عَنسٍ وَعَبسِ
نَقَلَ الدَهرُ عَهدَهُنَّ عَنِ   الجِدَّةِ حَتّى رَجَعنَ أَنضاءَ لُبسِ
فَكَأَنَّ الجِرمازَ مِن عَدَمِ الأُنـ   ـسِ وَإِخلالِهِ بَنِيَّةُ رَمسِ
لَو تَراهُ عَلِمتَ أَنَّ اللَيالي   جَعَلَت فيهِ مَأتَماً بَعدَ عُرسِ
وَهوَ يُنبيكَ عَن عَجائِبِ قَومٍ   لايُشابُ البَيانُ فيهِم بِلَبسِ

وَإِذا مارَأَيتَ صورَةَ أَنطا   كِيَّةَ إرتَعتَ بَينَ رومٍ وَفُرسِ
وَالمَنايا مَواثِلٌ وَأَنوشَر   وانَ يُزجى الصُفوفَ تَحتَ الدِرَفسِ
في اِخضِرارٍ مِنَ اللِباسِ عَلى أَصـ   ـفَرَ يَختالُ في صَبيغَةِ وَرسِ
وَعِراكُ الرِجالِ بَينَ يَدَيهِ   في خُفوتٍ مِنهُم وَإِغماضِ جَرسِ
مِن مُشيحٍ يَهوى بِعامِلِ رُمحٍ   وَمُليحٍ مِنَ السِنانِ بِتُرسِ
تَصِفُ العَينُ أَنَّهُم جِدُّ أَحيا   ءٍ لَهُم بَينَهُم إِشارَةُ خُرسِ
يَغتَلي فيهِم إِرتِيابي حَتّى   تَتَقَرّاهُمُ يَدايَ بِلَمسِ
قَد سَقاني وَلَم يُصَرِّد أَبو الغَو   ثِ عَلى العَسكَرَينِ شَربَةَ خُلسِ
مِن مُدامٍ تَظُنُّها وَهيَ نَجمٌ   ضَوَّأَ اللَيلَ أَو مُجاجَةُ شَمسِ
وَتَراها إِذا أَجَدَّت سُروراً   وَاِرتِياحاً لِلشارِبِ المُتَحَسّي
أُفرِغَت في الزُجاجِ مِن كُلِّ قَلبٍ   فَهيَ مَحبوبَةٌ إِلى كُلِّ نَفسِ
وَتَوَهَّمتُ أَنَّ كِسرى أَبَروِيـ   ـزَ مُعاطِيَّ وَالبَلَهبَذَ أُنسي
حُلُمٌ مُطبِقٌ عَلى الشَكِّ عَيني   أَم أَمانٍ غَيَّرنَ ظَنّي وَحَدسي
وَكَأَنَّ الإيوانَ مِن عَجَبِ الصَنـ   ـعَةِ جَوبٌ في جَنبِ أَرعَنَ جِلسِ
يُتَظَنّى مِنَ الكَآبَةِ إِذ يَبـ   ـدو لِعَينَي مُصَبِّحٍ أَو مُمَسّي
مُزعَجاً بِالفِراقِ عَن أُنسِ إِلفٍ   عَزَّ أَو مُرهَقاً بِتَطليقِ عِرسِ
عَكَسَت حَظَّهُ اللَيالي وَباتَ الـ   ـمُشتَري فيهِ وَهوَ كَوكَبُ نَحسِ
فَهوَ يُبْدي تَجَلُّداً وَعَلَيهِ   كَلكَلٌ مِن كَلاكِلِ الدَهرِ مُرسي
لَم يَعِبهُ أَن بُزَّ مِن بُسُطِ الديـ   ـباجِ وَاِستَلَّ مِن سُتورِ الدِمَقسِ
مُشمَخِرٌّ تَعلو لَهُ شُرُفاتٌ   رُفِعَت في رُؤوسِ رَضوى وَقُدسِ
لابِساتٌ مِنَ البَياضِ فَما تُبْـ   ـصِرُ مِنها إِلّا غَلائِلَ بُرسِ
لَيسَ يُدرى أَصُنعُ إِنسٍ لِجِنٍّ   سَكَنوهُ أَم صُنعُ جِنٍّ لِإِنسِ
غَيرَ أَنّي أَراهُ يَشهَدُ أَن لَم   يَكُ بانيهِ في المُلوكِ بِنِكسِ
فَكَأَنّي أَرى المَراتِبَ وَالقَو   مَ إِذا ما بَلَغتُ آخِرَ حِسّي
وَكَأَنَّ الوُفودَ ضاحينَ حَسرى   مِن وُقوفٍ خَلفَ الزِحامِ وَخُنسِ

وَكَأَنَّ القِيانَ وَسطَ المَقاصِيـ   ـرِ يُرَجِّعنَ بَينَ حُوٍ وَلُعسِ
وَكَأَنَّ اللِقاءَ أَوَّلَ مِن أَمْـ   ـسِ وَوَشكَ الفِراقِ أَوَّلَ أَمسِ
وَكَأَنَّ الذي يُريدُ اِتِّباعاً   طامِعٌ في لُحوقِهِم صُبحَ خَمسِ
عُمِّرَت لِلسُرورِ دَهراً فَصارَت   لِلتَعَزّي رِباعُهُم وَالتَأَسّي
فَلَها أَن أُعينَها بِدُموعٍ   موقَفاتٍ عَلى الصَبابَةِ حُبسِ
ذاكَ عِندي وَلَيسَت الدارُ داري   بِاِقتِرابٍ مِنها وَلا الجِنسُ جِنسي
غَيرَ نُعمى لِأَهلِها عِندَ أَهلي   غَرَسوا مِن زَكائِها خَيرَ غَرسِ
أَيَّدوا مُلكَنا وَشَدّوا قُواهُ   بِكُماةٍ تَحتَ السَنَّورِ حُمسِ
وَأَعانوا عَلى كَتائِبِ أَرِيا   طَ بِطَعنٍ عَلى النُحورِ وَدَعسِ
وَأَراني مِن بَعدُ أَكلَفُ بِالأَشـ   ـرافِ طُرّاً مِن كُلِّ سِنخٍ وَأُسِّ

p. 177

[قال البحتري من الكامل]

أَتُرى الزَمانُ يُعيدُ لي أَيّامي   بَينَ القُصورِ البيضِ وَالآطامِ
إِذ لا الوِصالُ بِخُلسَةٍ فيهِم وَلا   فَرطُ اللِقاءِ لَدَيهِمُ بِلِمامِ
ساعاتُ لَهوٍ ما تَجَدَّدَ ذِكرُها   إِلّا تَجَدَّدَ عِندَ ذاكَ غَرامي
وَهَوىً مِنَ الأَهواءِ باتَ مُؤَرِّقي   فَكَأَنَّهُ سَقَمٌ مِنَ الأَسقامِ

p. 178

[قال البحتري من المتقارب]

تَغَيَّرَ أَو حالَ عَن عَهدِهِ   وَأَضمَرَ غَدراً وَلَم يُبدِهِ
مَليءٌ بِأَن يَستَرِقَّ القُلو   بَ عَلى هَزلِهِ وَعَلى جِدِّهِ
وَأَن يوجَدَ السِحرُ في طَرفِهِ   وَأَن يُجتَنى الوَردُ مِن خَدِّهِ
يَشِفُّ القُلوبَ وَإِن أَكذَبَ الـ   ـظُنونَ وَأَخلَفَ في وَعدِهِ
بِما أَشبَهَ البَدرَ مِن حُسنِهِ   وَما شاكَلَ الغُصنَ مِن قَدِّهِ

p. 182

[قال محمد أبو العنبس الصَيْمَري من السريع]

يا وَحْشَةَ الدنيا على جعفرٍ   على الهمام الملك الأزهر
على قتيل من بني هاشمٍ   بين سرير الملك والمنبر
والله رب البيت والمَشْعَر   والله لو أن قتل البحتري
لثارَ بالشامِ له ثائرٌ   في ألف بغل من بني عض خرى
يَقْدُمُهُم كلّ أخي ذلة   على حمار دابر أعور

Notes

Introduction

1. Randel, "Lost in Translation," 16.
2. Glassie, *Passing the Time in Ballymenone,* 12.
3. Ibid.
4. Herder, *Against Pure Reason,* 46.
5. Jayyusi, *The Literature of Modern Arabia,* 10.
6. For more on the importance of literary imagination in public life, see Nussbaum, *Poetic Justice*; Rawls, *A Theory of Justice*; and Booth, *The Company We Keep.* While I would not subscribe to the Aristotelian notion that literature ought to adhere to principles of ethics, lest it corrupt the soul and society, I do agree with these authors that the act of interpreting cultivates ethics, empathy, and cognitive maturity.
7. The term *tradition* has many connotations and serves multiple uses, as Ben-Amos observes in his article "The Seven Strands of Tradition." In this study, I use it in three senses pertinent to the context: *tradition as canon* (selected ancestral knowledge considered authoritative), *tradition as process* (transmitted and transferred), and *tradition as performance* (summoned and reformed in performance). I propose to circumvent the supposed dichotomy

between tradition (stable) and performance (changing) by following Hymes's lead, which stresses the importance of performance for the aesthetic enjoyment of tradition ("Breakthrough into Performance," 19).

As a matter of practice, I have systematically avoided four senses: *tradition as mass* (inherited baggage passively transmitted), *tradition as culture* (synchronically shared traits without link to the past), *tradition as* langue (an abstract but malleable code or a system of rules by which people generate cultural performances), and *tradition as lore* (short narrations). See also Glassie, "Tradition," for comments on tradition in contrast to "heritage," "history," and "culture."

8. The oldest continuous literary traditions emerged from the great agrarian-trade imperial systems of the world that prospered along the major river valleys in the temperate zones of Africa and Asia. The two most comparable examples are the Chinese (*wenyan wen*) and Sanskrit traditions, which are about a millennium older than the Arabic literary tradition. They differ from Arabic in other important ways, though. Both *wenyan wen* and Sanskrit have historically been considered distinct languages, not dialects or registers, compared to the vernaculars and colloquials of their respective social contexts. Classical literary Arabic, however, figures as a dialect or register compared to various Arabic colloquials. The continuity of literary Arabic is worth noting, not for any argument of ethnocentric pride, but rather for the humanistic puzzle posed by a literary tradition that remains relatively comprehensible across three continents and over a millennium and a half.

9. Throughout this book, several studies on the *marzēaḥ* (found in the Near East, beginning in 1400 B.C. at Ugarit) and the *symposion* (found in ancient Greece) influence the course of the discussion. For the *marzēaḥ,* I have relied on Matthäus, "Greek Symposion and the Near East"; Beach, "Samaria Ivories, Marzeah, and Biblical Text"; Carter, "Thiasos and Marzeah"; Bordereuil and Pardee, "Le papyrus du marzeah"; Ackerman, "A Marzeah in Ezekiel 8:7–13?"; and Greenfield, "Marzeah as a Social Institution." For the *symposion,* I have relied on Murray, "Symposion as Social Organisation"; Murray, *Early Greece*; Murray, *Sympotica*; Steiner, "Private and Public"; McNiven, "Watching My Boyfriend with His Girlfriend"; and Pope, "Divine Banquet at Ugarit." Much of what we might consider Hellenic or Hellenistic was influenced by perpetual ties with the Near East during the Geometric period (900–700 B.C.) and Alexander the Great's (d. 323 B.C.) expansion of empire eastward into the Middle East and Central Asia, where major principles of social organization and ritual emerged in the fourth millennium B.C.—more than three thousand years before Classical Greece. My aim in this book is to highlight Greek and Middle Eastern studies that illustrate the

interconnections between Greece and the Near East both after and before Alexander. See also Kuhrt and Sherwin-White, *Hellenism in the East.*

10. In this study, I use *myth, mythology,* and *mythic* to characterize a type of narrative or group of narratives that relate or allude to the activities of a culture's sacral figures. As one definition has it, "These narratives are the product of communal and (often) sacred impulses to sanction and reflect the cultural order existing at the time of their creation . . . [and] they arouse . . . large-scale beliefs concerning either their veracity or meaningfulness" (Vickery, *New Princeton Handbook of Poetic Terms*). In addition, the category of myth is important in the realm of Middle Eastern literary studies where nineteenth- and twentieth-century Orientalists have scowled at the magical and supernatural aspects of narrative to the point of finding mythic references ridiculous or meaningless, at a time when Europe was rediscovering the supernatural in the form of the Grimms' tales, Roman and Greek mythology, *Beowulf,* and the *Nibelungenlied.* Note, for example, Nöldeke's unfortunate dismissal of the *Iranian Book of Kings* because the protagonist Rostam could not by any stretch have eaten a horse by himself or lifted a house over his head (*The Iranian National Epic*). Thus, one of my purposes for using the idea of myth is to recognize the literary appropriateness of the supernatural in sacral narratives and move toward a pragmatic interpretation. As Vickery notes, we should expect "fifty-headed monsters, shape-shifting deities, talking animals, descent into the underworld, chariot-drawn flights through the sky"; they "attest to myth's characteristic concern with experiences beyond the normal and natural" (*New Princeton Handbook of Poetic Terms,* 198).

11. The "great divide" theory of orality-literacy has been promoted principally by Ong (*Orality and Literacy*) and countered by Finnegan (*Literacy and Orality*).

one Literary Salons: From Ancient *Symposion* to Arabic *Mujālasāt*

1. The Abbasid era, fortunately, appeals to Arabs and Muslims of secular, religious, and fundamentalist temperaments because it can be cast in myriad ways to lend credibility to competing visions of the future. While fundamentalist regimes, like the Saudis, have their own conservative vision and interpretation of the Abbasid era, which expurgates its bacchic and hedonic aspects, surprisingly, it does serve as a model of society and government since it embodied the ideals of the caliphate. See Davidson, *Islamic Fundamentalism,* 53.

2. Wolfart Heinrichs charts the development of the concept of *^{c}ulūm ^{c}arabiyya* from the tenth to thirteenth centuries in the works of several medieval intellectuals. Until the eleventh century, there does not seem to be a formalized sense of *^{c}ulūm ^{c}arabiyya* that includes both religious (*dīnī*) and humanistic (*adabī*) knowledge, which suggests that *adab* might have developed as an alternative educational ideal distinct from those that were more religious (Heinrichs, "Classification of the Sciences and the Consolidation of Philology in Classical Islam," 119–39). In effect, as early as the mid-eighth century we see a literary-social ideal of *adab* and *ta'addub* (humanistic formation, education) centered on Arabic language (lexicography, syntax, morphology) and literature (including both *akhbār*-based prose, such as biography and history, and poetry), but it was not until the eleventh century that *adabī* and *dīnī* came to complement each other under the common rubric *^{c}ulūm ^{c}arabiyya.* See also Makdisi, *Rise of Humanism,* 89.

3. Makdisi, *Rise of Colleges,* 75–80. The historian Joel L. Kraemer (*Humanism in the Renaissance of Islam,* 10) notes that other terms were used for remembered knowledge, such as "knowledge of the forebears" (*^{c}ulūm al-awā^{c}il*), "knowledge of the Arabs" (*^{c}ulūm al-^{c}arab*), and "knowledge of humanities" (*^{c}ulūm al-insāniyyah*). Ibn Khaldūn also refers to Arabic knowledge with the phrase "speech of the Arabs" (*kalām al-^{c}Arab*), in *Muqaddima,* 1026.

4. Ibn Khaldūn, *Muqaddima,* 1025–26.

5. The term *adab* is discussed more fully later. In short, though, the term is complex and multifaceted, much like *discipline* or *school of thought: adab* can simultaneously or singly denote (1) a body of knowledge, (2) a particular genre of narrative (*akhbār*) literature, or (3) an appealing manner of thinking and behaving.

6. The exact content of *adab* knowledge varied by time and place, but it seems universally to have included poetry (*shi^{c}r*) and narrative of some sort (*sīra, akhbār, tārikh*). See Makdisi, *Rise of Humanism,* 89–94. That is to say, *adab* might include or exclude the supporting studies, such as grammar, lexicography, etymology, morphology, prosody, rhyme, or genealogy, but at a minimum it had to include the textual substance of the humanities, poetry and narrative. For reference to new poetry recited in *mujālasāt,* see al-Ṣūlī, *Akhbār Abī Tammām,* 14–16.

7. Makdisi, *Rise of Humanism,* 51–52; Najar, *La mémoire rassemblée,* 155–57.

8. Makdisi, *Rise of Humanism,* 48.

9. Ibid., 53–54.

10. Ibid., 54–59.

11. Ibid., 64–66. Note that the demand for chancery employees, as early as the eighth century, meant that participants in *adabī* culture had established the curricula and venues to train secretaries, as well as the standards for professional competence, long before participants in *dīnī* culture. For more on the cultural battles between the champions of *adab* and *dīn,* see Ali, "Early Islam—Monotheism or Henotheism?"

12. Makdisi, *Rise of Humanism,* 60–64.

13. Brookshaw, "Palaces, Pavilions and Pleasure-gardens," 200.

14. Ms. Spr. 1216, f. 12a. I have preferred the phrasing of the Berlin manuscript over the printed edition because the crucial last sentence of this quotation does not appear in my 1881 printed edition: Nawājī, *Ḥalbat al-Kumayt,* 20.

15. Lane, *Arabic-English Lexicon,* s.v. "s-m-r," "ḥ-ḍ-r," "dh-k-r," and "j-l-s"; Hava, *Al-Farāʾid al-Durriyyah,* s.v. "s-m-r," "ḥ-ḍ-r," "dh-k-r," "j-l-s," and "n-d-m." I have endeavored to discern substantive differences in the usage of the four terms *mudhākara, musāmara, mujālasāt,* and *munādama,* to no avail. Although each root foregrounds slightly different activity, they all amount to literary assemblies with implied banqueting and drinking at night. The one possible exception might be *munādama;* some piety-minded scholars might avoid using a term that explicitly denotes wine drinking on the grounds that they deem it taboo or indiscreet.

16. For recent scholarship on literary gatherings in more hierarchical settings, see Bencheikh's *Poétique arabe,* which examines gatherings at the courts of caliphs and state officials where poets or their designees perform for an elite audience; as well as Gruendler, *Medieval Arabic Praise Poetry* and "Motif vs. Genre." Najar, *La mémoire rassemblée,* 155–62, further delineates a variety of exclusive gatherings limited to caliphs, courtiers, and poets. This book focuses primarily on the nature and character of the egalitarian *mujālasāt,* often involving amateurs only, and their impact on the formation of a literary canon. I owe a debt to al-Karkhī, *Majālis al-Adab,* and Webber, *Romancing the Real.* Webber has worked on the *mujālasāt* in the modern era.

17. Abū Ḥayyān al-Tawḥīdī, *Kitāb al-Imtāᶜ wal-Muʾānasa.*

18. Al-Ṣūlī, *Akhbār al-Buḥturī wa Dhayl al-Akhbār.*

19. Al-Dīnawarī, *Kitāb al-Mujālasa wa-Jawāhir al-ᶜIlm.*

20. Al-Tanūkhī, *Nishwār al-Muḥāḍara wa-Akhbār al-Mudhākara.*

21. Al-Zamakhsharī, *Rabīᶜ al-Abrār wa-Nuṣūṣ al-Akhbār.*

22. Al-Amāsī, *Rawḍ al-Akhyār al-Muntakhab.*

23. Ibn al-ᶜArabī, *Kitāb Muḥāḍarat al-Abrār wa-Musāmarāt al-Akhyār fil-Adabiyyāt wal-Nawādir wal-Akhbār.*

24. Al-Ḥanbalī, *Nuzhat al-Musāmir fī Akhbār Majnūn Banī[c] Āmir* and *Nuzhat al-Musāmir fī Akhbār Laylā al-Akhyāliyya.*

25. Al-Suyūṭī, *Al-Wasā'il ilā Musāmarāt al-Awā'il.*

26. Nestorianism was a sect of Christianity that was well established in Iran and Central Asia in the ninth and tenth centuries. Nestorians stressed that Christ's two natures, the divine and the human, were independent, as two people in a dance. This was in contrast to the Jacobites of Egypt and Syria, who believed in two natures in one unified person. Not surprisingly, Nestorius was condemned by the councils of Ephesus (431) and Chalcedon (451), and his teachings branded a heresy. See Kidd, *A History of the Church to A.D. 461,* vol. 3. The Nestorian embrace of two independent natures enabled clergy and laity to sanctify the more carnal, sensual dimensions of mortal life. For tales of festivities at Nestorian monasteries in ninth- and tenth-century Iraq, see al-Shābushtī, *Kitāb al-Diyārāt.*

27. Joffe, "Alcohol and Social Complexity in Ancient Western Asia."

28. Reade, "*Symposion* in Ancient Mesopotamia," 38.

29. Ibid., 40.

30. Ibid.

31. Greenfield, "Marzeah as a Social Institution."

32. Carter, "Thiasos and Marzeah."

33. Amos 6:4–7 (NRSV).

34. Beach, "Samaria Ivories, Marzeah, and Biblical Text"; Carter, "Thiasos and Marzeah."

35. Greenfield, "Marzeah as a Social Institution"; Carter, "Thiasos and Marzeah"; and Pope, "Divine Banquet at Ugarit."

36. Greenfield, "Marzeah as a Social Institution"; Ackerman, "A Marzeah in Ezekiel 8:7–13?"

37. Carter, "Thiasos and Marzeah."

38. Ibid.

39. Boardman, "Symposion Furniture"; Carter, "Thiasos and Marzeah."

40. Morris, "Art of Citizenship"; Murray, *Early Greece,* 19–21.

41. Carter, "Thiasos and Marzeah."

42. Murray, *Early Greece,* 207–13.

43. Murray, *Sympotica,* 6.

44. Ibid., 6–7; Murray, *Early Greece,* 207.

45. Murray, *Early Greece,* 208.

46. Murray, *Sympotica,* 7.

47. Nagy, *Pindar's Homer,* 435–37; Nagy, *Poetry as Performance,* n85.

48. Reade, "*Symposion* in Ancient Mesopotamia," 40.

49. Boardman, "Symposion Furniture."

50. Peters, *Harvest of Hellenism,* 121, 128, 595, 699; al-Shābushtī, *Kitāb al-Diyārāt*; Mohammadi, "University of Jundishapur in the First Centuries of the Islamic Period."

51. Ibn Abī Uṣaybiʿa, *Kitāb Ṭabaqāt al-Aṭṭibāʾ,* 2:109–26.

52. Brockelmann, *Geschichte der arabischen Litteratur,* 2:486.

53. Ms. Esc. 1708., fols. 51r/v. The text in Arabic reads: "*hawaytu mudhākarat al-aḥbāb wa musāmarat dhawī al-ʿuqūl wal-albāb fa-kunnā naqʿudu lil-samar fī layālī al-qamar wa-naltaqiṭ min al-afwāh janīy al-thamar wa-lā namillu al-sahar ilā al-saḥar wa-idhā tajādabnā ṭirf al-ḥadīth tawridunā ẓarf al-qadīm wal-ḥadīth uʿjiba kull minnā bi-mā jāb wa-uʿizza bi-mā jāb . . . fa-akhadha kull minnā yufiḍ mā fīhī wa-ṭābahu wa-yuʿjib al-ḥāḍirīn bi-faḍl khiṭābihi.*"

54. Bauman, *Story, Performance, and Event,* 3, 39; Bauman, *Verbal Art as Performance,* 39–40; Lord, *Singer of Tales,* 16.

55. Al-Shābushtī, *Kitāb al-Diyārāt,* 16–17; al-Jāḥiẓ, *Kitāb al-Tāj fī Akhlāq al-Mulūk,* 32–42. Cf. Bauman, *Verbal Art as Performance,* 43.

56. Al-Shābushtī, *Kitāb al-Diyārāt,* 17–18.

57. Al-Ṣūlī, *Akhbār al-Buḥturī wa Dhayl al-Akhbār,* 80.

58. Al-Jāḥiẓ, *Kitāb al-Tāj fī Akhlāq al-Mulūk,* 36. Note also al-Ḥasan b. Rajāʾ responding to Abū Tammām with interjections, compliments, and standing in honor of the poet, who then stood as well to reciprocate the gesture and then finally embraced the poet. See al-Ṣūlī, *Akhbār Abī Tammām,* 168–70.

59. Al-Jāḥiẓ, *Kitāb al-Tāj fī Akhlāq al-Mulūk,* 42.

60. Al-Ṣūlī, *Akhbār al-Buḥturī wa Dhayl al-Akhbār,* 82–83, 94–95; al-Jāḥiẓ, *Kitāb al-Tāj fī Akhlāq al-Mulūk,* 32–42. For the pensive look and examples of caustic reactions that were probably embarrassing to the performer, see al-Ṣūlī, *Akhbār Abī Tammām,* 106, 250–53.

61. Bauman, *Verbal Art as Performance,* 45.

62. Nykl, *Historia de los amores de Bayad y Riyad,* 4–5, 16.

63. The following architectural information comes from fieldwork conducted by the author and a reference widely used by scholars of Islamic architecture, ArchNet: http://archnet.org/library/images/.

64. Al-Tanūkhī, *Al-Mustajād min Fiʿlāt al-Ajwād,* 199–201.

65. Ibn Shams al-Khilāfa Mujidd al-Mulk, *Kitāb al-Ādāb,* 29.

TWO *Adab* Principles for Artistic Speech in Assembly

1. The debate over the operative meanings of *adab* has revolved around the two senses of the word: first, *adab* as a content matter, a corpus

of exemplary manners (*sunna*) in pre-Islamic times, then texts, as well as a set of likely literary subjects; and second, *adab* as form or style, which meets standards of elegance and complexity, thus making it a kind of strategy for composition. See the 1910–11 Cairo lectures of Nallino, *Tarīkh al-Ādāb al-ᶜArabiyya min al-Jāhiliyya ḥattā ᶜAṣr Banī Umayya,* 1–40. Gustave von Grunebaum and Régis Blachère have both emphasized the concept of *adab* as an approach or a style; see Grunebaum, *Medieval Islam,* 255; and Blachère, "Un auteur d'Adab oublié," 46. When the debate moved away from the criteria of form or content, Ilse Lichtenstädter in 1943 affirmed the diversity of *adab* materials but added a more functional dimension to the definition: "Adab covers a variety of literary works dealing with a great number of heterogeneous topics, and almost the only factor that they have in common is their intention of bringing knowledge to the people in an entertaining manner" (Lichtenstädter, "On the Conception of Adab," 33–34). Charles Pellat augmented the functional aim of *adab,* stating that it ought to achieve the "formation of the average Muslims in the domains of religion, morals and culture," in his "Variations sur le thème de l'adab," 25. The effect of these definitions is to argue that the goal of education is to educate, which of course appears circular. Similarly, S. A. Bonebakker tells us that *adab* was the "scholarship of an educated man," in "Adab and the Concept of Belles-Lettres," 20. Fedwa Malti-Douglas contributed by examining the stylistic and organizational patterns that render certain monographic *adab* works *adab,* in her 1985 book, *Structures of Avarice.* The limitation of these definitions is that they fundamentally overlook or underestimate the influence of external validation in face-to-face performance at *adab* assembly and that performance qualities and effects were critical to making *adab* a category of emergent verbal art. Thus these definitions help us to determine what makes a text worthy of the descriptor *adab* in retrospect, but they tell us nothing about how a littérateur would have known *adab* if he or she saw it. Therefore, these definitions are not useful for understanding *adab* as an artistic form that emerges anew and reformulates structures in social interaction. The generative and regenerative aspects of *adab* speech are lost. Without some consideration of interaction and performance, it is also difficult to recognize how a subgenre like *mujūn* (bacchic-comic) literature, which can be bawdy, bodily, and sometimes grotesque, enters the canons of *adab.*

2. Hava, *Al-Farāʾid al-Durriyyah,* s.v. "aʾ-d-b." Lane, *Arabic-English Lexicon,* s.v. "aʾ-d-b."

3. Al-ᶜĀmirī, *Kitāb al-Iᶜlām bi-Manāqib al-Islām,* 96.

4. Makdisi, *Rise of Humanism,* 90. The scholar Abdelwahab Bouhdiba observes that Shahrazad, the heroine of the *Thousand and One Nights,*

illustrates and reaps the efficacy of such knowledge. She is a living encyclopedia who puts herself into social action. Through her knowledge of anecdotes, poetry, astronomy, *fiqh,* biography, and human history, she enchants the deranged king, despite standing orders to kill her, thereby delaying her own execution. More than buying time, however, night after night Shahrazad gradually converts her husband from a deranged misogynist to a responsive man with a diet of storytelling full of wonder (*Sexuality in Islam,* 134).

5. Makdisi, *Rise of Humanism,* 89–93, 104, 132, 161–70.

6. Such *adab*-minded histories are the norm, not the exception. Consider the poetically titled *Murūj al-Dhahab* (Meadows of Gold) by al-Masᶜūdī, which also counts as a compendium of Arabo-Islamic cosmology, geographic lore, proverbs, tribal rituals, animal and plant folklore, Arabian legend, apropos proverbs, and poems.

7. For more on the infancy of Islamic historiography, including the precarious position that historians occupied, see Robinson, *Islamic Historiography,* 3–8. Note in particular Robinson's characterization of historiography before any prestige that accrued in the modern era: "Almost to a man, Muslim historians made their living doing something other than history, especially tutoring, teaching . . . and writing—everything from copying out books to drafting letters for a patron. In fact . . . for much of the classical period, historians kept their *heads low,* choosing to follow the cultural and academic patterns set by those who did enjoy enormous social authority" (emphasis added).

8. The wonder and lyricism I mention can be witnessed in the way that poets spoke of human ruins and remains (literal and figurative). Consider, for example, Labīd's verse: "Rains reveal remains like / Palimpsests; their pens renew their texts" (*Muᶜallaqa of Labīd,* l. 8). And Abū Tammām's reflection: "It's in the nature of ruins not to answer, / so it's right for eyes to tear. / Go ahead, ask. Make your tears an answer. / You'll find that passion asks and answers" (*Dīwān Abū Tammām bi-Sharḥ al-Khaṭīb al-Tabrīzī,* 1:158).

9. There is at least one notable exception, where the historian Ibn ᶜAsākir (d. 1176) gingerly includes a list of Turkic soldiers who accompanied the caliph al-Mutawakkil to Damascus, thus debunking the widely held public notion that the caliph went there to flee his soldiers. See Paul Cobb's erudite article "Al-Muwakkil's Damascus." Until Cobb's article, however, Ibn ᶜAsākir's list seems to have had little or no impact on public perception of al-Mutawakkil's trip to Damascus, thus demonstrating the absence of appetite in medieval Islamic society for unartistic presentations of the past.

10. Noth, *Early Arabic Historical Tradition,* 6, 24.

11. The source-critical approach to *akhbār*-narratives is no straw man employed here to force an argument. Middle Eastern scholars remain di-

vided about how to use and interpret *akhbār*-narratives, whether in the discipline of history or literary studies. In the wake of postmodernist reflections on the ideologies and projects of the twentieth century, source-critical approaches have lost their luster in other branches of the modern humanities and social sciences, as evidenced by the "linguistic turn" in Kenneth Burke, *Permanence and Change* and *Attitudes toward History*; Hayden White, *Tropics of Discourse* and *The Content of the Form*; Natalie Zemon Davis, *Fiction in the Archives*; and Martin Kreiswirth, "Tell Me a Story." These theorists have reconfigured and problematized the modernist distinctions between history, reality (supposed fact), and literature (supposed fiction). And for once, theory was ahead of culture, prefiguring the rise of intermixed narratives that blur the distinction between myth and reality, such as the modern categories of historical fiction, science fiction, and magical realism, not to mention edutainment, entertainment news, and Jon Stewart's "fake news." However, the field of classical Arabic literature and historiography seems to be unsure about the linguistic turn. The modernist school, which has its roots in European Orientalism of the nineteenth century, is motivated by a need to reconstruct what actually happened (positivism) by taking *akhbār* sources to be historical, quasi-historical, or pseudohistorical, based on degrees of "reliability" and "authenticity." The debate over "historicity" has yielded two major positivist camps. First are those who consider Arabo-Islamic historiography a salvation narrative (*Heilsgeschichte*), and thus to them the whole Arabic enterprise is biased in favor of a particular ideology. These scholars use the source-critical approach to winnow the majority and reject all but a few "facts" (Conrad/Noth, Michael Cook, Patricia Crone). The second camp appreciates a good yarn with its literary indulgences, which can be examined on a case-by-case basis, but sees *akhbār*-sources, especially "history works," as largely accurate and referentially truthful, with rare fanciful exceptions. This camp is represented in the scholarship of Fred Donner, *The Early Islamic Conquests* and *Narratives of Islamic Origins*; ᶜAbd al-ᶜAzīz Dūrī, *The Rise of Historical Writing among the Arabs*; and Michael Morony, *Iraq after the Muslim Conquest.* Literary scholarship on Arabic *akhbār*-narrative sources also follows this line, such as Wolfhart Heinrichs, "Prosimetrical Genres in Classical Arabic Literature"; Hilary Kilpatrick, "The Genuine Ashᶜab"; Joseph Sadan, "An Admirable and Ridiculous Hero" and "Hārūn al-Rashīd and the Brewer"; Andras Hamori, "Tinkering with the Text"; and Stefan Leder, "Prosa-Dichtung in der akhbār Überlieferung," "Authorship and Transmission in Unauthored Literature," "Features of the Novel in Early Historiography," "The Literary Use of *Khabar*," and "Conventions of Fictional Narration in Learned Literature." Whereas the mainstream of academia has come to view narrative as an "instance of the mind," as innate to being as thought and breathing, modernist approaches to narrative fundamentally view narrative as a "product" or an "artifact" of history (Kreiswirth, "Tell Me a Story," 70). In practice, positivists mine narrative for facts and details representing actual people, places, and events, while the mainstream of academia interprets narratives as storied evaluations of people, places, and events. In short they do not represent the past but illustrate an interested reaction to it.

In response to positivist scholarship, a postmodernist trend in Middle East scholarship can be seen in the work of Marilyn Waldman, *Toward a Theory of Historical Narrative* and "'The Otherwise Unnoteworthy Year 711'"; Suzanne Stetkevych, *Mute Immortals Speak* and *Poetics of Islamic Legitimacy*; Paul Cobb, "Al-Mutawakkil's Damascus" and *White Banners*; Tayyib El-Hibri, *Reinterpreting Islamic Historiography*; Julie Meisami, *Persian Historiography to the End of the Twelfth Century*; Chase Robinson, *Islamic Historiography*; Beatrice Gruendler, "Meeting the Patron" and "Verse and Taxes"; and Samer Ali, "Singing Samarra (861–956)." These authors consider the literary devices present in *akhbār* sources not as indulgences but as narrative strategies inherent to thought and communication that must be decoded and interpreted. Perhaps the earliest leader in this vein was the late Marshall Hodgson in *The Venture of Islam.* His magisterial study of Islamic history is widely recognized for its Weberian concern for material conditions (a response to Orientalist essentialisms about spirit and nature) that shape history, but less widely appreciated for his uncanny sensitivity to the persisting power of linguistic and literary constructs to shape perceptions *and* realities (a rejoinder to Orientalist dismissals of indigenous rhetoric and artistry). The "narrative turn" that Kreiswirth examines—the shift from viewing narrative as a receptacle of information and structures to a medium for interpreting and understanding the people, places, and events the produce them—this has yet to become the norm in Middle Eastern studies ("Tell Me a Story"). The situation raises compelling questions about why the field has remained disconnected from broader debates in the humanities and social sciences.

12. Toorawa, *Ibn Abi Tahir Tayfur and Arabic Writerly Culture,* documents many instances of reliance on paper and the practice of self-study, which he argues replaced orality. For empirical field research that responds to the orality-literacy replacement school, often termed the great divide theory, see Finnegan, *Oral Poetry* and *Literacy and Orality.* In the context of medieval Europe, interdependence of orality and literacy has been documented and analyzed by Carruthers, *The Book of Memory*; and Coleman, *Public Reading and the Reading Public in Late Medieval England and France.* In

the Arabo-Islamic context, see Sprenger, "On the Origin and Progress of Writing Down Historical Facts among the Museulmans" and *Das Leben und die Lehre des Mohammad*; Ahmed, "The Institution of al-Mudhākara"; MacKay, *Certificates of Transmission*; Pedersen, *The Arabic Book*; Makdisi, *Rise of Humanism*; Berkey, *The Transmission of Knowledge in Medieval Cairo*; Chamberlain, *Knowledge and Social Practice in Medieval Damascus*; Gregor Schoeler, "Die Frage der mündlichen oder schriftlichen Überlieferung der Wissenschaften im frühen Islam," "Weiteres zur Frage," "Mündliche Thora und Ḥadīṯ," "Schreiben und Veröffentlichen," "Writing and Publishing," and *The Oral and the Written in Early Islam*; and Gruendler, "Arabic Script" and "Arabic Alphabet." These authors have amply attested to the bimodal interdependence (even interactivation) in the realm of Islamic education, as well as *adab*. Though the orality-literary replacement model fails to reflect social practice, Toorawa's study remains valuable since it documents more consistently than any other a group that promoted books and self-study, at the expense of oral, face-to-face modes of education and accreditation.

13. Note the exceptions in Makdisi, *Rise of Humanism,* 217–29; and Toorawa, *Ibn Abi Tahir Tayfur and Arabic Writerly Culture,* who discusses the bookish leanings of a noted bookmaker.

14. Makdisi, *Rise of Colleges,* 272.

15. Ibid., 342 n. 240. MacKay, *Certificates of Transmission.* Berkey, in his study of Mamluk education in Cairo (*Transmission of Knowledge in Medieval Cairo,* 31), notes that the *ijāza* was open to "abuses," but he does not refute its presence or importance as a certificate for transmitting knowledge. In the Mamluk educational system, *ijāza* remained an emblem of personal contact with a teacher and signified receiving knowledge directly from the teacher's mouth. In contrast, Chamberlain has explained that in medieval Damascus the *ijāza* was more a type of currency in the patron-client relationship that characterized that of the teacher-student (*Knowledge and Social Practice in Medieval Damascus,* 88–89). Rather than a result of examination and learning per se, it was an honor—a "benefit"—bestowed on a student for his devotion (*ḥubb*) and service (*khidma*) to the teacher in the hope that he would promote the teacher's legacy (110–16).

16. Petrosyan et al., *Pages of Perfection,* 36.

17. Ibid. Whereas the largest library in twelfth-century Europe housed a collection of 2,000 volumes, one college library in Baghdad had 10,400 books, the Fatimid royal library in Cairo had 120,000, and that in Cordoba had 150,000 or more (Gibb, *Arabic Literature,* 87; see also Morse, *Truth and Convention,* 23). Private collections, typically signs of status, housed in

Bukhara, Cairo, Cordoba, Damascus, and Shiraz held 10,000 volumes (Petrosyan et al., *Pages of Perfection,* 36). The ubiquity of paper correlates with the proliferation of Qur'an copying, the collection of current and ancestral literature, the translation of foreign works into Arabic, and the production of documents by state secretaries (46).

18. Petrosyan et al., *Pages of Perfection,* 53.

19. Ibid., 51, 53.

20. Ibid., 49.

21. Meyerhof, *Medico-Philosophical Controversy between Ibn Butlan of Baghdad and Ibn Ridwan of Cairo,* 50.

22. Ms. Esc. 1708, fols. 51r/v.

23. For more on the Arabic script, its development and usage, see Gruendler, "Arabic Alphabet," 148–65; and Gruendler, "Arabic Script," 135–44.

24. Meyerhof, *Medico-Philosophical Controversy between Ibn Butlan of Baghdad and Ibn Ridwan of Cairo,* 50–52.

25. Ibn Khaldūn, *Muqaddima,* 1235.

26. Quoted in Makdisi, *Rise of Humanism,* 213.

27. Ibn al-Nadīm, *Al-Fihrist,* 215; cf. Bulliet, *Islam,* 19.

28. Hodgson, *The Venture of Islam,* 352.

29. Bulliet, *Islam,* 15.

30. Ibid., 19–21. See Ahmed, "The Institution of the al-Mudhākara." Ahmed describes a more informal session wherein Hadith students would share reports from memory before or after formal class. The institution attests not only to the value placed on memorizing knowledge but also on being able to process it and use it.

31. Al-Ṣūlī, *Akhbār Abī Tammām,* 258: "*inna aḥsana al-ḥadīthi mā aḥdatha bil-qulub ᶜahdan.*"

32. Ibn Khaldūn, *Muqaddima,* 1235.

33. Versteegh, *The Arabic Language,* 55.

34. Ibid. Note also the necessity of public reading as a test of competence but also as a model for others. MacKay, *Certificates of Transmission.*

35. E.g., Bloom and Blair, *Islamic Arts,* 70, 72, 73, 74–75, 76; Hillenbrand, *Islamic Architecture,* 53, 66.

36. Cf. Foley, *Singer of Tales in Performance,* 2: "Time and again the South Slavic guslari questioned by Parry and Lord characterized a word not as a lexeme or a chirographically distinct item, but rather a unit of utterance in performance. The minimal 'atom' in their compositional idiom was the poetic line."

37. *EI*[2], s.v. "Khaṭṭ."

38. Ibn Khaldūn, *Muqaddima,* 1246.

39. See Makdisi, *Rise of Humanism,* 202–7, for the myriad ways in which students and teachers would cultivate memory capacity, as well as the ability to understand and manipulate knowledge in assembly.

40. Al-Shābushtī's *Kitāb al-Diyārāt* is organized according to places—monasteries primarily in Iraq. Each chapter focuses not on the monastery but on a particular personality related to the monastery. People are indexed by places, but that becomes a mere pretext for segues into the narratives of their lives. As the medievalist Mary Carruthers has noted, indexing people by places illustrates an organizational scheme for ordering an unruly cache of cultural information; moreover, the "shock value" of bawdy and rambunctious behavior at the monastery festivals aids memory (Carruthers, *The Book of Memory,* 129–31, 137). Note also Gruendler's argument that the *Kitāb al-Maᶜānī* of al-ᶜAskarī was organized as a mnemonic aid according to subjects that would befit a salon session. Manuscripts that have survived present themselves as accessible manuals (Gruendler, "Motif vs. Genre").

41. Al-Shābushtī, *Kitāb al-Diyārāt,* 79.

42. Ms. We. 1100, passim.

43. Ibn al-ᶜArabī, *Kitāb Muḥāḍarat al-Abrār,* 1:9.

44. Al-Ṣūlī, *Akhbār Abī Tammām,* 70, mentions one amateur littérateur who *might* have been deaf, Muḥammad b. Saᶜīd al-Aṣamm, who "narrates" an anecdote to a colleague from another colleague, but it is not clear how he would have "heard" the anecdote or "recited" it if the hearing impairment left a speech impediment. I personally know of no other cases of deaf or aphonic (aphasic) littérateurs, whether professional or amateur.

45. Al-Ṣūlī, *Akhbār Abī Tammām,* 89–93, 59–61.

46. Ibid., 258.

47. Ibid., 250.

48. Ibid., 137.

49. Ibid., 192.

50. For the ways in which the carpe diem theme was attached to sympotic and funerary practices in ancient Egypt, Greece, Palestine, and Syria, see Grottanelli, "Wine and Death—East and West." In the *Copa,* discussed by Grottanelli, the Syrian innkeeper-temptress presses the point in the voice of Death itself: "Set forth the wine and dice! Away with him who cares about tomorrow! Death plucks your ears and cries: Live; I come!"

51. Ibn Abī Uṣaybiᶜa, *Kitāb Ṭabaqāt al-Aṭṭibā',* 2:251.

52. Al-Buḥturī, *Dīwān,* ode 148. All citations to Al-Buḥturī's poetry are to the al-Ṣayrafī edition (1977), unless noted otherwise.

53. Ibid., ode 44.

54. For more on self-disclosure in the Greek *symposion,* see Rosler, "Wine and Truth in the Greek Symposion."

55. Ibn Rashīq al-Qayrawānī, *Kitāb al-ᶜUmda fī Ṣanᶜat al-Shiᶜr wa Naqdih,* 1:9–10.

56. Gruendler, *Medieval Arabic Praise Poetry,* 6; Kraemer, *Humanism in the Renaissance of Islam,* 4. Note also that in the tale of Bayāḍ and Riyāḍ, the Romeo in this love story is a Damascene merchant's son who happens to be in Andalusia conducting his father's business. See Nykl, *Historia de los amores de Bayad y Riyad,* 12.

57. Al-Ṣūlī, *Akhbār Abī Tammām,* 55, 184. For the cost of books, see Makdisi, *Rise of Humanism,* 70–76.

58. For more on the attribute of being pleasant and charming (*ẓarīf*), see Gruendler, *Medieval Arabic Praise Poetry,* 6.

59. Abū Ḥayyān al-Tawḥīdī, *Kitāb al-Imtāᶜ wal-Muʾānasa*; al-Dīnawarī, *Kitāb al-Mujālasa wa-Jawāhir al-ᶜIlm*; al-Ṣūlī, *Akhbār al-Buḥturī wa Dhayl al-Akhbār, Akhbār Abī Tammām, Akhbār al-Shuᶜarāʾ al-Muḥdathīn min Kitāb al-Awrāq, Ashᶜār Awlād al-Khulafāʾ wa Akhbāruhum min Kitāb al-Awrāq,* and *Akhbār al-Rāḍī bil-Lāh wal-Mutaqī lil-Lāh min Kitāb al-Awrāq*; and al-Tanūkhī, *Nishwār al-Muḥāḍara wa-Akhbār al-Mudhākara* and *Al-Mustajād min Fiᶜlāt al-Ajwād.*

60. Ibn Qutayba, *Al-Maᶜārif,* 2.

61. Cf. Gruendler, *Medieval Arabic Praise Poetry,* 6–9; al-Jāḥiẓ, *Kitāb al-Tāj fī Akhlāq al-Mulūk,* 31–39.

62. Blachère, *Un poète arabe,* 130.

63. Gruendler, *Medieval Arabic Praise Poetry,* 25.

64. Cf. Bauman, *Story, Performance, and Event,* 54.

65. Nagy, *Poetry as Performance,* 61.

66. Ibid., 85.

67. Al-Thaᶜālibī, *Yatīmat al-Dahr fī Maḥāsin Ahl al-ᶜAṣr,* 2:394. The story also appears in Yāqūt b. ᶜAbd Allāh al-Ḥamawī, *Kitāb Irshād al-Arīb fī Maᶜrifat al-Adīb,* 5:334.

68. Abū Ḥayyān al-Tawḥīdī, *Kitāb al-Imtāᶜ wal-Muʾānasa,* 2:60.

69. Douglas, *Constructive Drinking,* 4.

70. D'Arms, "Heavy Drinking and Drunkenness in the Roman World."

71. Murray, *Early Greece,* 210.

72. Ibid., 211, 212.

73. Pellizer, "Outlines of a Morphology of Sympotic Entertainment," 178–79.

74. Nykl, *Historia de los amores de Bayad y Riyad,* 9.

75. Bouhdiba, *Sexuality in Islam,* 130–31. As a whole, Bouhdiba's work argues that Islamic culture maintained a largely lyrical orientation toward life that humanized and legitimated sexuality. Although the book is riddled with minor errors, Bouhdiba has culled an astounding body of medieval

Arabic material to examine how Islamic culture reconciles the ideal and the practice of sexuality and religion.

76. Cf. Foucault, *History of Sexuality,* 12.

77. Najar, *La mémoire rassemblée*; Gruendler, "Qaṣīda: Its Reconstruction in Performance and Reception."

78. This book illustrates a literary culture that promoted competence by virtue of audience validation or scorn. Thus I propose to circumvent the supposed dichotomy between tradition (stable) and performance (corrupting) by following Hymes's lead, which stresses the importance of live performance in enabling audiences to aesthetically enjoy and engage tradition. His observation articulates the perspective of littérateurs who lived *adab* week after week in *mujālasāt:* "Tradition itself exists partly for the sake of performance; performance is itself partly an end" (Hymes, "Breakthrough into Performance," 19; cf. Nagy, *Poetry as Performance,* 29).

In his *Singer of Tales in Performance,* Foley adds that performance brings together text, tradition, and social-artistic event in the person of an animate thoughtful performer. Rather than view the performer as working *against* "original" texts and a "neat" tradition, he notes the role of the performance setting as "the event that frames the communicative exchange, and tradition, the body of immanent meaning that always impinges upon the linguistic integers of the metonymic idiom" (45). Put succinctly: "Tradition is the enabling referent, performance is the enabling event" (xiii). The audience plays a role as well in witnessing the communicative exchange, reacting with their approval or disapproval, thus shaping the performer's behavior. In this sense a live audience contributes to the delivery of the text and influences the trajectory of tradition (46).

79. Ms. Pet. 105, f. 221b.

80. Al-Iṣfahānī, *Kitāb al-Aghānī,* 21:50. In another instance, Abū Tammām recited his poetry while seated; see al-Ṣūlī, *Akhbār Abī Tammām,* 168, 271.

81. Ms. D992, D1196, and D1293.

82. Ms. We. 1100.

83. Al-Ṣūlī, *Akhbār Abī Tammām,* 141.

84. Nykl, *Historia de los amores de Bayad y Riyad,* 14–16.

85. Al-Ḥuṣrī al-Qayrawānī, *Zahr al-Ādāb wa Thamar al-Albāb,* 150.

86. Nykl, *Historia de los amores de Bayad y Riyad,* 12.

87. This case of text adjustment had implications for the making of cultural memory and is dealt with in that vein in chapter 4.

88. Nagy, *Poetry as Performance,* 109–12, 155. For more on the issue of a text's fixity or fluidity in the Bedouin context, see Blachère, *Histoire de la littérature arabe des origines à la fin du XVe siècle de J.C.,* 1:89–92.

89. For reference to the Qur'an's lines of transmission, see Saᶜīd, *Recited Koran.* Text adjustment in Abbasid poetry is addressed more thoroughly later in this book. For text adjustment in composition and performance, see also Blachère, *Histoire de la littérature arabe des origines à la fin du XVe siècle de J.C.,* 1:89.

90. Ms. Pm. 4, esp. f. 235b–238a.

91. Ms. Spr. 46, esp. f. 115a–240b.

92. Ms. Pm. 127. On Muᶜāwiya, see f. 60a–65b; on the civil war between al-Amīn and al-Maʾmūn, see f. 133b–135b.

93. Al-Ṣūlī, *Akhbār Abī Tammām,* 62.

94. Al-Tanūkhī, *Nishwār al-Muḥāḍara wa-Akhbār al-Mudhākara,* 10.

95. For more on the use of mythology in American advertising, see Goffman, *Gender Advertisements*; Lears, *Fables of Abundance*; and Randazzo, *The Myth Makers.*

96. Grunebaum, *Medieval Islam,* 281, 282.

97. Hodgson, *The Venture of Islam,* 1:353.

98. El-Hibri, *Reinterpreting Islamic Historiography,* 13; emphasis mine.

99. Ibid., 217.

100. Ibid., 218.

101. Ibid., 12, 13.

102. Bauman, *Story, Performance, and Event,* 21.

103. Khalidi, *Arabic Historical Thought in the Classical Period,* 76, 74.

104. Ibid., 13; Hodgson, *Venture of Islam,* 1:352.

105. Al-Ṭabarī, *Tārīkh,* 1:6.

106. Khalidi, *Arabic Historical Thought in the Classical Period,* 9.

107. Ibid., 25.

108. El-Hibri, *Reinterpreting Islamic Historiography,* 13.

109. Khalidi, *Arabic Historical Thought in the Classical Period,* 78; J. Stetkevych, *Zephyrs of Najd,* 170.

110. Khalidi, *Arabic Historical Thought in the Classical Period,* 9.

111. Al-Ṭabarī, *Tārīkh,* 1:6.

112. El-Hibri, *Reinterpreting Islamic Historiography,* 13.

113. Ibid., 15.

114. Morse, *Truth and Convention,* 128.

115. Al-Masᶜūdī, *Murūj al-Dhahab,* 4:121.

116. Morse, *Truth and Convention,* 128, 89, 86.

117. Ibid., 128.

118. The present approach takes *akhbār*-based histories to be laden with literary devices that subtly suggest attitudes, values, and beliefs about people, places, and events in the past. Note that such an approach should be distin-

guished from modernist scholarship that duly recognizes that historians and informants endow their narratives with attitudes and biases but does not interpret rhetorical strategies (Wellhausen, "Prolegomena zur ältesten Geschichte des Islams"; Petersen, *ᶜAli and Muᶜawiya in Early Arabic Tradition*; Dūrī, *The Rise of Historical Writing among the Arabs*; Crone, *Slaves on Horses*). Whereas modernist historians take literary devices to be either useless or obscuring, this study, along with El-Hibri's and Khalidi's, takes literary devices to be a figurative language regarded by medieval authors and their audiences as essential to encoding and decoding attitudes, beliefs, and values about the past. The task of the modern historian, then, is to learn the interpretive strategies employed by savvy medieval audiences to approximate how they might have received these narratives.

119. Khalidi, *Arabic Historical Thought in the Classical Period,* 26, 78–79, 9.

120. Morse, *Truth and Convention,* 111, 128.

121. Muslim, *Ṣaḥīḥ Muslim,* 2011.

122. Ibid.

123. Saᶜdī al-Shīrāzī, *Gulistān-i Saᶜdī,* 13–14.

124. Al-Ṣūlī, *Akhbār al-Buḥturī wa Dhayl al-Akhbār,* 106.

125. Ajami, *Neckveins of Winter,* 58.

126. Ibid., 59, 58; cf. Bürgel, *Feather of Simugh,* 68.

127. Ajami, *Neckveins of Winter,* 60.

128. Goodman, "The Sacred and the Secular."

129. ᶜAbbās, *Tārīkh al-Naqd al-Adabī ᶜind al-ᶜArab,* 38–39.

130. Cantarino, *Arabic Poetics in the Golden Age,* 36.

131. Ibid., 37.

132. Ibid.; cf. Bürgel, *Feather of Simugh,* 70.

133. Cantarino, *Arabic Poetics in the Golden Age,* 38.

134. Bürgel, *Feather of Simugh,* 61, 66.

135. Monroe, *Risālat at-Tawābiᶜ wa z-Zawābiᶜ,* 3.

136. Bürgel, *Feather of Simugh,* 70.

137. Al-Ṣūlī, *Akhbār al-Buḥturī wa Dhayl al-Akhbār,* 49–54.

138. Ibid.

139. Ibn al-Jawzī, *Akhbār al-Ḥamqā wal-Mughaffalīn,* 124.

140. The value of oratory for marking and bringing about manhood has been discussed by Nagy in the context of ancient Greece (*Poetry as Performance,* 163).

141. Ibn Rashīq al-Qayrawānī, *Kitāb al-ᶜUmda fī Ṣanᶜat al-Shiᶜr wa Naqdih,* 1:27.

142. Ibn al-ᶜImrānī, *Al-Inbāʾ fī Tārīkh al-Khulafāʾ,* 118.

143. Ibn Khaldūn, *Muqaddima,* 1277, 1289.
144. Ibid., 1252.
145. Ibid.
146. Ibn Rashīq al-Qayrawānī, *Kitāb al-ᶜUmda fī Ṣanᶜat al-Shiᶜr wa Naqdih,* 1:24.
147. Ibid., 1:27.
148. Al-Khaṭīb al-Baghdādī, *Tārīkh Baghdād,* 13:447.

THREE Poetry Performance and the Reinterpreting of Tradition

1. ᶜAlī b. al-Jahm's life is presented and represented in many medieval sources: al-Iṣfahānī, *Kitāb al-Aghānī,* 10:204; al-Khaṭīb al-Baghdādī, *Tārīkh Baghdād,* 7:240; Ibn Khallikān, *Wafayāt al-Aᶜyān,* 1:441; and al-Marzubānī, *Muᶜjam al-Shuᶜarāʾ,* 286. See also Sezgin, *Geschichte des arabischen Schrifttums,* 580–81.

2. This anecdote also represents a type or genre of anecdote (*khabar*) where the center and periphery meet, usually a caliph (or other high official) and a simpleton (Bedouin, farmer, wayfarer, etc.). Interestingly, the exchange is usually transformative for both parties, indicating a mutual redemption.

3. Ibn al-ᶜArabī, *Kitāb Muḥāḍarat al-Abrār,* 2:8–9. The full text states:

> Littérateurs (*udabāʾ*) narrate to us an anecdote about Abī [*sic*] al-Jahm, who was a coarse Bedouin when he came to al-Mutawakkil and chanted his praise in an ode (*qaṣīda*) to him in which he says—addressing the Caliph!—
>
> You are like a *dog* in maintaining your loyalty.
> You are like a *billy goat* in confronting your challenges!
> You are like a *hide-bucket*—may we never do without you
> as a bucket—one of the biggest buckets! Great in size!
>
> Despite the vulgarity of his diction, al-Mutawakkil realized his acumen and the charm of his intention. He understood that he must have known nothing but such [coarse] comparisons, for lack of wider interaction, and the daily life of the desert.
>
> He [al-Mutawakkil] then secured a beautiful home for him [Ibn al-Jahm] along the Tigris riverfront with a sweet breeze that pervades it and nourishes the soul. Near him there was the pontoon bridge, al-Jisr. And he also ordered fine food for him—for him to become familiar with it. ᶜAlī [Ibn al-Jahm] would ride most of the time. He would ven-

ture out to Baghdad's neighborhoods and would see the bustle of people and the beauty of greenery and then return to his home. He lived like this for six months, while littérateurs and nobles frequented his literary receptions and gatherings.

The caliph thereafter invited him back to perform for him. He came in and then recited (*fa-ḥaḍara wa anshada*):

Doe's eyes—between *Ruṣāfa* and *Jisr*—
import passion from where I know and I know not where.

Then al-Mutawakkil said, "Ah! I almost feared that he might lose his charm and subtlety."

4. The court littérateur Abū ᶜUthmān al-Jāḥiẓ reminds Abbasid courtiers that Sasanian kings warned courtiers to watch their tongues in a king's company, or lose their heads. A crier was sent by the chamberlain to the highest point in the palace and called out, "O tongue! Watch your head. You keep the company, on this day, of the King of Kings" (al-Jāḥiẓ, *Kitāb al-Tāj fī Akhlāq al-Mulūk,* 28). The implication of Ibn al-Jahm's verbal gaff is an accidental brush with death.

5. Ibn al-Jahm, *Dīwān,* 135.

6. Ibid., 6–7.

7. S. Stetkevych, *Mute Immortals Speak.*

8. Abū ᶜUbāda al-Walīd al-Buḥturī is said to have begun cultivating his talents by delivering praise hymns to eggplant and onion merchants in his native city of Manbij, Syria, near Aleppo. He also delivered a praise hymn to a noblewoman, a daughter of the Ḥumaydī family of Khurasan (Central Asia) that had relocated to Baghdad. See Ali, "Al-Buhturi."

9. On the problem of sincerity, see Meisami, *Medieval Persian Court Poetry,* 41–43; and S. Stetkevych, "Abbasid Panegyric and the Poetics of Political Allegiance," 35. On the rejection of the *qaṣīda* in the West, see Sells, "Qaṣīda and the West." Sells's article, though well documented, paints an overly bleak picture and might best be read in the context of J. Stetkevych's 1979 article, "Arabic Poetry and Assorted Poetics," which argues that German Orientalism enthusiastically engaged and assimilated the *qaṣīda,* including praise hymns, particularly in adaptations and translations, but then in the mid-nineteenth-century enthusiasm gave way to a technical, banalizing approach, where philologists sought to compile perfect editions. J. Stetkevych points out that over the past hundred years, this obsession with banalities has suspended a thoroughgoing engagement of the ode. For more on the rejection of the traditional ode by modern Arab poets and critics, see Jayyusi, *Trends and Movements in Modern Arabic Poetry,* "Tradition and Modernity in Arabic

Poetry," and "Persistence of the Qasida Form." One can find a paramount example of a Nasserist-socialist condemnation of the profession of praise in Shawqī Ḍayf's 1990 work, *Al-ᶜAṣr al-ᶜAbbāsī al-Thānī*. Ḍayf attributes al-Buḥturī's success as a poet to his "greed" (278, 279, 281) and his willingness to praise anyone for reward (280). Ḍayf tells us that the poet's cupidity had no limits (282, 283). Compare this with the work of Wahb Rūmiyya, who, critical of rejectionists, has posited specific functions for the courtly ode and has deemed it reasonable that poets would seek favors, money, and other material benefits from their patrons (Rūmiyya, *Binyat al-Qaṣīda al-ᶜArabiyya ḥattā Nihāyat al-ᶜAṣr al-Umawī*, 53–67).

10. Meisami, *Medieval Persian Court Poetry,* 43–46.

11. Gruendler, "Ibn al-Rūmī's Ethics of Patronage," 106; and *Medieval Arabic Praise Poetry,* 26.

12. Sperl, "Islamic Kingship and Arabic Panegyric Poetry," 33.

13. S. Stetkevych, "Abbasid Panegyric and the Poetics of Political Allegiance," 36–40; and "Pre-Islamic Panegyric and the Poetics of Redemption," 4–5. For more on the power of the poet to compel the patron to action, see S. Stetkevych, *Poetics of Islamic Legitimacy,* especially chapter 4, "Supplication and Negotiation: The Client Outraged, al-Akhtal and the Supplicatory Ode."

14. Ibn Rashīq al-Qayrawānī, *Kitāb al-ᶜUmda fī Ṣanᶜat al-Shiᶜr wa Naqdih,* 1:12.

15. Ibid., 1:73–88.

16. S. Stetkevych, "Pre-Islamic Panegyric and the Poetics of Redemption," 3.

17. Ibid., 36.

18. Al-Buḥturī, *Dīwān,* 2:1018.

19. Cf. Crotty, *Poetics of Supplication,* 5.

20. Ibid., 18–19.

21. S. Stetkevych, "Qaṣīdah and the Poetics of Ceremony."

22. Crotty, *Poetics of Supplication,* 19.

23. Al-Buḥturī's poem cited in Ibn Rashīq al-Qayrawānī, *Kitāb al-ᶜUmda fī Ṣanᶜat al-Shiᶜr wa Naqdih,* 1:81. Also al-Buḥturī, *Dīwān,* 1:365.

24. Ibid.

25. Bauman, *Verbal Art as Performance,* 43–44.

26. For more on the rise of figurative language in Abbasid court poetry and its political implications, see S. Stetkevych, *Abū Tammām and the Poetics of the ᶜAbbāsid Age*; and Meisami, *Medieval Persian Court Poetry.*

27. Ibn Shams al-Khilāfa Mujidd al-Mulk, *Kitāb al-Ādāb,* 29.

28. *EI²,* s.v. "Marāsim"; also al-Jāḥiẓ, *Kitāb al-Tāj fī Akhlāq al-Mulūk*; Ibn al-ᶜImrānī, *Al-Inbāʾ fī Tārīkh al-Khulafāʾ*.

29. Cf. Anderson, *Imagined Communities,* 15.

30. Ibn Shams al-Khilāfa Mujidd al-Mulk, *Kitāb al-Ādāb,* 28.

31. *EI*², s.v. "Marāsim"; al-Jāḥiẓ, *Kitāb al-Tāj fī Akhlāq al-Mulūk,* 7–8, 105; also Sourdel, *Medieval Islam,* 133; cf. Hammoudi, *Master and Disciple,* 72–73.

32. Ibn al-ᶜImrānī, *Al-Inbāʾ fī Tārīkh al-Khulafāʾ,* 115.

33. Hammoudi, *Master and Disciple,* 45.

34. Al-Jāḥiẓ, *Kitāb al-Tāj fī Akhlāq al-Mulūk,* 156–57.

35. Ibid.

36. Ibid., 93.

37. I thank the Islamic scholar Vincent Cornell for raising this point in conversation, June 1999.

38. Cf. Crotty, *Poetics of Supplication,* 92–95.

39. Cf. Foucault, *History of Sexuality,* 85, 86.

40. Ettinghausen and Grabar, *Art and Architecture of Islam,* 83–86; Creswell, *Short Account of Early Muslim Architecture,* 337; Bloom and Blair, *Islamic Arts,* 52; and Hillenbrand, *Islamic Architecture,* 398–406.

41. Hillenbrand, *Islamic Architecture,* 395.

42. Ibn al-ᶜImrānī, *Al-Inbāʾ fī Tārīkh al-Khulafāʾ,* 91; al-Jāḥiẓ, *Kitāb al-Tāj fī Akhlāq al-Mulūk,* 51–52.

43. Ibn Rashīq al-Qayrawānī, *Kitāb al-ᶜUmda fī Ṣanᶜat al-Shiᶜr wa Naqdih,* 1:14.

44. Al-Jāḥīẓ, *Kitāb al-Tāj fī Akhlāq al-Mulūk,* 90–91.

45. See, e.g., Ibn al-ᶜImrānī, *Al-Inbāʾ fī Tārīkh al-Khulafāʾ,* 128, also 69, 76, 77, 79. Cf. Gruendler, *Medieval Arabic Praise Poetry,* 23, who has described other methods of communicating a poem, depending on the state of the poet's rapport with a patron or would-be patron.

46. E.g., see Ibn al-Jahm, poem no. 127 (*Dīwān,* 179).

47. Men of authority simulated in their lives the tokens of authority the king exhibited. The king's subordinates also enjoyed "kingly" privileges in courts of their own that vary not in kind but in degree. For example, when al-Mutawakkil's vizier, al-Fatḥ b. Khāqān, survived a drowning accident while fishing, he held audience just as his superior would to receive visitors' well-wishes, and al-Buḥturī delivered a poem to document his relief (al-Ṣūlī, *Akhbār al-Buḥturī wa Dhayl al-Akhbār,* 96–97).

48. Ibn al-ᶜImrānī, *Al-Inbāʾ fī Tārīkh al-Khulafāʾ,* 117–18.

49. From Ibn al-ᶜImrānī, *Al-Inbāʾ fī Tārīkh al-Khulafāʾ* (117). The text describes the covenant of succession gala as follows:

> He [al-Mutawakkil] declared covenants of allegiance for his three sons and rendered them heirs apparent. It was an auspicious day. It was

Monday, the first of Muḥarram, 236. They are: Muḥammad, and his honorific is al-Muntaṣir [Made Victorious]; al-Zubayr, his honorific is al-Muᶜtazz [Made Mighty]; and Ibrāhīm, his honorific is al-Muᵓayyad [Given Support]. He [the father] set up a banquet area the length of four *parasangs* [about sixteen miles] in the garden that he planted in Samarra, known as the Jaᶜfarī, which was seven *parasangs* in length [about twenty-eight miles] stretching along the banks of the Tigris and one *parasang* wide [about four miles]. It was said that it was filled on that day with life. Statues of ambergris and camphor were set in the hands of people as well as censers for musk—in sum all aromatic goods and substances. They were transported from storage in baskets and sacks. Everyone who drank a bowl of wine got some of it, smelled it, tucked it in his sleeves or handed it over to his servant in waiting. Whenever a rod of scent burned out, it was replaced. It was so from sunrise to sunset.

Al-Mutawakkil himself sat upon a throne of gold set with gems weighing a thousand *mann* [two thousand "Baghdadi" pounds, i.e., elephantine]. The heirs apparent stood before him, wearing jeweled crowns. Meanwhile, people were sitting and standing according to their ranks (*ṭabaqātihim*). Sunrise glimmered on the golden vessels at each place setting, as well as on belts, swords, and shields adorned with gold—it was well-nigh blinding. On that day, Ibrāhīm Ibn al-ᶜAbbās al-Ṣūlī, the Prince of Men, rose and recited among the ranks of men (*bayn al-samāṭīn*):

"The Leaders of Islam—dependent upon 'Victory,'
'Might' and 'Support'—have unveiled
A Hashimite Caliph and three who safeguard
the caliphate as heirs apparent.
Their forefathers have safeguarded them, and they their
forefathers. Thus they proceed with the noblest of
souls and grandfathers."

For more on ceremony in various Islamic courts, see S. Stetkevych, "ᶜAbbāsid Panegyric and the Poetics of Political Allegiance" and "Qaṣīdah and the Poetics of Ceremony"; and Saunders, *Ritual, Politics, and the City in Fatimid Cairo.* See also Mez, *Renaissance of Islam.*

50. Al-Shābushtī, *Kitāb al-Diyārāt,* 150–56; Ibn al-ᶜImrānī, *Al-Inbāᵓ fī Tārīkh al-Khulafāᵓ,* 118–19.

51. Al-Buḥturī, *Dīwān,* ode 277.

52. S. Stetkevych, "Umayyad Panegyric and the Poetics of Islamic Hegemony," 95.

53. In al-Ṣūlī, *Akhbār al-Buḥturī wa Dhayl al-Akhbār,* 153.

54. S. Stetkevych, "Umayyad Panegyric and the Poetics of Islamic Hegemony," 22.

55. Ibid.; cf. S. Stetkevych, "Qaṣīdah and the Poetics of Ceremony," 90.

56. Al-Jāḥiẓ, *Kitāb al-Tāj fī Akhlāq al-Mulūk,* 70. Emphasis mine.

57. Abū Tammām, *Dīwān Abū Tammām bi-Sharḥ al-Khatīb al-Tabrīzī,* 3:183. Emphasis mine.

58. Al-Buḥturī, *Dīwān,* 2:1007.

59. Meisami, *Medieval Persian Court Poetry,* 46; cf. Morse, *Truth and Convention,* 130.

60. Al-Jāḥiẓ, *Kitāb al-Tāj fī Akhlāq al-Mulūk,* 102.

61. S. Stetkevych, *Mute Immortals Speak,* 7; cf. S. Stetkevych, "Pre-Islamic Panegyric and the Poetics of Redemption," "Abbasid Panegyric and the Poetics of Political Allegiance," "ᶜAbbāsid Panegyric," "Qaṣīdah and the Poetics of Ceremony," and "Umayyad Panegyric and the Poetics of Islamic Hegemony."

62. S. Stetkevych, *Mute Immortals Speak,* 7.

63. I have relied on Khalīl Mardam's "version 3" of the ode (*Dīwān ᶜAlī Ibn al-Jahm,* 252–56), which is based on al-Shayzarī's recension in his *Jamharat al-Islām Dhāt al-Nathr wal-Niẓām.* Mardam's other versions seem to be revised composites by him, based on renditions and excerpts from Berlin manuscripts and classical anthologies. The result is a modern rendition of the ode, based on the editor's early-twentieth-century preoccupation with completeness and his judgment of flow and sequence (136, 252). These modern composites are valid forms of reception that illustrate the vitality of poetry to audiences over the generations; however, they do not serve our purposes for interpreting the impact of a coherent ode on the Middle Ages. Version 3 (from al-Shayzarī's *Jamharat al-Islām*) has the advantage of circulation as a structurally rich ode during al-Shayzarī's era of the thirteenth century. Mardam relies on a manuscript of *Jamharat al-Islām* at the University of Leiden (ms. 480) with a scribal date of 699 A.H. or A.D. 1299/1300, thus plausibly stretching that circulation into the fourteenth century. While versions and variations must have abounded among medieval audiences, both in manuscript and face-to-face performance, which suggests the ode's appeal, we can consciously take al-Shayzarī's version as a point of departure or at least as a well-known revival of the ode. The ode is composed in the *ṭawīl* meter and uses the end-rhyme *ra.*

64. The beloved is nicknamed Ẓalūm, the intensive of Ẓālim (unjust one). Thus it has been rendered *in-Justine,* which accentuates, I hope, the Arabic poetic conceit of the unjust beloved with whom the poet-lover pleads.

65. The phrase "but the veil is torn" means that the affair becomes public.

66. I.e., none add to his repute.

67. These are puns on al-Mutawakkil's three heirs apparent: Muʾayyad bil-lāh (Aided by God), Muʿtazz bil-lāh (Made Mighty by God), and Muntaṣir bil-lāh (Made Victorious by God).

68. A quotation of Qur'an 4:59.

69. Abū Naḍla, "father of toil," became a nickname for Hāshim b. ʿAbd Manāf (Ibn Manẓūr, *Lisān al-ʿArab,* s.v. "n-ḍ-l").

70. Lit., "the graying man of praise," i.e., the Prophet Muhammad's grandfather, ʿAbd al-Muṭṭalib b. Hāshim.

71. Jabbur, *Bedouins and the Desert,* 110.

72. Ibid.

73. Le Strange, *Baghdad during the Abbasid Caliphate,* 187.

74. J. Stetkevych, *Zephyrs of Najd,* 109.

75. Ibid.

76. Al-Jurjānī, *Al-Wasāṭa bayna al-Mutanabbī wa Khuṣūmih,* 21–23.

77. Ibid.

78. El Tayib, "Pre-Islamic Poetry," 35.

79. Ibid.

80. Al-Jurjānī, *Al-Wasāṭa bayna al-Mutanabbī wa Khuṣūmih,* 21–23.

81. In the *Thousand and One Nights* the story of the Bedouin girl and the caliph Hārūn al-Rashīd illustrates a literal marriage between the Bedouin and the cosmopolitan. She recites spontaneous poetry, which represents the legendary virtue of desert dwellers, and invites the caliph to understand and want her (Sallis, *Sheherazade through the Looking Glass,* 113). Eva Sallis has described this pairing as a "satisfying union of images of excellence from the two worlds of Arabic folklore" (ibid.).

82. Ibn al-ʿArabī, *Kitāb Muḥāḍarat al-Abrār,* 2:9.

83. J. Stetkevych, "Name and Epithet," 108.

84. Ibid.

85. Sperl, "Islamic Kingship and Arabic Panegyric Poetry," 32. On occasion, courtly praise hymns present Fate as rightful (such as Abū Nuwās, *Dīwān,* 166), but the overwhelming trope shows Fate as humanity's antagonist (see Sperl, "Islamic Kingship and Arabic Panegyric Poetry," 32).

86. Sperl, "Islamic Kingship and Arabic Panegyric Poetry," 32. For more on Fate in pre-Islamic and early Islamic society, see Watt, *Free Will and Predestination in Early Islam*; Graham, *Divine Word and Prophetic Word in Early Islam*; Ringgren, *Studies in Arabian Fatalism*; and Homerin, "A Bird Ascends the Night."

87. Sperl, "Islamic Kingship and Arabic Panegyric Poetry," 33.

88. Ibn al-ᶜImrānī, *Al-Inbāʾ fī Tārīkh al-Khulafāʾ*, 77.

89. The amount was equivalent to the cost of a modest home in the Abbasid economy or the price of purchasing a highly skilled slave.

90. McEwan, *Oriental Origin of Hellenistic Kingship,* 26; emphasis mine.

91. Al-Iṣfahānī, *Kitāb al-Aghānī,* 16:360–61.

92. Ibid., 16:370–71. The idiom *al-muslim al-fāqir* refers to a back-breaking event.

93. Ibn Hudhayl, *ᶜAyn al-Adab wal-Siyāsa,* 33.

94. Al-Iṣfahānī, *Kitāb al-Aghānī,* 16:360–61.

95. Crotty, *Poetics of Supplication,* 90.

96. Ibid., 91, 92.

97. Ibn Hudhayl, *ᶜAyn al-Adab wal-Siyāsa,* 21.

98. Abu-Lughod, *Veiled Sentiments,* 110.

99. Ibid., 104, 109.

100. In the Abbasid period, candidates to the throne were expected to show the utmost submission before the monarch, perhaps more than other servants. Suggesting the seriousness of the subject, al-Jāḥiẓ placed his discussion on the son's deference immediately after a section on the king's anxiety over sleeping arrangements and the need to strictly follow measures to ensure the king's security (*Kitāb al-Tāj fī Akhlāq al-Mulūk,* 124). He says, "The king has the right to have his son treat him as slaves do . . . and that the chamberlain (*al-ḥijāb*) be stricter on him than on those who are beneath him among the king's intimates and servants" (125; see also 127). The anthropologist Abdellah Hammoudi reports a similar dynamic in contemporary Moroccan kingship: "Before reaching supreme dignity the candidate to the sultanate must, like everyone else, ostensibly demonstrate submission: downcast eyes, service to the reigning prince, relinquishing of any display of authority or even virility in his presence" (*Master and Disciple,* 76).

101. Abu-Lughod, *Veiled Sentiments,* 115. Al-Jāḥiẓ notes that deference also has other unexpected implications. Courtiers and visitors should alter their names in the presence of the king if it might exalt them above the king. They should also eschew statements of age, seniority, or privilege that might appear to match or challenge the king (al-Jāḥiẓ, *Kitāb al-Tāj fī Akhlāq al-Mulūk,* 88–89).

102. S. Stetkevych, "Abbasid Panegyric and the Poetics of Political Allegiance," 38.

103. Ibid., 40.

104. Al-Azmeh, *Muslim Kingship,* 8, 35, 77, 122.

105. Anderson, *Imagined Communities*, 13; cf. Eliade, *Sacred and the Profane*, 149.

106. Lovejoy, *Great Chain of Being*, 59.

107. Al-Azmeh, *Muslim Kingship*, 28, 59, 75, 76, 155; al-Iṣfahānī, *Kitāb al-Aghānī*, 23:210.

108. Al-Azmeh, *Muslim Kingship*, 58.

109. Anderson, *Imagined Communities*, 13.

110. Ibid., 13–15.

111. Ms. Esc. 724, f. 28b.

112. Ibid.

113. Hammoudi (*Master and Disciple*, 53), in reference to Moroccan kingship, says bluntly: "The monarch is definitely hated when he does not distribute favors." Interestingly, Hammoudi observes that Islamic law and ethics (derived by the Ulema) sought to curtail court spending on gifts, thereby threatening the sultan's popularity. Having interests and perspectives at variance with the court, the Ulema realize that without gifts to his servants, the sultan "loses their loyalty and takes the chance that his troops will choose to serve a more generous prince" (53).

114. Ms. Esc. 724, f. 28b.

115. Ibn Hudhayl, ʿAyn al-Adab wal-Siyāsa, 105.

116. Ibid. In this context one can appreciate the remark by al-Jāḥiẓ that posits generosity (*al-sakhāʾ*) and self-restraint (*al-ḥayāʾ*) as complementary virtues in the king. After describing the paramount importance of generosity—that he knows of no successful king in history who was not—he turns to self-restraint. He says, "As for self-restraint, it is a form of mercy. It is a duty on the king, if he is a shepherd (*al-rāʿī*) to show mercy on his flock (*raʿiyya*), if he is a prayer leader (*imām*) to have pity on the followers, and if he is a master (*al-mawlā*) to have mercy on his slave (*al-ʿabd*)" (al-Jāḥiẓ, *Kitāb al-Tāj fī Akhlāq al-Mulūk*, 139). Note also how the littérateur Abū al-Faraj Qudāma b. Jaʿfar categorized generosity. He found that human beings are distinct from other animals in four main qualities: sense (*al-ʿaql*), courage (*al-shajāʿa*), chastity (*al-ʿiffa*), and justice (*al-ʿadl*). He sees generosity as a form of justice (Ibn Jaʿfar, *Naqd al-Shiʿr*, 66–67).

117. The oft-quoted Hadith states, "Embody the characteristics of God" (*takhallaqū bi-khuluq illāh*); cf. Bürgel, *Feather of Simugh*, 17.

118. Ms. Esc. 725, f. 93a.

119. Al-Tanūkhī, *Al-Mustajād min Fiʿlāt al-Ajwād*, 201.

120. Ms. Esc. 725, f. 70b, margins.

121. Al-Ṣūlī, *Akhbār al-Buḥturī wa Dhayl al-Akhbār*, 154. Emphasis mine.

122. Ibn Shams al-Khilāfa Mujidd al-Mulk, *Kitāb al-Ādāb,* 8.

123. Ms. Esc. 725, f. 1b.

124. Foucault, *History of Sexuality,* 101.

125. S. Stetkevych, "Qaṣīdah and the Poetics of Ceremony," 31; Crone and Hinds, *God's Caliph,* 21, 27.

126. Al-Azmeh, *Muslim Kingship,* 15.

127. Al-Buḥturī, *Dīwān,* 2:728–29.

128. S. Stetkevych, "Abbasid Panegyric and the Poetics of Political Allegiance," 40.

129. Crone and Hinds, *God's Caliph,* 27–28, 82; Fowden, *Empire to Commonwealth,* 156; Sperl, "Islamic Kingship and Arabic Panegyric Poetry," 33.

130. Al-Azmeh, *Muslim Kingship,* 75; Sperl, "Islamic Kingship and Arabic Panegyric Poetry," 33.

131. Cf. Qur'an 4:59.

132. S. Stetkevych, "Qaṣīdah and the Poetics of Ceremony," 31.

133. Mardam, *Dīwān ᶜAlī Ibn al-Jahm,* 140n.

134. Al-Azraqī, *Akhbār Makka,* 1:17.

135. Ibid., 2:125–26, cf. 156.

136. Fowden, *Empire to Commonwealth,* 91. See also p. 157: "The Islamic Empire consummated rather than contradicted the themes of late Roman history. For a time, it succeeded where Rome had failed." Fowden's work is lacking in primary textual evidence, but his thesis is corroborated by ᶜAbd al-Karīm (*Quraysh*) and Al-Azmeh (*Muslim Kingship,* 8), both of whom rely heavily on primary sources. All of these studies have the advantage of suggesting discernible intercultural exchange in the Mediterranean region.

137. ᶜAbd al-Karīm, *Quraysh,* 37.

138. Ibid., 37, 38–39, 44, 53, 109, 123, 127–29.

139. Cf. S. Stetkevych, *Mute Immortals Speak,* 42–54.

140. ᶜAbd al-Karīm, *Quraysh,* 69–76.

141. Al-Azraqī, *Akhbār Makka,* 1:112.

142. Al-Buḥturī, *Dīwān,* 2:1018.

143. Nagy, *Poetry as Performance,* 61.

144. Cf. Bauman, *Verbal Art as Performance,* 44.

145. Bürgel, *Feather of Simugh,* 57.

146. Ibid., 57; cf. Ibn Rashīq al-Qayrawānī, *Kitāb al-ᶜUmda fī Ṣanᶜat al-Shiᶜr wa Naqdih,* 20, 60.

147. Ibn Rashīq al-Qayrawānī, *Kitāb al-ᶜUmda fī Ṣanᶜat al-Shiᶜr wa Naqdih,* 20; cf. Bürgel, *Feather of Simugh,* 53.

148. Anderson, *Imagined Communities,* 13.

149. Crotty, *Poetics of Supplication,* 8.

150. Mardam based his edition (*Dīwān ᶜAlī Ibn al-Jahm*) primarily on Ms. Esc. 369, a manuscript of Moroccan provenance in the Maghribī script dated 1002 A.H. Although it is only a partial collection or *dīwān,* this manuscript constitutes the most comprehensive extant collection of Ibn al-Jahm's poetry.

151. Bauman, *Verbal Art as Performance,* 9.

152. I am taking guidance here from the folklorist Richard Bauman. In his study of Quaker modes of communication in the seventeenth century, Bauman predicates his analysis not on abstract formulations of language, such as a substructural "code" (a *langue,* in Ferdinand de Saussure's terms), but on the functions of language in a social setting (Bauman, *Let Your Words Be Few,* 5). In practical terms this approach shifts attention from language as an abstract code to "the role of language as structured by and giving structure to ideology, social relations, groups, and institutions. This is not only language as thought, but language as *used* by society . . . to enact or negotiate social identities and to accomplish social goals" (5).

153. Al-Mutanabbī, *Dīwān al-Mutanabbī,* 1:12–31.

154. The earliest known work by a Malamatiyya scholar is that of ᶜArrām b. al-Asbagh al-Sulamī (d. 1021). His translation of his treatise can be found in al-ᶜAfīfī, ed. and trans., *Al-Malāmatiyya wal-Ṣūfiyya wa Ahl al-Futuwwa*; this translation was originally published as al-Sulamī and al-ᶜAfīfī, ed. and trans., "Al-Risāla al-Malāmatiyya," in the May 1942 issue of *Majallat Kulliyat al-Ādāb Jāmiᶜat Fuʾād al-Awal.* For general reference to the development of Sufism, I have referred to Lewisohn, *Heritage of Sufism*; and al-Sulamī, *Ṭabaqāt al-Ṣūfiyya.* See also the biography of al-Sulamī in his *Ṭabaqāt al-Ṣūfiyya,* and in al-Sulamī, *Early Sufi Women,* 15–70. For later Moroccan Sufism, I have relied on Cornell, *Realm of the Saint.* For more on the Malamatiyya, see Schimmel, *The Mystical Dimensions of Islam,* 86–87. For the Malamatiyya in late Egypt, see Winter, *Society and Religion in Early Ottoman Egypt,* 82–91.

155. When reframed, third-person speech can undergo fundamental changes in meaning, not simply through text adjustments, but through delivery techniques such as intonation, gesture, and facial expression. M. M. Bakhtin has observed, "Another's discourse . . . enters the speech that frames it not in a mechanical bond but in a chemical union (on the semantic and emotional expressive level)" (Bakhtin, *Dialogic Imagination*, 340).

156. Ibn Hudhayl, *ᶜAyn al-Adab wal-Siyāsa,* 33.

157. Ibn al-ᶜArabī, *Kitāb Muḥāḍarat al-Abrār,* 2:9.

158. Ibn al-Jahm, *Dīwān,* 178.

159. Ms. Esc. 369, f. 1a, attributed to Muḥammad b. Sulaymān al-Shābb al-Zarīf (d. 1289).

160. Ibid., f. 74a. The verses belong to Muḥammad b. Aḥmad al-Wāʾwāʾ al-Dimashqī (d. 995).

161. The sacrality of the Beloved is linked through a tradition of love poetry (ghazal) to the ancient Arabian practice of venerating goddesses. In pre-Islamic Arabia virgin-mothers such as al-Lāt (akin to Ishtar and Aphrodite) were worshiped for their powers of procreation, tenderness, and sensuality (Smith, *Lectures on the Religion of the Semites,* 57). According to the Arabist Ibrāhīm Salāma, the practice of adoring goddesses and venerating femininity continued under the guise of *ghazal* well into the Islamic era (Salāma, *Tayyārāt Adabiyya bayn al-Sharq wal-Gharb,* 27–28).

FOUR The Poetics of Sin and Redemption: Performing Value and Canonicity

1. El-Hibri, *Reinterpreting Islamic Historiography,* 192–93; cf. al-Ṭabarī, *Tārīkh al-Ṭabarī,* 9:225; al-Masʿūdī, *Murūj al-Dhahab,* 4:115–22. See also Gordon, *Breaking of a Thousand Swords,* 82, where the author contends, based on numismatic analysis by the historian Michael Bates, that al-Mutawakkil genuinely favored al-Muʿtazz as heir. Tayeb El-Hibri, however, following Abū Jaʿfar al-Ṭabarī's material, reaches the conclusion that the caliph supported al-Muntaṣir but shifted under pressure.

2. Al-Buḥturī, *Dīwān,* 2:1047. As noted earlier, all references are to the al-Ṣayrafī edition (1977), unless stated otherwise.

3. Al-Maʿarrī, *Al-Luzūmiyyāt,* 2:610; al-Ṣūlī, *Akhbār al-Buḥturī wa Dhayl al-Akhbār,* 101.

4. Al-Buḥturī, *Dīwān,* 2:849–50.

5. Al-Masʿūdī, *Murūj al-Dhahab,* 4:122, 135; al-Ḥuṣrī al-Qayrawānī, *Zahr al-Ādāb wa-Thamr al-Albāb,* 215–16; al-Thaʿālibī, *Thimār al-Qulūb,* 191; al-Ṣūlī, *Akhbār al-Buḥturī wa Dhayl al-Akhbār,* 101.

6. The question of sincerity might also be viewed from the theoretical perspective formulated by Foucault: genuine human emotions and impulses encompass not only the beautiful and the delicate but also the enraged and hateful. When social beings internalize societal expectations (power relations), they implicitly begin to regulate their own behavior (self-policing) in order to render their behavior acceptable, responsible, or professional to others. In the ethical realm, coming home stressed and deciding to "kick the dog" would be a truly sincere emotional expression, but is this what society expects

of its members? In the artistic realm as well, artists who fail to be playful—deploying figurative distortions, narrative patterns, allegory, metonymy, and so on—risk earning the labels "banal," "heavy handed," or "grinding an ax" in conveying sincere thoughts and feelings. His concepts of internalized power and self-policing are best articulated in his *Discipline and Punish.* According to Foucault in *The History of Sexuality,* vol. 1, even the realm of sexuality, putatively the most private and sincere area of human psychology, is subject to societal expectations and acculturated attitudes toward pleasure and guilt that encourage members of society to police their own thoughts, feelings, and behaviors, or risk derision. If societal pressures shape self-presentation in the bedroom, then a fortiori the argument can be applied to other ostensibly "sincere" aspects of life, such as love and art.

7. Ḍayf, *Al-ᶜAṣr al-ᶜAbbāsī al-Thānī,* 278; al-Buḥturī, *Dīwān,* 5:2792.

8. Ḍayf, *Al-ᶜAṣr al-ᶜAbbāsī al-Thānī,* 278.

9. Cf. S. Stetkevych, "Pre-Islamic Panegyric and the Poetics of Redemption" and "ᶜAbbāsid Panegyric."

10. Al-Ṣūlī, *Akhbār al-Buḥturī wa Dhayl al-Akhbār,* 101.

11. Ibid.

12. Al-Masᶜūdī, *Murūj al-Dhahab,* 4:135.

13. B. H. Smith, "Contingencies of Value."

14. Cf. S. Stetkevych, "Pre-Islamic Panegyric and the Poetics of Redemption" and "Abbasid Panegyric and the Poetics of Political Allegiance."

15. Bauman, *Verbal Art as Performance,* 43–44.

16. Ibn Rashīq al-Qayrawānī, *Kitāb al-ᶜUmda fī Ṣanᶜat al-Shiᶜr wa Naqdih,* 1:81; and al-Buḥturī, *Dīwān,* 1:365. The influence and prestige of al-Buḥturī in particular is discussed further in chapter 5.

17. Foucault, *History of Sexuality,* 101.

18. Bauman and Briggs, "Poetics and Performance as Critical Perspectives," 60.

19. Ibid., 61.

20. Gordon, *Breaking of a Thousand Swords,* 50; *EI²,* s.v. "Sāmarrāᵓ."

21. *EI²,* s.v. "Sāmarrāᵓ."

22. Gordon, *Breaking of a Thousand Swords,* 141.

23. Ettinghausen and Grabar, *Art and Architecture of Islam,* 83–86; Creswell, *Short Account of Early Muslim Architecture,* 337; Bloom and Blair, *Islamic Arts,* 52; and Hillenbrand, *Islamic Architecture,* 398–406.

24. Hillenbrand, *Islamic Architecture,* 339.

25. Ibid.

26. Al-Shābushtī, *Kitāb al-Diyārāt,* 9.

27. Ibn ᶜAbd Rabbih, *Al-ᶜIqd al-Farīd,* 5:344; and Northedge, "Creswell, Herzfeld, and Samarra," 78.

28. Ya^c^qūbī, cited in Creswell, *Short Account of Early Muslim Architecture,* 367.

29. See the architectural plans in Hillenbrand, *Islamic Architecture,* 575–77; Northedge, "Creswell, Herzfeld, and Samarra," 78; Northedge, "The Palace at Iṣṭabulāt, Sāmarrāʾ," 81; and Northedge, "An Interpretation of the Palace of the Caliph at Samarra," 143–70.

30. Hillenbrand, *Islamic Architecture,* 406–7. For an earlier dating, see Creswell, *Short Account of Early Muslim Architecture,* 339–42; and Northedge, "The Palace at Iṣṭabulāt, Sāmarrāʾ," 68.

31. Measurements of Bulkuwārā, Iṣṭabulāt, and al-Jawsaq al-Khā cited in Hillenbrand, *Islamic Architecture,* 575; Creswell, *Short Account of Early Muslim Architecture,* 337; Bloom and Blair, *Islamic Arts,* 52.

32. Lane, *Arabic-English Lexicon,* s.v. "f-n-y." Note the paronomasia (*jinās*) between *fināʾ* (courtyard) and *fanāʾ* (death).

33. S. Stetkevych, "Pre-Islamic Panegyric and the Poetics of Redemption," 3; "Abbasid Panegyric and the Poetics of Political Allegiance," 44; *Mute Immortals Speak,* 7. Bulkuwārā embodied the symbolism through elevation. The axis of procession traversed three planes (Hillenbrand, *Islamic Architecture,* 398–406), so that a visitor proceeded upward through the symbolic rite of passage.

34. Al-Jāḥiẓ, *Kitāb al-Tāj fī Akhlāq al-Mulūk,* 8. Note how bodily orientation and choreography express the claims of authority on the performer (see Connerton, *How Societies Remember,* 71).

35. Hillenbrand, *Islamic Architecture,* 395, 574.

36. Hodgson, *The Venture of Islam,* 283.

37. For examples of the ways that piety-minded groups symbolically rejected the court and courtly culture, see the important article by the historian Christopher Melchert, "Piety of the Hadith Folk." Most interesting, Melchert documents many of the ways that piety-minded men and women eschewed *adab* humanism along with its promotion of savvy, curiosity, and wonder, as well as inquiry into seemingly fun but useless matters.

38. McEwan, *Oriental Origin of Hellenistic Kingship,* 18.

39. Sperl, "Islamic Kingship and Arabic Panegyric Poetry," 23.

40. Al-Nu^c^aymī, *Al-Usṭūra fil-Shi^c^r al-^c^Arabī qabl al-Islām,* 92.

41. Ibid. Abū Qābūs was the Lakhmid king of al-Ḥīra, al-Nu^c^mān III b. Mundhir (r. 580–602).

42. Cole, *Nomads of the Nomads,* 47.

43. J. Stetkevych, "Toward an Arabic Elegiac Lexicon," 66. The psychological and semiotic richness of *rabī^c^* can perhaps be captured in a scene of both subjective space and time. It is therefore useful to link it with Bakhtin's idea of chronotope: "Time, as it were, thickens, takes on flesh, becomes

artistically visible; likewise, space becomes charged and responsive to the movements of time" (Bakhtin, *Dialogic Imagination,* 84). Similarly, Theodor Gaster has expressed a space-time image with his term *topocosm.* With it he indicates anxiety and joy as the earth dies and comes back to life with the seasonal waning and waxing of daylight (Gaster, *Thespis,* 24). See also J. Stetkevych, "Toward an Arabic Elegiac Lexicon," especially the section on *rabᶜ* (vernal encampment).

44. Four months were considered noncombat periods, the first three being consecutive: Dhū l-Qaᶜda, Dhū l-Ḥijja, al-Muḥarram, and Rajab (Ibn Manẓūr, *Lisān al-ᶜArab,* s.v. "ḥ-r-m").

45. Graves, *Greek Myths,* 415.

46. Ibid., 420.

47. Aeschylus (d. 455 B.C.), *Libation Bearers,* lines 129–39.

48. Graves, *Greek Myths,* 420, 419.

49. S. Stetkevych, *Mute Immortals Speak,* 244.

50. Aeschylus, *Libation Bearers,* lines 129–39.

51. Al-Iṣfahānī, *Kitāb al-Aghānī,* 19:310.

52. Al-Maqdīsī, *Kitāb al-Badʾ wal-Taʾrīkh,* 6:123.

53. Ibn al-Jahm, *Dīwān,* 116, verses 30–31.

54. Al-Masᶜūdī, *Murūj al-Dhahab,* 4:120; for the idiom *ᶜalā wujūhihim,* see Hava, *Al-Farāʾid al-Durriyyah,* s.v. "w-j-h"; and Lane, *Arabic-English Lexicon,* s.v. "w-j-h."

55. Ibn al-ᶜImrānī, *Al-Inbāʾ fī Tārīkh al-Khulafāʾ,* 120.

56. Ibn Kathīr, *Al-Bidāya wal-Nihāhaya fil-Tārīkh,* 10:804.

57. S. Stetkevych, *Mute Immortals Speak,* 55, 57, 56, 75.

58. Al-Ṭabarī, *Tārīkh,* 9:229.

59. S. Stetkevych, *Mute Immortals Speak,* 57.

60. Ibn Rashīq al-Qayrawānī, *Kitāb al-ᶜUmda fī Ṣanᶜat al-Shiᶜr wa Naqdih,* 2:839.

61. Ibid., 2:831.

62. I have relied here on the text of al-Ṣayrafī's 1977 edition (al-Buḥturī, *Dīwān,* 2:1045). The ode is composed in the *ṭawīl* meter with the rhyme *-ruh.* The complete Arabic text is included in this book's appendix.

63. Al-Muᶜtazz b. al-Mutawakkil would have been the rightful heir to the throne; see *EI*^{2}, s.v. "al-Muᶜtazz bi 'llāh."

64. Al-Fatḥ b. Khāqān, the caliph's confidant, died shielding him with his own body; see *EI*^{2}, s.v. "al-Fatḥ b. Khāḳān." Ṭāhir b. ᶜAbd Allāh was the Abbasid governor of Khurasan from 844 to 862; see *EI*^{2}, s.v. "Ṭāhirids."

65. ᶜUbaydallāh b. Yaḥyā b. Khāqān served al-Mutawakkil and, later, al-Muᶜtamid as vizier; see *EI*^{2}, s.v. "al-Fatḥ b. Khāḳān."

66. S. Stetkevych, *Mute Immortals Speak,* 82. Ibn al-Jahm indicates the importance of the oral circulation of poetry as a means of broadcasting the news of al-Mutawakkil's death, when he says, "Verses came to us screaming his loss; / their folk and courtly meters were self-mutilated [out of grief]" (*Dīwān,* 117, verse 39).

67. Cf. J. Stetkevych, *Zephyrs of Najd,* 62.

68. S. Stetkevych, *Abū Tammām and the Poetics of the ᶜAbbāsid Age,* 8.

69. Ibid., 69.

70. Lane, *Arabic-English Lexicon,* s.v. "gh-ḍ-ḍ"; cf. S. Stetkevych, *Abū Tammām and the Poetics of the ᶜAbbāsid Age,* 114, 124.

71. Ibn Munqidh, *Al-Manāzil wal-Diyār,* 200–201. Al-Maqqarī, in *Nafḥ al-Ṭīb,* also considers it proverbial (2:47).

72. Aeschylus, *Libation Bearers,* lines 129–39.

73. W.R. Smith, *Lectures on the Religion of the Semites,* 344, 349.

74. S. Stetkevych, *Mute Immortals Speak,* 72.

75. Ibid.

76. Al-Marzubānī, *Al-Muwashshaḥ,* 418.

77. A discussion of the textual adjustments in verses 27, 28, and 30 follows later in this chapter.

78. Monroe, *Risālat at-Tawābiᶜ wa z-Zawābiᶜ,* 13.

79. S. Stetkevych, "Abbasid Panegyric and the Poetics of Political Allegiance," 43, 59.

80. Al-Nuᶜaymī, *Al-Usṭūra fil-Shiᶜr al-ᶜArabī qabl al-Islām,* 69–70.

81. Cf. S. Stetkevych, "Abbasid Panegyric and the Poetics of Political Allegiance," 59.

82. Lord, *Singer of Tales,* 16; Bauman, *Verbal Art as Performance,* 39–40; and Nagy, *Poetry as Performance,* 19.

83. B.H. Smith, "Contingencies of Value." See also Blachère, *Histoire de la littérature arabe des origines à la fin du XVe siècle de J.C.,* 1:89–92; Nagy, *Poetry as Performance,* 34, 36.

84. Al-Ṣūlī, *Akhbār al-Buḥturī wa Dhayl al-Akhbār,* 102.

85. Al-Masᶜūdī, *Murūj al-Dhahab,* 4:122.

86. Al-Ḥuṣrī al-Qayrawānī, *Zahr al-Ādāb wa Thamar al-Albāb,* 1:215–16. Verses 4–5, 7–8, 6, 13–14, 22, 25–26, and 28 are cited in this order and with several textual variations.

87. Al-Maᶜarrī, *Al-Luzūmiyyāt,* 610.

88. Ibid.; al-Buḥturī, *Dīwān,* 2:849.

89. Al-Ṣūlī, *Akhbār al-Buḥturī wa Dhayl al-Akhbār,* 100.

90. S. Stetkevych, *Mute Immortals Speak,* 7.

91. Hubert and Mauss, *Sacrifice,* 13.

92. Al-Ṣūlī, *Akhbār al-Buḥturī wa Dhayl al-Akhbār,* 100.

93. See al-Ṣayrafī's 1977 edition (al-Buḥturī, *Dīwān,* 2:848). The ode is composed in the *al-mutaqārib* meter with the rhyme *-r,* and a non-vocalized (*sākin*) consonant (*ḥarf mayyit*), which together echo the rhyme of the elegy to al-Mutawakkil. The complete Arabic text is included in this book's appendix.

94. I have preferred here to use the alternate reading of al-Buḥturī's *Dīwān,* edited by Ḥannā᾽ al-Fākhūrī in 1995 (2:420, verse 16): *wa-thannā bi-shar.* Here al-Ṣayrafī's edition (*thannā bi-khayr*) is inconsistent with the idea of one moral character elaborated in lines 15–18.

95. J. Stetkevych, *Zephyrs of Najd,* 9.

96. Lane, *Arabic-English Lexicon,* s.v. "a-sh-r" and "d-r-r." *Ushur* denotes sharp jagged teeth, which occur naturally among children or may be affected artificially with a file. In either case, *ushur* connotes immaturity or childish folly, as in the expression "*aᶜyaytanī bi-ushur fa-kayfa bi-durdur*"—that is, you wore me down when you were a child (lit., "having jagged teeth"), so all the more when you are grown (lit., "having sound teeth"). Both Lane (*Arabic-English Lexicon*) and Hava (*Al-Farā᾽id al-Durriyyah,* s.v. "a-sh-r") suggest there is a hint of gloating or exulting in this root. Note also that full teeth connote maturity in other contexts as well: *sinn* (age, equal or match), *sanan* (good conduct), *sana* (year), *sunna* (tradition, precedent, model). See Hava, *Al-Farā᾽id al-Durriyyah,* s.v. "s-n-n."

97. S. Stetkevych, "Abbasid Panegyric and the Poetics of Political Allegiance," 46.

98. Lane, *Arabic-English Lexicon,* s.v. "s-r-yā."

99. Grunebaum, *Muhammadan Festivals,* 30.

100. Lane, *Arabic-English Lexicon,* s.v. "s-ᶜ-yā."

101. Grunebaum, *Muhammadan Festivals,* 33, 23, 29.

102. Ibid., 19; Ibn ᶜAbd Rabbih, *Al-ᶜIqd al-Farīd,* 7:249.

103. Lane, *Arabic-English Lexicon,* s.v. "m-s-ḥ."

104. Al-Iṣfahānī, *Kitāb al-Aghānī,* 20:291; al-Ṭabarī, *Tārīkh,* 9:253.

105. Al-Ṭabarī, *Tā᾽rīkh,* 9:252–55.

106. *EI²,* s.v. "Fitna."

107. Garrison, *Dryden and the Tradition of Panegyric,* 7–8.

108. Ibid., 141–42.

109. S. Stetkevych, "Abbasid Panegyric and the Poetics of Political Allegiance," 43.

110. Caton, *"Peaks of Yemen I Summon,"* 95.

111. In this vein the praise hymn is considered an "insignia" of political authority (S. Stetkevych, "Umayyad Panegyric and the Poetics of Islamic

Hegemony," 90; S. Stetkevych, "ᶜAbbāsid Panegyric," 135), much like the ruler's ring, seal, and ritual clothing, although much more responsive to emergent situations and worthy of broadcast. Yet to be examined is the impact of this "insignia" in coloring and texturing the ideals of Arabo-Islamic leadership, manhood, and personhood, even to the present day.

112. Hava, *Al-Farāʾid al-Durriyyah,* s.v. "s-f-w."

113. Bayyūmī, et al., *Muᶜjam Taṣrīf al-Afᶜāl al-ᶜArabiyya,* 310.

114. S. Stetkevych, *Mute Immortals Speak,* 180.

115. Cf. S. Stetkevych, *Abū Tammām and the Poetics of the ᶜAbbāsid Age,* 206.

116. Al-Ṣūlī, *Akhbār al-Buḥturī wa Dhayl al-Akhbār,* 101; al-Masᶜūdī, *Murūj al-Dhahab,* 4:135; al-Iṣfahānī, *Kitāb al-Aghānī,* 23:206; and Ibn al-Sāᶜī, *Tārīkh al-Khulafāʾ,* 84.

117. Hodgson, *Venture of Islam,* 486; al-Iṣfahānī, *Kitāb al-Aghānī,* 23:206; and al-Ṭabarī, *Tārīkh al-Ṭabarī,* 9:185.

118. *EI*[2], s.v. "Fitna."

119. Qur'an 82:1–5.

120. Cf. Sperl, "Islamic Kingship and Arabic Panegyric Poetry," 32–33.

121. Ibid., 23.

122. Garrison, *Dryden and the Tradition of Panegyric,* 141.

123. Ḍayf, *Al-ᶜAṣr al-ᶜAbbāsī al-Thānī,* 278.

124. See S. Stetkevych, *Poetics of Islamic Legitimacy,* 1–79.

125. Al-Ṣūlī, *Akhbār al-Buḥturī wa Dhayl al-Akhbār,* 101.

126. Turner, *From Ritual to Theatre,* 83.

127. Ibid., 81–82.

128. Frye, *Fables of Identity,* 52.

FIVE Al-Buḥturī's Īwān Kisrā Ode: Canonic Value and Folk Literacy in the *Mujālasāt*

1. El-Hibri, *Reinterpreting Islamic Historiography,* 192–93; cf. al-Ṭabarī, *Tārīkh al-Ṭabarī,* 9:225; al-Masᶜūdī, *Murūj al-Dhahab,* 4:115–22. See also Gordon, *Breaking of a Thousand Swords,* 82.

2. Although many odes by al-Buḥturī are readily set to an occasion, this one is not, indicating that the exact occasion was not aesthetically relevant to the text. Al-Ṣayrafī speculates that the ode was composed in 883, though 861 is equally likely; see al-Buḥturī, *Dīwān* (ed. al-Ṣayrafī), 5:2753.

3. Al-Ṣayrafī, in al-Buḥturī, *Dīwān,* 2:1152, 5:2753, 2755; Ḍayf, *Al-ᶜAṣr al-ᶜAbbāsī al-Thānī,* 229–31; Motoyoshi, "Reality and Reverie," 96;

and Serrano, "Al-Buḥturī's Poetics of Persian Abodes," 69, 79. Serrano's thesis is reworked in Serrano, "Al-Buhturi's Poetics of Persian Abodes," in his *Neither a Borrower,* 8–48.

4. Serrano, "Al-Buḥturī's Poetics of Persian Abodes," 69, 86; see also Meisami, "Poetic Microcosms," 175.

5. Biographies of al-Buḥturī may be found in the following sources: al-Ashtar, "Un poète arabe"; al-ᶜAbbasī, *Maᶜāhid al-Tanṣīṣ ᶜalā Shawāhid al-Talkhīs,* 1:234–47; al-Iṣfahānī, *Kitāb al-Aghānī,* 21:37–53; Ibn Khallikān, *Wafayāt al-Aᶜyān,* 6:21–31; al-Khaṭīb al-Baghdādī, *Tārīkh Baghdād,* 13:446–50; *EI²,* s.v. "al-Buḥturī,"; al-Samᶜānī, *Al-Ansāb,* 2:101–2; al-Ṣūlī, *Akhbār al-Buḥturī wa Dhayl al-Akhbār*; Yāqūt b.ᶜAbd Allāh al-Ḥamawī, *Kitāb Irshād al-Arīb fī Maᶜrifat al-Adīb,* 1:81; 2:295, 423; 5:252, 339; 7:226–333; and Ali, "Al-Buhturi."

6. Ibn Khallikān, *Wafayāt al-Aᶜyān,* 6:30.

7. Ibid., 6:22.

8. Ali, "Al-Buhturi."

9. Ali, "Praise for Murder?"

10. Ali, "Al-Buhturi."

11. Ibn al-ᶜImrānī, *Al-Inbāʾ fī Tārīkh al-Khulafāʾ,* 136.

12. *EI²,* s.v. "al-Buḥturī."

13. Al-Buḥturī, *Dīwān,* ode 19.

14. Ibn Shams al-Khilāfa Mujidd al-Mulk, *Kitāb al-Ādāb,* 29.

15. For al-Buḥturī's endorsement of al-Muᶜtazz, see al-Shābushtī, *Kitāb Al-Diyārāt,* 150–56; Ibn al-ᶜImrānī, *Al-Inbāʾ fī Tārīkh al-Khulafāʾ,* 118–19; and his praise ode jointly to al-Muᶜtazz and al-Mutawakkil, in al-Buḥturī, *Dīwān* (ode 277), on the occasion of al-Muᶜtazz's circumcision and seating at Bulkuwārā. For al-Buḥturī's failure to serve al-Muntaṣir as state poet, see Ibn al-ᶜImrānī, *Al-Inbāʾ fī Tārīkh al-Khulafāʾ,* 117. Note also his decision to stigmatize, then redeem al-Munstaṣir (chap. 4). Although this may seem on the surface an about-face, it is telling that he suffered no negative consequences for besmearing the caliph, and he was never expected to offer an ode of apology (*iᶜtidhār*) for his assault, because al-Muntaṣir needed his poetic services. In effect, the two odes stand as a token of his preeminence.

16. Webber, "On Canonicity, Literacy and Middle Eastern Folk Narrative," 41. This chapter benefited tremendously from Webber's article, which challenges the supposed divide between canonical and folk literatures by making a compelling case for their interinfluence in the form of ideas, motifs, character types, and the literacies that audiences summon to interpret both.

17. al-Buḥturī, *Dīwān,* ode 340.

18. The traditional northern border of the empire between the Caspian and Black Sea.

19. Bedouin camps and abodes. He contrasts the delicacy of Sasanian abodes with the bleakness of Bedouins'.

20. Two major Bedouin tribes. ᶜAns is of the Qaḥṭānī line from Yemen, and ᶜAbs descends from the ᶜAdnānī line from Najd (today near Riyadh).

21. S. Stetkevych, *Mute Immortals Speak,* 153. For more on brigand poetry, see Khulayyif, *Al-Shuᶜarāᵓ al-Ṣaᶜālik fī al-ᶜAṣr al-Jāhilī.*

22. S. Stetkevych, *Mute Immortals Speak,* 88, 91.

23. This translation of al-Shanfarā's *Lāmiyat al-ᶜArab* is from S. Stetkevych, *Mute Immortals Speak,* 144.

24. Al-Ṣayrafī, in al-Buḥturī, *Dīwān,* 5:2755; Ḍayf, *Al-ᶜAṣr al-ᶜAbbāsī al-Thānī,* 229.

25. Ḍayf, *Al-ᶜAṣr al-ᶜAbbāsī al-Thānī,* 231.

26. Hodgson, *The Venture of Islam,* 1:282–83.

27. The caliph al-Manṣūr (r. 754–75) is said to have plundered Ctesiphon to use its materials for his new imperial city, Baghdad. When he sought to dismantle the Īwān Kisrā of the Sasanian palace, however, the goal proved too daunting and expensive to accomplish. The caliph was forced to abandon the project, having left barely a dent; see al-Thaᶜālibī, *Thimār al-Qulūb,* 181. Nevertheless, caliphs would continue to make excursions to the nearby ruins, as did al-Mutawakkil (al-Ṭabarī, *Tārīkh,* 9:166).

28. Qur'an 67:3–4.

29. Serrano, "Al-Buḥturī's Poetics of Persian Abodes," 69; Motoyoshi, "Reality and Reverie," 109. For more on the function of epic and epic-like praise hymns in supporting empire, see Quint, *Epic and Empire,* 133; and S. Stetkevych, *Poetics of Islamic Legitimacy.*

30. Sperl, "Islamic Kingship and Arabic Panegyric Poetry," 32.

31. Al-Dīnawarī (Abū Ḥanīfa), *Al-Akhbār al-Ṭiwāl,* 69; al-Ṭabarī, *Tārīkh,* 2:102, 149.

32. Hodgson, *Venture of Islam,* 1:282.

33. Al-Dīnawarī, *Al-Akhbār al-Ṭiwāl,* 69.

34. Ibid., 70, 73.

35. Motoyoshi, "Reality and Reverie," 106, 107.

36. See S. Stetkevych, "Intoxication and Immortality."

37. See S. Stetkevych, *Mute Immortals Speak,* 41–42.

38. See S. Stetkevych, "Intoxication and Immortality," 35.

39. Al-Dīnawarī, *Al-Akhbār al-Ṭiwāl,* 107.

40. Ibid., 108.

41. Ibid., 107.

42. S. Stetkevych, *Mute Immortals Speak,* 219.
43. Ibid., 199.
44. Al-Ṭabarī, *Tārīkh,* 2:129; al-Dīnawarī, *Al-Akhbār al-Ṭiwāl,* 62.
45. Al-Ṭabarī, *Tārīkh,* 2:147.
46. Ibid., 2:129–31; al-Dīnawarī, *Al-Akhbār al-Ṭiwāl,* 62.
47. Anderson, *Imagined Communities,* 13.
48. Ibid., 13–24, 36.
49. DeWeese, *Islamization and Native Religion,* 24.
50. Ibid.
51. Ibid., 26; Anderson, *Imagined Communities,* 14–15.
52. *EI*[2], s.v. "Shu^c^ūbiyya."

SIX Singing Samarra (861–956): Poetry, Reception, and the Reproduction of Literary Value in Historical Narrative

1. El-Hibri, *Reinterpreting Islamic Historiography,* 188, 192, 198.
2. Ibid., 198.
3. Ibn Qutayba, *Al-Ma^c^ārif,* 393.
4. The terms *plot* and *story* are used in the most literary technical sense: the former is a sequence of events conveying a sense of causality; the latter is simply a sequence of events.
5. Al-Ya^c^qūbī, *Tārīkh al- Ya^c^qūbī,* 2:492.
6. See also Morse, *Truth and Convention,* 128.
7. B.H. Smith, "Contingencies of Value."
8. Al-Ṭabarī, *Tārīkh,* 9:154.
9. Kraemer, *History of al-Ṭabari*, vol. 34, *Incipient Decline,* xii–xiii; al-Ṭabarī, *Tārīkh,* 9:210. On al-Mutawakkil's trip to Damascus, see Paul Cobb's important reinterpretation, "Al-Mutawakkil's Damascus." Although Cobb's focus is not mythmaking, he does show that later historical accounts deploy the Damascus story for rhetorical ends—namely, to prefigure an attack on the caliph's life (246). He found a rare list of al-Mutawakkil's entourage in Ibn ^c^Asākir's history of Damascus, which shows plainly that nearly every prominent member of his Turkic force accompanied him (248), thus casting doubt on the *adab*-based theory that he fled them. Most important, Cobb's careful analysis of sources illustrates how historical narratives are invented to serve the important function of addressing profound lingering questions about what happened and why.
10. Saliba, *History of al-Ṭabarī,* vol. 35, *Crisis of the ^c^Abbāsid Caliphate,* 1.

11. Ibn al-ᶜImrānī, *Al-Inbāʾ fī Tārīkh al-Khulafāʾ,* 137.

12. Waines, *History of al-Ṭabari*, vol. 36, *Revolt of the Zanj,* xvi.

13. Ibn al-ᶜImrānī, *Al-Inbāʾ fī Tārīkh al-Khulafāʾ,* 137.

14. Hodgson, *The Venture of Islam,* 1:488; Kennedy, *The Prophet and the Age of the Caliphate,* 175.

15. Kennedy, *The Prophet and the Age of the Caliphate,* 175.

16. See Ali, "Reinterpreting al-Buḥturī's Īwān Kisrā Ode."

17. Ibn Khallikān, *Wafayāt al-Aᶜyān,* 1:42; Yāqūt b.ᶜAbd Allāh al-Ḥamawī, *Muᶜjam al-Buldān,* 3:173–78.

18. J. Stetkevych, *Zephyrs of Najd,* 52, 62. See also Ibn Munqidh, *Al-Manāzil wal-Diyār,* 200.

19. Al-Buḥturī, *Dīwān,* odes 262, 395, 750, 771.

20. Al-Ṣayrafī, in al-Buḥturī, *Dīwān,* 5:2793.

21. Al-Buḥturī, *Dīwān,* ode 771, lines 1–4.

22. Ibid., line 5.

23. Kennedy, *The Prophet and the Age of the Caliphate,* 174.

24. Al-Buḥturī, *Dīwān,* 2:656, lines 1–5.

25. Hillenbrand, *Islamic Architecture,* 398.

26. Ibid., 406.

27. Ibn al-ᶜImrānī, *Al-Inbāʾ fī Tārīkh al-Khulafāʾ,* 137; Yāqūt b.ᶜAbd Allāh al-Ḥamawī, *Muᶜjam al-Buldān,* 3:178.

28. Kraemer, *History of al-Ṭabari,* 34:223; Yāqūt b.ᶜAbd Allāh al-Ḥamawī, *Muᶜjam al-Buldān,* 3:178.

29. Yāqūt b.ᶜAbd Allāh al-Ḥamawī, *Muᶜjam al-Buldān,* 3:178.

30. Ibid., 3:176; cf. Meisami, "Palace-Complex as Emblem," 69–78.

31. In Meisami, "Palace-Complex as Emblem," 69–70.

32. According to Ibn Rashīq, poets were notorious for their artifice and mendacity, as would be expected in an artistic profession. He tells one anecdote in which it is framed as a complaint: A wise man was once asked about poets. He said, "What can you say about these folks? Modesty is honorable except among them, and lying is dishonorable except among them." See Ibn Rashīq al-Qayrawānī, *Kitāb al-ᶜUmda fī Ṣanᶜat al-Shiᶜr wa Naqdih,* 1:18.

33. Al-Ṣūlī, *Akhbār al-Buḥturī wa Dhayl al-Akhbār,* 49–54.

34. Ibid.

35. Al-Ṣūlī, *Akhbār al-Buḥturī wa Dhayl al-Akhbār,* 49.

36. Ibn Khallikān, *Wafayāt al-Aᶜyān,* 6:28. In addition to al-Buḥturī's two collectors, there were at least five men who orally transmitted his poetry. They were Muḥammad b. al-Mubarrad (d. 898), Muḥammad b. Khalaf al-Marzubān (d. 921), al-Huṣayn b. Ismāᶜīl al-Muḥāmilī (d. 941), Muḥammad b. Aḥmad al-Ḥakīmī (d. 947), and ᶜAbd Allah b. Jaᶜfar b. Darastawayh al-Naḥwī (d. 958); see al-Khaṭīb al-Baghdādī, *Tārīkh Baghdād,* 13:447.

37. Ibn Khallikān, *Wafayāt al-Aʿyān,* 5:389.

38. Ibid.

39. Al-Samʿānī, *Al-Ansab,* 2:102.

40. For an interpretation of al-Buḥturī's ode pair, stigmatizing and then praising al-Muntaṣir, see Ali, "Praise for Murder?"

41. Ibn Khallikān, *Wafayāt al-Aʿyān,* 6:30.

42. Al-Iṣfahānī, *Kitāb al-Aghānī,* 21:53; al-ʿAbbasī, *Maʿāhid al-Tanṣīṣ ʿalā Shawāhid al-Talkhīs,* 1:243.

43. Ibn Bassām al-Shantarīnī, *Al-Dhakhīra fī Maḥāsin Ahl al-Jazīra.*

44. Sibṭ al-Jawzī, *Mirʾāt al-Zamān*; al-Dhahabī, *Tārīkh al-Islām.*

45. See Ali, "Reinterpreting al-Buḥturī's Īwān Kisrā Ode."

46. Al-Masʿūdī, *Murūj al-Dhahab,* 4:118.

47. *EI²,* s.v. "Khabar."

48. Al-Masʿūdī, *Murūj al-Dhahab,* 4:118.

49. Ibid., 4:121.

50. Ms. Spr. 48, f. 595.

51. Al-Masʿūdī, *Murūj al-Dhahab,* 4:118:

> Al-Buḥturī said: We gathered that night with boon-companions (*nudamāʾ*) at al-Mutawakkil's gathering (*majlis*) and we began to mention the topic of swords. One of the people present said, "O Commander of the Faithful, I heard that a man from Basra happened upon a sword from India without equal, and nothing like it was seen." Al-Mutawakkil ordered that a letter be written to the governor of Basra, asking him to buy it [the sword] at whatever price. The letter was sent through the post and a letter from the governor of Basra returned saying that a man from Yemen [had] bought it. Al-Mutawakkil then ordered a message to Yemen asking for the sword and [the opportunity to] purchase it. And the letter was sent.
>
> Al-Buḥturī added: While we were still with al-Mutawakkil, ʿUbayd Allāh suddenly entered with the sword. He let him know that it was purchased from its owner in Yemen for 10,000 dirhams. He [al-Mutawakkil] was pleased with its arrival; he thanked God for facilitating the matter. He drew it and liked it. Each of us said what he liked, and he placed it under the fold of his mattress. When morning came, he said to al-Fatḥ [his vizier and lover], "Bring me a slave-boy whose courage and valor you trust. Charge him with this sword, so he may hold it over my head, never parting from me by day so long as I reign."
>
> He [Al-Buḥturī] said: Talking did not resume until Bāghir the Turk came and al-Fatḥ said, "O Commander of the Faithful, this is Bāghir

the Turk. He was recommended to me for his courage and valor. He is fit for what the Commander of the Faithful wishes." Al-Mutawakkil called him and charged him with the sword, and ordered him according to his wishes. He offered to elevate his station and increase his income.

Al-Buḥturī said: By God, that sword was not drawn nor unsheathed from the time it was charged to him until the night that Bāghir struck him with that sword.

52. El-Hibri, *Reinterpreting Islamic Historiography,* 193.
53. Ibid., 210.
54. Ibid.
55. Al-Masᶜūdī, *Murūj al-Dhahab,* 4:119:

Then al-Buḥturī said: I noticed a strange thing about al-Mutawakkil the night that he was slain. We were mentioning haughtiness and what kings used to do by way of insolence. We engaged the topic, but he abstained. Then he turned his face toward the Qibla [Mecca] and prostrated and rolled his face in the dust in humility to God, Mighty and Majestic be He. Then he took dust and sprinkled it on his beard and head. He erupted, "I am a slave of God, and he who is destined to dust must humble himself and not wax haughty."

Al-Buḥturī said: I took it as a bad omen for him, and downplayed what he did in sprinkling dust on his head and beard. Then he sat for drinking. When one of the singers sang a tune, he liked it. He turned to al-Fatḥ and said, "O Fatḥ, there is no one who hears this song who is noble except you and me." Then he started to weep.

Al-Buḥturī said: I took a bad omen from his weeping and said [to myself], "Here's the second one." While we were in the midst of that, a servant came—one of Qabīḥa's [the caliph's wife] servants—carrying a cloth bundle. Inside of it was a robe of honor sent to him by Qabīḥa. The messenger said, "O Commander of the Faithful, Qabīḥa says to you, 'I had this ceremonial coat (*khilᶜa*) made for the Commander of the Faithful and I liked it, so I sent it to you that you may wear it.'" He [al-Buḥturī] said: In it was a red coat (*darrāᶜa*) the likes of which I have never seen, and a red silk gown (*muṭraf*). It was so delicate it looked like [Egyptian] *Dabīqī* silk.

He [al-Buḥturī] said: He wore the coat on the *inside* and then wrapped himself in the gown. I chased him to warn him of a jutting object that might cause his gown to catch. Al-Mutawakkil moved into it and the gown coiled around him. It thus pulled him once and ripped the gown from end to end.

He [al-Buḥturī] said: He took it, wrapped it, and gave it to the servant of Qabīḥa who brought it. He said, "Tell her, keep this gown with you so that it may be a burial shroud when I die."

I said to myself, "Verily, we are from God, and to Him we return. By God, this reign is over." Al-Mutawakkil then became severely drunk. He [al-Buḥturī] said: It was his custom that if he keeled over when drunk, the servants at his head set him upright. As we were doing that—and some three hours of the night had passed!—Bāghir suddenly approached accompanied by ten soldiers of the Turks. Swords were in their hands sparkling in the light of the candle. They then attacked us and headed toward al-Mutawakkil so that Bāghir climbed the throne with other Turks. Fatḥ cried out, "How dare you! Your master!"

When the slave-boys and others present, as well as boon-companions, saw them, they fled in haste. No one else remained in the gathering except Fatḥ. He fought them and pushed them. Al-Buḥturī said: Then I heard al-Mutawakkil's death-cry (*ṣayḥa*). Bāghir had struck him with the sword with which al-Mutawakkil had charged him. He struck him on the right side, cut him open to his waist, then turned him over for the left side and did the same.

Al-Fatḥ approached, pushing them away, and one of them stabbed him with his sword in his stomach and it exited his back. He nevertheless remained steadfast, neither leaning nor dying. Al-Buḥturī said: I never did see a man with a stronger spirit nor one more noble. He threw himself on al-Mutawakkil, and they died together.

They were rolled together in the carpet in which they died. They were put off to the side in that state all night and most of the day until the caliphate rested in al-Muntaṣir. He gave orders and they were buried together. It is said that Qabīḥa wrapped him in the exact gown that was ripped.

56. Ahsan, *Social Life under the Abbasids,* 39, 40–41.

57. Al-Ṭabarī, *Tārīkh,* 9:224.

58. Ibn al-Jawzī, *Al-Muntaẓam fī Tārīkh al-Mulūk wal-Umam,* 11:356.

59. Whereas Ibn al-Jawzī introduces the mother as a delegate of Fate in carrying the symbol of al-Mutawakkil's death, al-Masᶜūdī prefers to introduce the mother in a different way. He prefaces the murder story of al-Mutawakkil by saying ominously, just lines from al-Buḥturī's alarming story, "In the year 247 [861], Shujāᶜ, the mother of al-Mutawakkil, died . . . then al-Mutawakkil died six months after her death." See al-Masᶜūdī, *Murūj al-Dhahab,* 4:118. To him, the literary force of the mother's role is more important than slavish consistency.

60. Al-Thaᶜālibī, *Thimār al-Qulūb,* 190; al-Ṭabarī, *Tārīkh,* 9:226; Ibn al-ᶜImrānī, *Al-Inbāʾ fī Tārīkh al-Khulafāʾ,* 119; and Ibn al-Sāᶜī, *Tārīkh al-Khulafāʾ,* 79.

61. Al-Thaᶜālibī, *Thimār al-Qulūb,* 191.

62. Al-Masᶜūdī, *Murūj al-Dhahab,* 4:121.

Conclusion

1. Alexis de Tocqueville, *Democracy in America,* trans., edited, and with introduction by Harvey Mansfield and Delba Winthrop (Chicago: University of Chicago Press, 2000), ch. 25.

2. Gregory Orfalea and Sharif Elmusa, eds., *Grape Leaves: A Century of Arab-American Poetry* (New York: Interlink Books, 2000), 22.

3. Edgar Allan Poe, "The Thousand-and-Second-Tale of Scheherazade," in *The Complete Works of Edgar Allan Poe* (New York: G. P. Putnam's Sons, 1902), 6:130.

4. Some in the field of Arabic literature may reject the use of theory and comparisons to complement textual gaps. Such reactions are a matter not of scholarly integrity but of personal temperament. The humanities in America have by and large embraced the use of theory and comparisons to fill gaps in textual evidence, especially in literary studies.

Bibliography

ʿAbbās, Iḥsān. 1997. *Tārīkh al-Naqd al-Adabī ʿind al-ʿArab: Naqd al-Shiʿr min al-Qarn al-Thānī ḥattā al-Qarn al-Thāmin al-Hijrī.* Rev. ed. Amman: Dār al-Shurūq.

al-ʿAbbasī, ʿAbd al-Rahīm b. Aḥmad. 1947. *Maʿāhid al-Tanṣīṣ ʿalā Shawā-hid al-Talkhīs.* Edited by Muḥammad Muḥyī al-Din. Cairo: Maṭbaʿat al-Saʿāda.

ʿAbd al-Karīm, Khalīl. 1997. *Quraysh: Min al-Qabīla ilā al-Dawla al-Markaziyya.* Cairo: Sīnā lil-Nashr.

Abrahams, Roger D. 1977. "Toward an Enactment Centered Theory of Folklore." In *Frontiers of Folklore,* edited by William R. Bascom, 79–120. American Association for the Advancement of Science, Selected Symposia Series, no. 5. Boulder, Colo.: Westview Press.

Abū Ḥayyān al-Tawḥīdī, ʿAlī b. Muḥammad. 1939. *Kitāb al-Imtāʿ wal-Muʾānasa* [Book of Delight and Good Company]. Edited by Aḥmad Amīn and Aḥmad Zayd. 3 vols. Cairo: Lajnat al-Taʾlīf wal-Tarjama wal-Nashr.

Abu-Lughod, Lila. 1986. *Veiled Sentiments: Honor and Poetry in a Bedouin Society.* Berkeley: University of California Press.

Abū Nuwās, al-Ḥasan b. Hānī. 1992. *Dīwān.* Edited by Badr al-Dīn Ḥaḍriyy and Muḥammad Ḥammāmī. Beirut: Dār al-Sharq al-ʿArabī.

Abū Tammām, Ḥabīb b. Aws. 1982–83. *Dīwān Abū Tammām bi-Sharḥ al-Khaṭīb al-Tabrīzī* [Poetry Collection of Abū Tammām with the Commentary of al-Tabrīzī]. Edited by Muḥammad ʿAbduh ʿAzzām. 4 vols. Dhakhāʾir al-ʿArab, 5. Cairo: Dār al-Maʿārif.

Ackerman, Susan. 1989. "A Marzeah in Ezekiel 8:7–13?" *Harvard Theological Review* 83: 267–81.

Aeschylus. 1960. *The Libation Bearers.* Translated by Richmond Lattimore. In *Greek Tragedies,* vol. 2, edited by David Grene and Richmond Lattimore, 91–131. Chicago: University of Chicago Press.

al-ʿAfīfī, Abū al-ʿIlā. 1945. *Al-Malāmatiyya wal-Ṣūfiyya wa-Ahl al-Futuwwa* [The Malamatiyya Order, the Sufis, and the People of Chivalry]. Muʾallafāt al-Jamʿiyya al-Falsafiyya al-Maṣriyya, 5. Cairo: ʿĪsā Bābī al-Ḥalabī.

Al-Aḥādīth al-Qudsiyya. 1991. 8th ed. 2 vols. Cairo: al-Majlis al-Aʿlā lil-Shuʾūn al-Islāmiyya.

Ahmed, Munir ud-Din. 1969. "The Institution of al-Mudhākara." *Zeitschrift der Deutschen Morgenländischen Gesellschaft,* Supp. 1 [No. 17, Deutscher Orientalistentag, 21–27 July, 1968]: 595–630.

Ahsan, M. M. 1979. *Social Life under the Abbasids, 170–289 A.H., 786–902 A.D.* London: Longman.

Ajami, Mansour. 1984. *The Neckveins of Winter: The Controversy over Natural and Artificial Poetry in Medieval Arabic Literary Criticism.* Leiden: E. J. Brill.

Al-Azmeh, Aziz. 1997. *Muslim Kingship: Power and the Sacred in Muslim, Christian, and Pagan Polities.* London: Tauris Publishers.

Ali, Samer Mahdy. 2004. "Praise for Murder? Two Odes by al-Buḥturī Surrounding an Abbasid Patricide." In *Writers and Rulers: Perspectives on Their Relation from Abbasid to Safavid Times,* edited by Beatrice Gruendler and Louise Marlow, 1–38. Series Literaturen im Kontext, vol. 16. Wiesbaden: Verlag Reichert.

———. 2005. "Al-Buhturi." In *Dictionary of Literary Biography: Arabic Literary Culture, 500–925,* edited by Michael Cooperson and Shawkat M. Toorawa, 98–107. Detroit: Thomas Gale.

———. 2006a. "Reinterpreting al-Buḥturī's Īwān Kisrā Ode: Tears of Affection for the Tragic Cycles of History." *Journal of Arabic Literature* 37: 46–67.

———. 2006b. "Singing Samarra (861–956): Poetry and the Burgeoning of Historical Narrative upon the Murder of al-Mutawakkil." *Journal of Arabic and Islamic Studies* 6: 1–23.

———. 2008. "Early Islam—Monotheism or Henotheism? A View from the Court." *Journal of Arabic Literature* 39: 14–37.

al-Amāsī, Muḥammad b. Qāsim. 1279 A.H. [A.D. 1862 or 1863]. *Rawḍ al-Akhyār al-Muntakhab min 'Rabī^c al-Abrār' fī ^cIlm al-Muḥaḍarāt fī Anwā^c al-Muḥāwarāt min al-^cUlum al-^cArabiyya wa-al-Funun al-Adabiyya* [Garden of the Best, Selected from 'Vernal Gardens for the Virtuous' on Knowledge at Literary Gatherings, and the Varieties of Discourse on Arabic Knowledge and Literary Art]. [Cairo?]: Ḥuṣayn al-Ṭarābulusī.

al-^cĀmirī, Abū al-Ḥasan. 1967. *Kitāb al-I^clām bi-Manāqib al-Islām.* Edited by Aḥmad ^cAbd al-Ḥalīm Ghurāb. Cairo: Dār al-Kātib al-^cArabī.

Anderson, Benedict. 1991. *Imagined Communities: Reflections on the Origin and Spread of Nationalism.* Rev. ed. London: Verso.

Arberry, A. J., ed. 1965. *Arabic Poetry: A Primer for Students.* Cambridge: Cambridge University Press.

al-Ashtar, Ṣāliḥ. 1953. "Un poète arabe du IIIe siècle de l'hégire (IXe de J.-C.), Buhturi." Ph.D. dissertation, Sorbonne University.

Ashtiany, Julia, et al., eds. 1990. *^cAbbāsid Belles-Lettres.* Cambridge: Cambridge University Press.

al-^cAskarī, Abū al-Hilāl al-Ḥasan. 1988. *Kitāb Jamharat al-Amthāl* [Reference of Proverbs]. Edited by Aḥmad ^cAbd al-Salām and Muḥammad Zaghlūl. 2 vols. Beirut: Dār al-Kutub al-^cIlmiyya.

^cAttār, Farīd al-Dīn. 1988. *The Conference of the Birds.* Translated by Afkham Darbandi and Dick Davis. New York: Penguin.

al-Azraqī, Abū al-Walīd. 1983. *Akhbār Makka* [Lore of Mecca]. Edited by Rushdī al-Ṣāliḥ Malḥas. 2 vols. Beirut: Dār al-Andalus.

Badawī, Aḥmad Aḥmad. 1996. *Usus al-Naqd al-Adabī ^cind al-^cArab.* Cairo: Nahḍat Miṣr.

Badawi, El-Said, and Martin Hinds. 1986. *A Dictionary of Modern Egyptian Arabic: Arabic-English.* Beirut: Librarie du Liban.

Badawi, Muhammad Mustafa. 1988. *Early Arabic Drama.* Cambridge: Cambridge University Press.

Bakhtin, M. M. 1981. *The Dialogic Imagination: Four Essays.* Edited by Michael Holquist. Translated and edited by Caryl Emerson and Michael Holquist. University of Texas Press Slavic Series, no. 1. Austin: University of Texas Press.

Barret, W. S., ed. 1964. *Euripedes: Hippolytus.* Oxford: Oxford University Press.

Bascom, William. 1984. "The Forms of Folklore: Prose Narratives." In *Sacred Narrative: Readings in the Theory of Myth,* edited by Alan Dundes, 5–29. Berkeley: University of California Press.

Bauman, Richard. 1977. *Verbal Art as Performance.* Rowley, Mass.: Newbury House.

———. 1983. *Let Your Words Be Few: Symbolism of Speaking and Silence among Seventeenth-Century Quakers.* Cambridge: Cambridge University Press.

———. 1986. *Story, Performance, and Event: Contextual Studies of Oral Narrative.* Cambridge Studies in Oral Literate Culture, no. 10. Cambridge: Cambridge University Press.

Bauman, Richard, and Charles Briggs. 1990. "Poetics and Performance as Critical Perspectives on Language and Social Life." *Annual Review of Anthropology* 19: 59–88.

Bayyūmī, Ḥasan, et al. 1989. *Muᶜjam Taṣrīf al-Afᶜāl al-ᶜArabiyya.* Cairo: Elias.

Beach, Eleanor Ferris. 1993. "The Samaria Ivories, Marzeah, and Biblical Text." *The Biblical Archeologist* 56: 94–104.

Beckwith, Christopher. 1984a. "Aspects of the Early History of the Central Asian Guard Corp in Islam." *Archivum Eurasiae Medii Aevi* 4: 29–43.

———. 1984b. "The Plan of the City of Peace: Central Asian Iranian Factors in the Early ᶜAbbāsid Design." *Acta Orientalia* 38: 143–64.

Beeman, William O. 1986. *Language, Status, and Power in Iran.* Bloomington: Indiana University Press.

Beeston, A. F. L., et al., eds. 1983. *Arabic Literature to the End of the Umayyad Period.* Cambridge: Cambridge University Press.

Ben-Amos, Dan. 1984. "The Seven Strands of Tradition: Varieties in Its Meaning in American Folklore Studies." *Journal of Folklore Research* 21: 97–131.

Bencheikh, Jamel-Eddine. 1975. *Poétique arabe: Essai sur les voies d'une creation.* Paris: Éditions Anthropos.

Berkey, Jonathan Porter. 1992. *The Transmission of Knowledge in Medieval Cairo: A Social History of Islamic Education.* Princeton Studies on the Near East. Princeton, N.J.: Princeton University Press.

Blachère, Régis. 1935. *Un poète arabe du IVe siècle de l'Hégire (Xe siècle de J.-C.): Abou t-Ṭayyib al-Motanabbî (essai d'histoire littéraire).* Paris: Adrien-Maisonneuve.

———. 1952. *Histoire de la littérature arabe des origines à la fin du XVe siècle de J.-C.* Vol. 1. Paris: Adrien-Maisonneuve.

———. 1963. "Un auteur d'Adab oublié: al-ᶜUtbī, mort en 228." In *Mélanges d'orientalisme offerts à Henri Massé.* Tehran: University of Tehran.

Bloom, Jonathan, and Sheila Blair. 1997. *Islamic Arts.* Art and Ideas Series. London: Phaidon.

Boardman, John. 1999. "Symposion Furniture." In *Sympotica: A Symposium on the Symposion,* edited by Oswyn Murray, 122–31. Oxford: Oxford University Press.

Boas, Franz. 1955. *Primitive Art.* New York: Dover Publications.

Bonebakker, S. A. 1990. "Adab and the Concept of Belles-Lettres." In *ᶜAbbāsid Belles-Lettres,* edited by Julia Ashtiany, 16–30. Cambridge: Cambridge University Press.

Booth, Wayne. 1988. *The Company We Keep: An Ethics of Fiction.* Berkeley: University of California Press.

Bordereuil, P., and D. Pardee. 1990. "Le papyrus du marzeah." *Semitica* 38: 49–68.

Bouhdiba, Abdelwahab. 1998. *Sexuality in Islam.* Translated by Alan Sheridan. London: Saqi Books.

Briggs, Charles L. 1988. *Competence in Performance: The Creativity of Tradition in Mexicano Verbal Art.* Philadelphia: University of Pennsylvania Press.

Brockelmann, Carl. 1943–49. *Geschichte der arabischen Litteratur.* 2 vols. and 3 supp. Leiden: E. J. Brill.

Brookshaw, Dominic. 2003. "Palaces, Pavilions and Pleasure-gardens: The Context and Setting of the Medieval *Majlis.*" *Middle Eastern Literatures* 6: 199–223.

Brown, Francis, S. R. Driver, and Charles Briggs. n.d. *A Hebrew and English Lexicon of the Old Testament.* Oxford: Clarendon Press.

al-Buḥturī, Abū ᶜUbāda al-Walīd. 1977. *Dīwān* [Poetry Collection]. Edited by Ḥasan Kāmil al-Ṣayrafī. 5 vols. Dhakhāʾir al-ᶜArab, 34. 2d ed. Cairo: Dār al-Maᶜārif.

———. 1995. *Dīwān* [Poetry Collection]. Edited by Ḥannā al-Fākhūrī. 2 vols. Beirut: Dār al-Jīl.

Bulliet, Richard W. 1994. *Islam: The View from the Edge.* New York: Columbia University Press.

Bürgel, Johann Christoph. 1988. *The Feather of Simugh: The "Licit Magic" of the Arts in Medieval Islam.* New York: New York University Press.

Burke, Kenneth. 1935. *Permanence and Change: An Anatomy of Purpose.* New York: New Republic.

———. 1937. *Attitudes toward History.* New York: New Republic.

Cannadine, David, and Simon Price, eds. 1987. *Rituals of Royalty: Power and Ceremonial in Traditional Societies.* Cambridge: Cambridge University Press.

Cantarino, Vincente. 1975. *Arabic Poetics in the Golden Age.* Studies in Arabic Literature 4. Leiden: E. J. Brill.

Carruthers, Mary. 1994. *Book of Memory: A Study of Memory in Medieval Culture.* Cambridge: Cambridge University Press.

Carter, Jane B. 1997. "Thiasos and Marzeah: Ancestor Cult in the Age of Homer." In *New Light on a Dark Age: Exploring the Culture of Geo-*

metric Greece, edited by S. Langdon, 72–112. Columbia: University of Missouri Press.

Caton, Steven Charles. 1990. *"Peaks of Yemen I Summon": Poetry as Cultural Practice in a North Yemeni Tribe.* Berkeley: University of California Press.

Chamberlain, Michael. 1994. *Knowledge and Social Practice in Medieval Damascus, 1190–1350.* Cambridge: Cambridge University Press.

Cobb, Paul M. 1999. "Al-Mutawakkil's Damascus: A New ᶜAbbāsid Capital?" *Journal of Near Eastern Studies* 58: 241–57.

———. 2001. *White Banners: Contention in ᶜAbbāsid Syria, 750–880.* Albany: State University of New York Press.

Cole, Donald Powell. 1975. *Nomads of the Nomads: The Āl Murrah Bedouins of the Empty Quarter.* Arlington Heights, Ill.: Harlan Davidson.

Coleman, Joyce. 1996. *Public Reading and the Reading Public in Late Medieval England and France.* New York: Cambridge University Press, 1996

Connerton, Paul. 1994. *How Societies Remember.* Cambridge: Cambridge University Press.

Cornell, Vincent. 1998. *Realm of the Saint: Power and Authority in Moroccan Sufism.* Austin: University of Texas Press.

Creswell, K. A. C. 1989. *A Short Account of Early Muslim Architecture.* Revised and supplemented by James W. Allan. Cairo: American University Press.

Crone, Patricia. 1980. *Slaves on Horses: The Evolution of the Islamic Polity.* Cambridge: Cambridge University Press.

Crone, Patricia, and Michael Cook. 1977. *Hagarism: The Making of the Islamic World.* Cambridge: Cambridge University Press.

Crone, Patricia, and Martin Hinds. 1987. *God's Caliph: Religious Authority in the First Centuries of Islam.* Cambridge: Cambridge University Press.

Crotty, Kevin. 1994. *The Poetics of Supplication: Homer's "Iliad" and "Odyssey."* Ithaca, N.Y.: Cornell University Press.

al-Daḥdāḥ, Anṭūn. 1989. *Muᶜjam Qawāᶜid al-Lugha al-ᶜArabiyya.* Beirut: Maktabat Libnān.

D'Arms, John H. 1995. "Heavy Drinking and Drunkenness in the Roman World: Four Questions for Historians." In *In Vino Veritas,* edited by Oswyn Murray and Manuela Tecusan, 304–17. London: British School at Rome.

Davidson, Lawrence. *Islamic Fundamentalism.* Westport, Conn.: Greenwood Press, 1998.

Davis, Natalie Zemon. 1987. *Fiction in the Archives: Pardon Tales and Their Tellers in Sixteenth-Century France.* Stanford: Stanford University Press.

Ḍayf, Shawqī. 1990. *Al-ᶜAṣr al-ᶜAbbāsī al-Thānī.* 7th ed. Tārīkh al-Adab al-ᶜArabī, 4. Cairo: Dār al-Maᶜārif.

DeWeese, Devin. 1994. *Islamization and Native Religion in the Golden Horde: Baba Tūkles and Conversion to Islam in Historical and Epic Tradition.* Hermeneutics: Studies in the History of Religion, Kees W. Bolle, series editor. University Park: Pennsylvania State University Press.

al-Dhahabī, Muḥammad b. Aḥmad. 1987. *Tārīkh al-Islām* [History of Islam]. Edited by ᶜUmar Tadmurī. 37 vols. Beirut: Dār al-Kitāb al-ᶜArabī.

al-Dīnawarī, Abū Ḥanīfa Aḥmad. [1959]. *Al-Akhbār al-Ṭiwāl* [The Long Lore]. Edited by ᶜAbd al-Munᶜim ᶜĀmir and Jamāl al-Dīn al-Shayyāl. Turāthunā. Baghdad: Maktabat al-Muthannā.

al-Dīnawarī, Aḥmad b. Marwān. 1997. *Kitāb al-Mujālasa wa-Jawāhir al-ᶜIlm* [Book of Literary Gathering and Jewels of Knowledge]. Edited by ᶜAbd al-Raḥmān Mujīd al-Qaysī. 2 vols. Beirut: Muʾassasat al-Rayyān.

Dīwān al-Amīn wal-Maʾmūn [Poetry Collection of al-Amīn and al-Maʾmūn]. 1998. Edited by Wāḍiḥ al-Ṣamad. Beirut: Dār Ṣādir.

Donner, Fredrick. 1981. *The Early Islamic Conquests.* Princeton, N.J.: Princeton University Press.

———. 1998. *Narratives of Islamic Origins: The Beginnings of Islamic Historical Writing.* Princeton, N.J.: Darwin Press.

Douglas, Mary, ed. 1987. *Constructive Drinking: Perspectives on Drink from Anthropology.* Cambridge: Cambridge University Press.

Dūrī, ᶜAbd al-ᶜAzīz. 1983. *The Rise of Historical Writing among the Arabs.* Edited and translated by Lawrence I. Conrad. Introduction by Fred M. Donner. Princeton, N.J.: Princeton University Press.

EI¹ = Encyclopaedia of Islam. 1913–38. 1st ed., s.v. "Ḳaṣīda" and "Shᶜir." Leiden: E. J. Brill.

EI² = Encyclopaedia of Islam. 1954–. 2d ed., s.v. "al-Buḥturī," "al-Fatḥ b. Khāḳān," "Fitna," "Khabar," " Ibn Khāḳān," "Madjlis," "Malik," "Marāsim," "al-Muᶜtazz bi 'llāh," "Sāmarrāʾ," "Shuᶜūbiyya," "Ṭāhirids." Leiden: E. J. Brill.

El-Hibri, Tayeb. 1999. *Reinterpreting Islamic Historiography: Harun al-Rashid and the Narratives of the Abbasid Caliphate.* Cambridge: Cambridge University Press.

Eliade, Mircea. 1959. *The Sacred and the Profane: The Nature of Religion.* Translated by Willard R. Trask. San Diego: Harcourt Brace Jovanovich.

El Tayib, Abdulla. 1983. "Pre-Islamic Poetry." In *Arabic Literature to the End of the Umayyad Period,* edited by A. F. L. Beeston et al., 27–113. Cambridge: Cambridge University Press.

Ettinghausen, Richard, and Oleg Grabar. 1994. *The Art and Architecture of Islam, 650–1250*. Pelican History of Art. New Haven, Conn.: Yale University Press.

al-Fākihī, Abū ʿAbd Allāh Muḥammad. 1986. *Akhbār Makka* [Lore of Mecca]. Edited by ʿAbd al-Malik b. ʿAbd Allāh. 6 vols. Al-Nahḍa al-Ḥadītha.

Finnegan, Ruth. 1977. *Oral Poetry: Its Nature, Significance, and Social Context*. Cambridge: Cambridge University Press.

——. 1988. *Literacy and Orality: Studies in the Technology of Communication*. Oxford: Basil Blackwell.

Foley, John Miles. 1995. *The Singer of Tales in Performance*. Bloomington: Indiana University Press.

Foucault, Michel. 1990. *The History of Sexuality: An Introduction*. Vol. 1. Translated by Robert Hurley. New York: Vintage Books.

——. 1995. *Discipline and Punish: The Birth of the Prison*. Translated by Alan Sheridan. New York: Vintage Books.

Fowden, Garth. 1993. *Empire to Commonwealth: Consequences of Monotheism in Late Antiquity*. Princeton, N.J.: Princeton University Press.

Franklin, John Curtis. 2007. "'A Feast of Music . . .': The Greco-Lydian Musical Movement on the Assyrian Periphery." In *Anatolian Interfaces: Hittites, Greeks, and Their Neighbors: Proceedings of an International Conference on Cross-Cultural Interaction, September 17–19, 2004, Emory University, Atlanta, Georgia*, edited by B. J. Collins, M. Bachvarova, and I. Rutherford. Oxford: Oxbow Books.

Frye, Northrop. 1963. *Fables of Identity: Studies in Poetic Mythology*. New York: Harcourt.

Garrison, James D. 1975. *Dryden and the Tradition of Panegyric*. Berkeley: University of California Press.

Gaster, Theodor. 1961. *Thespis: Ritual, Myth, and Drama in the Ancient Near East*. Foreword by Gilbert Murray. Garden City, N.Y.: Anchor.

——. 1984. "Myth and Story." In *Sacred Narratives: Readings in the Theory of Myth*, edited by Alan Dundes, 110–36. Berkeley: University of California Press. First printed in *Numen* 1 (1954): 184–212.

Gibb, H. A. R. 1963. *Arabic Literature*. 2d ed. Oxford: Clarendon Press.

Glassie, Henry. 1982. *Passing the Time in Ballymenone: Culture and History of an Ulster Community*. Philadelphia: University of Pennsylvania Press.

——. 1995. "Tradition." *Journal of American Folklore* 108: 395–412.

Goffman, Erving. 1979. *Gender Advertisements*. New York: Harper & Row.

Goodman, L. E. 1983. "The Greek Impact on Arabic Literature." In *Arabic Literature to the End of the Umayyad Period*, edited by A. F. L. Beeston et al., 460–82. Cambridge: Cambridge University Press.

———. 1993. "The Sacred and the Secular: Rival Themes in Arabic Literature." In *Literary Heritage of Classical Islam: Arabic and Islamic Studies in Honor of James A. Bellamy,* edited by Mustansir Mir with Jarl E. Fossum, 287–330. Princeton, N.J.: Darwin Press.

Gordon, Matthew. 2001. *The Breaking of a Thousand Swords: A History of the Turkish Military of Samarra (A.H. 200–275/815–889 C.E.).* Albany: State University of New York Press.

Graham, William A. 1977. *Divine Word and Prophetic Word in Early Islam: A Reconsideration of the Sources, with Special Reference to the Divine Saying or Hadīth Qudsī.* The Hague: Mouton.

———. 1987. *Beyond the Written Word: Oral Aspects of Scripture in the History of Religion.* Cambridge: Cambridge University Press.

Graves, Robert. 1955. *The Greek Myths.* Combined ed. New York: Penguin.

Greenfield, J. 1974. "The Marzeah as a Social Institution." *Acta Antiqua Academiae Scientiarum Hungaricae* 22: 450–55.

Grottanelli, Cristiano. 1995. "Wine and Death— East and West." In *In Vino Veritas,* edited by Oswyn Murray and Manuela Tecusan, 62–89. London: British School at Rome.

Gruendler, Beatrice. 1996. "Ibn al-Rūmī's Ethics of Patronage." *Harvard Middle Eastern and Islamic Review* 3 (1–2): 104–60.

———. 2000. "ᶜAbbāsid Praise Poetry in the Light of Speech Act Theory and Dramatic Discourse." In *Understanding Near Eastern Literatures: A Spectrum of Interdisciplinary Approaches,* edited by B. Gruendler and V. Klemm, 157–69. Wiesbaden: Reichert.

———. 2001. "Arabic Script." In *Encyclopedia of the Qurᵓān (EQ),* edited by J.D. McAuliffe, W. al-Kadi, C. Gilliot, A. Rippin & W. Graham, 1:135–44. 4 vols. Leiden: E.J. Brill.

———. 2003. *Medieval Arabic Praise Poetry: Ibn al-Rumi and the Patron's Redemption.* London: Routledge Curzon.

———. 2005a. "Meeting the Patron: An *Akhbār* Type and Its Implications for *Muhdath* Poetry." In *Ideas, Images, Methods of Portrayal: Insights into Arabic Literature and Islam,* edited by Sebastian Günther, 51–77. Wiesbaden: Harrassowitz.

———. 2005b. "Motif vs. Genre: Reflections on the *Dīwān al-Maᶜānī* of Abū Hilāl al-ᶜAskarī." In *Ghazal as World Literature I: Transformations of a Literary Genre,* edited by Thomas Bauer and Angelika Neuwirth, 57–85. Beirut/Stuttgart: Ergon.

———. 2005c. "Verse and Taxes: The Function of Poetry in Selected Literary *Akhbâr* of the 3rd/9th Century." In *On Fiction and Adab in Medieval Arabic Literature,* edited by Philip Kennedy, 85–124. Wiesbaden: Harrassowitz.

———. 2006. "Arabic Alphabet: Origin." In *Encyclopedia of Arabic Language and Linguistics,* edited by Kees Versteegh, 148–65. Leiden: E. J. Brill.

———. 2007. "Qaṣīda: Its Reconstruction in Performance and Reception." In *Classical Arabic Humanities in Their Own Terms: Festschrift for Wolfhart Heinrichs on His 65th Birthday,* edited by Beatrice Gruendler with Michael Cooperson, 1–65. Leiden: E. J. Brill.

———. Forthcoming. "Abstract Aesthetics and Practical Criticism in Ninth-Century Baghdad." In *Takhyîl: Source Texts and Studies,* edited by Marlé Hammond and Geert J. van Gelder. 2 vols. Oxford: Oxford University.

Grunebaum, Gustave von. 1951. *Muhammadan Festivals.* New York: Schuman.

———. 1962. *Medieval Islam: A Study in Cultural Orientation.* 2d ed. Chicago: University of Chicago Press.

Hammoudi, Abdellah. 1997. *Master and Disciple: The Cultural Foundations of Moroccan Authoritarianism.* Chicago: University of Chicago Press.

Hamori, Andras. 1998. "Tinkering with the Text: Two Variously Related Stories in the *Faraj Baᶜd al-Shidda.*" In *Story-Telling in the Framework of Non-Fictional Arabic Literature,* edited by Stefan Leder, 61–78. Wiesbaden: Harrassowitz.

al-Ḥanbalī, Yūsuf b. Ḥasan. 1994. *Nuzhat al-Musāmir fī Akhbār Majnūn Banī ᶜĀmir* [The Joy of the Late-Night Raconteur for the Lore of Majnūn Banī ᶜĀmir]. Beirut: ᶜĀlam al-Kutub.

———. 1996. *Nuzhat al-Musāmir fī Akhbār Laylā al-Akhyāliyya* [The Joy of the Late-Night Raconteur for Anecdotes about Laylā al-Akhyāliyya]. 1st ed. Edited by Muḥammad al-Ṭunjī. Beirut: ᶜĀlam al-Kutub.

Hava, J. G. 1970. *Al-Farāʾid al-Durriyyah* [Al-Faraid: Arabic-English Dictionary]. 4th ed. Beirut: Dār al-Mashriq.

Heinrichs, Wolfhart. 1995. "The Classification of the Sciences and the Consolidation of Philology in Classical Islam." In *Centres of Learning: Learning and Location in Pre-Modern Europe and the Near East,* edited by Jan Willem Drijvers and Alasdair A. MacDonald, 119–39. Leiden: E. J. Brill.

———. 1997. "Prosimetrical Genres in Classical Arabic Literature." In *Prosimetrum: Crosscultural Perspectives on Narrative in Prose and Verse,* edited by Joseph Harris and Karl Reichl, 249–75. Woodbridge: Brewer.

Herder, Johann Gottfried. 1993. *Against Pure Reason: Writings on Religion, Language, and History.* Translated and edited by Marcia Bunge. Minneapolis: Augsburg Fortress Press.

Hillenbrand, Robert. 1994. *Islamic Architecture: Form, Function, and Meaning.* Edinburgh: Edinburgh University Press.

Hobsbawm, Eric, and Terence Ranger. 1983. *The Invention of Tradition.* Cambridge: Cambridge University Press.

Hodgson, Marshall G. S. 1974. *The Venture of Islam: Conscience and History in a World Civilization.* 3 vols. Chicago: University of Chicago Press.

Holy Bible. Revised Standard Version. 1953. New York: Thomas Nelson.

Homerin, Th. Emil. 1990. "A Bird Ascends the Night: Elegy and Immortality in Islam." *Journal of the American Academy of Religion* 58: 541–73.

Howell, Mortimer Sloper. *A Grammar of the Classical Arabic Language.* 4 vols. Delhi: Gian Publishing House, 1986.

Hubert, Henri, and Marcel Mauss. 1981. *Sacrifice: Its Nature and Function.* Translated by W. D. Halls. Chicago: University of Chicago Press.

Humphreys, R. Stephen. 1992. *Islamic History: A Framework for Inquiry.* Rev. ed. Cairo: American University Press.

al-Ḥuṣrī al-Qayrawānī, Abū Isḥāq. 1969. *Zahr al-Ādāb wa Thamar al-Albāb* [Blossoms of Humanistic Arts and Fruits of the Heart]. 2d ed. Edited by ᶜAlī Muḥammad al-Bijāwī. 2 vols. Cairo: ᶜĪsā Bābī al-Ḥalabī.

Hutton, Partick H. 1993. *History as an Art of Memory.* Hanover: University Press of New England.

Hymes, Dell. 1975. "Breakthrough into Performance." In *Folklore: Performance and Communication,* edited by Dan Ben-Amos and Kenneth S. Goldstein, 11–74. The Hague: Mouton.

Ibn ᶜAbd Rabbih, Aḥmad b. Muḥammad. n.d. *Al-ᶜIqd al-Farīd* [The Unique Necklace]. Edited by Muḥammad al-ᶜAryān. 8 vols. Cairo: Dār al-Fikr.

Ibn Abī Uṣaybiᶜa, Aḥmad b. al-Qāsim. 2001. *Kitāb Ṭabaqāt al-Aṭṭibāʾ* [Prosopography of Physicians]. Edited by ᶜĀmir al-Najjār. 6 vols. Cairo: Al-Hayʾa al-Maṣriyya al-ᶜĀmma lil-Kitāb.

Ibn al-ᶜArabī, Muḥyī al-Dīn. 1968. *Kitāb Muḥāḍarat al-Abrār wa-Musāmarāt al-Akhyār fil-Adabiyyāt wal-Nawādir wal-Akhbār* [Book of Repartee with the Virtuous and Late-Night Talk with the Elect on Humanities, Stories, and Anecdotes]. 2 vols. Beirut: Dār al-Yaqẓa al-ᶜArabiyya.

Ibn Bassām al-Shantarīnī, Abū al-Ḥasan ᶜAlī. 1997. *Al-Dhakhīra fī Maḥāsin Ahl al-Jazīra* [Treasury of the Virtues of the (Iberian) Peninsula's People]. Edited by Iḥsān ᶜAbbās. 8 vols. Beirut: Dār al-Thaqāfa.

Ibn Ezra, Moses. 1985–86. *Kitāb al-Muḥāḍara wal-Mudhākarah* [Book of Literary Gatherings and Remembrances]. Edited by Montserrat Abumalhan Mas. Madrid: Consejo Superior de Investigaciones Científicas, Instituto de Filología.

Ibn Ḥabīb, Muḥammad. 1991. *Kitāb Man Nusiba ilā Ummihi min al-Shuᶜarāʾ* [Poets Who are Descended from Their Mothers]. In *Nawādir al-Makhṭuṭāt* [Rarities among Manuscripts], edited by ᶜAbd al-Salām Hārūn, 2:90–106. 2 vols. Beirut: Dār al-Jīl.

Ibn Hudhayl, ᶜAlī b. ᶜAbd al-Raḥmān. n.d. *ᶜAyn al-Adab wal-Siyāsa wa Zayn al-Ḥasab wal-Riyāsa* [The Epitome of Humanities and Politics and the Best of Personal Merit and Leadership]. 2d ed. Beirut: Dār al-Kutub al-ᶜIlmiyya.

Ibn al-ᶜIbrī [Bar Hebraeus]. 1994. *Tārīkh Mukhtaṣar al-Duwal* [Abridged History of Nations]. 2d ed. Edited by Antūn Ṣaliḥānī al-Yāsūᶜī. Ḥāzimiyya, Lebanon: Dār al-Rāʾid al-Lubnānī.

Ibn al-ᶜImrānī, Muḥammad. 1973. *Al-Inbāʾ fī Tārīkh al-Khulafāʾ* [Announcing the History of Caliphs]. Leiden: Netherlands Institute; Cairo: ᶜĪsā al-Bābī al-Ḥalabī.

Ibn Iskandar, Kai Kāʾūs. 1951. *A Mirror for Princes: The Qābūs Nāma.* Translated by Reuben Levy. New York: Dutton.

Ibn Iyās, Muḥammad b. Aḥmad. 1992. *Badāʾiᶜ al-Zuhūr fī Waqāʾiᶜ al-Duhūr* [The Most Wondrous of Blossoms: The Events of the Ages]. Edited by Saᶜīd al-Laḥḥām. Beirut: Al-Maktaba al-Ḥadītha.

Ibn Jaᶜfar, Abū al-Faraj Qudāma. 1978. *Naqd al-Shiᶜr* [Poetry Criticism]. 3d ed. Edited by Kamāl Muṣṭafā. Cairo: Maktabat al-Khānjī.

Ibn al-Jahm, ᶜAlī. 1996. *Dīwān* [Poetry Collection]. Edited by Khalīl Mardam Bay. Beirut: Dār Ṣādir.

Ibn al-Jawzī, Abū al-Faraj. 1983. *Akhbār al-Ḥamqā wal-Mughaffalīn* [Anecdotes about Idiots and Fools]. 3d ed. Cairo: Zāhid al-Qudsī.

———. 1992. *Al-Muntaẓam fī Tārīkh al-Mulūk wal-Umam* [Strung Pearls: On the History of Kings and Nations]. Edited by Muḥammad and Muṣṭafā ᶜAbd al-Qādir ᶜAṭā. 18 vols. Beirut: Dār al-Kutub al-ᶜIlmiyya.

Ibn Kathīr, Ismāʾīl b. ᶜUmar. 1998. *Al-Bidāya wal-Nihāhaya fil-Tārīkh* [The Beginning and End of History]. Edited by ᶜAbd al-Raḥmān al-Lādqī and Muḥammad al-Bayḍūn. 13 vols. Beirut: Dār al-Maᶜārifa.

Ibn Khaldūn, ᶜAbd al-Raḥmān b. Muḥammad. n.d. *Muqaddima* [The Introduction]. Edited by ᶜAlī ᶜAbd al-Wāḥid Wāfī. Cairo: Dār Nahḍat Miṣr.

Ibn Khallikān, Abū al-ᶜAbbās. 1968–72. *Wafayāt al-Aᶜyān* [Obituaries of Nobles]. Edited by Iḥsān ᶜAbbās. 8 vols. Beirut: Dār al-Thaqāfa.

Ibn Manẓūr, Muḥammad b. Mukarram. 1990. *Lisān al-ᶜArab* [Tongue of the Arab]. 15 vols. Beirut: Dār Ṣādir.

Ibn Munqidh, Usāma. 1994. *Al-Manāzil wal-Diyār* [Stations and Places]. Edited by Muṣṭafā Ḥijāzī. Cairo: Wizārat al-Thaqāfa [Ministry of Culture].

Ibn al-Nadīm, Muḥammad b. Isḥāq. n.d. *Al-Fihrist.* Cairo: Maktaba al-Tijāriyya al-Kubrā.

Ibn Qutayba, Abū Muḥammad ᶜAbd Allāh b. Muslim. 1966. *Al-Shiᶜr wal-Shuᶜarāʾ* [Poetry and Poets]. Edited by Aḥmad Muḥammad Shākir. 2 vols. Cairo: Dār al-Maᶜārif.

——. 1992. *Al-Ma^c^ārif* [Types of Knowledge]. Edited by Tharwat ^c^Akkāsha. Cairo: Dār al-Ma^c^ārif.

Ibn Rashīq al-Qayrawānī, al-Ḥasan. 2000. *Kitāb al-^c^Umda fī Ṣan^c^at al-Shi^c^r wa Naqdih* [The Mainstay of the Profession of Poetry and Its Criticism]. Edited by al-Nabawī Sha^c^lān. 2 vols. Cairo: Maktabat al-Khānjī.

Ibn al-Sā^c^ī, ^c^Alī b. Anjab. 1968. *Nisā^ʾ^ al-Khulafā^ʾ^* [Womenfolk of the Caliphs]. Edited by Muṣṭafā Jawād. Dhakhā^ʾ^ir al-^c^Arab, 28. Cairo: Dār al-Ma^c^ārif.

——. 1993. *Tārīkh al-Khulafā^ʾ^ al-^c^Abbāsiyyīn* [History of Abbasid Caliphs]. Edited by ^c^Abd al-Raḥīm Yūsuf al-Jamal. Cairo: Maktabat al-Ādāb.

Ibn Shams al-Khilāfa Mujidd al-Mulk, Abū al-Faḍl Ja^c^far. 1993. *Kitāb al-Ādāb* [Book of Humanistic Arts]. 2d ed. Edited by Muḥammad Amīn al-Khānjī. Cairo: Maktabat al-Khānjī.

al-Ibshīhī, Shihāb al-Dīn. n.d. *Al-Mustaṭraf fī Kull Fannin Mustaẓraf* [The Most Novel in Each Charming Art]. Beirut: Dār al-Jīl.

Irwin, Robert. 2006. "Ibn Zunbul and the Romance of History." In *Writing and Representation in Medieval Islam: Muslim Horizons,* edited by Julia Bray, 3–15. London: Routledge.

al-Iṣfahānī, Abū al-Faraj. 1992–93. *Kitāb al-Aghānī* [The Book of Songs]. Edited by al-Najdī Nāṣif, under Muḥammad Abū al-Faḍl Ibrāhīm. 24 vols. Cairo: Al-Hay^ʾ^a al-Maṣriyya al-^c^Āmma lil-Kitāb.

al-Itlīdī, Muḥammad b. Diyāb. 1998. *Nawādir al-Khulafā^ʾ^* [Stories of the Caliphs]. Edited by Ayman ^c^Abd al-Jābir al-Buḥayrī. Cairo: Dār al-Āfāq al-^c^Arabiyya.

Jabbur, Jibrail S. 1995. *The Bedouins and the Desert: Aspects of Nomadic Life in the Arab East.* Translated by Lawrence I. Conrad. Edited by Suhayl J. Jabbur and Lawrence I. Conrad. Albany: State University of New York Press.

al-Jāḥiẓ, Abū ^c^Uthmān. 1914. *Kitāb al-Tāj fī Akhlāq al-Mulūk* [The Book of the Crown on the King's Etiquette]. 1st ed. Edited by Aḥmad Zakī Bashā. Cairo: Al-Maṭb^c^a al-Amīriyya.

——. 1990. *Kitāb al-Bukhalā^ʾ^* [The Book of Misers]. 5th ed. Edited by Ṭāhā al-Ḥājirī. Dhakhā^ʾ^ir al-^c^Arab, 23. Cairo: Dār al-Ma^c^ārif.

Jayyusi, Salma Khadra. 1977. *Trends and Movements in Modern Arabic Poetry.* 2 vols. Leiden: E.J. Brill.

——, ed. 1989. *The Literature of Modern Arabia: An Anthology.* Austin: University of Texas Press.

——. 1994. "Tradition and Modernity in Arabic Poetry: The Constant Challenge, the Perennial Assertion." In *Tradition and Modernity in Arabic Language and Literature,* edited by J.R. Smart, 27–48. London: Curzon.

———. 1996. "The Persistence of the Qasida Form." In *Qasida Poetry in Islamic Asia and Africa,* vol. 1, *Classical Traditions and Modern Meanings,* edited by Stefan Sperl and Christopher Shackle, 1–19. Studies in Arabic Literature 20. Leiden: E. J. Brill.

Joffe, Alexander H. 1989. "Alcohol and Social Complexity in Ancient Western Asia." *Current Anthropology* 39 (June): 297–322.

al-Jurjānī, ʿAlī b. ʿAbd al-ʿAzīz. 1913/1331. *Al-Wasāṭa bayna al-Mutanabbī wa Khuṣūmih* [Arbitration between al-Mutanabbī and His Opponents]. Edited by Aḥmad ʿĀrif al-Zayn. Sidon, Lebanon: Imprimerie al-Irfan.

al-Karkhī, Ḥusayn Ḥātim. 2003. *Majālis al-Adab fī Baghdād.* Beirut: al-Muʾassasa al-ʿArabiyya lil-Dirāsāt wal-Nashr, al-Markaz al-Raʾīsī.

Kennedy, Hugh. 1986. *The Prophet and the Age of the Caliphate: The Islamic Near East from the Sixth to the Eleventh Century.* London: Longman.

Khalidi, Tarif. 1994. *Arabic Historical Thought in the Classical Period.* Cambridge: Cambridge University Press.

al-Khaṭīb al-Baghdādī, Abū Bakr. [1966?]. *Tārīkh Baghdād* [History of Baghdad]. 14 vols. Beirut: Dār al-Kitāb al-ʿArabī.

Kidd, B. J. 1922. *A History of the Church to A.D. 461.* Vol. 3. Oxford: Clarendon Press.

Kilpatrick, Hilary. 1998. "The Genuine Ashʿab: The Relativity of Fact and Fiction in Early Adab Texts." In *Story-Telling in the Framework of Non-Fictional Arabic Literature,* edited by Stefan Leder, 94–117. Wiesbaden: Harrassowitz.

Kraemer, Joel L. 1986. *Humanism in the Renaissance of Islam: The Cultural Revival during the Buyid Age.* Leiden: E. J. Brill.

———, trans. and annot. 1992. *The History of al-Tabari.* Vol. 34, *Incipient Decline.* Albany: State University of New York Press.

Kreiswirth, Martin. 1995. "Tell Me a Story: The Narrativist Turn in the Human Sciences." In *Constructive Criticism: The Human Sciences in the Age of Theory,* edited by Martin Kreiswirth and Thomas Joseph Daniel Carmichael, 61–87. Toronto: University of Toronto Press.

Kroeber, A. L. 1948. *Anthropology.* New York: Harcourt, Brace.

Kuhrt, Amelie, and S. Sherwin-White, eds. 1987. *Hellenism in the East: The Interaction of Greek and Non-Greek Civilizations from Syria to Central Asia after Alexander.* London: Duckworth.

Lambton, Ann. 1981. *State and Government in Medieval Islam: An Introduction to the Study of Islamic Political Theory: The Jurists.* Oxford: Oxford University Press.

Lane, Edward William. 1842. *An Account of the Manners and Customs of the Modern Egyptians.* London: Ward, Lock and Co.

——. 1984. *Arabic-English Lexicon.* 2 vols. Cambridge: Islamic Texts Society.

Lapidus, Ira M. 1979. "Islam and the Historical Experience of Muslim People." In *Islamic Studies: A Tradition and Its Problems,* edited by Malcolm H. Kerr, 89–101. Seventh Giorgio Levi Della Vida Conference. Malibu, Calif.: Undena Publications.

Lears, T. J. Jackson. 1994. *Fables of Abundance: A Cultural History of Advertising in America.* New York: Basic Books.

Leder, Stefan. 1987. "Prosa-Dichtung in der akhbār Überlieferung: Narrative Analyse einer Satire." *Der Islam* 64: 6–41.

——. 1988. "Authorship and Transmission in Unauthored Literature: The Akhbār Attributed to al-Haytham ibn ᶜAdī." *Oriens* 31: 67–81.

——. 1990. "Features of the Novel in Early Historiography—the Downfall of Xālid al-Qasrī." *Oriens* 32: 72–96.

——. 1992. "The Literary Use of *Khabar*: A Basic Form of Historical Writing." In *The Byzantine and Early Islamic Near East: Problems in the Literary Source Material,* edited by Averil Cameron and Lawrence I. Conrad, 277–315. Princeton, N.J.: Darwin Press.

——. 1998. "Conventions of Fictional Narration in Learned Literature." In *Story-Telling in the Framework of Non-Fictional Arabic Literature*, edited by Stefan Leder, 34–60. Wiesbaden: Harrassowitz.

Le Strange, G.E. 1924. *Baghdad during the Abbasid Caliphate from Contemporary Arabic and Persian Sources.* 2d ed. Oxford: Clarendon Press.

Levy, Reuben. 1929. *A Baghdad Chronicle.* Cambridge: Cambridge University Press.

Lewis, Bernard. 1988. *The Political Language of Islam.* Chicago: University of Chicago Press.

Lewisohn, Leonard, ed. 1999. *The Heritage of Sufism.* 3 vols. Oxford: Oneworld.

Lichtenstädter, Ilse. 1943. "On the Conception of Adab." *Moslem World* 33: 33–38.

Lord, Albert B. 1960. *The Singer of Tales.* Harvard Studies in Comparative Literature, no. 24. Cambridge, Mass.: Harvard University Press.

Losensky, Paul. 1998. *Welcoming Fighānī: Imitation and Poetic Individuality in the Safavid-Mughal Ghazal.* Costa Mesa, Calif.: Mazda.

Lovejoy, Arthur. 1973. *The Great Chain of Being: A Study in the History of an Idea.* Cambridge, Mass.: Harvard University Press.

al-Maᶜarrī, Abū al-ᶜAlāᵓ. n.d. *Al-Luzūmiyyāt* [The Prescribed Poems]. 2 vols. Beirut: Dār Ṣādir.

MacKay, Pierre A. 1971. *Certificates of Transmission on a Manuscript of the Maqamat of Hariri.* Philadelphia: American Philosophical Society.

Makdisi, George. 1981. *The Rise of Colleges: Institutions of Learning in Islam and the West.* Edinburgh: Edinburgh University Press.

———. 1990. *The Rise of Humanism in Classical Islam and the Christian West: With Special Reference to Scholasticism.* Edinburgh: Edinburgh University Press.

Malti-Douglas, Fedwa. 1985. *Structures of Avarice: The Bukhalāʾ in Medieval Arabic Literature.* Leiden: E. J. Brill.

al-Maqdīsī, Muṭahhar b. Ṭāhir. [1960s?]. *Kitāb al-Badʾ wal-Taʾrīkh* [The Beginning and Historiography]. 6 vols. Baghdad: Maktabat al-Muthannā.

al-Maqqarī, Aḥmad b. Muḥammad. 1968. *Nafḥ al-Ṭīb min Ghusn al-Andalus al-Raṭīb.* 8 vols. Beirut: Dār Ṣādir.

Mardam, Khalīl, ed. 1996. *Dīwān ᶜAlī Ibn al-Jahm* [Poetry Collection of ᶜAlī Ibn al-Jahm]. Beirut: Dār Ṣādir.

Maritain, Jacques. 1953. *Creative Intuition in Art and Poetry.* New York: Pantheon Books.

al-Marzubānī, Muḥammad b. ᶜImrān. 1960. *Muᶜjam al-Shuᶜarāʾ* [Lexicon of Poets]. Edited by ᶜAbd al-Sattār Aḥmad Farrāj. Cairo: ᶜĪsā al-Bābī al-Ḥalabī.

———. 1965. *Al-Muwashshaḥ* [The Adorned]. Cairo: Dār Nahḍat Miṣr.

al-Masᶜūdī, Abū al-Ḥasan. [1948?]. *Murūj al-Dhahab* [Meadows of Gold]. Edited by Muḥammad Muḥyi al-Dīn ᶜAbd al-Ḥamīd. 4 vols. Beirut: al-Maktaba al-Islāmiyya.

Matthäus, H. 1999. "The Greek Symposion and the Near East: Chronology and Mechanisms of Cultural Transfer." In *Proceedings of the Fifteenth International Congress of Classical Archaeology, Amsterdam, July 12–17, 1998: Classical Archaeology Towards the Third Millennium: Reflections and Perspectives,* edited by R. F. Docter and E. M. Moormann, 1: 256–60. 2 vols. Amsterdam: Allard Pierson Museum.

Mauss, Marcel. 1967. *The Gift: Forms and Functions of Exchange in Archaic Societies.* Translated by Ian Cunnison. New York: Norton.

McEwan, Calvin. 1934. *The Oriental Origin of Hellenistic Kingship.* Studies in Ancient Oriental Civilization, no. 13. Chicago: University of Chicago Press.

McNiven, Timothy J. 2001. "Watching My Boyfriend with His Girlfriend: The Eromenos and the Hetaira in Athenian Vase Painting." *American Journal of Archaeology* 105: 255–56.

Meisami, Julie Scott. 1987. *Medieval Persian Court Poetry.* Princeton, N.J.: Princeton University Press.

———. 1996a. "The Palace-Complex as Emblem: Some Samarran Qaṣīdas." Paper presented at the colloquium Interdisciplinary Approaches to Samarra, May 10–11, Wolfson College.

——. 1996b. "Poetic Microcosms: The Persian Qasida to the End of the Twelfth Century." In *Qasida Poetry in Islamic Asia and Africa,* vol. 1, *Classical Traditions and Modern Meanings,* edited by Stefan Sperl and Christopher Shackle, 137–82. Studies in Arabic Literature 20. Leiden: E.J. Brill.

——. 1999. *Persian Historiography to the End of the Twelfth Century.* Edinburgh: Edinburgh University Press.

Melchert, Christopher. 2002. "The Piety of the Hadith Folk." *International Journal of Middle East Studies* 34: 425–39.

Meyerhof, Joseph Schacht Max. 1937. *The Medico-Philosophical Controversy between Ibn Butlan of Baghdad and Ibn Ridwan of Cairo: A Contribution to the History of Greek Learning among the Arabs.* Cairo: Fouad I University, Faculty of Arts.

Mez, Adam. 1973. *The Renaissance of Islam.* Beirut: United Publishers.

Mohammadi, Mohammad. 1969. "The University of Jundishapur in the First Centuries of the Islamic Period and Its Role in the Transmission of the Intellectual Sciences and Medicine to the Arab World and Islam." *Journal of the Regional Cultural Institute* [Iran, Pakistan, Turkey] 2: 152–66.

Monroe, James T., trans. 1971. *Risālat at-Tawābiᶜ wa z-Zawābiᶜ: The Treatise of Familiar Spirits and Demons by Abū ᶜĀmir ibn Shuhaid al-Ashjaᶜī al-Andalusī.* Berkeley: University of California Press.

Moreh, Shmuel. 1992. *Live Theatre and Dramatic Literature in the Medieval Arab World.* New York: New York University Press.

Morony, Michael. 1984. *Iraq after the Muslim Conquest.* Princeton, N.J.: Princeton University Press.

Morris, Ian. 1997. "The Art of Citizenship." In *New Light on a Dark Age: Exploring the Culture of Geometric Greece,* edited by S. Langdon, 9–43. Columbia: University of Missouri Press.

Morse, Ruth. 1991. *Truth and Convention: Rhetoric, Representation, and Reality.* Cambridge: Cambridge University Press.

Motoyoshi, Akiko. 1999. "Reality and Reverie: Wine and Ekphrasis in the ᶜAbbāsid Poetry of Abū Nuwās and al-Buḥturī." *AJAMES: Annals of Japan Association for Middle East Studies* 14: 85–120.

Mottahedeh, Roy P. 1980. *Loyalty and Leadership in an Early Islamic Society.* Princeton, N.J.: Princeton University Press.

Ms. D992, *Dīwān al-Mutanabbī.* Bibliothèque Générale (Moroccan National Archive), Rabat, Morocco.

Ms. D1196, *Dīwān Imruʾ al-Qays.* Bibliothèque Générale (Moroccan National Archive), Rabat, Morocco.

Ms. D1293, *Dīwān al-Mutanabbī.* Bibliothèque Générale (Moroccan National Archive), Rabat, Morocco.

Ms. Esc. 369. *Dīwān ᶜAlī b. al-Jahm* [Poetry Collection of ᶜAlī b. al-Jahm]. Real Biblioteca del Monasterio, San Lorenzo de El Escorial, Madrid, Spain.

Ms. Esc. 724. *Kitāb al-Ādāb* [Book of Literary Materials]. Real Biblioteca del Monasterio, San Lorenzo de El Escorial, Madrid, Spain.

Ms. Esc. 725. Untitled. Real Biblioteca del Monasterio, San Lorenzo de El Escorial, Madrid, Spain.

Ms. Esc. 732. *Madkhal al-Sulūk ilā Manāzil al-Mulūk* [Introduction to Decorum for the Homes of Kings]. Real Biblioteca del Monasterio, San Lorenzo de El Escorial, Madrid, Spain.

Ms. Esc. 1708. *Al-Maqāma al-Badīᶜiyya fī Waṣf Jamāl al-Maᶜālim al-Makkiyya* [The Wondrous Story Session Describing the Beauty of Mecca's Landmarks]. Real Biblioteca del Monasterio, San Lorenzo de El Escorial, Madrid, Spain.

Ms. Pet. 39. *Kitāb al-Siyāsa wal-Imāma* [Book on Politics and Leadership]. Staatsbibliothek, Berlin, Germany.

Ms. Pet. 105. *Muḥāḍarāt al-Udabāʾ* [Salons of Littérateurs]. Staatsbibliothek, Berlin, Germany.

Ms. Pm. 4. *Al-Inbāʾ bi-Anbāʾ al-Anbiyāʾ wa Tawārīkh al-Khulafāʾ* [The Announcing of News of Prophets and the History of Caliphs]. Staatsbibliothek, Berlin, Germany.

Ms. Pm. 127. *Tārikh Shāh-nah* (*sic*). Staatsbibliothek, Berlin, Germany.

Ms. Spr. 46. Untitled. Staatsbibliothek, Berlin, Germany.

Ms. Spr. 48. *Murūj al-Dhahab* [Meadows of Gold]. Staatsbibliothek, Berlin, Germany.

Ms. Spr. 1142. Untitled. Staatsbibliothek, Berlin, Germany.

Ms. Spr. 1216. *Ḥalbat al-Kumayt* [The Racing Formation of the Bay Horse/ The Gathering for Bay-Colored Wine]. Staatsbibliothek, Berlin, Germany.

Ms. Spr. 1239. Untitled. Staatsbibliothek, Berlin, Germany.

Ms. Spr. 1242. Untitled. Staatsbibliothek, Berlin, Germany.

Ms. We. 17. *Tārīkh Makka al-Mukarrama* [A History of Honored Mecca]. Staatsbibliothek, Berlin, Germany.

Ms. We. 183. Untitled. Staatsbibliothek, Berlin, Germany.

Ms. We. 1100. *Kitāb al-Diyārāt* [Book of Monasteries]. Staatsbibliothek, Berlin, Germany.

Al-Muᶜjam al-Wasīṭ. n.d. 3d ed. 2 vols. Cairo: Majmaᶜ al-Lugha al-ᶜArabiyya.

Murray, Oswyn. 1983. "The Symposion as Social Organisation." In *The Greek Renaissance of the Eighth Century B.C.: Tradition and Innovation*, edited by Robin Hägg, 195–99. Stockholm: Svenska institutet i Athen.

——. 1993. *Early Greece.* 2d ed. Cambridge, Mass.: Harvard University Press.

——, ed. 1999. *Sympotica: A Symposium on the Symposion.* Oxford: Clarendon Press; New York: Oxford University Press.

Muslim, Abū al-Ḥusayn. n.d. *Ṣaḥīḥ Muslim.* Edited by Muḥammad Fu᾽ād ᶜAbd al-Bāqī. 5 vols. Cairo: Fayṣal ᶜĪsā al-Bābī al-Ḥalabī.

al-Mutanabbī, Abū al-Ṭayyib. 1971. *Dīwān al Mutanabbī bi-Sharḥ al-ᶜUkbarī.* 4 vols. Cairo: Muṣṭafā al-Bābī al-Ḥalabī.

Nagy, Gregory. 1990. *Pindar's Homer: The Lyric Possession of an Epic Past.* Baltimore: Johns Hopkins University Press.

——. 1991. *Best of the Achaeans: Concepts of the Hero in Archaic Greek Poetry.* Baltimore: Johns Hopkins University Press.

——. 1996. *Poetry as Performance: Homer and Beyond.* Cambridge: Cambridge University Press.

Najar, Brahim [Najjār, Ibrāhīm]. 1987. *La mémoire rassemblée. Poètes arabes "mineurs" des IIe/VIIIe et IIIe/IX siècles: Approche confrontative et évaluative du corpus.* Clermont-Ferrand: Française d'Édition et d'Imprimerie.

Nallino, Carlo Alfonso. 1970. *Tarīkh al-Ādāb al-ᶜArabiyya min al-Jāhiliyya ḥattā ᶜAṣr Banī Umayya.* 2d ed. Introduction by Ṭāhā Ḥusayn. Cairo: Dār al-Maᶜārif.

Nawājī, Muḥammad b. al-Ḥasan. 1881. *Ḥalbat al-Kumayt fī Adab al-Nawādir al-Mutaᶜalliqa bil-Khamriyyāt* [The Racing Formation of the Bay Horse/The Gathering for Bay-Colored Wine: On Humanities and Stories Related to Wine Poetry]. Bulaq: Maṭbaᶜat Idārat al-Waṭan.

Nicholson, Reynold A. 1966. *A Literary History of the Arabs.* Cambridge: Cambridge University Press.

Nöldeke, Theodor. 1930. *The Iranian National Epic, or, The Shahnamah.* Philadelphia: Porcupine Press.

Noorani, Yaseen. 1997. "A Nation Born of Mourning: The Neoclassical Funeral Elegy in Egypt." *Journal of Arabic Literature* 28: 38–67.

Northedge, Alastair. 1991. "Creswell, Herzfeld, and Samarra." *Muqarnas* 8: 74–93.

——. 1992. "The Palace at Iṣṭabulāt, Sāmarrā᾽." *Archéologie islamique* 3: 61–86.

——. 1993. "An Interpretation of the Palace of the Caliph at Samarra (Dar al-Khilafa or Jawsaq al-Khaqani)." *Ars Orientalis* 23: 143–70.

Noth, Albrecht. 1994. *The Early Arabic Historical Tradition: A Source-Critical Study.* With Lawrence I. Conrad. Translated by Michael Bonner. 2d ed. Princeton, N.J.: Darwin Press.

al-Nuᶜaymī, Aḥmad Ismāᶜīl. 1995. *Al-Usṭūra fil-Shiᶜr al-ᶜArabī qabl al-Islām.* Cairo: Sīnā.

Nussbaum, Martha Craven. 1995. *Poetic Justice: The Literary Imagination and Public Life.* Boston: Beacon Press.

al-Nuwayrī, Aḥmad b. ᶜAbd al-Wahhāb. 1964–. *Nihāyat al-Arab fī Funūn al-Adab* [The Utmost in Types of *Adab*]. Edited by Saᶜīd ᶜAbd al-Fattāḥ ᶜAshūr. 33 vols. Cairo: al-Muᵓassasa al-Maṣriyya al-ᶜĀmma.

Nykl, A. R., trans. 1941. *Historia de los amores de Bayad y Riyad, una chantefable oriental en estilo persa (Vat. ar. 368).* New York: Hispanic Society of America.

Ong, Walter J. 1982. *Orality and Literacy: The Technologizing of the Word.* London: Methuen.

Orfalea, Gregory, and Sharif Elmusa, eds. *Grape Leaves: A Century of Arab-American Poetry.* New York: Interlink Books, 2000.

Pedersen, Johannes. 1984. *The Arabic Book.* Translated by Robert Hillenbrand. Princeton, N.J. : Princeton University Press.

Pellat, Charles. 1964. "Variations sur le thème de l'adab." *Correspondance d'Orient: Études* 5–6: 19–37.

Pellizer, Ezio. 1999. "Outlines of a Morphology of Sympotic Entertainment." In *Sympotica: A Symposium on the Symposion,* edited by Oswyn Murray, 177–84. Oxford: Oxford University Press.

Peters, F. E. 1970. *The Harvest of Hellenism: A History of the Near East from Alexander the Great to the Triumph of Christianity.* New York: Simon and Schuster.

Petersen, Erling Ladewig. 1974. *ᶜAli and Muᶜawiya in Early Arabic Tradition.* Odense: Odense University Press.

Petrosyan, Yuri, et al. 1995. *Pages of Perfection: Islamic Paintings and Calligraphy from the Russian Academy of Sciences, St. Petersburg.* With essays by Marie Lukens Swietochowski and Stefano Carboni. Lugano, Switzerland: ARCH Foundation.

Pinault, David. 1992. *Story-telling Techniques in the Arabian Nights.* Leiden: E. J. Brill.

Poe, Edgar Allan. 1902. *The Complete Works of Edgar Allan Poe.* Edited and with an introduction by Charles F. Richardson. New York: G. P. Putnam's Sons.

Pope, M. H. 1972. "A Divine Banquet at Ugarit." In *The Use of the Old Testament in the New and Other Essays: Studies in Honor of William Franklin Stinespring,* edited by William F. Stinespring and James M. Efird, 170–203. Durham, N.C.: Duke University Press.

al-Qazwīnī, Zakariyya b. Muḥammad. n.d. *Athār al-Bilād wa-Akhbār al-ᶜIbād* [The Heritage of Nations and the Lore of Humans]. Beirut: Dār Ṣādir.

Quint, David. 1993. *Epic and Empire: Politics and Generic Form from Virgil to Milton.* Princeton, N.J.: Princeton University Press.

Randazzo, Sal. 1995. *The Myth Makers.* Chicago: Probus.

Randel, Don Michael. "Lost in Translation." *University of Chicago Magazine,* April 2006, 16.

Rawls, John. 1971. *A Theory of Justice.* Cambridge, Mass.: Harvard University Press.

Reade, Julian E. 1995. "The *Symposion* in Ancient Mesopotamia: Archeological Evidence." In *In Vino Veritas,* edited by Oswyn Murray and Manuela Tecusan, 35–56. London: British School at Rome.

Ringgren, Helmer. 1955. *Studies in Arabian Fatalism.* Uppsala: Lundequistska Bokhandeln.

Robinson, Chase. 2003. *Islamic Historiography.* Cambridge: Cambridge University Press.

Rosenthal, Franz. "'Of Making Many Books There Is No End': The Classical Muslim View." In *The Book in the Islamic World: The Written Word and Communication in the Middle East,* edited by George N. Atiyeh, 33–56. Albany: State University of New York Press.

Rosler, Wolfgang. 1995. "Wine and Truth in the Greek Symposion." In *In Vino Veritas,* edited by Oswyn Murray and Manuela Tecusan, 106–12. London: British School at Rome.

Rūmiyya, Wahb. 1997. *Binyat al-Qaṣīda al-ᶜArabiyya ḥattā Nihāyat al-ᶜAṣr al-Umawī.* Damascus: Dār Saᶜd al-Dīn.

Sadan, Joseph. 1989. "An Admirable and Ridiculous Hero: Some Notes on the Bedouin in Medieval Arabic Belles-Lettres, on a Chapter of *Adab* by al-Rāghib al-Iṣfahānī, and on a Literary Model in Which Admiration and Mockery Coexist." *Poetics Today* 10: 471–92.

———. 1998. "Hārūn al-Rashīd and the Brewer: Preliminary Notes on the Adab of the Elite and Ḥikāyāt." In *Studies in Canonical and Popular Arabic Literature,* edited by Shimon Ballas and R. Snir, 1–22. Toronto: York Press.

Saᶜdī al-Shīrāzī. 1969. *Gulistān-i Saᶜdī.* Edited by Nūr Allāh Irānparast. Tehran: Danish.

al-Saffūrī, ᶜAbd al-Raḥmān b. ᶜAbd al-Salām. 1993. *Nuzhat al-Majālis wa-Muntakhab al-Nafāʾis* [The Joy of Gatherings and the Chosen Precious Few]. Edited by ᶜAbd al-Raḥīm Mardīnī. Damascus: Dār al-Maḥabba.

Saᶜīd, Labīb. 1975. *The Recited Koran: A History of the First Recorded Version.* Princeton, N.J.: Darwin Press.

Salāma, Ibrāhīm. 1952. *Tayyārāt Adabiyya bayn al-Sharq wal-Gharb.* Cairo: Anglo-Egyptian Bookstore.

Saliba, George, trans. and annot. 1985. *The History of al-Ṭabarī*. Vol. 35, *The Crisis of the ʿAbbāsid Caliphate*. Albany: State University of New York Press.

Sallis, Eva. 1999. *Sheherazade through the Looking Glass: The Metamorphosis of the Thousand and One Nights*. Richmond, Surrey: Curzon.

al-Samʿānī, ʿAbd al-Karīm. 1962–82. *Al-Ansāb* [Lineages]. Edited by ʿAbd al-Raḥmān al-Yamānī. 13 vols. Hyderabad, India: Maṭbaʿat Majlis Dāʾirat al-Maʿārif al-ʿUthmāniyya.

Saunders, Paula. 1994. *Ritual, Politics, and the City in Fatimid Cairo*. Albany: State University of New York Press.

Schimmel, Annemarie. 1975. *The Mystical Dimensions of Islam*. Chapel Hill: University of North Carolina Press.

Schoeler, Gregor. 1985. "Die Frage der mündlichen oder schriftlichen Überlieferung der Wissenschaften im frühen Islam." *Der Islam* 62: 201–30.

———. 1989a. "Weiteres zur Frage der mündlichen oder schriftlichen Überlieferung der Wissenschaften im frühen Islam." *Der Islam* 66: 38–67.

———. 1989b. "Mündliche Thora und Ḥadīṯ: Überlieferung, Schreibverbot, Redaktion." *Der Islam* 66: 213–41.

———. 1992. "Schreiben und Veröffentlichen: Zu Verwendung und Funktion der Schrift in den ersten islamischen Jahrhunderten." *Der Islam* 69: 1–43.

———. 1997. "Writing and Publishing: On the Use and Function of Writing in the First Centuries of Islam." *Arabica* 44: 423–35.

———. 2006. *The Oral and the Written in Early Islam*. Translated by Uwe Vagelpohl. Edited by James Montgomery. London and New York: Routledge.

Sells, Michael A. 1987. "The Qaṣīda and the West: Self-Reflective Stereotype and Critical Encounter." *Al-ʿArabiyya* 20: 307–24.

Serrano, Richard. 1997. "Al-Buhturi's Poetics of Persian Abodes." *Journal of Arabic Literature* 28: 68–87.

———. 2002. *Neither a Borrower: Forging Traditions in French, Chinese and Arabic Poetry*. Oxford: Legenda.

Sezgin, Fuat. 1975. *Geschichte des arabischen Schrifttums* [History of Arabic Writings]. Band 2, *Poesie bis ca. 430 H*. Leiden: E. J. Brill.

Shabazi, A. Shapur. 1991. *Ferdowsī: A Critical Biography*. Costa Mesa, Calif.: Mazda Publishers.

al-Shābushtī, Abū al-Ḥasan. 1986. *Kitāb al-Diyārāt* [Book of Monasteries]. Edited by Kūrkīs ʿAwwāḍ. Beirut: Dār al-Rāʾid al-ʿArabī.

al-Shayzarī, Muslim b. Maḥmūd. 2005. *Jamharat al-Islām Dhāt al-Nathr wa-al-Niẓām.* Ed. Muḥammad Ibrāhīm Ḥūwar. Abu Dhabi: Al-Majmaᶜ al-Thaqāfī.

Sibṭ b. al-Jawzī, Yūsuf b. Qizughlī. 1985. *Mirʾāt al-Zamān* [Mirrors of the Ages]. Edited by Iḥsān ᶜAbbās. Beirut: Dār al-Shurūq.

al-Sīrāfī, Abū al-Saᶜīd. 1995. *Kitāb Ṣanᶜat al-Shiᶜr* [The Profession of Poetry]. Edited by Jaᶜfar Mājid. Beirut: Dār al-Gharb al-Islāmī.

Slyomovics, Susan. 1987. "The Death-Song of Amir Khafaji: Puns in an Oral and Printed Episode of Sirat Bani Hilal." *Journal of Arabic Literature* 18: 62–78.

Smith, Barbara Herrnstein. 1983. "Contingencies of Value." *Critical Inquiry* 10: 1–35.

Smith, W. Robertson. 1894. *Lectures on the Religion of the Semites. First Series: The Fundamental Institutions*. New ed. London: A. & C. Black.

——. 1903. *Kinship and Marriage in Early Arabia*. Boston: Beacon Press.

Sourdel, Dominque. 1983. *Medieval Islam.* Translated by J. Montgomery Watt. London: Routledge and Kegan Paul.

Sperl, Stefan. 1977. "Islamic Kingship and Arabic Panegyric Poetry in the Early Ninth Century." *Journal of Arabic Literature* 8: 20–35.

Sperl, Stefan, and Christopher Shackle, eds. 1996. *Qasida Poetry in Islamic Asia and Africa.* Vol. 1, *Classical Traditions and Modern Meanings.* Studies in Arabic Literature 20. Leiden: E. J. Brill.

Sprenger, Alois. 1856a. "On the Origin and Progress of Writing Down Historical Facts among the Musulmans." *Journal of the Asiatic Society of Bengal* 25: 303–29, 375–81.

——. 1856b. "Über das Traditionswesen bei den Arabern." *Zeitschrift der Deutschen Morgenländischen Gesellschaft* 10: 1–17.

——. 1869. *Das Leben und die Lehre des Mohammad.* Vol. 3. Berlin: Nicolaische Verlagsbuchhandlung.

Steiner, Ann. 2002. "Private and Public: Links between Symposion and Syssition in Fifth-Century Athens." *Classical Antiquity* 21: 347–90

Stetkevych, Jaroslav. 1979. "Arabic Poetry and Assorted Poetics." In *Islamic Studies: A Tradition and Its Problems,* edited by Malcolm H. Kerr, 103–23. Seventh Giorgio Levi Della Vida Conference. Malibu, Calif.: Undena Publications.

——. 1986. "Name and Epithet: The Philology and Semiotics of Animal Nomenclature in Early Arabic Poetry." *Journal of Near Eastern Studies* 45 (2): 89–124.

——. 1993. *The Zephyrs of Najd: The Poetics of Nostalgia in the Classical Arabic* Nasīb. Chicago: University of Chicago Press.

———. 1994. "Toward an Arabic Elegiac Lexicon: The Seven Words of the *Nasīb*." In *Reorientations /Arabic and Persian Poetry,* edited by Suzanne Pinckney Stetkevych, 58–129. Bloomington: Indiana University Press.

———. 1996. *Muḥammad and the Golden Bough: Reconstructing Arabian Myth.* Bloomington: Indiana University Press.

Stetkevych, Suzanne Pinckney. 1989. "Intoxication and Immortality: Wine and Associated Imagery in al-Maᶜarrī's Garden." In *Critical Pilgrimages: The Arabic Literary Tradition,* edited by F. Malti-Douglas, special issue of *Literature East and West* 25: 29–48. Reprinted in *Homoeroticism in Classical Arabic Literature,* ed. J.W. Wright and Everett K. Rowson, 210–32. New York: Columbia University Press, 1997.

———. 1991. *Abū Tammām and the Poetics of the ᶜAbbāsid Age.* Series in Arabic Literature, 13. Leiden: E.J. Brill.

———. 1993. *The Mute Immortals Speak: Pre-Islamic Poetry and the Poetics of Ritual.* Ithaca, N.Y.: Cornell University Press.

———. 1994. "Pre-Islamic Panegyric and the Poetics of Redemption: Mufaḍḍalīyah 119 of ᶜAlqamah and Bānat Suᶜād of Kaᶜb b. Zuhayr." In *Reorientations/Arabic and Persian Poetry,* edited by Suzanne Pinckney Stetkevych, 1–57. Bloomington: Indiana University Press.

———. 1996a. "Abbasid Panegyric and the Poetics of Political Allegiance: Two Poems of al-Mutanabbī on Kāfūr." In *Qasida Poetry in Islamic Asia and Africa,* vol. 1, *Classical Traditions and Modern Meanings,* edited by Stefan Sperl and Christopher Shackle, 35–63. Studies in Arabic Literature 20. Leiden: E.J. Brill.

———. 1996b. "ᶜAbbāsid Panegyric: The Politics and Poetics of Ceremony in al-Mutanabbī's ᶜĪd-Poem to Sayf al-Dawlah." In *Tradition and Modernity in Arabic Language and Literature,* edited by J.R. Smart, 119–43. London: Curzon.

———. 1997a. "The Qaṣīdah and the Poetics of Ceremony: Three ᶜĪd Panegyrics to the Cordoban Caliphate." In *Language of Power in Islamic Spain,* edited by Ross Brann, 1–48. Bethesda, Md.: CDL Press.

———. 1997b. "Umayyad Panegyric and the Poetics of Islamic Hegemony: Al-Akhṭal's Khaffa al-Qaṭīnu ('Those That Dwelt with You Have Left in Haste')." *Journal of Arabic Literature* 28: 89–122.

———. 2002. *The Poetics of Islamic Legitimacy: Myth, Gender, and Ceremony in the Classical Arabic Ode.* Bloomington: Indiana University Press.

al-Sulamī, ᶜArrām b. al-Asbagh. 1991. "Kitāb Asmāᵓ Jibāl Tahāma wa-Sukkanihā [The Names of Tahāma's Mountains and Residents]." In *Nawādir al-Makhṭuṭāt* [Manuscript Rarities], edited by ᶜAbd al-Salām Hārūn, 2:419–72. 2 vols. Beirut: Dār al-Jīl.

al-Sulamī, Muḥammad b. al-Ḥusayn. 1969. *Ṭabaqāt al-Ṣūfiyya* [Prosopography of Sufis]. Edited by Nūr al-Dīn Shurayba. Cairo: Maktabat al-Khānjī.

——. 1999. *Early Sufi Women: Dhikr an-Niswa al-Muta*ᶜ*abbidāt aṣ-Ṣūfiy yāt.* Edited and translated by Rkia Elaroui Cornell. Louisville, Ky.: Fons Vitae.

al-Sulamī, Muḥammad b. al-Ḥusayn, and Abū al-ᶜAlāʾ al-ᶜAfīfī, ed. and trans. 1942. "Al-Risāla al-Malāmatiyya." *Majallat Kulliyat al-Ādāb Jāmi*ᶜ*at Fuʾād al-Awal* 6 (May): 47–103.

al-Ṣūlī, Abū Bakr b. Yaḥyā. 1958. *Akhbār al-Buḥturī wa Dhayl al-Akhbār* [Anecdotes about al-Buḥturī]. Edited by Ṣāliḥ al-Ashtar. Damascus: Al-Majmaᶜ al-ᶜIlmī al-ᶜArabī.

——. [1960s?]. *Akhbār Abī Tammām* [Anecdotes about Abū Tammām]. Edited by Khalīl Maḥmūd ᶜAsākir et al. Introduction by Aḥmad Amīn. Beirut: al-Maktab al-Tijārī lil-Ṭibāᶜa wal-Tawziᶜ wal-Nashr.

——. 1979a. *Akhbār al-Shu*ᶜ*arāʾ al-Muḥdathīn min Kitāb al-Awrāq* [Anecdotes about Modern Poets from the Book of Pages]. Edited by J. Heyworth Dunne. Beirut: Dār al-Masīra.

——. 1979b. *Akhbār al-Rāḍī bil-Lāh wal-Mutaqī lil-Lāh min Kitāb al-Awrāq* [Anecdotes about al-Raḍī from the Book of Pages]. Edited by J. Heyworth Dunne. Beirut: Dār al-Masīra.

——. 1979c. *Ash*ᶜ*ār Awlād al-Khulafāʾ wa Akhbāruhum min Kitāb al-Awrāq* [Poetry of the Children of Caliphs and Anecdotes about Them from the Book of Pages]. Edited by J. Heyworth Dunne. Beirut: Dār al-Masīra.

al-Suyūṭī, Jalāl al-Dīn. n.d. *Tārīkh al-Khulafāʾ* [History of Caliphs]. Cairo: al-Maktaba al-Tawfīqiyya.

——. 1950. *Al-Wasāʾil ilā Musāmarāt al-Awāʾil* [Techniques for Holding Late-Night Conversations with Ancestors]. Edited by Asᶜad Talas. Baghdad: Maktabat al-Zawrāʾ.

——. 1986. *Nuzhat al-Julasāʾ fi-Ash*ᶜ*ār al-Nisāʾ* [The Joy of Attendees for the Poetry of Women]. Edited by ᶜAbd al-Laṭīf ᶜĀshūr. Cairo: Maktabat al-Qurʾān.

al-Ṭabarī, Abū Jaᶜfar. 1990. *Tārīkh al-Ṭabarī: Tārīkh al-Rusul wal-Mulūk* [Ṭabarī's History; The History of Prophets and Kings]. 11 vols. Dhakhāʾir al-ᶜArab, 30. Cairo: Dār al-Maᶜārif.

——. 1991. *The History of al-Tabari*. Vol. 33, *Storm and Stress along the Northern Frontiers of the* ᶜ*Abbāsid Caliphate.* Translated by C. E. Bosworth. Albany: State University of New York Press.

——. 1992. *The History of al-Tabari.* Vol. 34, *Incipient Decline.* Translated and annotated by Joel L. Kraemer. Albany: State University of New York Press.

al-Tanūkhī, al-Muḥassin b. ᶜAlī. 1971. *Nishwār al-Muḥāḍara wa-Akhbār al-Mudhākara* [Recollections of the Assembly and Anecdotes of the Salon]. Edited by ᶜAbbūd al-Shājī. Beirut: Dār Ṣādir.

———. 1985. *Al-Mustajād min Fiᶜlāt al-Ajwād* [The Best about the Deeds of the Munificent]. Edited by Yūsuf al-Bustānī. Cairo: Dār al-ᶜArab.

Tarn, W. W. 1952. *Hellenistic Civilization*. Rev. 3d ed. New York: New American Library.

al-Thaᶜālibī, ᶜAbd al-Malik. 1983. *Yatīmat al-Dahr fī Maḥāsin Ahl al-ᶜAṣr* [The Wonder of the Ages: On the Virtues of the People of This Age]. 2d ed. Edited by Mufīd Muḥammad Qumayḥa. 5 vols. Beirut: Dār al-Kutub al-ᶜIlmiyya.

———. 1985. *Thimār al-Qulūb fil-Muḍāf wal-Mansūb* [Fruits of the Heat: On Nouns and Their Attributes]. Muḥammad Abū al-Faḍl Ibrāhīm. Dhakhā᾿ir al-ᶜArab, 57. Cairo: Dār al-Maᶜārif.

Tocqueville, Alexis de. *Democracy in America*. Translated, edited, and with introduction by Harvey Mansfield and Delba Winthrop. Chicago: University of Chicago Press, 2000.

Toorawa, Shawkat M. 2005. *Ibn Abi Tahir Tayfur and Arabic Writerly Culture: A Ninth-Century Bookman in Baghdad*. London: Routledge Curzon.

Turner, Victor. 1982. *From Ritual to Theatre: The Human Seriousness of Play*. New York: Performing Arts Journal Publications.

Versteegh, C. H. M. 1997. *The Arabic Language*. New York: Columbia University Press.

Vickery, John B. 1994. s.v. "Myth." *The New Princeton Handbook of Poetic Terms*. Princeton, N.J.: Princeton University Press.

Waines, David, trans. and annot. 1992. *The History of al-Tabari*. Vol. 36, *The Revolt of the Zanj*. Albany: State University of New York Press.

Waldman, Marilyn Robinson. 1980. *Toward a Theory of Historical Narrative: A Case Study in Perso-Islamicate Historiography*. Columbus: Ohio State University Press.

———. 1981. "'The Otherwise Unnoteworthy Year 711': A Reply to Hayden White." *Critical Inquiry* 7, no. 4 (Summer): 784–92.

al-Washshā᾿, Muḥammad b. Isḥāq. n.d. *Al-Muwashshā aw al-Ẓarf wal-Ẓurafā᾿* [The Variegated: On Charm and the Charming]. Beirut: Dār Ṣādir.

Watt, Montgomery W. 1948. *Free Will and Predestination in Early Islam*. London: Luzac.

Webber, Sabra J. 1991. *Romancing the Real: Folklore and Ethnographic Representation in North Africa*. Philadelphia: University of Pennsylvania Press.

———. 1993. "On Canonicity, Literacy and Middle Eastern Folk Narrative." *Edebiyāt* 4: 35–48.

Wellhausen, Julius. 1899. "Prolegomena zur ältesten Geschichte des Islams." In *Skizzen und Vorarbeiten.* Berlin: Georg Reimer.

White, Hayden. 1978. *Tropics of Discourse: Essays in Cultural Criticism.* Baltimore: Johns Hopkins University Press.

———. 1987. *The Content of the Form: Narrative Discourse and Historical Representation.* Baltimore: Johns Hopkins University Press.

Winter, Michael. 1982. *Society and Religion in Early Ottoman Egypt: Studies in the Writings of ᶜAbd al-Wahhāb al-Shaᶜrānī.* New Brunswick, N.J.: Transaction Books.

Wright, J.W. 1997. "Masculine Allusion and the Structure of Satire in Early ᶜAbbāsid Poetry." In *Homoeroticism in Classical Arabic Literature,* edited by J.W. Wright and Everett K. Rowson, 1–23. New York: Columbia University Press.

al-Yaᶜqūbī, Aḥmad b. Abī Yaᶜqūb. 1960. *Tārīkh al-Yaᶜqūbī* [History of al-Yaᶜqūbī]. 2 vols. Beirut: Dār Ṣādir.

Yāqūt b.ᶜAbd Allāh al-Ḥamawī, Shihāb al-Dīn. n.d. *Muᶜjam al-Buldān* [Lexicon of Lands]. 5 vols. Beirut: Dār Ṣādir.

———. 1923–25. *Kitāb Irshād al-Arīb fī Maᶜrifat al-Adīb* [The Intelligent Guide for Knowing Littérateur]. 2d ed. Edited by D.S. Margoliouth. 6 vols. London: Luzac.

———. 1936–38 [1355–57]. *Muᶜjam al-Udabāʾ* [Lexicon of Littérateur]. 20 vols. Cairo: Dār al-Maʾmūn.

al-Zamakhsharī, Maḥmūd b. ᶜUmar. 1976–81. *Rabīᶜ al-Abrār wa-Nuṣūṣ al-Akhbār* [Vernal Gardens for the Virtuous and Texts of Anecdotes]. Edited by Salīm al-Nuᶜaymī. [Baghdad]: Riʾāsat Dīwān al-Awqāf.

Index

9/11. *See* September 11, 2001; trauma

Abbasid society, 13, 19, 26, 48–49, 82, 127, 167, 169, 174, 186, 195, 212n1; and al-Buḥturī, 123, 181, 187; and the caliphate, 99, 103–4, 155, 175; and courtiers, 229n4; historians of, 36; as ideological successors to Sasanians, 162; and Īwān Kisrā ode, 154; and kings, 157, 235n100; loftiness in, 149; and al-Mutawakkil's assassination, 171; and palaces, 124–27; and performance, 77; redemption of, 175; in the *Ruṣāfiyya,* 107

ʿAbd al-Karīm, Khalīl, 106, 237n136

ʿAbd Manāf (Ibn Quṣayy), 104, 106, 234n69

ʿAbd al-Muṭṭalib (Muhammad's Grandfather), 104–5, 106–7

Abū al-ʿAnbas al-Ṣaymarī (d. 888), 182

Abū al-ʿAtāhiya (d. 825), 104, 179

Abū al-Ghawth (al-Buḥturī's son), 165

Abū Hayyān al-Tawḥīdī (d. tenth cent.), 18, 48, 51

Abu-Lughod, Lila, 97–98

Abū Nuwās (d. ca. 810), 72, 234n85

Abū Tammām (d. 842), 45, 53–56, 86–87, 97, 135, 155, 181, 218n8; and "Bedouinness," 93

Academy of Jundishapur, 26

adab, 14–15, 19, 27, 31–32, 34, 48, 184, 192, 196, 213nn2, 5, 6, 214n11, 216n1; and

Bauman, Richard, 28–29, 61, 110, 238n152; on persuasion, 124. *See also* performance
Bayāḍ and Riyāḍ, 29–30, 52, 54, 224n56
Bedouins, 45, 73, 75–76, 97, 128, 161, 225n88, 228nn2, 3, 234n81; abodes of, 162, 154, 247n19; and Bedouinness, 93; compared to Sasanians, 158, 247n19; culture of, 74; as idealized, 93; poetics of, 162; and the *Ruṣāfiyya,* 92; tribes of, 247n20; women, 98
beloved, 25, 47, 92, 94–95, 97, 112, 115, 178–79, 233n64; immaturity of, 144, 243n96; sacrality of, 239n161
beneficial lying, 65–68. *See also* history; knowledge; truth
Blachère, Régis, 49
blindness, 45, 142
Blossoms of Humanistic Arts and Fruits of the Heart (al-Ḥuṣrī al-Qayrawānī), 140
Book of Monasteries, The (al-Shābushtī), 44, 52–53, 125
Book of Songs, The, 95, 130
Book of the Crown on the King's Etiquette, The (al-Jāḥiẓ), 86
books, 4, 8, 38–39, 218n7, 220n12; and audience attention, 44; and teachers, 40. *See also* self-study
Bouazza, Moulay (Abu Wanalgut; d. 1177), 111
Briggs, Charles, 124
buffoonery, 110–12. *See also* Sufism
Bughā al-Ṣaghīr al-Shirābī, 177
al-Buḥturi (d. 897), 6, 29, 46–47, 53, 68, 74, 79, 80, 87, 102, 127, 150, 174–75, 180, 229n8; and Abbasid patronage, 155; and Abbasid public image, 123; and allegiance to Tulunids, 155, 156; and ʿAlwa bint Zurayqa, 154; as cultural icon, 181; dyad of, in the *mujālasāt,* 150–52; and elegy to al-Mutawakkil, 132–39, 149, 242n62; and embellishments, 168; and endorsement of al-Muʿtazz, 246n15; and engaged resistance, 156; as expert on al-Mutawakkil's assassination, 180–82; on glory in praise hymns, 107; and greed, 229, 230n9; on influence, 80; and al-Mutawakkil's assassination, 119–20, 252n55; and al-Mutawakkil's "covenant of succession," 85; personal interests of, 154–56; poem 771, 177; poem 262, 177–78; poetic role of, 173; on his poetry, 86; post-Mutawakkil poems of, 176–77; and praise hymn to al-Muntaṣir, 141–50, 244n93; questions raised by, 183, 185; and rapport with al-Fatḥ b. Khāqān, 182; and rapport with al-Mutawakkil, 182; and redemption of Abbasid society, 175; and sacrifice, 131–32; and textual adjustments, 55; and trans-mission of poetry of, 249n36; and vengeance, 132, 148. *See also* Īwān Kisrā ode

oral tradition, 3, 4, 104. *See also* *adab;* face-to-face interaction; knowledge; performance
orality and writing, 7, 9, 44, 212n11, 220n12
Orestes, 129–30. *See also* vengeance (*tha'r*)
Orient, 190
"other," the, 190

paideia, 33
palaces, 125–27, 133; and Bulkuwārā, 125–26, 178–79, 241nn31, 33, 246n15; Iṣṭa-blulāt, 125–27, 241n31; al-Jawsaq Khāqānī, 125, 241n31; Qaṣr al-Jiṣṣ, 126–7. *See also* Īwān Kisrā (Arched Hall)
Palestine, 190, 223n50
paper: development and use of, 39, 220n12, 221n17. *See also* books; self-study
patrons, 79, 81, 86, 108; relationship to poet, 87, 101–3, 231n45; role of, 81–87. *See also* king; poetry; poets; supplication
Pellizer, Ezio, 52
performance, 14, 27–28, 61, 73, 109, 123, 225n78; and *adab,* 74; adjustment in, 52–57, 192, 225n78; benefits of, 32, 86; of al-Buḥturī's dyad, 150–51; and emotions, 46–52, 57; in group, 36, 122, 193; to heal trauma, 194; and improvisation, 43; and invention, 66; motive of, 194; of poetry, 81; and reframing and ode, 193; theory of, 5, 28, 191, 192; tradition as, 210n7; and words, 222n36. *See also adab;* audience; style adjustments; textual adjustments
performative, 36, 45, 57; approach, 62; norms, 74; sense, 192; speech, 79
Persians, 5, 14, 16, 19, 65–66, 84, 158, 168, 170, 185
Phoenicians, 22–24
Poe, Edgar Allan, 1, 190–91, 194; and "The Thousand-and-Second Tale of Scheherazade," 1–2, 190–91
poetry, 68, 108; authenticity in, 69–71; and children, 73; instrumentality of, 79; and invention, 69–71; and morality, 70; and narrative, 68; and social interaction, 181
poets, 70, 79, 86–87, 123, 146, 151; and audience, 139; authority of, 184; brigand (*su'lūk*), 154, 157, 160–63; and decision making, 85; as healers, 193; and influence, 80, 123, 156; and mendacity, 249n32; performance of, 86; and poet-hero as redeemer, 128–32, 150; prerogatives of, 81, 84–85; and relationship to patron, 87, 100, 101; and rhetorical strategy, 184; role of, 77–81; as supplicant, 80; as transmitters of cultural texts, 181; and verbal art, 122–24; as victim of fate, 94. *See also* al-Buḥturī; king; poetry; supplication
positivism, 37, 218n11

samer M. ALI

is associate professor of Arabic Studies at the University of Texas at Austin.

CPSIA information can be obtained at www.ICGtesting.com
Printed in the USA
LVOW10s1441040516

486529LV00025BA/117/P

9 780268 020323